Around the world in 80 girls

\-

The epic 3 year round the world trip

of a backpacking Casanova

For the girls that fell in love with me

I hope you never read this book

Contents

Tips and trips section for picking up girls home and abroad

About this Book

Great, yet another book on world travel....

The narrow road is deeply rutted and dusty. It is dark when we arrive at the floating village of Chong Kneas. Houses on stilts line the narrow road, which is strewn with artifacts of daily–plastic, aluminum cans and empty water vessels.

If you like to read texts like this, then you are reading the wrong book and I advise to you to visit your local bookstore and get a real travel book. If you want to read long, boring descriptions of the landmarks and cultural stuff, your local bookstore or library is the place to go. This is not one of those books. I had to leave parts of the trip and thousands of little details out to keep this book readable. I could have easily filled 2000 pages.

If there are thousands of books on travelling, what makes this one so special?

While there are many books on travelling and also on picking up girls, there are only a few books combining the two subjects. Books on (round the world) travel are often politically correct books written by guys who know how to travel but know nothing about girls. I dare to say that 95% of guys travelling are satisfied with an occasional drunken lay in a hostel, preferably with someone of their own "kind".

So, that means I can just buy a book about picking up girls, read it and go abroad. Right?

No. You *could* do that but the problem is that most of those books are written by marketers or "Pick up artists" who may be good at teaching this stuff and selling it but suck when it comes to actually picking up girls. Those pick-up books are interesting reads but custom-suited for the western world. The world you're about to say goodbye to. The world where witty "routines" don't work since the exotic hottie you're speaking with barely knows English or not very familiar with western culture except what she sees on television.

So who should read your book?

• Anyone interested in travelling to exotic countries who wants to read real, crazy stories of the kind you won't find in regular travel books. If you've ever been on a pre-packaged tour, and stared out the window of your air-conditioned bus, packed to the rafters with overfed Western tourists, being pushed around by travel guides who keep you to a strict schedule, and wondered what it's *really* like out there, and what it would be like to actually get off that bus and go into the real life of the country, I can give you an idea of that too.

• Anyone who wants to travel to exotic places and pick up the local girls whether they are White, Asian, Latin, Black, Brown or whatever exotic mix you can think of.

• This book is mainly focused to cheap-ass backpacker bum travelling, but the tips will also help out the traveler on a bigger budget. In fact, more money equals more honey, but not for the obvious reasons known in the western world.

• Anyone shy who wants to improve his life by travelling and meeting people from other cultures, including, yes, girls.

Who should NOT read this book?

• Anyone who expects a great piece of literature. I'm not a literary stylist, and I'm not going to pretend to be.

In fact, I'm breaking the show/don't tell rule in every possible way. Why, you ask? Because I want to tell you the story like I'm having a beer with you in a smoky bar. A place where serious talk is easily followed up by hilarious laughter or stuff that need whispering when there are women around.

• Anyone who is easily offended or overly politically correct. I very much doubt you'll enjoy this book. What's in here is three years of my life. Three years of wandering, and three years of girls. There will be travel, there will be booze, there will be (at times) utter debauchery. And at times there will also be those moments when I found myself at some of the lowest points of my life – and how I got out of them. If this doesn't sound like your cup of tea, save yourself the bother and go read something from Oprah's Book Club.

Thwack! The dull sound of a hard punch to the face. Dara's pupils swam and she stumbled on her feet for half a second before her surprised look at Nina turned vicious. Without hesitating she threw herself at Nina and grabbed her by the hair, both of them kicking and punching, screaming in a language I didn't understand as they tried to tear each other's scalp off. I tried to pull them apart but their fingers were all tangled up in each other's hair, and they had no intention of letting go. All the people in the guesthouse were staring, and quickly two guys who worked there rushed over to help stop the fight, with a method rather more effective than mine: they started beating the girls all over until they gave in and stopped. One of the guys was hitting Nina so hard I had to pull him off her.

When the fight was broken up, Dara gave me a desperate look and walked away crying. Even coming out of a fight she still looked gorgeous. Her shirt was torn and showed a bit of the big beautiful breasts I had touched so many times before. I looked inside my room and saw Nina lying on the floor, crying and still soaking wet from that crazy jump she'd made into the filthy lake a little earlier. I closed the door and dragged Nina into the shower, took her clothes off and turned the water on. Her everlasting smile was gone, her eyes looked straight through me and she lay there like a ragdoll. I was washing the dirty water off her naked body and looked at her bruises and suddenly it hit me: I was shocked at how easily I was fixing up this bruised and naked twenty-three year old Vietnamese girl like it was an everyday thing.
What the hell did I get myself into? And more importantly….

What the hell had happened to me?

To answer that, I have to go back to the beginning

Prologue: You know it's time to leave when...

My name's not actually Neil Skywalker. That part you probably figured out already, considering that I don't think there's anyone out there who actually has that last name. And I was never the type of guy you'd expect to find surrounded by screaming, cat-fighting Asian girls battling over him.

Rather the opposite, in fact. I was born and raised in Holland or, as it's officially called, the Netherlands. My small country used to be famous for its excellent cheese, wooden shoes and windmills. Now it's famous for legal marijuana being sold in coffee shops and tax-paying prostitutes in the red light district.

I didn't start out as a total chump, like most guys who write about picking up girls, but I've just been a regular dude for most of my life. During my high school years I was the bad influence in class and wasn't interested in learning anything. I changed high schools three times. I lost my virginity when I was thirteen years old on a family holiday in France. The girl was English, and therefore my first lay was also my first flag. That might sound like the start of a promising Casanova career but it was a one hit wonder and nothing happened for the next four years.

As far as I know, no one had sex at my high school. If they did, they hid it well. At the last school dance I made out with a girl named Tammy. A blond and smiley girl with melon sized breasts. They were truly huge. Unfortunately the rest of her body was slightly on the heavy side too. She was a sweet girl but impossible to get in the sack. It lasted three weeks. Never been a patient guy.

I soon found another girl. She lived in quite a rough neighborhood. Just like her daughter, her overly friendly/horny mom couldn't keep her hands of me which was more than a bit weird when you're a seventeen year old boy. In those times you had to wait till your parents were out of the house if you wanted to have sex. Something that didn't happen often. We had sex just three times before we broke up.

I didn't date any girls for two years after that. At age nineteen, I could count the times I had sex on one hand. A fact my "friends" and colleagues at the construction site were happily using to make fun of me.

After getting my driver's license, a nice convertible, a better paycheck and by hitting the gym on a daily basis my confidence got a big boost. For the next five years I had four girlfriends and one one-night stand in a park behind a club. If you would rate them on beauty then they would probably be 6.5's. No fuglies but not head turners either.

Things were looking up until I decided to break up with the half Russian girl I was with for nearly two years. A lot of (non girl-related) shit had happened in the last few years including hanging out with the wrong crowd and frequent and serious trouble with the law. Something I won't go into.

I was always too hard-headed and foolish to get a college education, and after basic high school I worked at all kinds of jobs. Unlike some guys, luckily I had some skills and wasn't just lifting boxes. For many years I was working in construction as a carpenter, and for a little while as a tiler.

It would have been great for the self-esteem – I'm pretty proud of some of the carpentry projects I did – if it hadn't been for the fact that any kind of manual labor is looked down on, even the skilled, well-paying stuff. Or at least, that's what I thought. I felt I wasn't good enough to get a beautiful girl with a job like that. Putting girls high upon a pedestal. I assumed beautiful girls only liked the educated and well dressed manager type of guy.

Well, let's face it. As a major movie fan, Hollywood wasn't the greatest source of information on how to get an attractive girlfriend. I didn't see many blue collar guys picking up the babes. It's always the slick marketing executive or financial expert you'd see spending lots of money in clubs or bars. A sexy dressed babe with long luscious hair makes flirty eye contact, our handsome hero spews a few quick witted lines and not much later they end up in bed in some luxurious apartment with a great overview.

And if you do see a blue collar guy in a movie, then he has a cool job as a bartender or surf/ dive instructor or he fixes race cars or something. I wasn't any of those guys.

No, I had my hopes set on being that guy who by some

miracle ended up with that totally hot girl at the end of the movie. A girl who by real life standards would be a million miles out of his league. The late nineties were full of crappy rom-coms like that.

I lost my (fifth) construction job, and quit going to the gym and doing martial arts. I had wrecked my left shoulder by overtraining and overworking six days a week. It's still an injury that comes back from time to time.

No job, no money, no girl and no gym. A horrible and depressive dry spell was inevitable. I would classify myself as a "totally frustrated and cowardly mess" during that time. I would make up excuses not to chase girls or would lose all incentive to do so. For the next year I was unemployed, injured and sat at home; an old but spacious apartment in the city center. I bought it at the age of twenty-two, and completely renovated it by myself in the evenings and weekends for almost nine months while working a full time job.

Since I didn't have much money and wasn't in the mood for going out, I can't say I remember doing much that period of time besides watching lots of movies, browsing the web to kill time and having a daily wank.

A friend suggested me to work as a taxi driver just like him. There were no jobs available in my city at that time and thus I went to work in a nearby city where I didn't know anything besides maybe the main street. You can imagine the trouble I got myself into by not knowing any streets at all. This was before navigation in cars or on phones so I had to use a paper map.

There were always tons of college girls around the bus and train station but since I didn't have much game, I did nothing with all those opportunities walking by. I also felt that I wasn't good enough for college educated girls since I had such a low income job. I did however have a one night stand with a colleague after which I tried to avoid her as much as possible since the sex was pretty bad. She however had a thing for me so that I had to use a system of scouts and phone calls to see if she was at the train station.

I had a short relationship with a young platinum blond

girl (actually a college student I met through a friend) during that time so technically I was cheating during that one night stand. The relationship only lasted four weeks anyway, more on that later in the book. Later on I met a girl during work and she became my girlfriend for the next 3.5 years.

After a year I was pretty bored with the taxi driving and wanted more out of life. My contract had just been renewed and I stayed at home pretending to have back problems (which wasn't a complete lie btw). I wanted to get an office job and an uncle told me about me being a professional buyer just like him. It sounded pretty good to me.

The only problem was the expensive course I had to follow. I couldn't afford it so I managed to pretty much blackmail the taxi company to pay for half my education if I volunteered to quit my job. A trade which basically saved me about 1700 dollars at the time and the taxi company paying for an employee that didn't work. Corporate laws are a bit different (read better) in Northern Europe and the employee is well protected from being fired.

I took a job at a local bread factory/bakery and worked a three shift job packing all kinds of bakery products off the conveyer belt. It was a truly depressing, dead end job but hell, it paid the bills and I had time to study and follow the course.

After six month I got laid off and received unemployment money again (70% of your net salary per month) and did some cash in hand tiling jobs.

I sat at home for almost a year before I got a big break when a government recruitment office gave me an internship at a company that designed and manufactured machines. After six months they gave me a year contract. I became quite popular at the company for being able to do the job even though I didn't have the academic education everyone thought was required for the job. I got into the strategic buying department and went about buying parts for machines from all over the world – though since I was an assistant, I never got to travel.

Around then I was also a fanatic at trading stock options and spent a lot of time and money on that, dreaming of what a fantastic lifestyle I would have once I had some big money to spend. Instead of buying cool clothes, going to bars and socializing I was wasting my precious time and money on bad investments and a relationship that wasn't going anywhere. It ended in a fight and her packing up and leaving. Never saw her again and good riddance. It was a 3.5 year mistake.

Well, at least my investments were going not all that bad. Like any half-assed investor I made some money and lost some too. At one point, though, it looked like it might all have been worth it. For years I'd been anticipating the big crash in 2008, and bought lots of put options, that means you make money when the market goes down. Options are high risk/high reward investments. But I didn't realize just how bad it would be, so when the stock market had already bounced up and down a few times and I was becoming disappointed in the outcome and was afraid the market might even go up again and I would lose all my invested money, I sold everything, clearing a cool 10,000 Euros profit. It was a reasonable profit considering the original money I put in my account but then disaster struck and the Dutch stock market crashed in an all out panic. The panic I had anticipated for years. I could have made 150,000 Euros if I'd held on for just three or four weeks longer.

I wasn't cut out for this and my hopes and dreams of having an easy life went out the door and it depressed me for months. Of course I had to smile at work and couldn't talk about it. It was this depressing time that planted a seed in my mind about wanting to leave everything behind. I just didn't know how to give form to my escapism needs.

For years I thought that if I saved enough money or became rich the hot girls and successful life would come to me. This dream was now gone and then one day I saw some poor-looking guy with a really hot girl on the back of his bicycle. They were laughing and having fun and suddenly reality hit me in the face. It wasn't money that was keeping me from success; it was me and my social behavior. I wasn't an easy-talking or popular guy – I've always been very self-conscious and reacted way too much to other people's opinions about me, arguing every time I disagreed with someone, taking comments about me far too seriously, virtually unable to take a joke. Although I was able to get a girl from time to time, the periods in between girlfriends were full of depression and low self esteem. I was way too hung up on following "the rules" and my happiness depended on having a girlfriend and living happily ever after.

A colleague told me about the trips he had made to India and some other countries and I was briefly introduced to an intern who had just traveled for six months in Australia. I remember seeing him only once or twice. I didn't to talk to him much but his cool and laid back appearance intrigued me. Dare I say, I was fucking jealous of this young and confident surfer dude type of guy. Jealousy is a very rare emotion for me so it hit me extra hard.

Suddenly I became interested in traveling and remembered that in the ten previous years my only vacations were one weekend in Paris in 2002 with a girlfriend and two weeks in Greece in 2007 with my long term girlfriend. Every other time my summer holidays rolled around I was either single or my lousy friends backed out of our plans to go somewhere. Two trips in ten years: that sounds really pathetic and it was. I spent my vacation days at home surfing the internet or watching movies. Did I already mention that for years I was a major pussy by not even wanting to listen to people telling me to travel by myself? The thought of traveling alone had horrified me for nearly a decade but now I decided to do something about it.

In the summer of 2008 I signed up for a group tour to India and Nepal and went there with about twenty other Dutch people for twenty-four days. At least I wouldn't be totally alone. The trip was amazing and disastrous at the same time. I got so sick that I lost 25 pounds and by the end looked like a concentration camp survivor. But despite my terrible attempts of getting with a few girls in my group and all the horror of being sick for weeks and being forced to keep travelling in stinking hot buses and disgusting trains in the most unhygienic country in the world, I still got a taste of travelling and I liked it a lot. I discovered that other cultures fascinated me.

After spending a month recovering, I was back working

at the office. Well, working is an overstatement; most of the time I had a pretty easy life there. The company was doing poorly because of the financial crisis, though in my opinion it was mostly due to bad management. In the two and a half years I worked there we had six re-organizations and I survived them all. I had five different bosses and I managed to get a lot of stuff out of them, something most colleagues didn't appreciate, especially the ones who'd been working there for years but were too dumb or timid to profit from their job. I was getting paid a great salary, got a suitcase, a laptop, and company phone, bought myself a good car and a quality suit – but most importantly, for the first time in my life I felt like a somebody instead of a nobody.

My social skills were improving fast but not with girls; I didn't have a girlfriend for a one and a half year. Although I was dating a lot via dating sites, I was getting no results, except for a few fuglies and one attractive girl who lived in another city and broke my heart after a few weeks. I highly pedistalized her.

One day I went out with an extremely hot girl who had travelled a lot in South East Asia. We went for a drink but I couldn't keep a fun conversation going with her and things died out fast. I realized this was my major weak point. I was a typical boring beta male with bad traits like neediness and nice behavior. Nice guys don't get laid. Ever notice how all the hot girls keep complaining about guys they got laid with who turned out to be an asshole? You could be that guy!

It was the week before New Year's Eve 2008/2009 when I found out that most of my few friends were staying at home with their girlfriends and children. I was looking at two options: sit at home alone like some pathetic loser or man up and do something about it.

Two days before New Year's I jumped in my car at seven in the morning with only a small backpack and some food. It was minus twelve degrees Celsius outside and my wiper fluid was frozen because I was too cheap to buy some decent anti-freeze fluid. Half the ride I couldn't see a damn thing and was driving on the German autobahn, the only highway in the world where you can drive as fast as you want. I drove for eight hours straight to Prague in the Czech Republic. I parked my car in a sketchy underground garage and after a while and a discussion with a sketchy cab driver I found a hostel.

Those were the best three days of my life to date. I met lots of people of all nationalities and enjoyed hanging out with them, especially thanks to Jonathan, the Peruvian-Norwegian guy who got me involved in most of the activities. He's still a friend and visits me from time to time.

On New Year's Eve I was dancing, kissing and touching a big-boobed Singaporean girl all night. I didn't get the Singapore flag, but I still had one hell of a time in Prague. I mean, I'd never stayed in a hostel before and suddenly there were hot nineteen-year-olds walking around in their underwear in front of me. Lots of people were asking if I had Facebook, which wasn't very popular in Holland at the time. I quickly set up an account and got fifteen friends instantly.

From this moment on I was certain what was really missing in my life: Fun and Adventure. I couldn't believe how it was pretty much normal for every European or Australian college student to go abroad and have lots of fun. How much had I missed out all of those years?

When the company I worked for finally went bankrupt, 125 people lost their job and I was the only one kind of happy about it. This was my chance and my excuse. I figured that if I could backpack alone for three days and have fun, I could also do it for three years. Apparently a decent three days in Prague didn't keep me from being clueless; it never occurred to me that Prague would be a walk in the park compared to what I was about to experience.

My last few months at home, I was anxious to leave it all behind and saw only the negatives of staying any longer in this adventureless life. My friends were not going out much anymore because they already had girlfriends and children. And if I went out with one of them, we basically stood around and watched other people have fun, downing a few beers and/or being too stoned to even talk to girls. We had fun but together as buddies, not with girls. Sometimes we were so zombified by the insanely strong Dutch weed that if we started speaking to each other, it felt like we were coming out of another dimension. Like someone just violently woke you up in the middle of the night.

Needless to say, I wasn't at all successful at getting girls.

A few weeks later I started dating a nice but pretty plump girl. I met her online, the way I met most girls back then. My "girlfriend" was fat but had some huge melons and could give hella blowjobs. I guess she was hungry all the time. Coming out of a long dry spell, I was fine with it. She was five years younger than me, had her own place and was a pretty good singer and guitar player. I like it when girls sing for me. She tried to teach me to play guitar but after a few weeks I got bored with the slow progression and gave up. I was pretty good at giving thing up back then.

Having this "girlfriend" was like hitting an all-time low and I was embarrassed to be seen with her. We never went anywhere together, just met up for sex at our houses so I guess she was more a fuckbuddy than a girlfriend anyway.

After informing my friends that I was going away for a long time, I told her that I was leaving for a while and broke up with her. She wasn't happy with it and tried to convince me to try a long-distance relationship. I was thinking of all the hot girls I was going to meet and said no to that.

So at this point, I was out of a job and single again. By day I was planning my trip and getting rid of everything connected to me. I started sending letters to every company or website that had my address. Basically I made myself disappear off the radar. In the evenings I played darts with my buddies, smoked a lot of weed and had some beers and chips while listening to the greatest reggae singer still alive: Alpha Blondy. Those days were great, getting stoned and having fun with my friends every day of the week. Yes, at 31 years old I still wasn't very mature.

For those wondering how I was planning to afford to travel around the world without working; as said I owned an apartment in the city center of my home town. I had bought it in 1999 at the age of twenty-two, just when the real estate boom started in Holland. It took me nine months to totally renovate the whole place, something I did 95% on my own since my "good" friends were somehow never around to help.

I sold it in 2006 with a 40K Euro profit, months before the market started to collapse. Those who did their homework in those years could see the collapse coming and got out when I did. I'd been sitting on that money ever since and from then on had just rented a decent house and bought a nice car. I set my moving-out date at just two days before I left on my trip, so I had plenty of time to sell a lot of stuff and box up the rest.

There was a lot of stuff. You may remember me mentioning that I spent a lot of time at home watching movies. I had a specialized home cinema room in my house which took me months to build. It had a hundred-inch projector screen, a top quality projector, Cinema love seats, a 7.1 sound system with big JBL speakers, special cinema lighting and carpet and about three thousand DVDs. It was my first dream come true, and I couldn't bear to sell it, so I boxed everything up and stored it at my sister's house. The DVDs alone filled twenty-one boxes.

I went to city hall and registered myself as a homeless person and told them I was leaving for at least a year. This is the only way in Holland to get out of the expensive health insurance. So the only thing I had left in Holland was a bank account. During my last week I sold my beloved car, sorted out a few last things and said goodbye to my family and friends. It was time to see what I had in me and prove myself to the world.

It was time to break up with old habits and improve myself in every way possible.

Chapter One – Going East

All my life I've been fascinated by Russia and its cold, dark past. I grew up in the eighties and was always intrigued by the cold war and the military stand-off between NATO and the Warsaw Pact. My father once visited St Petersburg for his work in 1984, when it was still called Leningrad. It was a short visit but the stories he brought back fascinated me – the monotone and grey lifestyle of the people, the whole communist system and its many flaws. Coming from the West it just seemed like another world.

I have always been very interested in military history and since Russia did the most of the fighting (and suffering) in World War II, I had a great interest in seeing this country. After visiting several war museums and famous places throughout Germany, Poland and the Baltic states, I'd made it to Mother Russia. This is where my trip would really start. I had raced through the first six countries, doing nothing more than high-speed sightseeing and some lame flirting with local or backpacker girls. Still, I was already proud of myself for the two cold approaches I'd done on local girls in clubs.

These were things I barely ever did at home. The first one I tried was in Warsaw, in Poland. I had been looking for a bar to go to for the whole evening and finally found one. I sat down at the bar next to a couple of very hot-looking girls. Girls I would never dare to speak to back home. They told me they were Ukrainian students and I talked with them for a little while. I even quoted a funny Russian line to them. I had met a Russian guy in Berlin who taught me the phrase "Idite na guy", which is basically the Russian way of saying "Fuck you". What it literally means is "Go to the dick". The girls laughed hard but warned me never to say it out loud, because Polish or Russian guys would beat the crap out of me if I did. The conversation died out quickly and our glasses were empty. After excusing myself I never returned. What the hell could I talk about with these girls? I was never a student so my knowledge of university life is zero, and at that time I had no pick-up skills whatsoever. Avoiding an expensive round of cocktails was the best thing I could do.

Still, even if it wasn't a success, it was a start. You can't boost your self-confidence all at one go. The second time I did a cold approach was on a local girl in Vilnius, the capital of Lithuania. I went to a club named Tarentino's with a big group from the hostel. It was an awesome place to go. I approached two girls but the hottest one, named Edita, barely understood English. I took her by the hand to a quiet spot to avoid the loud music. She spoke some words of German but my German was terrible and so was my beta style of picking up. If I had a time machine and went back there now, I could do way better on both those approaches, but looking back on it it was still a giant leap from online dates with average-looking Dutch girls. At least travelling made me feel like somebody and not so socially awkward in clubs and bars. It was a bad start but at least it was a start. I was trying.

Russia – St Petersburg

The bus finally drove into St Petersburg after a ten-hour ride from Tallinn in Estonia. Russian Customs were surprisingly easy – they didn't even check my bag or give me any trouble. *So much for the strict Russian borders*, I thought. After being dropped off somewhere, I had to find my way to the hostel, which isn't easy in a country that uses a completely different alphabet. Most places in Europe, you can work out the sounds, like 'hôtel' in France, but how on earth is the innocent tourist supposed to know that he's looking for the 'общежитие'? Still, though it took me a while (and the metro was super-crowded), I finally found the hostel. It was a simple one, with the crappiest beds I'd seen in three weeks on my trip. The bed had no bedsprings; it was just a wooden board with a two-centimeter mattress on it. You might as well sleep on the floor. Welcome to Russia.

During the day, I met an Australian and two Finnish guys. That night, after drinking a bunch of vodka shots, we went out to a club called Achtung. It was a fun night. I noticed a hot girl with model-quality looks glancing at me a few times from the dance floor, and after a vodka shot of courage I went over to talk to her. Her name was Sofia, and she came from Uzbekistan. She was studying and modeling in St Petersburg. We danced for a while and I got a quick kiss out of her. She was at least an 8.5 on the hotness scale, but after a while she lost interest. In other words, I didn't have the skill set to keep things going. Also, I think she was looking for a rich dude rather than a backpacker.

The guys and I tried another bar before going back to the hostel. They were going on about what a good job I did talking to that hot girl – and that is just what beta guys do. Congratulate each other on nothing. I was actually proud for having the balls to walk up to a strange hot girl and saying "Hi, how are you doing?" Saying that is nothing. It's just a simple opening line, one anyone can use on anyone. All it does is what it's designed to: open a conversation. It's nothing to be proud of. What's worth being proud of is managing to keep the conversation up.

St Petersburg is a beautiful city with far too much in it to see in only four days, even with the almost inexistent nights and endless days where the sun comes up in the East almost while it's still shining in the West, a city of palaces and canals and incredible history. Just as an example, I went to the Hermitage, one of the biggest museums in the world. It's been calculated that The Hermitage has so many art objects on display that if you look at every item for just eight seconds, then it would take seven years to see everything. And the basement is filled with about fifteen times more stuff! There's so much in storage that people with access can just walk in and carry things out – there's no way of cataloguing it all, and no-one will ever notice that the object's gone missing.

Sightseeing in St Petersburg is not cheap, but luckily, I studied at the University of Driver's License, which got me massive discounts everywhere. My Dutch driver's license is a pink plastic card with my picture on it. It also has symbols of cars, motorcycles, and trucks, and says "Driver's License" in five different languages. None of them, however, was Russian, or written in Cyrillic, and since the employees at the museums didn't speak any other language than Russian or read the western alphabet, I got away with using it as a student card every time. The entrance fee for the Hermitage alone costs about sixteen dollars but is free for students, lucky me!

Not everything's beautiful, though. The city is full of old Ladas, the ugliest and crappiest cars ever. They look like nothing so much as the old T-34 tanks from Stalin's days. The weirdest one I saw was parked and had a giant dildo for a shift stick. I asked no questions.

But to make up for the cars, there were three Russian girls at the hostel, and one was very good looking. I asked her if she spoke English and she said no. Sometime later, I ran into the second one, and I asked the same question. Again the answer was no. I had almost given up on them, but the third one turned out to speak very good English and the four of us talked all evening while she translated everything. They were from Yakutsk, a city in the northeast of Russia where in winter time, it drops to seventy degrees below zero, unbelievable temperatures. When I told them that I had wanted to go dancing with them a few days before but didn't ask because I thought they didn't speak English, they were disappointed, because they loved to dance. Soon after that, the English-speaking girl left, and the two others moved to my dorm. I used my Russian language pocket book and had fun with the naughty sentences in there. The hot blond girl already had a boyfriend; the second girl, Anna, was definitely interested in me but wasn't that good-looking.

The day after, the four of us walked around the city and visited some places together. That evening, I had to take the train to Moscow, and the three of them showed up at the train station, bringing an extra girl with them. She spoke a little bit of English and said she wanted a picture with me because she wanted a picture with a handsome guy. I looked around, but she actually was talking about me. Naturally I let her take it. The girls even went on the train to make sure that everything was alright and that I got the right sleeping bunk in the overnight train. We said goodbye, and that's the last I saw of them – but I noticed I was sharing the compartment with a hot MILF in her early thirties and her young daughter. The woman slept in the bed next to me and was barely covered by the blanket, wearing only a thong and bra. So I'd say I had a good start in Russia. It would only get better from there.

Russia – Moscow

The train ride to Moscow took about nine hours and all the time I could enjoy the view of this half-naked woman sleeping in front of me, so I was in a pretty good mood when we arrived. It didn't last. The metro system in Moscow, with its ten lines and almost two hundred stations, is huge. And of course everything was spelled in the Cyrillic alphabet and I couldn't understand a word. It took a while before I found some people who spoke a bit of English and could help me out.

Arriving at the hostel I got a new surprise – it was another rathole! There was one toilet for a whole hostel with about twenty-five people. The toilet seat was just lying loose on the toilet – I nearly fell off the first time I used it. The door had a little hook to lock it, but the hook didn't fit in the little metal ring so you needed to leave a little crack to lock it. So there I was taking a big dump, the door doesn't close well, the couch was one meter away from the toilet door and there was no radio or television in the hostel to cancel out the noise I was are making. This is one of the most embarrassing things that can happen to me. I ended up going to the McDonalds every time I needed to crap.

The whole hostel was a dump and the grumpy young girl working there wasn't any fun either. I had booked this hostel because the two guys from Chile I'd met in Lithuania and later in Estonia had told me they'd be staying there. So in St Petersburg I told the Australian guy and the two Finnish guys I was hanging out with to go there too. Well, let's say they thanked me for booking this dump.

I in turn thanked the Chilean guys for it. Still, when I arrived already knew five people there, no need to make new friends.

That night I went to the famous Red Square with Gustavo and Nico from Chile. It was amazing; Red Square is huge, just below the Kremlin, and the wildly-colored St Basil's Cathedral looks spectacular when it's lit up at night. Of course seeing shitloads of hot Russian girls adds to the fun.

On the way back to the hostel, the three of us got stopped by a policeman. He stopped in front of us and when he got out of his car, he first looked around to check if anyone was watching us. Then he asked for our passports. Gustavo and Nico's passports were in order, but mine had no visa registration. It turns out you have to register if you're going to stay in the city longer than seventy hours after arriving. Though I'd only just arrived, we didn't understand the rules. The policeman became very serious and told me I had to come with him to the police station. Gustavo spoke a bit of Russian and translated what he could for me, while the copper just stood there playing with his whistle. He kept repeating "Gustavo, nje problemi, Nico nje problemi, Neil PROBLEMI!" He looked quite relaxed but also rather serious. I asked Gustavo to ask him if he wanted a bribe but Gustavo, a law student, was a bit anxious about asking him directly. In the end I took my Dutch/Russian travel book from my pocket and showed the cop a line which said "can I pay the fine on the spot?" He smiled and agreed. I asked him how much the fine would be, and he said "I don't know". I flipped to the section on numbers and pointed to the number five hundred. His smile got even broader as he agreed with it. So I paid five hundred rubles (about fifteen dollars in 2009) and we went on our way. Gustavo told me that before we left, the cop said that the money was for his family. At a guess his children's names are Vodka and Bottle.

When we got back to the hostel we woke up the girl who was working there. She was now even grumpier than before and explained to us that I didn't have to pay a fine at all. I had already kind of figured that.

The next day the hostel girl, Julia, was in a way better mood, and told me she'd had a major hangover the day before. Me and the two guys from Chile couldn't stop joking around with her about the night before, and kept pointing out things about the hostel and bellowing PROBLEMI! This pretty much covered the whole hostel.

After our shameless adventure in bribing a public official, the Chileans and I visited numerous sites throughout the city.

On our second trip to Red Square we saw one of the hottest girls ever. Soon they were using the time during our long walks to teach me a bit of Latin Spanish – but only the words to describe a woman. As a test of how well I was learning, with every smoking hot girl that walked by I had to give them a full description in Spanish.

One day we had an unexpected city tour when an eighty-four year old guide just walked up to us in the street and started talking. He spoke excellent English and had lived through the Second World War and Stalin's days. After he had showed us around the city we gave him a generous tip. He was doing tours because his retirement money had almost completely disappeared in the 1998 Ruble crash. That old geezer was definitely in better shape than us: we'd walked many miles and were dead tired afterwards, while he was probably going to do the same again. He was probably snickering at the wimpy young tourists that we were as he left us. I couldn't blame him.

Meanwhile, back home, my family received a new bank card for me and sent it by FedEx to the hostel in Moscow. An ATM in Estonia had eaten my ING bank card and since then I'd been paying in cash only. The card arrived the day after my family sent it, but Customs kept the card for a whole five days. Great fun, what with my funds running out.

The Chilean guys had to move on, and I promised I'd visit them once and if I reached Chile. Meanwhile I stayed in the hostel and practiced my Russian with Julia. During the day most backpackers went sightseeing, so I was alone with her most of the time, which gave me enough time to game her. She taught me the Cyrillic alphabet by letting me read the newspaper out loud. We were sitting closer and closer together and started touching and flirting a bit.

Later that day we went out together with a group from the hostel and visited a small club called Papa's Place. That Monday was Happy Hour night, and at one point we were getting four drinks for the price of one. No need to say we all ended up shitfaced. I walked back to the hostel with Julia but stopped at a small park close to it. We started kissing and things got pretty steamy pretty quick. When I put my hand under her short dress I felt she was really wet and ready to go. She wanted me then and there but it was already daylight, so I asked where she lived. We took a one-hour ride on the metro to the suburbs. To me it looked like a Russian ghetto, with countless grey concrete buildings straight out of Soviet times. I made a fool of myself by asking her about it and she looked surprised and said that the really bad neighborhoods were further outside the city. Coming from a western country, I had never seen a neighborhood like this and had no interest in seeing the "really" bad neighborhoods.

I had to pay a bribe to the guard to let me inside the building. Her apartment was small and old, but she had a bed and that was the most important thing. We both took a quick cold shower and jumped in bed to warm each other. She was the first bang on my trip. One down, many more to follow. Julia was smart, twenty-three years old, a working student and nice girl who had a beautiful slim body and a butter face. This means nice body, BUT HER FACE. Still, for four days we shagged like there was no tomorrow, but then my bank card finally arrived. I only had a 25-day visa, so after one last romantic get-together I had to move on to the next destination.
When I told them I was shagging a twenty–three year old Russian girl, my friends back home went crazy. Especially since I was already in my early thirties.

Russia – Kazan

Kazan is a medium-sized city, which in Russia means it only has well over a million people. I arrived late at night and luckily the owner of the hostel was waiting for me. She was a young woman, about twenty-seven years old, and she lived in an apartment on the outskirts of the city. The hostel itself was basically just an apartment with one room that served as a dorm. I was the only one there. The next day was a Friday and I went to the city center by bus. The buses were dirt cheap, only thirty rubles a ride. Every bus has a girl collecting the money and I pissed mine off because I only had a thousand-ruble note with me. It didn't help that I couldn't speak back to her and just kept shrugging my shoulders as she tried to find 970 rubles change. That's one girl I did *not* manage to add to my shagging diary.

That day and the next day I walked all over the city centre and was taking pictures of everything. The Kazan Kremlin is very beautiful, and since it was the weekend there were a lot of weddings going on, with all the bridesmaid-eye candy that implies. Kazan is one of Russia's Islamic provinces, with a lot of Turkish-descended people around. That can mean only one thing: Döner kebab places. There's nothing better than burying your face into a giant kebab after a long day of walking around.

In the main shopping street I sat down next to some cute girls who didn't pay attention to me until I pulled out my street map and it became obvious I was a tourist. Their attitude changed immediately and they started talking to me. Of course they didn't speak English and I tried to talk some extremely bad Russian but that didn't help either. I bailed out the moment it became awkward to try to talk to them any longer, and later I went to the train station and bought a ticket to Yekaterinburg for the next day.

Back in the hostel some boring backpackers had arrived but they didn't want to go out at night. I had a look in the Russian Lonely planet and read there was a small salsa bar named Cuba Libre not too far away. I thought, *What the hell,* and went there. It was a small place indeed, with just one bar and a small dance floor. I talked to a platinum blonde girl with big boobs at the bar who looked interested at first. She spoke a little bit of English, but she lost interest after she found out I was not going to stay long. So I walked up to two girls on the dance floor and started dancing with them. The cuter of the two was a skinny girl from Moscow. She was nice and spoke reasonable English, but she also had absolutely no interest in flirting.

At the table next to us there were three girls who were drinking and dancing a lot. One of them had massive knockers that were almost falling out of her dress. One of the others was skinny and had a cute sexy face; the third girl was skinny but not that good-looking. I danced a bit with them, but that was it: I couldn't get the conversation going and the one with the big knockers danced with some other guy. At least I tried, I thought to myself, and decided to go back to the hostel. Things weren't going anywhere, and I didn't expect anything to happen. I was wrong.

I was waiting for the toilet to be free when the three girls pulled me out of the line and outside the bar to smoke a cigarette. We all lit one up and one of the first things they asked me was: "Do you want to go home with us?" Now, I don't get asked home by three young hot Russian girls often but I was surprisingly relaxed about it. I thought that I was either getting mugged or in for great night. If you want to have fun you have to take risks, and since the whole point of the trip was to have fun, I jumped in a taxicab with them and we drove off.

We went to the apartment of the big-boobed and very drunk blonde girl. She lives there with her father but he wasn't in. They cooked me a midnight meal (try to find a girl in the west who will do that) and we had some more beers. After an hour the two skinny girls went to bed and I was alone with the girl with the big rack. Her name was Julia, just like the girl back in Moscow. She was twenty-two and worked as an English teacher. We talked all night and I tried to make a move on her but she wasn't that easy. I left at nine in the morning; it took me two hours and a lot of buses to find my way back to the hostel.

After sleeping for a few hours, I went to meet her in a park. We walked around a bit, and sat down at a bench. We kissed and later we talked about the fact I was leaving that same evening. I asked her if she wanted me to stay. Julia told me that she actually had a boyfriend and wasn't sure about the whole thing. But then she said that she wouldn't be seeing her boyfriend until next weekend, and I jumped on that, pointing out that we could have the whole week together. Since it wasn't vacation-time (except for me), she had to work during the week, and I told her that if she wanted to see me, she'd have to make some time for me in the evenings. She agreed but said, "But how, you already have a train ticket". I took the ticket I had paid twenty-five dollars for out of my jacket and I ripped it up in front of her. She looked me in the eyes to see if I was serious, and then we kissed again.

Julia asked me to meet her at work the next day. She taught English at a building in the city center. When I got there, she asked me if I would make an appearance in the class to talk with the students a bit. She didn't tell me that it was a surprise visit for the students, so I was a bit shocked when I walked in and she said something like "Tadaaa, a real foreigner who is travelling around the world!" I had no idea what kind of students she had – I didn't even know if I should be expecting kindergarteners or geriatrics – but I saw they were all in their twenties. Out of fifteen persons, there was only one guy and about seven or eight good looking girls. At first they were shy about speaking English in front of a foreigner, but they loosened up after a while. Julia introduced me as just a friend and I noticed the girls in the class were quite interested in me. One girl named Svetlana, who was a ballet dancer and stunningly hot – a 9 on the scale of 10 – asked all kinds of questions about travelling. I told her to come with me and flirted a bit with her. Julia kicked me under the table.

I started to tease her more and more and it drove her nuts. Clearly, though, it worked, because she couldn't stop kissing after the class ended, and started asking me sexual questions.

She invited me to stay with her in a dacha, the Russian version of a summerhouse. That Wednesday I met up with her and some of her friends, two guys and two girls who were both named Irina. The wooden dacha was near the river Volga and looked quite nice; one of the guys owned it and had built it himself. To make a long story short, we had a barbeque, lots of vodka – this was Russia, after all – and then went for a swim in the river. Julia took off her bra and went in the water while covering her boobs with her hands. By now she had been cock-teasing me for four days, and she was good at it, always talking about sex and asking me all kinds of sex-related questions – how many girls had I been with? Did I masturbate? Did I like to eat pussy? Did I do anal? How big was I? I told her she'd find out soon enough.

When we went back to the summerhouse, there was some confusion as to who was going to sleep where. One of the two

Irinas was pretty hot and kind of on a date with one of the guys, but she didn't actually want to sleep alone in a room with him. The Irinas wanted to share the only bedroom with Julia, but I managed to talk her into spending the night in that bedroom with me.

We went to bed and of course I was assuming we're going to have sex: she'd been talking my ears off about it all week. But once we were in bed she became very shy and didn't want to do much other than talk about it. After almost two hours of talking and trying I was getting really fed up and make an angry comment to her, telling her to leave me alone because I wanted to sleep. I was still quite drunk off the vodka and irritated by her holding off.

She left the room and came back a few minutes later. Her attitude had switched 180 degrees and she jumped on me and started making out. Within a few minutes we were having sex, which was actually only kind of average: she was a bit thick and her big boobs were very saggy once they came out of her bra. Half an hour later we did it again, this time breaking the condom in the process. I only realized that out after I was done, but I'd already been wondering why it had suddenly started to feel so good. Her face was red as a tomato the next day when we bought a morning-after pill at a pharmacy. I tried to have sex with her at her school that day when all the students and her girlfriend Irina had left, but though things got steamy she wouldn't do it.

On my last day I spent some time with her at her apartment. We had to take a cold shower because the heater was broken. My willy nearly disappeared when she washed it with ice-cold water and it was my turn to have a tomato-colored face when she made a comment about it. She'd turned out to be a real whiner and even complained during sex. Now, before then I'd never had any complaints about my performance and that much whining and bitching made me angry. She was the one who was very inexperienced and this whining of hers made me insecure (and soft). The sex was terrible. An hour later we had anal sex and afterwards she told me she was finally completely satisfied.

It was weird that she complained that much, because she

seemed to really be into me and held back her tears a bit when she said goodbye in the train. Or maybe she faked that a bit. Either way, it doesn't matter. She's married with an American, had his (?) baby and lives somewhere in the States now.

Russia – Yekaterinburg

Because I was really late buying my new ticket to Yekaterinburg, I could only get a ticket for a four-person compartment instead of a cheap ticket for a fifty-five bed wagon. There were three Russian guys in the compartment and they worked out I was a tourist as soon as they saw my backpack. They didn't speak much English, almost none in fact, but with my pocket language book I could make myself understandable. One guy was a football referee, another one was an engineer and the last one was a young soldier who already had three kids. After a while the soldier pulled out a one-liter bottle and put it on the table. It was some black liquid that he assured me was an herbal elixir that would make me very strong. Well, the only thing strong was the alcohol percentage: fifty percent and we drank straight from the bottle. We drank half the night and by the time the bottle was empty I didn't need the translation book anymore: I spoke fluent Russian and they spoke fluent English, or at least that's how it seemed. We were all speaking the herbal elixir language. The next morning the train rolled into the station and I said goodbye to my drinking buddies. I had a massive headache and was sick all weekend.

The only things I remember are remember are eating in a local restaurant with the guy who worked at the hostel (there were no other visitors), getting a 5000 Ruble note from an ATM and not being able to use it anywhere and visiting the place where the whole Romanov imperial family was brutally murdered during the 1918 communist revolution and canceling a date with a girl I had met in St Petersburg.

Kazakhstan – Astana

The train ride to the new capital of Kazakhstan, Astana, took twenty-four hours. The train was filled with people with lots of gold teeth, a girl from Kyrgyzstan with a moustache and a drunken and annoying Uzbek couple. I arrived in the country of Borat, one of the only countries I had read a few books about since I wanted to be prepared for travelling in a country that was a former Soviet state and had been home to the infamous gulags and nuclear test sites. Most Russian and other former Soviet Union train stations have dorms for overnight travelers so it was easy to find a bed. The dorms are cheap and comfortable and you meet a wide selection of characters there.

During the day I walked around for a bit and in the evening I went to an eating place next to the train station. It was an outside place with a barbeque and a tent built over it. I sat down and ordered two giant chicken skewers and a pint of beer. A few minutes later a Kazakh guy sat down at the same table and started talking to me. He spoke some English and some bad German. He started telling me all kinds of bullshit; like that he was married, except I didn't see a ring on his finger. He was a schoolteacher but didn't know anything about teaching when I asked. It was obvious that he was trying to scam me in some way. We talked about girls a bit and then he told me that he was picking up his mother from the train station. He asked me to come with him and he would introduce some girls to me. I said OK and wanted to pay the bill but the Kazakh guy took care of it. We went to the station, this idiot took about a five-second look around for his mother (!) and said "She's not here, lets go to meet the girls".
I was sure he was trying to sucker me into something I had no interest in and told him no. I went back to the station dormitory, leaving him behind with a dumb look on his face. Thanks for the free beer and food, dumbass.

Beyond looking around, I had some business to attend to: I needed to get a new Russian double entry visa, and that was going to be a real task to obtain. I went to look for the Russian embassy but couldn't find it that day. I can't really say the streets were clearly signed. That night I met two Dutch guys, which was quite a surprise: next to no tourists at all visit Kazakhstan, so meeting two of your countrymen is exceptional. Koert and Marco were a couple of nice guys travelling around Kazakhstan and Russia. Luckily for me, they also had to go to the embassy to change the date on their visas. They'd met a Kazakh girl who was helping them out with translating and filling in the forms. The Kazakh language was banned during the Soviet occupation, so the spoken language in Kazakhstan is Russian. About 25% of people living in this country are of Russian descent. I don't remember the girl's name, but she was short and attractive in a cute sort of way.

We all went to the embassy the next day (Wednesday) only to find out that it was closed.

We came back the next morning. There was a long line of Russians waiting at the embassy gates. We stood in line for about four hours: it was about thirty-five degrees Celsius and there was no shade. After four hours we hadn't even made it to the gates and they shut for the day. So on Friday we went back again and finally got inside. On Thursday, I had bought a new Russian invitation on the Internet.

Maybe I should explain that. To travel in Russia, you need an invitation from someone already in the country – relative, business partner, travel agency, whatever. It's just the sort of thing that's always gone on in Russia, a country that practically invented bureaucracy and has never liked people being able to move around without officials knowing about it. These days, though, the system doesn't work very well, since you can buy invitations on the Internet for something like $30.

So I had my invitation, my passport and enough money so I thought it would be easy enough to get a new visa. Ha. I soon found out that I also needed to have a train ticket to prove I really was leaving Kazakhstan and entering Russia. So I rushed out of the embassy, jumped into a taxi, got to the train station, stood in line, bought a ticket for some town on the Kazakhstan-Russia border, jumped back into another taxi, returned to the embassy, fought my way back in through the crowd of impatient and shouting Russians, made it to the desk and showed the guy my ticket. He simply looked at it and told me I also needed a copy of the ticket. Even though he had a copy machine right behind him he refused to make a copy for me, even when I offered him some money. This was pathetic. So I raced out of the embassy again, jumped into yet another taxi, rushed to an internet cafe, made some copies – actually, just in case, I copied every piece of paper I had – got back into a taxi, went back to the embassy, fought my way through the crowd of angry and shouting Russians – well, you get the picture. Back at the desk, I was finally able to pay a lot of money – I think it was around a hundred dollars – and we were told to come back the same day and pick up our passports. The other two Dutch guys had also had a lot of trouble with their paperwork. We were all very lucky to have our cute translator girl with us. We came back later and luckily everything was okay this time, we paid and got a new visa sticker in a passport. Normally it's nearly impossible to get a Russian visa outside your own country, and I was incredibly happy to get it. If I hadn't, I'd have had to fly to Mongolia and from there on to Japan, which would both be very expensive and mean I'd miss out on the best part of Russia: Siberia and the Russian Far East.

My remaining days in Astana I visited different parts of the city, taking a lot of pictures. The only bars I saw were very high-end and I skipped visiting them to save money. Astana is a very modern and expensive city with lots of shiny new buildings. The most noticeable landmark, for instance, is the Bayterek tower, a giant shiny golden ball on top of a tall tower. The whole area is brand new and full of massive buildings that must have cost a fortune.

I didn't really know where to go or what to see, so I never went out at night, something I now regret. Still, I was excited about being in Kazakhstan and after a lot of hassle about some required migration papers, I bought a train ticket to Al maty, the old capital in the south.

Kazakhstan – Almaty

The long train ride to the far south started with a piece of luck – I was put in a four-person compartment with two young sisters, who were very nice (though one was only 17) and spoke quite good English. I suppose it couldn't last. The conductor added a fourth person to the cabin, a guy called Nariman. I was a bit pissed-off – there I was, just getting started, and this cock-block shows up, a guy who didn't even have a ticket but made a deal with the conductor. I wasn't very happy about this.

As it turned out, though, Nariman was a cool guy who spoke very good English. He was enthusiastic about meeting a foreigner travelling in his country. It was nice to be able to speak some English again instead of attempting bad Russian.

Aigeriem, the elder of the two sisters, had a boyfriend, and when we arrived he drove me to a guesthouse. It was a total dump and they noticed; within an hour they had found me a quite expensive hotel instead. It cost forty dollars a night, but after looking at that guesthouse I didn't care, though I told them I couldn't afford it for long.

The room was nice but had no hot water in the shower. After twenty hours on a hot and dusty train I didn't care and showered anyway. That night I met up with Nariman again, and we decided to smoke some weed together with his buddies. They told me to wait at a crossroad a few blocks from my hotel. I waited for a while and suddenly a big Mercedes stopped next to me. Nariman was sitting inside with two friends and one was quite a big guy. It all looked very dodgy.

I asked myself how well I knew this Nariman fellow: after all, I'd just met him on the train, where he'd told me he was a banker and worked crazy hours, but I had no proof of any of that. Still, because he spoke good business English I decided to take a gamble and trust him and his friends, so despite the fact my mother always told me not to get in cars with strangers, I climbed in.

We drove around a bit and Nariman showed me the weed. It was stuffed in a matchbox and it was the crappiest looking bush weed I ever saw. I asked him how much they paid for it and he said something like twenty dollars.

When I offered them to pay my share they refused. We all sneaked into my hotel room and sat down. The other two guys didn't speak much English. The biggest guy started rolling the joints and was constantly talking about the police. He was freaking me out and at one point I told him to either say he was a police officer who was going to arrest me or to shut up about it. They all laughed and I relaxed a bit. Smoking weed in Kazakhstan is highly illegal and they will throw you straight into jail if they catch you, tourist or not. The only way out is a thousand-dollar bribe, and I wasn't planning to pay that amount of money and go through a lot of trouble just for smoking a joint.

We started to smoke and got through something like four big fat joints. The Kazakhs were super proud to smoke weed with a foreigner and especially someone from the marijuana capital of the world: Holland. We smoked everything and the Kazakhs were as high as kites, laughing their asses off. I almost didn't feel a thing; I was still used to the strong weed from the Netherlands. The Kazakhs were very impressed.

The next day, Aigeriem called me and told me she'd found a new place for me to stay. I checked out immediately and took one of those big fluffy towels from the hotel to compensate for not having had warm water. The room Aigeriem had found was with an old Russian lady. She looked like she was a thousand years old, spoke only Russian and was half deaf and blind. I paid only forty-five dollars for eight days and had my own room with a bed, television and a table.

The rest of the week was kind of boring. I spent my days visiting some museums and war monuments. I didn't have a laptop back then so instead of wandering through the Internet I just learned some Russian during the day.

Aigeriem stopped calling – I guess her boyfriend was jealous or something. Also, she was a bit of a goody-two-shoes and I'd refused to pay a huge fine at the police station to get some immigration paper they thought I needed, since I'd got my visa back in Holland and knew my papers were in order. The immigration officers even wanted an official invitation paper from the old grandma I was staying. I was like "fuck that, I'll take my chances"

On Friday Nariman called me and asked me to go out with him. He said he knew four girls who were dying to meet a world-travelling foreigner. Of course I said yes to this. Everyone found it really interesting that I was travelling around Russia and Kazakhstan without speaking sufficient

Russian. People there can't usually afford to travel abroad, and even if they can it's a hassle with the Russian and Kazakh governments.

We all met in a big club and they all bought me mojitos. After the club we went to a smaller bar where we smoked the big shish (water pipe). Nariman had told me he had a crush on a girl working at his bank, and she was there that night. She was a 7.5 at least. The girl sitting next to me was only a 6.5, but she had an amazing body. Her name was Dana. After we left the bar Nariman and the girls waited for a taxi and I assumed that Dana was going with them, but she surprised me by saying she wanted to walk with me.

We were making out within minutes and she got quite horny, but she didn't want to take it any further. I got home at seven in the morning and quickly fell asleep.

I had one more date with her and a girlfriend but not much happened that night except for going to a cinema. And that was the end of that. No Kazakh flag, but at that point I wasn't really bothered with flags or even particularly concerned with getting laid. I was still in touch with both Julias and kind of missed the one from Kazan. Of course, I wouldn't say no to an opportunity, but I was focusing most of my attention on surviving a trip to unknown places where I hardly understood a word people were saying. Not many people or tourists visit places in the Russian federation other than St Petersburg or Moscow.

A few days later I took a (Russian) tour to Charyn National Park, the Kazakh equivalent of the Grand Canyon. It was a two-hour drive and I met two Dutch girls in the tour bus. There must be something about Kazakhstan that attracts Dutch people, because weirdly I didn't meet tourists from any other nationalities while I was there, only ones from Holland. One of the girls was of Chinese descent but had a great pair of knockers.

I hung out with them all day while climbing rocks and taking walks through the astonishing natural scenery. The views were amazing and it was nearly forty degrees outside. It was tough climbing the rocks there but definitely worth it. The guides even forced the Russian seniors who took the tour to climb the dangerously loose mountain sides. I needed both hands to climb up and they were even with walking canes. Later that weekend I met up with Nariman again and we had some beers and smoked some shish. The next day I left Almaty and headed back to Russia – a land I'd been interested in that now I loved, seduced by the friendliness of the people, their endless curiosity about foreigners, and the stunning architecture.

Train ride from Almaty to Irkutsk

That being said, the train ride back to Russia and further to Irkutsk was the ride from hell. Welcome back to Russia. (I love Russia, but like everything really worth getting bothered over, it has its share of issues.) Let's start with the first part of the trip, the forty-hour ride to the Russian city of Novosibirsk.

Getting the train ticket was a piece of cake this time: the woman behind the counter didn't ask for any migration papers and didn't even make a problem when I bought a ticket for a train ride after my visa ended. I did this because I didn't want to arrive in a major Russian city at three in the morning, which is definitely not recommended if you're interested in keeping your skull or ribs (or life) undamaged. So I bought a ticket for a later train that arrived at ten in the morning.

The ticket purchase went super fast because I got help from an English-speaking lady waiting in line. After I had the ticket she tried to convince me to join a church with a full demonstration of Jesus-freak preaching. Nice of her, but eh, no thanks, I don't believe in fairy tales told by grown men in dresses.

Finding a ride in Kazakhstan is dead simple: you just stand at the side of the road and stick your arm out. So far it's similar to lots of countries, the only difference is that while there are taxis, any car will stop in the hope of making an extra buck. Then you have to haggle (ten words of Russian and using your fingers for counting) with the locals to get a ride. I've taken lots of trips with complete strangers for just a few dollars this way. It's a win-win situation for the both of us. They get some extra gasoline money in a country where gasoline is dirt cheap thanks to their enormous oil industry and I get a cheap ride to wherever I want.

After buying the ticket I went back to my room to pack my bag and buy some food for the trip. I said goodbye to the Russian grandma (who's toilet sounds I won't miss) and went to the station.

I thought it would be smart to have some money in case I needed to bribe the railway police so I took about 150 dollars worth of Kazakh Tenge out of the ATM. I got on the train and after a while the railway police at some station checked me out. Finding out my visa had expired that day, they started to make problems. I started to negotiate a bribe by writing numbers on my translation book since they didn't speak any English. At one point they agreed on twenty dollars but told me, as far I could understand, that I couldn't leave the country. I said I was going to the border anyway, and suddenly they didn't want the bribe anymore and let me go.

I was happy not to pay a dime to those hicks, not knowing what a surprise was waiting for me at the border.

Once again, the train was filled with all kinds of characters. No good-looking single women, though, that was for sure. Things started to get really interesting a few hundred kilometers before the border, when the whole train wagon came alive. I had already noticed that a few people had enormous bags with them. They started to unpack those bags and out came the t-shirts, jeans and dresses. Others had massive amounts of alcohol with them. You'd think this was all done out of sight of the officials, but no: the train conductor was the great leader in all this. He even tried to stash four bottles of whiskey in my bag. I told him "No way!" Let him do his own smuggling. All the mattresses were lifted and got a pile of jeans under them. All the pillowcases were filled with t-shirts and dresses. This whole process took about an hour, and by the end the whole wagon was one gigantic contraband-stuffed carriage.

When we finally reached the Kazakh/Russian border, the train was raided by customs soldiers. They started checking all the passports. I remembered that the officers before wanted dollars instead of their own currency, so I reached into my bag and looked for my hidden pocket. Normally I would wear the money belt/pocket under my clothes but in Almaty it was so hot that I left it in my bag a few times. I found my money belt but the money was gone. I suspect that the grandson of the Russian grandma I stayed with took it. He was a scumbag, always asking me for small change and cigarettes. I often heard him yell at the old lady. Like I said, just before I got on the train I bought some groceries for the long train ride, and didn't pay attention to my bag. This was probably the moment the bastard stole my money. 165 USD gone.

Luckily for him I didn't check before I left, because I'm not the forgiving type or the average schoolboy backpacker. I would have beaten the living daylights out of him right there in his own house. I've been my own judge a couple of times before and I've never regretted it, even though I ended up with a criminal record because of it.

Anyway, the money was gone, I was hundreds of kilometers away from Almaty, and I couldn't do a damn thing about it. When a customs officer looked at my passport and saw my visa was expired, he told me to get off the train. From the moment I stepped off the train there were a few mean-looking soldiers surrounding me. One had a big German Shepherd dog on a leash that was nearly biting me and another soldier stuck his AK-47 in my back. He pushed me in front of him towards a small office while yelling commands I couldn't understand at me in Russian. I had to walk past the train and absolutely everyone was watching me. The train nearly fell on its side because everyone was pressing against the windows to see me.

Inside the office I was questioned as to why I had overstayed my visa. They wanted to know everything about why I was in Kazakhstan, what I'd done there, where I'd been. Then they told me they had to send me back to Almaty to get another visa. It sounds ridiculous, to make me take a thirty-five hour train ride back to Almaty jus to get a hundred-dollar visa for a single day. But they were dead serious about it. This carried on for half an hour; four different officers were constantly asking me difficult questions in

Russian, making phone calls and faxing my picture around.

Finally, at some point an officer from the Russian side of the border walked in, probably to find out what was holding the train up so long. He had a lot of stripes on his shoulder and a massive hat; he looked impressive, was clearly high-ranking, and spoke reasonable English. He asked me where I was from, and I told him Holland. As soon as I said that he cracked a huge smile and got all enthusiastic. Apparently he was a major Football fan, and he said that since the Russian national team hired a Dutch coach they had started to have some great successes on the field, for the first time in years. I joined in his enthusiasm about the famous coach Guus Hiddink and kept talking about Football. He started talking to the Kazakhs and apparently convinced them to let me go, because that's just what they did. All I had to do was sign some documents and that was it. I didn't even get a fine or anything!

I got back on the train and everyone asked what happened. The train was moving again and I explained while people unpacked all their smuggled stuff from everywhere in the wagon and put it back in their bags. Some hours later we arrived in Novosibirsk. At this point I was running short on time to visit; I had to go to Mongolia before a specific date or my Mongolian visa wouldn't be valid anymore. The next train to Irkutsk, a mere 1,850 km away, was leaving in a few hours and I bought a ticket for it, just in case I hadn't spent enough time on trains of late. Because I didn't end up using the Kazakh money for bribery, and since I was out of USD thanks to that bastard in Almaty, I wanted to change it to Russian rubles. Funnily enough, I couldn't find an exchange booth anywhere. I tried several banks next, but none of them could or would change it. No bank would take the money, not in Russia, Japan or China.

After Hong Kong I gave up, and to this day I'm still stuck with $150 worth of Kazakh money. I'll have to go back.

This train ride took yet another forty hours and I slept for most of it. The trains are interesting at first, since they were all made back in the Soviet era, but the Soviet propaganda imagery gets pretty boring after a while. Bear in mind that the trains I took in Russia were never the "real" Trans-Siberian train, an overpriced tourist trap. These were the real trains that real people took, who always got wide eyes when they saw my huge backpack, since they'd almost never seen a tourist in among them before. They got interested and it was easy to strike up conversations – well, at least as much of a conversation as my limited Russian allowed. Everyone gets their own bed, and the toilets are reasonably clean, though the sink there is the only one and everyone has to freshen up and do their teeth there, which seeing as there are 48 beds per carriage can make for a bit of a lineup.

There were a few shady characters in the train wagon, particularly two Siberian truck drivers who for some reason needed to be on the train. One was wearing a black eye patch and looked pretty beat up and the other one was a drunk. Other passengers warned me not to hang out with them but there was no escaping. They just kept sitting close to me and I decided to make the best of it and we drank some vodka together. The next morning when I woke up they were gone but all my stuff was still there, so everything worked just fine.

Normally the girls/women called provodnitsas who work on the trains – serving drinks, looking after passengers, all that – are fucking horrible but this time there was a nice-looking girl working and she was super friendly. She brought me free tea the whole day and we chatted a lot. Her English wasn't good enough for a normal conversation but we got along. The last ten hours the wagon was almost empty and I was so bored that I actually helped her clean and fold all the sheets and blankets. After almost eighty hours and lots of trouble I finally arrived in Irkutsk.

Russia – Irkutsk and Ulan Ude

On arriving in Irkutsk I took a taxi to the nearest hostel, where luckily they still had a bed available. I found four guys in the kitchen, three English and one American. We had a lot of drinking fun that night; after my trip I was definitely in need of a shot, or two or three. The guys invited me to come with them to Lake Baikal and to Ulan Bataar, the capital of Mongolia, and the next day the five of us went to the train

44

station to buy tickets. I had some doubts about doing this because I thought I might want to stay longer in Irkutsk and go out a bit, but I bought the ticket anyway and we went to Listyanka, a small tourist town next to the famous Baikal by minivan.

Lake Baikal is the deepest and biggest freshwater lake in the world; it's the size of a small country and it's legendary – there's a great Russian folk song about it. We walked and climbed a bit along the shoreline and took some great pictures of this endless, clear blue lake. After that we bought some beers and rested a bit on the small beach.

Although the Russian summer is hot, the water was freezing cold and we only swam for a few minutes.

There were two local girls hanging around us and they giggled a lot when they saw me mooning passing boats. Who can resist such a work of performance art? They came closer and I splashed some water on them, and we got talking. One girl didn't speak any English but the other one, who was a stunning blonde, spoke a little. We chatted for a while until the guys wanted to go back to the hostel.

We walked back to the bus stop and ate some delicious smoked fish along the way. Close to the bus stop we were eating and drinking some more and I ran into the two girls again. They said wanted to go to a club with me. "With us?" I asked them. "No, with you" they replied. It was pretty clear they were not attracted by the shy behavior of the others. I still had to say no to them, unfortunately, because I'd already checked out of the hostel and had a train ticket. They were very disappointed. I tried to convince the guys to change the tickets and stay just one day longer but they wanted to go.

We went back to the hostel, took our bags and got on the train to Ulan Ude. There's never a guarantee about anything, but I was pretty sure I could have at least kissed that cute one on a night out. Oh well.

That night we drank lots of beer on the train. In Russian trains, drinking beer is quite normal, there's a guy walking around with a little shopping cart selling it.

We arrived quite early and we walked around the city a bit. One of the guys, the baby of the bunch, was named Chris, and when I found out he was nineteen I told him I was old enough to be his father. After all, I was thirty-two and I first had sex when I was thirteen with an English girl named Rachel. At that he shouted out: "O my god, my mom's name is Rachel". I burst out laughing and made quite a few jokes about that, telling him we'd hadn't been very safe and so it was entirely possible that I'd knocked her up. Actually, I checked, and his mother was older than the Rachel I was with. Still, we all laughed about it, and from that moment I called him son and occasionally had a portentous father/son conversation with him, dispensing sage advice. Because you really want your fatherly advice to come from a guy who sold his house to bum around the world for three years and pick up girls.

We bought some more beers at a supermarket and started drinking again. It was eleven in the morning and we were already downing beers like idiots. We all took a minibus ride to a Buddhist monastery (yes, Russia has those too) and were surprised to see just how poor everything was, while the monks were walking around with mobile phones and gameboys.

At night our group went to a Mongolian restaurant recommended by Lonely Planet. The food tasted very good but the next day I was sick as fuck. That evening we went to an Internet cafe/bar/casino where we almost had a fight with an annoying drunk army captain. He was fun at first but got more annoying and aggressive as the evening went on.

That night I said goodbye to two of the three English guys. Too bad, because those guys were the most fun in our group. The other English guy, James and an American guy also named James and I went on the train to the Mongolian border and spent the night in the train station's dorm. We watched some TV series on a laptop and drank a bottle of vodka.

Mongolia – Ulan Bataar

My trip to Mongolia wasn't without trouble. When I woke up in the dorm at the Russian train station in Naushki I was quite hungover and had to run for the toilet. My stomach was fucked up, either from the Mongolian food and/or the bottle of vodka we drank the night before.

The two Jameses and I got into a taxi that took us to the border. There we found a family with a minivan who would take us across for a few dollars each. We cramped ourselves into the van with the whole Mongolian family and lots of bags and went across the border. There we found a guy/taxi to drive us to Ulan Bataar. I think we paid around sixty dollars for it, which in my opinion was way too much for a five-hour drive, but the others wanted to go and I had to tag along.

On the way there we drove through the countryside, which was quite spectacular. The country has lot of mountains and grassy fields everywhere; we saw cows, wild horses and sheep all the time. There were lots of gers, the traditional Mongolian tents that a lot of people mistakenly think are called yurts. I was not in the mood to take pictures because of my fucked-up stomach. I assumed I would take pictures another day, something I didn't do because I was sick for days over there and didn't want to repeat my near-death disaster in India and Nepal the year before. I will do whatever it takes to avoid making the same mistakes I made there.

We arrived in Ulan Bataar, the capital of Mongolia, and went to the famous golden Gobi hostel only to find out it was fully booked. They sent us to the Golden Gobi 2 hostel, which was not as good but fun anyway. By now, along with my stomach troubles I had also developed a cold, so my misery was complete. The two Jameses went on a three-day tour but I didn't join them. The tour consisted of one day of sightseeing, one of horse riding and staying with a nomadic family in a tent, and then some more sightseeing. The idea of horse riding and the eating of sheep intestates/guts didn't appeal to me and my stomach. I just stayed in the hostel and watched some movies. There was a nice Mongolian girl named Deeggi working as a maid there and I tried to get with her, she showed interest but the language barrier and the family watching all the time wouldn't make it a successful pick-up. Deeggi was a young girl but also a single mom and I didn't want her to lose her job over it.

Anyway, later that week when I was feeling a bit better I

went out with some people from the hostel. We went to a bar called Strings, which had a good live band and reasonably-priced beer. After I ate a meal there I hit the dance floor. There were plenty of good-looking Mongolian girls dancing around. Within a minute I was dancing with a slutty-looking chick in an ultra-short skirt. She started grinding her ass up to my dick like crazy. I thought to myself, *Wow, they must really like white foreigners.* How naïve of me in a city visited by hundreds of thousands of tourists every year. She pulled me off the dance floor and took me by the hand to the side. The following conversation was very short and went something like this:

Girl: You like me?

Me: Sure I like you!

Girl: Want to have fun with me? Let's go have sex!

Me: (thinking) Damn, that's easy, I already like it here.

Me: Yeah sure, let's go!

Girl: Ok, fifty dollars!

Me: Eh what? Hmmm, no way!

Girl: Why? You like me yeah, you pretty boy, have fun with me! I give you good time.

Me: Eh, No thanks!

That was the first time I encountered an Asian prostitute. I still had so much to learn. Me and the sleazebag German guy I was hanging out with returned to our table and drank some more beer. I went to the dance floor again to dance with some other girls and the first girl/prostitute got jealous and started grinding her hot little bum on me again. That's when I realized that probably all the girls in there were prostitutes. We left not much later.

The next day the German guy and I went to hear a sort of rock/folklore band in a big theatre. It was pretty pricy and filled with tourists. I didn't like the show much because in my opinion the music sucked and it was ridiculously loud. It was so loud that we went to sit in the back of the hall and the German guy even put pieces of paper in his ears to avoid ear damage. It was a mix of opera, Mongolian chanting, loud rock and hip hop. Strangest concert I've ever seen.

Later that night we went to Strings club again. This time we were able to meet some "normal" (i.e., non-professional) Mongolian girls and sit down with them. Nothing happened that night but at least we had some fun. The little bum grinder was also there and tried to steal me a few times but I told her to go away after a while.

Although Mongolia is a very poor country, the city center is very nice, with an enormous square and giant statues of Genghis Khan, the father of the country and one of the most successful warlords in history. The Mongolian empire once stretched from Pacific Ocean to Hungary. The Mongols were feared all over the world and famous for their technique of shooting arrows from horses sprinting at full speed.

After a while I had to say goodbye to everyone there and take the train back to Russia. I was forced to buy a ticket for the tourist wagon, because I wasn't allowed into other wagons with Mongols in it. When I entered the small four-person compartment there were two Mongolian guys sitting in there. They looked like decent people and were well-dressed. They helped me to put my heavy backpack on the rack above the beds. It took a while before the train left. I went out of the compartment and smoked a cigarette, and then talked to some Scottish guy I met.

When I came back to my compartment the two Mongolian guys were gone. I didn't think anything of it until I looked at my bag. It looked different than before.

I looked inside and saw that my expensive Ralph Lauren jacket was gone. I was furious and tried to talk to the train lady, but she didn't speak English. Luckily there was a Mongolian tourist guide on board who did. She explained what happened to the train lady but she didn't seem to care. I became angrier and told her I was going to search the train for those bastards. I was going to knock their teeth out as soon as I saw them.

I searched the whole train but didn't see them. When I got back to my compartment there were two train cops and they asked what happened. Again the tourist guide explained things and then the two cops and I went looking for my jacket. We searched the whole train together and every time there were two guys without families, the cops roughly opened their bags and searched through. It was quite a spectacle. In the end we didn't find the guys or my jacket. I let the train cops write a paper confirming that my stuff had been stolen, and they handwrote a paper in Mongolian. I asked the train lady to put some stamps on it to make it look more official. Months later, this helped me get a bit of insurance money back, but not nearly as much as the jacket was worth. If that were the worst thing that was gonna happen to me, then I would be more than OK with it. It wasn't.

Russia (Far East) – Chita

After that partly unfortunate week in Mongolia I was back in my beloved Russia. I quickly bought a ticket to Chita and soon fell asleep on the train. When I woke up the next morning I got to talking with a Russian guy who was sleeping in the bunk below me. After I'd answered a few of his questions he told me I was a hero for travelling alone in Russia. He spoke a bit of English and I spoke a bit of Russian so together we managed a conversation.

Sergei was a guy in his forties who was visiting his family for a few days, and he got me a fully-furnished two bedroom apartment for only five hundred rubles a day. That was about fifteen dollars back in 2009. Super cheap if you compare it to the crappy hostel in Moscow where I paid the same for a shitty dorm with sixteen beds and a toilet I couldn't bring myself to use. That day I walked around Chita a bit and in the evening Sergei and his girlfriend showed me around different places in the city.

The next day was pretty much the same. We went to some forest where Sergei proudly showed Russia's pride: the massive taiga, that endless spread of conifers that covers about half the country. Sergei paid for just about everything, including the food and drinks; I almost had to fight to manage to pay something in return. I did finally succeed in buying us some beers.

The next day was a weekday, so there wasn't much to do till the evening, when I went out to meet some girls. I met two hot girls on the street and got to talking with them. It wasn't the most peaceful of conversations: about ten meters away there was a fight going on, with a guy getting severely beaten up by three other guys. The girls wondered I wasn't scared, but I pointed out that it wasn't my ass getting kicked. Still, when the guys walked by us I thought it was better to stay quiet and not let them know I was a foreigner. It's a technique I often use when cops are walking by. I asked the girls for their phone numbers, and they said "Give me yours". Doing that's a stupid mistake I don't make nowadays. Always get the number of the girl and don't only hand out your own. I typed my number into her phone but was fucking the numbers up because her phone had the Russian alphabet.

Later in my room I realized I forgot to type in one number and was screwed. And not the fun kind of screwed I was hoping for, either.

I went back to where I'd met them, but I didn't see them again. Still, I wasn't going to waste too much time on something hopeless, so while walking back to the apartment I approached two girls. They didn't speak English at all but somehow I got them to a bar. I paid shocking prices for three beers and tried to make the best of it. The personnel were happy to see a foreigner and we joked around a bit as we drank. When we were done we started walking back towards my apartment and I tried to convince them to join me. This is not an easy task if you only speak very bad Russian. Unfortunately, the ugly one of the two was cockblocking me and wouldn't stop whining to her friend that she wanted to go home. I thought, *Do or die*, and looking at the hot one, a skinny girl named Ilona, I said the Russian word for kiss. "Da", she said and her red lips touched mine. We kissed. She definitely liked it, but her crazy and probably jealous girlfriend was pulling her arm, looked shocked and yelling "Ilona, stop it". We parted ways pretty soon after. Another almost sure thing ruined by someone else. The look in Ilona's eyes had already told me she was up for anything, and I had my own apartment close by.

Russia – The wedding in Chita

When I told Sergei I was about to leave because my visa was running out, he burst out "No way! Tomorrow's my cousin's wedding, you've got to see a Russian wedding!" How could I refuse? The next morning I bought a big bouquet of flowers and we went to the bride's house. It was still only ten in the morning and when we entered the house the bride was still walking around in her underwear. She was a totally hot girl, the kind they only make in Russia. Her bridesmaids kicked us out of the house. A bit later when she was dressed we went back inside and I was introduced to the whole family. The groom was a biker and all his biker buddies came over on their motorcycles.

Luckily I found out that one of the bridemaids (Natalia) spoke perfect English and I talked with her for a while.

In the afternoon we went to a park where the couple had the pictures taken. There was a lot of food and people started drinking vodka. Welcome to Russia. I had at least five double shots of vodka before we moved on. There was a whole truckload of hot girls there, but unfortunately most of them didn't speak English. Still, when we drove to a small church for more pictures I ended up in a large SUV with the hottest girls from the wedding crowd. We were sitting in the back of the car and suddenly the girls opened the small rooftop and stood up and started shouting and cheering like something out of the movies. I just sat there with the two finest asses a man could ever see waving in my face. I took a sneaky picture, because my friends back home would never believe me if I told them about this.

Later that night we all went to the wedding party where I kind of felt like a wedding crasher. But still, most people seemed to like it that I was there: at one point people almost stood in a line to toast with the foreigner. I was downing so many vodka shots that I had to switch to champagne so that I wouldn't get completely wasted. I danced with some girls and Sergei did half a drunken striptease. I got the feeling that Sergei was the disreputable uncle of the family, the one his brothers and sisters probably warned their kids about. I still found it almost unbelievable I was just attending a Russian wedding in the countryside like it was something perfectly natural.

I got talking with one of the bikers who had studied English once, and after the wedding he and a few other bikers drove me to a garage in some back alley. It all looked pretty dodgy but once inside they showed me their bikes and we drank some beers. After a while we smoked weed.

They had some sort of weed oil that they smoked with a sawed off plastic bottle and a bucket of water. I had never used that sort of bong before. Needless to say, after all that vodka and champagne and now this, I was pretty fucked up that day. Afterwards three of the rough bikers brought me home in a car and walked me all the way to the door of my apartment. At first it looked a bit sketchy when they walked up the stairs with me but they were just being nice and making sure I got indoors alright. Just as well, too. Russian people hardly ever smile but are among the nicest, friendliest people I met around the world.

I had a massive hangover the next morning but Natalia and a lot of young people from the wedding picked me up anyway, and we went with four or five cars to some lake a few hours away. It was still very hot outside. We all lay on the beach that day, eating leftover food from the wedding and drinking vodka again. (Welcome to Russia.) I made a sorry attempt to score with one of the girls but no success – I really wasn't in any state to carry it off anyway. Natalia was watching from a distance and acted like she didn't mind, but to this day she asks me to return to Russia and hang out with her. And one day I will and who knows what will happen then.

Russia (Far East) – Khabarovsk

After the wedding in Chita I spent two nights on the train

to reach Khabarovsk, the second-largest city in Russia's Far East. When I got off the train I dropped my bag in a locker and started exploring the city. It was hot outside and I walked around the city most of the afternoon. The first thing I noticed was the extremely high number of hot girls in the city. Having already been in Russia for already six weeks I was getting used to seeing quite a lot of attractive girls around but here it was unreal. Out of every ten girls you saw at least seven or eight were highly bangable. Almost every girl was at least a 7 on a scale of 10. It was at least thirty degrees in the sun and they were all dressed in short skirts and high heels. For some reason they were all big-breasted. I don't know what they eat there but they should introduce that diet to other parts of the world. I decided then and there that I would live in Khabarovsk after returning from my word trip.

Later that day I returned to the train station, since there are no hostels or cheap hotels in Khabarovsk. My plan was to stay in the train station's dorms, but as soon as she found out I was a foreigner the fat old lady behind the counter just said "Nyet". There were people just walking around behind me and I could see all the empty dorm beds. That fat old pig of a woman, who came straight from Stalinist times, just kept saying "Nyet" and I didn't really know what to do.

I went to the information desk and asked what was going on, but that didn't help much. But a security guard overheard my story and walked with me to the hostel's desk and tried to get me in. He didn't succeed. He started calling around for me and I was hopeful I might get a nice apartment the way I had in Chita. Unfortunately he couldn't find me anything, but he said I could sleep in the VIP waiting room for free. I offered him a beer in thanks, but he (Andrei) said: "I don't drink, I'm a sportsman, I run marathon". Although he looked like a low life with teeth missing I believed him.

Andrei worked a twelve-hour night shift and the next morning when I woke up he offered me a place in his house with his family. Obviously I accepted and we went there on an old, clunky bus to drop off my bag. After getting off the bus to the suburbs we walked over to his house. Although "house" is a bit of an overstatement. All of the two-story buildings were made of wood and looked like barracks from a WWII concentration camp. I finally understood what Moscow-Julia meant by a "really" bad look. But I hadn't had a shower in three days, so I was fine with it. The only problem was that there was no shower, only a sink. Still, I made the best of it with a bar of soap.

Andrei's wife was a lot younger than him; I think she was in her late twenties, but she was quite ugly for a Russian girl. I guess Andrei was already in his mid-forties. Anyway, after cleaning up I dropped my bag and Andrei and I went back to the city for a "tour". Since Andrei didn't have any money I bought him some food and he asked if he could get a beer with that. Communication was difficult because he didn't speak much English and I needed my pocket translation book a lot as we walked around the city and visited all the sites. Andrei was drinking more and more. In the afternoon we went to visit a childhood friend of him.

We went to an office where he introduced me to Vitaly. Vitaly had a business getting visas for Russians who wanted to work abroad, and had two girls working there. One of them, Tanya, was very good-looking and her dress showed maximum cleavage. She didn't speak much English. Natasha, the other one, was average-looking but spoke very good English. Both were in their early twenties. Vitaly was very interested in my travel story and invited me, the girls and Andrei to go to a Japanese restaurant. He had a thing for Japan and Buddhism.

He asked me if I'd be going to countries like Cambodia and Laos, and when I said yes he asked me to get him some information about meditation once I was there. I didn't have to pay for the food that night.

Later that night Andrei and I took another walk and we bought some vodka. He was getting drunk and annoying when I tried to speak with some girls, and I got the idea he was not exactly translating what I told him, so I suggested we went back to his house and sleep. And so we did. His wife put a mattress on the floor and gave me an old blanket. When I woke up their dirty dog was sleeping next to me on my pillow. At a guess I'd stolen its blanket.

The next morning, Andrei, his son and I went to a banya, a Russian bathing house. It was the only thing I hadn't experienced yet in Russia, and since it's a typical Russian thing to do I wanted to try it. The banya was very expensive by Russian standards and I was quite pissed that we only stayed for 1.5 hours while I paid about thirty dollars for it. Except for finally getting to take a decent shower after four days, I didn't like it much. It was basically a small spa with a pool table and couches in the other room and wasn't very interesting, or fun.

Andrei had to work the afternoon shift and his wife was supposed to bring me back to Vitaly's office, since Vitaly had offered to drive me to Vladivostok. Obviously, I thought, *Nice, a free ride*. On the way back from the banya I bought Andrei some beers because he was insisting so much. Beer is cheap but he got damn annoying, asking for a gift. He didn't know the English word for it and said it in Russian instead, but I pretended that I didn't understand him. I was thinking that in just a few more minutes I'd be rid of this clown.

Back in his home he wanted money for the night I stayed there. His wife was kind of pissed that I'd bought him beers. I refused to give him a single cent because I'd just paid a shitload of money for the banya and his beers in the last two days, and he'd never said anything about paying when he invited me to his house. We started arguing, and in the end I just packed my bags and took the bus to the city center with his wife. I could see that she was very ashamed of him, and told her she could do much better than him.

When I got to Vitaly's office it was full of hot girls applying for European visas. I told Vitaly all about my time with Andrei, and he agreed with me that Andrei was a strange character.

Vitaly told me his car was broken and that we'd have to go to Vladivostok by train. He gave me the keys to an apartment he owned or rented, and his office girls walked me there. I tried to game Tanya but she didn't bite. She left later and I went to a bar with Natasha, where we met up with her boyfriend, a big guy who looked like a Football hooligan.

Luckily he had to work at the local carnival and didn't

stay long; Natasha and I drank a few half-liters of beer and then went to a cinema in the afternoon, the movie was super boring and we both fell asleep with our 3D glasses on. We said goodbye later and I went back to the apartment, but instead of going out and bringing a hot girl back to the fancy apartment I just watched some television and went to sleep. If only I had more confidence and game back then.

The next morning Vitaly and I got on the train to Vladivostok. Andrei called to say he was very sorry for what happened. Some people are really nice until they start drinking, and I guess he's one of them. Tanya came to see goodbye but though I didn't realize it then, it wasn't a real goodbye: I would see Vitaly and Tanya again later in my trip.

Russia (Far East) – Vladivostok

Vladivostok, the last stop on my two-month trip in Russia, is a medium-sized city close to the borders of both China and North Korea. The train ride from Khabarovsk to Vladivostok took only one night, and in the morning Vitaly was talking my ears off about Buddhism. I was more interested in some hot-looking girls in the train wagon. One of them made a lot of eye contact with me and we touched a few times while passing in the hall. When the train had nearly arrived in the station, I thought *What the hell, I'll give it a try*. I asked her if she spoke any English and she answered that she'd been an English teacher for a while a few years back. When I asked for her name she said … Julia. The one in Moscow had studied English and the one in Kazan was an actual English teacher. Meeting a third Julia, another English teacher, I thought, *This can't go wrong*.

We talked for a short while and I got her phone number. When we got off the train, she nearly shouted out: "Call me!"

Vitaly and I tried to find a room for me from hawkers around the train station, but all we found was a drunken old lady renting out a room. Vitaly said that it was best to find something else, and we ended up in a street with a few strip clubs and went inside one of them. Vitaly said he was friends with the owner and had a room there. We went inside and dropped off his bags. He then told me that we could visit the strip club backstage later. I was looking forward to that.

Then we went to his Vladivostok office, which like the one in Khabarovsk was a really nice-looking place. He had one girl working there and she was pretty hot also. We talked for a while and I saw a few very attractive girls applying for European visas. Vitaly said it was to do household work. I thought to myself, *I'm not that stupid. The only people I've seen applying for your visas are really hot girls, and you're friends with strip-club owners.* I was pretty sure he was sending the girls to strip clubs or something. I didn't know that was a part of Buddhism.

There was only one hostel in Vladivostok at that time but we couldn't reach them by phone. Later a few of Vitaly's friends from his running club joined us. Two of them were quite good marathon runners and had run marathons all over the world. We all went for a sightseeing walk and later to a restaurant. After a massive dinner I didn't have to pay a cent. Have I mentioned that Russians are friendly?

Vitaly and his friends were discussing my room problem and Eduard, a policeman, offered me to stay at his place. He said that his wife was working the nightshift and only he and his two daughters would be there. I said: "Hmm I don't know, maybe I can find a place at the train station". Then I asked how old his daughters were, and he answered nineteen and twenty years old. I started glowing from inside and waited a few minutes before saying, "OK, I will stay with you".

We went to his apartment and when I walked in I saw cups and medals literally everywhere: the walls were filled with them. I asked him if they were all his and he told me that a lot of them were his daughters', who were international athletes. Needless to say by now I was ever gladder I'd accepted his invitation.

When I met the daughters they turned out to be very hot girls. I went out with the older daughter of the two, Natalya, and some of her friends. One of her admirers/orbiters got into a small car accident and I felt bad because he was showing me around the city, but on the other hand he hadn't really been paying much attention to what he was doing.

We went to a place called Beerhaus and drank a few beers

there, where I met a girl called Lisa who had her eyes on me.

That night I slept in Darya's room, though unfortunately not with her. She was truly beautiful and fun to be around. I would have ended my trip then and there if there'd been any chance with her, but she already was engaged to a Footballer.

The next morning Eduard made a big breakfast, and later a friend of his drove me all over the city to the hostel now that we had finally found the proper address. His friend didn't want any money for this long ride and by this point I didn't expect him to ask either. As I said, even though they don't smile much in public, Russians are incredibly nice and friendly people.

I settled in at the hostel, where I was the only guest, and texted the Julia I'd met on the train. We met up that evening.

Julia was a good-looking girl with a killer body who was still dressed in her office clothes but was still sexy in her tight purple dress.We walked along the beach road a bit and then I suggested we get some coffee and visit a cinema. She agreed, and we went to see *Bruno*, a brutally offensive but hilarious comedy with Sasha Baron Cohen. Because it was advertised as a comedy many people showed up with their children. They soon left, loudly complaining after the ridiculous sex scene with a small Thai gay boy. Julia didn't like the movie at all but I laughed my ass off even though I couldn't understand the dubbed Russian voices.

One technique I use with girls in the cinema to test how interested she is is to just grab her hand or simply say "Give me your hand" (being alpha), and gently rub my thumb on her fingers. If she doesn't pull away, and especially if she rubs back, then you know for sure she's willing to kiss you. Let your hand rest on her lap when you do this. If she doesn't mind your hand close to her pussy then you know she's an easy catch.
She was very eager to kiss me that night.

Afterwards back on the streets I walked a bit with her and then pulled her into an alley. She was quite surprised by it and quickly flushed. I kissed her again and she started to get really horny. She kept saying I was a fairytale/dream prince come true and we made out pretty heavily. She rubbed her body on me and that was my cue to ask her to show me the place she lived. She shared a one-room apartment with another girl but luckily for me the roommate was out of town.

Her apartment was in the suburbs, in a typical dark concrete building left over from Soviet times. We kissed some more and I took a quick shower. The bathroom was horrible and a lot was broken inside. After that she took a shower and we kissed some more on the bed. She was not willing to go all the way on the first night but I got a good blowjob out of it. I stayed over at her place.

Russia is an expensive country with low salaries; Julia worked in accounting and couldn't afford her own place. She shared her apartment and even the bed with the other girl. To my cheeky question about whether they spooned at night she just laughed. She asked me if I was a "pick upper". Of course I denied it and played dumb. I wasn't even lying, really: at that point I had actually never heard of pick-up artists.

After saying goodbye in the morning I walked around the city center with Darya and visited a boring museum. She told me that Natalya's friend Lisa was eager to see me again. I said to Darya that I was already with another girl and she was surprised. She asked me if I'd a Russian girlfriend before and I told her about the two Julias in Moscow and Kazan, and mentioned the girl in Kazakhstan. She immediately called Lisa and the two talked wildly about it, I couldn't understand much of the quick Russian conversation but enough to hear that they were excited about me. This was the moment of revelation that I found out that being with lots of girls is a major attraction spike for most girls and not a turn-off the way it was programmed in my beta mind. In pick-up terms this is called pre-selection and it would be become one of my strongest beliefs.

That day I also bought new jeans at a Chinese market, since my old pair was nearly falling apart and was all ripped up at the crotch and knees. Who says you need to dress nice to pick up a hot girl? In the evening I saw Julia again and we had coffee and some chicken at the local cafeteria before going back to her house. That night I had mind-blowing sex with her. It was the best I had ever had up to that point. She was very flexible, had a killer bikini model body and the craziness of a porn star. She looked very similar to the girl on the cover of this book, who is also a Russian model. She kept saying it must have been a magical event for us to meet in the train and being together now. She was head over heels in love with me (and still is).

Russia (Far East) – Trouble at Vladivostok Airport

When I was in Khabarovsk I had to plan my way out of Russia. My initial idea was to take a boat to Japan, but I changed my mind because the last boat left three days before my visa expired, and I didn't want to leave my beloved Russia before I had to. Other than the boat, the only option was taking a plane, so I started checking out websites. The only "cheap" flight I could find was one with Air Vladivostok to Niigata in Japan. I put "cheap" in quotation marks because it still came to about five hundred dollars for a one-hour flight. Of course, looking for a flight only five days before your visa expires is really not the most recommended way of travelling, but I really do travel on the fly – I never know how long I'll stay somewhere or when I'll move on to the next destination. In this case, there was only one problem: the flight I found was the day after my Russian visa expired.

There I was, overstaying my visa again; the first time I'd done that was in Kazakhstan. But I didn't worry, figuring that if I had managed to talk my way out of *that* situation, I could do it again in Russia. I presumed they wouldn't wave AK-47s around at me at an airport. What can I say, sometimes you have to take risks.

On departure day, I woke up next to Julia, who was already awake and looking at me. Her perfect naked body looked amazing in the morning sunshine that was coming in through the window. We talked about saying goodbye and she asked if we could keep in touch by email. I was ok with that but didn't give it much chance of actually happening; usually you keep in touch for a while and then things eventually die out. It's the natural order of things, I guess. Still, we exchanged Facebook names and email addresses anyway.

After saying goodbye to Julia I had to rush to get to Vladivostok airport on time. I took a bus and arrived only one hour before the flight. Because I already knew I was going to be in trouble, I cut in front of the line and showed my passport to the custom official. Her eyes widened when she saw my visa date. She called for her superior and a uniformed guy walked in.

He was unfriendly from the start. After one look at my visa he told me I was in Russia illegally and that he was putting me in the airport prison until further notice, talking about sending me back to Moscow for an emergency visa. So far, this was pretty much the same situation as back in Kazakhstan – except for the machine-gun pressing into my back and pushing me forward. With time ticking away I asked him if he could make an exception because I paid five hundred dollars for the ticket and had mixed up the dates when booking, but he didn't want to hear any of that. He kept saying that I was going to the prison, and that he would contact the embassy. He was determined that I wouldn't make the flight, and I was getting really worried. Had I gone too far this time? Was I going to be some big guy's girlfriend in prison?

But apparently there's someone up there whose job is to look out for lucky bastards like me: another custom official walked in and she was hot!! I guess she was somewhere in her late twenties. She had long blonde hair with red extensions woven into it. Her uniform couldn't hide her nice-looking breasts. I looked at her shoulders and saw the same stripes as the guy who was giving me a hard time. I thought to myself: *You are exactly the one I need right now.*

I started explaining my situation to her and she spoke very good English. For the next half-hour I completely ignored the tough guy and just praised Russia to her. I told her how much I loved the country and how nice everyone was to me, I talked about my experiences with the people I met along the way, the wedding I was invited to and the big bouquet of flowers I bought for the bride. When I said that, she put her hand on my shoulder and gave me a massive smile. Mixing up English and Russian words, I told her that I'd fallen in love with a

Russian girl and that I wanted to live in Russia after I finished my trip.

Well, I wasn't lying – not a single word of it. I had plans to live in Khabarovsk and work as an English teacher or something. I was truly in love with Russia. The whole story impressed her a lot – I had totally won her over. She even playfully touched me a few times while I was telling my story. I was charming her all the way. The hard-ass customs guy walked off and the hot one told me she could make an exception if I was willing to pay a fine and pay for a one-day emergency visa. Of course I said yes to this. We were pressed for time at this point – there were only a few minutes till the plane took off and she had a big pile of papers I had to sign. I signed at least twelve documents while she filled in all the forms for me because they were all in the Cyrillic Russian alphabet. To this day I have no idea what I agreed to in those forms but at that moment I didn't care. Now I kind of worry I might have promised my first-born son to Russia or something. The fine was a whopping nine Euros. I had to hold back my laugh when she told me that.

I had only a few minutes left, and other officials were searching through my backpack. When they finished she told me to hurry to the airplane, which was waiting on the airstrip.

In one last bold move I asked if I could take a picture with her. She looked around at her colleagues, especially the guy who had given me a lot of problems, than she looked at me, gave me a big smile and said: "Don't push your luck, get on that airplane!"

From the way she looked at me, I was pretty sure she wanted to take that picture with me, but didn't want to embarrass herself in front of her strict colleagues. With a quick "Bye and a wink!" I ran to the plane with my backpack on my back. As soon as I got one foot in the plane, they closed the door behind me and I had to leave my backpack the flight attendants' area. I was so happy that I didn't miss that flight. But I made it, all thanks to one hot Russian Customs agent. I'm pretty sure she had a lot of fun telling the story of the charming, illegal tourist over the next few weeks.

Actually, I had one more trump card up my sleeve when

the whole customs drama went down, if nothing else had worked out. Vitaly, the sketchy businessman I'd met in Khabarovsk and Vladivostok had told me to give him a phone call if I ever got in trouble. He runs a visa agency and had already promised me a free Russian visa for one or two years if I decided to live in his city. He'd solve any problems with Customs if needed. He also said that once I finished my trip round the world, if I did come back to Khabarovsk he would get me on Russian local television (local, but still a million viewers), because he was impressed with my story and knew people at the network. I think Vitaly had enough connections to actually talk me out of trouble. It didn't matter anymore. I was on my way to a whole new world. A world unknown to me but that I was dying to find out about. Asia had always fascinated me, and when exploring, what better country to start with than Japan, the craziest country of them all.

Chapter Two – Northern Asia

Japan – Niigata

The flight from Vladivostok in Russia to Niigata in Japan took only a little over an hour. I felt great setting foot in Asia, a whole new world waiting to be explored. At arrival the customs checked my temperature in case I had the bird flu, which was the big worry at the time. They took my picture, my fingerprints and went through my backpack. I couldn't find a working ATM and couldn't change my Russian rubles, which made for a great start for a new country. Luckily I had twenty dollars left in a hidden place in my bag and was able to exchange that and buy a bus ticket to the city center.

There was a guesthouse in town and I wrote down the address. When I asked for directions, the girls at the tourist office told me I'd have to take three separate buses and walk for twenty minutes. I thought to myself that I'd go straight to Tokyo and went to the train station. The prices were horrendous, so I looked for the bus station instead. I found it, but there were no more tickets for the night bus so I bought a ticket for the first bus in the morning at 06.00.

That evening I walked around Niigata a bit. Since I had my backpack I couldn't go to bars or anything, and frankly I didn't feel like it much. Niigata was impressive: it was my first contact with Japanese culture and of course I finally saw the teenage girls in their little school uniforms. Everything you might think about it is true: they do look sexy in those short skirts and big white socks.

The next amazing thing I saw were the toilets at the local McDonalds. I went in there for a burger and I needed to take a dump. I went into the toilets and saw that the toilet had a lot of buttons on it. The first button I tried turned out to be for the automatic toilet seat, which would go up or down without you needing to touch it. I sat down and did my thing. I took my time because I wanted to try all the buttons. One was turning on music and another turned on the bidet. A beam of water hit my bum; another beam of water hit me in the nuts. Apparently that one was for the ladies. A little blow-drying later and I was all done and ready for action.

That evening I tried to stay at the local train station to pass the time and get some sleep but the guards kicked me out around midnight. I walked the streets a bit and decided to get some sleep in the park. There were a few homeless people around sleeping on the park benches, and I found an empty one and lay down. The bums looked weirdly at me but left me alone. A few hours later I went back to the bus station because I couldn't catch any sleep. I found a bench to sleep on there, set my alarm and when I woke up there were already a bunch of people around me waiting for the same bus. Some were staring and pointing at me, and one even took a picture. They'd probably never seen a white guy sleeping on a bench before.

I jumped on the bus and went to see one of the biggest cities in the world: Tokyo.

Japan – Tokyo

Arriving in Tokyo created the usual effect: total disorientation, exhaustion, and not having a clue where I was. I had swapped the Russian Lonely Planet for the Japanese one in the hostel in Vladivostok, so at least I had a map of the city, but the Japanese alphabet is even crazier than the Russian one. After finding out where the hell I was, I was able to find my way to a hostel. Not that it was easy: luckily I got some help in the metro from a friendly woman, but once I was outside I walked for about an hour and a half to find the hostel. I walked in dripping with sweat; the humidity was killing in Tokyo. The hostel was very luxurious, but I wasn't expecting anything less for about twenty-eight dollars a night.

After a few days on my own I'd gathered a small group to hang out with. There were two Danish girls, an American girl, another Dutch guy and a Scottish guy who looked like a mix between a leprechaun and a Hobbit. We visited a museum together and went to a nearby bar called the Samurai Café a couple of times. Going to clubs was out of the question. Taxis were unaffordable and so were the prices in the clubs. Too bad, because it meant I didn't get any contact with local chicks. The two Danish girls (Julie and Lisa) were just average-looking but one of them had the biggest tits ever.

One night we all got drunk at the Samurai bar and at one point we were talking about doing a motorboat on them.
The Danish girl didn't think I'd do it but I grabbed those enormous knockers, stuck my head between them and motorboated her for half a minute. I couldn't get enough of it. Meanwhile the Scottish guy was on my tail, he wanted her too. He was butt-ugly but also quite funny. The race was on.

After a while we all went back to the hostel which was close to the bar. I talked with the Danish girl when we walked over and all of us stayed around in the hostel a bit more. The two girls went to bed and stayed behind with the Dutch guy.

A few minutes later I went to my bed in the dorm and got my toothbrush. When I walked into the bathroom I saw clothes lying on the floor and heard the big-boobed girl and the Scottish Gnome talk and laugh in one of the shower cubicles. I felt really pissed off and learned a lesson that day: it isn't over till the fat (Danish) lady sings. I don't remember if they were staying in the same dorm. Maybe they were and things got started that way, but most importantly I missed a lay and a flag that day.

The next day she mentioned she had to explain things to him while having sex. The leprechaun couldn't even bang her right! Thinking about this night now, I made so many beginner mistakes it isn't even funny.

I visited a lot of places the next day, including the famous crossroads you often see on television and a lot of temples. The problem with the temples is that when you've seen one you've seen them all.

I bought an Acer laptop because of the high prices for Internet in Tokyo. You'd think the most digitalized country in the world would have cheap Internet rates but I had to pay four dollars an hour for it. At least Wi-Fi was free in the hostel. I really needed to start using Skype because my time in Russian and Kazakhstan cost me an 1100-dollar phone bill. I had called Julia from Kazan and my friends and family quite a few times on my Dutch mobile, and of course it was like making a long-distance call from Holland each time. Only I could be that stupid. Those phone calls cost me a month of travelling. I had never used Skype back home and didn't bother to make an account before I left on my trip. I did however do lots of other planning and printing of information which I never used in the end. Talk about pennywise, pound foolish.

One night I decided to stay in one of the famous capsule hotels. Capsules are one-by-one meter wide and two meter deep sleeping places. It's a bit like sleeping in a coffin. The price was about the same as the hostel. It took a bit of getting used to living in Japan, especially coming from Russia. Everything was so clean. Japanese people are highly disciplined and don't throw rubbish on the street, they put their trash in their pockets and throw it away at home. The only places with trashcans were the 7-11s in the street. Some of the stereotypes about Japanese people are true but I prefer not to mention them. You can figure it out for yourself ig you ever visit. Still, despite all the cultural differences and the high prices I loved being in Japan and wouldn't have missed it for the world.

At first I missed Russia and all the people I met there, but I was slowly getting used to having left. I still emailed a lot with girls I met in Russia, especially Julia from Vladivostok.

Japan – Climbing Mount Fuji

One Friday night I climbed the famous Mount Fuji (or as the Japanese say, Fuji-san) with Dave and Sander, two Dutch guys I'd met in Tokyo. A bus took us to the base of the mountain and as usual we were totally unprepared. No warm clothes or rain gear and almost no food or water. This was the first time I used my hiking shoes and I was glad I found a reason to because I'd been carrying those heavy fuckers around for three months. Dave and Sander were just wearing sneakers. When we arrived at the base camp (Fifth station), there were loads of professionally-equipped Japanese people. I bought a flashlight at the base store because I'd forgotten mine. That sucked because now I had to spend twelve dollar on something I already had. Japanese prices were killing at that time.

We started climbing at 8:15 PM and rushed up the mountain; we passed whole groups of tiny Japanese and took giant steps with our long Dutch legs. I had no problems keeping up with the two Dutch guys even though they were ten years younger than me and I had black lungs from smoking and had just spent two months on the vodka drip in Russia.

We had to be careful in the dark; on some parts of the mountain you had to use your hands and your feet to climb, though at other parts there were steps cut out of the rocks.

After a few hours it was pitch black and it started to get very cold, and we had to rest a bit more often. Around 1:00 AM we reached the top of Fuji-san – just before a rain storm. So, there we were; tired, cold and wet. There was almost no place to hide from the rain and unlike the Japanese, who clearly knew what they were getting into, we hadn't brought any rain clothes.

At the very top of the mountain there was a wooden shack where people could stay during the night at extremely high prices. The roof stuck out a bit and we stood under it with our backs to the wall to avoid the rain. We stood like that for hours. No need to say it was really cold up there. I was only wearing a shirt and a very thin jacket and was very hungry and thirsty. Funnily enough there were some vending machines along the way and at every level the price of a small bottle of water went up a hundred yens (a dollar).

After a while the door to the wooden shack opened and we went in there to sit around the fire. We ate some horribly expensive noodles but we didn't care about the price, we were starving and too cold. Around 5:30 the sun came up and we saw the most amazing sunrise ever. The view was absolutely stunning. The morning sunshine is called Go Rei Kou, which means "spiritual light", and it's easy to see why.

I was really proud of myself. Mount Fuji is 3776 meters high and it was quite an accomplishment to have climbed in the dark, in less than five hours. It takes most Japanese climbers way over six hours to get to the top.

But we were already dead tired, and the worst part was still to come. It turns out that getting down Mount Fuji is a lot harder than getting up. Mount Fuji is a volcanic mountain covered with sandy ash. You have to brace yourself with every step you take. After a few hours of descending your legs really hurt. But we made it without injuries, and after two hours of expensive bus and trains I was back at the hostel. I didn't sleep all night and thought I'd be knackered the next day but I ended up being quite awake the rest of the day.

Dave went straight from the mountain to some DJ-ing convention and night party that followed. He looked pretty rough when I say him again.

I checked out the next morning and just hung around the city till 11:00 at night, when I took the last metro to the train station. I stayed the most of the night at a McDonalds where they handed out free water to bums like me and took the train for Kyoto at five in the morning.

Japan – Kyoto

Arrival in Kyoto was a classic bum-trip. I left the train station and walked around for over an hour with my backpack on. The humidity was killing me. I had stayed in the McDonalds the whole night before and the last time I'd had a shower was the previous morning. Since I was late buying a ticket I had to change trains at small stations about five times. When I arrived in the hostel, I stank so much that people were running out of the dorm room. The first thing I did was taking a long shower and then spray on a lot of deodorant to show them all that I was actually a clean guy.

Within a few hours I'd connected with a couple of people and after drinking some beers in the hostel we all went out to find a bar. The one we ended up at wasn't a bad place – we even got to play some darts, my favorite pastime in Holland.

We met a Japanese boy and girl and joined their table. The girl was drunk as fuck and kept repeating the same questions: "Wheee you fom? Wha you name? Why youuu here?" It was fun at first but it soon became really annoying. I sat down next to her and decided to see how far I could go with her. I remember one of us asking the Japanese teenager next to her if he was her boyfriend. She laughed hard and said "Noooooooooooooooooooooo!!" very loudly and I almost felt sorry for the guy. He was clearly not amused.

Meanwhile I gamed her a bit and was able to touch her a lot under the table. The Japanese guy never noticed a thing.

At one point the group wanted to leave, so we all got up to go. The Japanese girl gave me a wink and that was that. I was pretty sure I could do more with her but didn't know how to isolate a girl and had no place to bring her anyway.

That night I met a cute Japanese girl in the hostel named Sayuri. She had studied in the States and was more westernized and liberal than most Japanese girls; she also had a nice pair of knockers, especially for an Asian girl. Even so, she was damn hard to pick up. Girls were so conservative and I didn't have the money to go to nightclubs to find the wilder ones. We went with a small group to a nearby park and drank our beers there. On the way we walked hand in hand but she backed out when I tried to kiss. I'm still in touch with her from time to time.

Japan – rest of the trip

For the next eight days I travelled with an Austrian guy named Mark. He was a tall 6.5ft bodybuilder but still complained he was small compared to his training buddies. He looked pretty massive to me. He was a compulsive tooth-brusher. Every morning he would brush his teeth for no less than twenty minutes.

From Kyoto we made daytrips to Kobe and Nara with a few other people. Then we went to a few other cities together, including Hiroshima and Nagasaki, where we visited the Atomic bomb memorial museums. We mostly travelled by Shinkansen bullet train, which was one of the world's fastest trains at that time, reaching a good 300km/h – which seems pretty fast till you realize that they're now experimenting with trains that can reach 581km/h. It was quite impressive to see the world flashing by while sitting in a luxury leather seat. Of course, this came at a price: my funds were getting depleted daily and my budget was shot to hell as a result. I spend about 2500 dollars in just twenty-four days there while staying in hostels, capsule hotels and eating cheap food from the local 7-elevens. It was the public transport that killed your daily budget. Every metro ride cost a few bucks and you had to make loads of rides a day. The system in Tokyo is insanely complicated, with all sorts of different operators who don't necessarily work together, so buying a day pass didn't really help. Taking the trains between cities was horribly expensive too. It wasn't money wasted, since I did get to see lots of places and attractions, but compared to Russia it was murder.

Mark and I are both tall blond guys and we got a lot of looks from schoolgirls, but it was hard to take a picture with them. I'd already found out that talking to those hot Japanese schoolgirls is almost a waste of time. First because most of the time they're very young. The second reason is that they're super shy and sometimes just run off when you approach them. The third reason is the enormous language barrier you're dealing with, that makes even a basic conversation impossible.

We ended up in Fukuoka, which is where I said goodbye to him. I was taking the ferry to the Asian mainland, beginning with South Korea. In retrospect I regret not going out because I heard Fukuoka has a decent nightlife. But I was still more focused on travelling than on picking up girls, so I just stayed at the hostel that night, buying some beers and having fun with the other guests. I did some minor flirting with a young French girl from Paris.

South Korea – Busan

My first day in South Korea was also the most fun. I got onto the ferry at Fukuoka in Japan and I spotted a nice-looking girl in the crowd. She approached me before boarding and we got talking. This Canadian girl was teaching English in South Korea and did a visa run to Japan. On the boat we shared stories and downed shitloads of beer during the five-hour boat ride. She told me that she had also travelled large parts of the world. She worked on giant private yachts owned by millionaires, mostly in South America. They had crazy parties on board with lots of hookers and blow. She told me she was a lesbian and got offered girls (pros) all the time.

Then she told me about how her ship got hijacked and robbed by pirates on the coast of Honduras and she barely survived. Next up was a shark attack. After this she worked as a paparazzo and she told me some crazy stories about some celebs.

When we drunkenly stumbled off the ferry, we agreed to see each other again in Seoul, which unfortunately didn't actually happen – she worked crazy hours.

I had arrived in Busan, the second-largest city in South Korea, with a population of 3.6 million. I took the metro to the hostel and got talking with a Korean guy. He was very impressed with my plans to travel the world and invited me for dinner. His brother-in-law owned a restaurant and we ate a huge amount of food there and drank some Soju, Korean rice wine. After this he took me to a karaoke place. I became a bit skeptical at so much friendliness.

Inside the karaoke place we sat down in a private room and drank some more Soju. After a while a few girls walked in and my Korean buddy told me to choose. I chose a tall girl, but I was getting a bit worried what was going on. I didn't want to get landed with a huge hooker bill at the end of the night. Apparently the girls were there to keep us company. They poured our drinks and spoonfed us fruits. Later the girls started singing and dancing and you could touch them a bit but not too much. The Korean guy was getting drunk and he paid the bill. After this we walked through the lobby and there was a Kung-Fu movie playing on TV. The Korean guy wanted to show off and dared me to spar with him. I said OK because I'd done about ten years of martial arts myself and the Korean dude was pretty drunk. To my surprise he was lightning fast and pretty much kicked my ass in that little play fight. I wasn't sober myself but still, that was impressive. We took a taxi to my hostel and said goodbye.

Looking back at this experience, I should have boldly asked for a girl in a Korean schoolgirl outfit. I loved the Japanese schoolgirl look and it's the same in South Korea, although girls there are build a bit huskier.

I was hungover as fuck the next morning and spend most of the time in bed. The owner of the hostel later told me that the Korean guy and a friend were at the door but he had sent them away. The owner wanted to keep his place secret and only for backpackers and not have it become a place for drunken businessman looking for a late-night sleeping place.

That afternoon I went sightseeing with two guys I met at the hostel, one from Switzerland and one from New Zealand. We took a cable ride up a nearby mountain and got a spectacular view over the city. At night we went out with a small group. I remember sitting outside the 7-11 and drinking the cans of beer we bought there while Robin, a Korean/American guy, told us an insane story about an English guy in a hostel he stayed at in Rio de Janerio. It's a long story but let me sum it up: one English guy, two transvestite Brazilian "girls", lots of coke, a fight about one of the trans chicks having too small a cock and the English guy therefore not wanting to have sex with them, angry drugs dealers waving guns around, the trans chicks sitting out the whole day in front of the hostel waiting for the English guy to come out and pay them, and sketchy cops looking for bribes. And the English guy didn't care that the whole hostel knew what happened! As Robin described it, the guy was a Zen master of not caring. He just sat in the hostel reading a book.

My last day in Busan I spent with the New Zealand guy, Greg. We went to a local fish market and ate a lot. You could just point at live fish in basins and a few minutes later it was on your plate. The food in South Korea is a lot cheaper than in Japan and you could eat a decent-sized meal for just five dollars. At one point there was no place in the hostel for Greg and me because of prior reservations, so we found an all-night bath house to stay at for only seven dollars a night. You could bathe and soak for hours in the large complex and then sleep in a capsule. As I was almost the only white guy, I got a lot of stares from the Korean guys, especially below the belt. I'm not saying I'm hung like a horse, but I was compared to them.

South Korea – Seoul

After six hours on the train Greg and I arrived in Seoul, the capital of South Korea. Greg is an English teacher there and went home to his place in the suburbs. I went looking for a hostel because I hadn't booked anything this time. When I reached a hostel the woman/owner said she had no bed available for me but also said she'd just opened a new hostel that week. She drew up a route description and gave me the security door code, and I walked over there. When I arrived I saw that it was a massive villa, and all for me because I was the only one there except the guy who worked there, Bong. He was so bored that he kept making me sandwiches all the time just to have something to do.

That night I went out to the Monkey Beach Bar (go there if you're in Seoul), where I met up with Greg and four others from the hostel in Busan. That was a great night out. We had lots of drinks and around 3 in the morning, the bar staff handed out super-soakers and everyone started shooting at each other. It was funny to see how some guys turn into hyperactive Rambos as soon as they're handed a water gun. Grow up, dudes. After this, everyone was soaked in water and it was getting cold outside. I tried to pick up one of three drunk, crazy girls from the USA I met outside, but of course I failed, having no game and never even having heard of pick-up artists or techniques at that point. I'd taught myself a few tricks during my trip but they weren't going to be not good enough. A lot more happened that night but I'd best keep it short.

After a few days I had to leave the hostel because a group of thirty Dutch engineering students had booked the villa. I went to the other hostel. After checking in I walked outside for some food and a blonde Swedish girl approached me. She had just arrived and was going to stay a semester to study. We started talking and had some coffee. Johanna was a pretty girl and we visited a lot of places together that day. Sightseeing was still high on my priority list. At one point we had to cross a busy street and at that moment I came up with some touching techniques. At first I put my hand on the middle of her back: ok, no negative reaction. Then I grabbed her hand and we sprinted across the street. Once on the other side I didn't let go of her hand and she held on to mine. From that day on I always use this technique. It's a perfect way to "protect" the girl, and yes, girls like this. It's a good way to test if the girl has interest in you.

After visiting a palace Johanna and I sat down in a small park together and something crazy happened. We were just sitting on a bench, looking at the map and all of a sudden an enraged red-headed Korean guy showed up about forty meters away. He was about forty-five years and he was shouting at us: "This is Korea, get out, go away!" I's been warned that a lot of Koreans are (silent) racists but this was just insane. He walked towards and I got up in front of Johanna.

Some other Korean guys got of their benches and tried to calm the situation down. The crazy guy was furious for no reason at all. Johanna started pulling my arm. "Let's go," she pleaded. One old Korean guy tried to reason with the mad man and got slapped in the face really hard. At this moment I stepped forward to do something about it but got pushed away by the other Korean guys telling me it was better to leave. Johanna pulled my arm again and I walked off with her.

When walking away I got really angry because I kept thinking of the poor old man getting slapped that hard because of us. I wanted to go right back and kick that fucker's ass but Johanna didn't understand why and asked me why I was so aggressive. At that very moment I realized it must have been a huge turn-off for her and I calmed down a bit.

A day later I met her again and we went to a park. We were lying in the grass close to each other and I looked her deep in her big blue eyes. She asked me: "Are you flirting with me?" All I could think of was: "Maybe". This triggered another thought in me and I've been using this line ever since, although slightly changed.

Me: Are you flirting with me? (Look her deep in the eyes and smile at her, aka a flirty look)
Girl: Eh… no
Me: Are you sure? (Keep looking flirty at her, touch her somewhere)
Girl: Eh… eh yes
Me: Sure you're sure? (Keep flirting)

Ok, now you just have to size up the situation. If she answers "Yes" or "maybe" after the first or second question, go for the kiss. If she keeps denying, say you're just joking and try something else later. Don't give up!

Did I kiss Johanna? No, I got the LJBF (let's just be friends) speech from her when we sat in a bus and curled up together to keep warm. I tried to kiss her there but she said she'd just arrived in Seoul and didn't want a relationship now. Most of the time that means "I don't want a relationship with YOU". But then again, she had got there just a day before and had a lot on her mind, starting with a new study program and looking for a place to stay.

This marked the beginning of a lot of struggling with Scandinavian girls.

Back in the hostel I met a few people in the dorm. There was a Mexican/American guy we nicknamed him El Mariachi, a black guy we nicknamed Young Obama and an American/Puerto Rican girl we nicknamed Dirty Jersey. Her nickname came from the fact she was from New Jersey and used the foulest language ever. My nickname was Holland because I had hung up a small Dutch flag in the dorm. It was a two-level room and I had the top level for myself. I hung up the small plastic flag I had and joked about how I colonized that spot.

Dirty Jersey was blond and fat but had the biggest pair of boobs I'd ever seen in life. And I've had some big ones since I was a teenager, not to mention on this trip. Remember the girls of Khabarovsk? Jersey must have had the same diet. When we walked out the dorm, I stood with my back to her and purposely grazed her boobs twice with my elbow. She said, "Hey that's the second time you touched my boobs". I turned around and said: "O, I'm sorry, did I touch your boobs?" while poking them with my finger. This was a very ballsy move and she could've slapped me in the face. But she didn't and just laughed and said "O, stop it!" "Stop what?" I said, "doing this?" and poked her boobs again. The tone was set for that night.

We all went for dinner and Dirty Jersey was wearing a black dress with cleavage was so deep that you could lose a whole Korean in there. El Mariachi and I were joking about it. We went to a club and I was dancing with Dirty Jersey, grabbing her boobs all the time in front of everyone. All the Koreans were looking at us, especially the girls, who are mostly flat-chested; some even took pictures of her. Her boobs were that big.

When we were leaving the club some Korean guys pushed her and she slapped one of them. The dude got angry and wanted to fight her, but I stepped in and pushed one of them really hard back into the crowd. They backed off after that. Being about a foot taller than anyone around and a lot stronger does help push sixty-kilogram guys around. It happened so fast that the others with us didn't even notice the five-second scramble.

I went to a love hotel with Dirty Jersey but she was drunk and just wanted to sleep. I tried a lot but she didn't give in to me. When I say that I tried a lot it doesn't mean I was saying stuff like "Oh baby please let me touch you, baby baby please". Have some pride, I always say. She said she was only into Asian guys and I wondered how she had sex with them. As I said before she was fat and I don't think Asian guys have enough "reach" down there to satisfy her. Hell, I was wondering about my own reach with her. Still, in the morning I got to play with her giant hooters. I didn't even want to have sex with her anymore, just play around a bit with those basketball-sized knockers. When we returned to the hostel she kept embarrassing me in front of the others, saying I'd been begging her.

Although I pushed really hard with her (also because I paid twenty–five dollars for the room, my half), begging is not in my vocabulary, and her saying that started to annoy me. Then at three o'clock in the morning she made a really loud Skype call to America, just to piss me off. I told her to "shut the fuck up" and she got all crazy, started throwing stuff at me and ripping up my Dutch flag.

The following days there was a lot of tension in the dorm room. I told the hostel owner to hurry up with my application for the Chinese visa. I was so fucking angry with Dirty Jersey that I even deleted all the pictures of that night out, including the ones of me holding her big boobs. We wanted to kill each other and there was verbal jousting all the time.

At night I went out with the guys. No one ever scored with a Korean girl although we tried. One German/Irish guy claimed to have had sex with a Korean girl but that was highly doubtful because he said he went to her place and she was twenty years old. In South Korea and all over Asia in general all girls live with a (large) family. So it's nearly impossible to bone a girl at their homes. He told some other highly doubtful stories too. I went to the other hostel a few times and heard the story of the drunken French guy who got a blowjob from a girl with a busted-up wooden leg. Afterwards he threw up in her bed. I knew the girl with the wooden leg: the leg was painted pink to look real but the paint was coming off and it looked like zombie leg. Her face wasn't anything to look at either. Although I really liked South Korea I had to move on, and agreed to see El Mariachi and his girl again in China where they worked as English teachers.

China – Beijing

I had printed out the hostel's address in Chinese characters, and just as well, because otherwise I would still be standing in Beijing airport. You'd expect that at such an enormous airport *someone* would speak English, but you'd be wrong. Thanks to my print-out I managed to find where I was meant to go, though calling it a hostel might not be the right word: it was more of a hotel that had some dorm/family rooms. Although I had booked, they had no bed for me in the dorm, and they gave me a normal room at reduced price but still double the price of a dorm room.

The room had a giant heart-shaped bed and lots of mirrors on the walls. Clearly it wasn't normally used by backpackers. Or perhaps it was.

There were no other travelers around and I decided to look for another hostel for the next day. I found one which looked very nice, with many backpackers around, but the rooms were dirty and damp and the toilets were disgusting. I decided to stay in my clean hotel.

The next day I went to the Peace Square, the largest square in the world. Then I visited Mao's mausoleum, where you can look at Mao in a glass casket. He looks like a wax statue. I had to stand in line for over an hour for half-a-minute of Mao. The lines were crazy and everyone had to hurry up. Everyone was frisked and scanned upon entry because it was strictly forbidden to take pictures.

I didn't manage to visit the Forbidden City because it was closed that day for the celebration of sixty years of "democracy". On the street a good-looking Chinese girl approached me and started asking me all kinds of questions in perfect English. I'd been warned to watch out for this scam, where they invite you to drink tea at their house and then present a five-hundred dollar bill afterwards, and decided to have some fun with her. I gave her bogus answers and when she asked me my age and acted very surprised when I told her, she asked me how I kept looking young. I said that my secret was fucking lots of different girls (which I wasn't even doing at this point). She was very shocked but still invited me for tea. I said no and went on my way. Go scam some dumb idiot, not me.

I decided to go to the Olympic stadium, and when I got on the bus it was already full and I had to stand. At every stop a new horde of people pushed themselves on the bus, and every time I thought it couldn't get any more crowded, the bus stopped and more people came in. At one point I was almost sitting on the driver's lap, the stick shift almost up my ass.

When I saw the stadium I had a hard time managing to get off the bus. The Olympic stadium is located in an Olympic park with several other stadiums, the famous Birds' Nest being by far the most impressive.

On the way back when trying to enter the bus there was lots of pushing and shoving, and I felt a hand sneak into my back pocket. My camera was almost outside my pocket and I felt some fingers on the camera cord.

Without looking I grabbed the hand and started crushing the fingers. I did several years of Jiu Jitsu before I started my trip and had trained myself to perfect a death grip. I squeezed the life out that hand. I couldn't see who it was, I was pushed inside the bus and had to let go, but I'm sure he or she will remember me.

I already changed to a dorm room in the hotel and in the evening a girl walked in. She had a beautiful face but was quite chubby and I didn't pay much attention to her. After she came out of the shower in only a towel, though, I noticed that she had quite a pair of knockers. She started talking to me and asking me questions about my trip. Pretty much standard backpacker talk. I told her that I was going to eat Beijing/Peking duck and invited her to join me. We went to a restaurant and ate some duck. I didn't like it so much, it tasted like greasy chicken and the skin was way too thick, but I could cross eating Beijing duck in Beijing off my list of things to do.

We had a few beers and back in the dorm we sat next to each other and started making out. We were the only ones there and that was great because we had sex that night. Let's call her Lisa. She was super horny and as said before had a great pair of knockers. They felt a bit weird, though, and in the end I asked her if they were real. She was shocked that I asked, but admitted they were fake boobs. She even said: "Real? Yeah, real expensive". We banged a lot that night. Canadian flag captured.

We switched to the room with the mirrors and the heart-shaped bed. She was crazy horny, wanted to have sex all day and asked me to use all holes. To which I did not say no.

A day later Lisa and I went to the Forbidden City, which had now re-opened. It's a huge and impressive complex, a must-see if you're in Beijing. On the way back we booked a tour to the Great Wall of China. We booked it with a guy who approached us on the street. You have to be very careful with this because many tours will take you first to all kinds of shops and jewelry stores or sometimes to "traditional Chinese doctors" who diagnose you with all kinds of horrible deceases but fortunately they also have the medicine you need, at an extreme price of course. At the end they take you to see the Great Wall for just half an hour. This guy had a book of handwritten recommendations, though, and I read good stories about him in five different languages. It looked solid and we took the gamble.The guide was not lying.

In the morning he took us to a forbidden part of the Great Wall with about twelve others, and had to give some money to villagers to let us pass through their villages. Normal tours to the Great Wall include thousands of other tourists and there's no way to take a picture without anyone in it, but we got a deserted spot. The guide was very friendly and not pushy at all, so we had all the time in the world to see this wonder. The views were stunning and spectacular. This part of the Wall wasn't restored, though, and it was a hell of a climb sometimes. Lisa was tough and only wore flip flops.

At one point Lisa and I fell very far behind, after first shaking off two German guys who were trying to secretly take pictures of Lisa's boobs. I gave them an angry look and they stopped. Lisa and I started making out on the Wall and as soon as no one was around off came my pants. Lisa was giving me a blowjob on the Great Wall of China, how awesome was that? I was enjoying myself until I saw two Chinese guys on a nearby tower. One was looking in our direction with a pair of binoculars glued to his face. Just our luck to get caught by two lost guys on a trek. Lisa was very embarrassed when I told her and we hurried to another tower on the wall. She finished the job there.

After catching up with the group and finishing the tour, we all sat down in a small village open restaurant. We were all drinking a well-deserved beer and I saw the German guys looking and laughing at us. I took a look at Lisa and saw that she had some of my leftover man yoghurt on her breast; all dried up but it was clearly visible what it was. I whispered it in Lisa's ear and she ran off to the toilets with a flaming red face. Hahaha, I will never forget that day.

We went to a local market later that week where they sold the strangest street food. We ate fried spider, some sort of super spicy fish, silk worms (mushy liquid inside, yuk!), sheep penis and balls which did not taste bad, a snake and then we ate some fried scorpions which actually tasted very good, a bit like walnuts. I even tried to eat fried starfish: you eat the inside of the legs, but it was disgusting and almost made me vomit. I know what my limit for weird food is now.

The next morning I had to say goodbye to Lisa. She had nearly killed me in the bedroom the night before. Up till that moment I had not met many girls with a higher sex drive than her. Her hand was still down my pants when I had one foot in the taxi. I promised to visit her whenever I made it to Canada

Lisa is now married to the guy who was her boyfriend back home then and they have a son together now in a medium sized city in Canada.

China – Suifenhe

Suifenhe is a small border city and almost solely survives on the clothes business with Russia. Every day busloads of Russians arrive and buy as much clothing as possible. In fact there are so many that Russia's now got a 35-kilogram per person limit since Russia is not happy with their local markets being flooded with cheap knockoff clothes. Russians do not need a visa to visit this town, so Julia from Vladivostok could join a group to go to Suifenhe – on condition she brought back a 35 kg bag with her.

I arrived in Suifenhe at six in the morning after taking two 24-hour trains with a short stop in Harbin. I didn't sleep much because the Chinese people on the train went to bed at 9:00 at night and woke up at 4:00 in the morning grabbing their mobile phones and making loud phone calls next to you. There's nothing bad about the Chinese trains though; the ones I took were very modern, people were friendly and very curious and tried to make conversation with you.

Fifteen minutes after arriving, I'd made it to the point where Julia and I had agreed to meet. The only thing was that she wasn't going to arrive till 1:00 in the afternoon, so I had a lot of time to kill.

I walked around a bit, ate some weird-looking street food and talked to some people. Chinese people are used to the white Russian faces but almost never see a whitie from another country, especially with a giant backpack.

I discovered a KFC in a side street of the square; strangely enough they sold a lot of food made of shrimp. I sat down, ordered some food and found out there was free Wi-Fi there so I just used the Internet till one o'clock rolled round. Julia was extremely happy to see me and started crying as soon as she ran towards me.

We had been emailing almost twice a week ever since I left Vladivostok some two months before. I didn't feel bad for having sex for five days with the Canadian girl; in fact I had tried to pick up a South African girl when I was in Harbin the day before. It's not that I didn't care for Julia or that I hadn't missed her, but it wasn't enough to keep faithful to her – especially because I was never ever really sure I'd ever see her.

We took a nice hotel room and I figured Julia wanted to walk around town a bit or eat but no, she just jumped on me. After our shower I didn't even get the chance to put my clothes back on. The sex was amazing; she's so good in bed.

We ate after; Julia had brought imported Dutch cheese and candy with her from Russia. That night we went to a restaurant where we met up with her mom, who had joined Julia on her trip to Suifenhe.

After the restaurant we locked ourselves in our room and banged like wild animals. When I put it in the "wrong" hole, it looked like Julia was going to pass out from ecstasy and I will never forget the look on her face.

The next day we bought another pair of jeans for me

because the one I bought in Vladivostok just two months before was already falling apart. Chinese quality. The rest of the day we shopped a bit and spent a lot of time between the sheets.

In the evening we ate something at a restaurant and I was so hungry that I kept ordering. I ate a four-egg omelet, two boiled eggs, a quarter chicken, rice and salad and drank a big coffee and half a liter of beer. I loaded up on proteins as much as possible. It all tasted great but when I stood up, my stomach was instantly fucked. I almost had to run back to the hotel. Julia wanted to go up to the room with me but I told her not to because I wanted some privacy. She was upset about it but I didn't care. She even wanted to be near to me when I was taking a crap, but I sent her away to do something else. I went up to the room and almost exploded in the bathroom.

Since then Julia and I have had the agreement that she'll leave the room when I need to use the "office". I've used this expression with other girls too. I'm always fucking embarrassed to take a dump when someone is near. One of the reasons I don't couchsurf.

The next morning she had to leave at 7:00 in the morning and we hugged goodbye. It was not the last time I saw her.

I went back to Harbin as a stopover to Dalian where I would see El Mariachi again. I'd been hoping to go to North Korea as well, but by now that was definitely off. I'd bought a double-entry visa for China, but all the tours to North Korea from Beijing were insanely expensive. I'd asked Julia if she could book me into a Russian tour I could join after they crossed the border. I didn't care how legal it was, I just really wanted to be able to say I'd been there. But that would have been crazily expensive too. It costs about 300 dollars a day to visit North Korea, no matter what country you book a tour from, and going with a tour is the only way to even get in. Even if you go alone you're stuck with a guide and a driver 24 hours a day and you can only stay in a government-owned 5-star hotel with the price to match. In hindsight I just should have done it. It would have been an once-in-a-lifetime experience.

China – Dalian

After arriving by night train I took a taxi to the apartment of the friend I'd met in Seoul. El Mariachi (a young war veteran) was living in Dalian with a girl/fuck buddy named Sheila, and I had a great time with them. They were both English teachers.

I had to sleep on the couch but I didn't mind because it was free and I was looking forward to hanging out with El Mariachi. It was a typical student house and the toilet was so dirty that I couldn't believe there was also a woman living there.

Dalian is a very young city, it's only a hundred years old or so. It's a harbor city and there's a fresh breeze wherever you go. It's a great contrast to most Chinese cities which are all smogged up. During the day El Mariachi and his girl showed me around the city a bit.

That night he and I went out to a bar but it wasn't too crowded. There were a few gold diggers/pros around and drinks were very expensive. I remember El Mariachi telling me to "just get your lips wet" when taking a sip of the beer, which I found very funny and still use from time to time. We bailed after a while.

The morning after, El Mariachi and his girl had to work and I stayed in the flat when Dan arrived and took the last bedroom. Dan was a tall American guy and another English teacher. The three of us went out to a big club where you had to pay about fourteen dollars to get in but after that got free drinks all night as long as you held on to your glass. There were loads of (Far East) Russian students in the club because China is a booming country. Everywhere you look people are building new roads, railways, bridges and buildings. I spoke to people from cities I visited when in Far East Russia. I couldn't pull a girl but I didn't try so hard either.

After waking up with a hangover the next day I went to a local street food place with El Mariachi and ate some weird stuff, though not as gross as the stuff in Beijing. The chicken hearts on a stick were delicious.

After this we went to a park where he showed me some marijuana plants growing along the roads. He wanted me to confirm it was real as I was a Dutch expert on weed, aka The Bongmeister. It was real marijuana and we took a few handfuls back to the apartment. I sorted it out and microwave dried it and rolled it up. This sounds bad and it was. The only buzz I got was being dizzy from the horrible crap we were smoking that evening.

That night I wanted to go out again but El Mariachi went to bed early and wouldn't join me, so I went out alone and spoke to lots of Russians again in the same club.

At the end of the night a Chinese girl named Carol walked up and started talking to me. We flirted a bit and when the club closed I took her back to the apartment, where we slept on the couch. It was almost daylight and getting cold when I heard Dan get up, but before he left the house he took a blanket and put it over us. Yeah, Dan was a nice guy.

As soon as he left I got up and took the girl to his room and banged her in his bed. Carol was quite young, only twenty-one years old. She had a rock hard body and was quite inexperienced in bed. It was my first Asian girl ever and I took that opportunity to bang her well.

After the deed I noticed there was a giant blood stain on the sheet. We took the sheet off the bed, talked a bit and fell asleep. We woke up in the afternoon and Carol left. I was quite hungover from lots of drinks and lack of sleep and didn't know what to do with the bloody sheet and just hung it outside without cleaning it.

That evening I hurried to the train station to get a train ticket. I gave El Mariachi some money for a new sheet and got the fuck out of town. I didn't know how Dan would react but for sure he wouldn't be happy. Dan, if you ever read this, I'm sorry for being such a dick. I still have contact with Carol and El Mariachi on Facebook. Carol now lives in Singapore. El Mariachi really got into The Lord and married a pretty girl and lives on the west coast of California.

China – Xian

A short stay in Beijing and a few long train rides later I arrived in Xian. Xian is a major tourist destination because of the discovery of the terracotta warriors some thirty-five years ago. I slept in a dorm and heard there was a Dutch girl staying there but I didn't see her that day.

The next morning as I was eating breakfast I all of a sudden saw Nicole, a Dutch girl I met in Mongolia, walk by. I tapped her on the shoulder and she was even more surprised than I was. What was even weirder was that just two days before in Beijing I'd met up with Odette, an American girl who looked like Brooke Shields and had been in the same Mongolian hostel as Nicole. Nicole and I talked for quite some time that morning. I explored the city a bit but it was not that interesting, just another giant Chinese city.

I woke up early the next morning and I got on the bus to the area where the famous terracotta warriors were. It was an enormous park with three giant halls filled with archeological finds. I started with the smallest one and worked my way to the biggest one, which was most impressive. There were thousands of statues and it was hard to imagine that everything was over 2200 years old. The statues were made of clay and were originally fully painted, but the paint came off when the statues came into contact with oxygen when they were excavated.

The nine thousand statues were discovered in 1974 by a Chinese farmer who was digging a water well. There was no history of the statues – no-one knew they'd ever existed – and it was one of the biggest discoveries of that time. All the statues are about 1.70m high and very detailed; they were modeled after real servants and soldiers and they all have different facial expressions. Legend has it that they were buried with the emperor to protect him in the afterlife, instead of burying the actual servants alive the way they would have done in earlier times.

In the evening I met an American woman named Christa in the hostel. I'd moved dorms and she was staying in my new one. I gathered some free beer tickets from the hostel and Christa gave me hers too. Christa had also travelled for a few months in Russia and we shared some stories. She told me a crazy story about how she took a train with hundreds of drunken Russian soldiers on it and was the only (foreign) woman. Christa was about thirty-three years old and chubby.

Not a looker but she was nice and had tits the size of watermelons. They were hard to miss and I couldn't keep my eyes off them, especially since she was wearing a low-cut shirt.

That night I had quite a few beers and later talked and flirted with Christa again in the dorm. When we went to sleep I asked her if I could sleep in her bed but she said no because of the couple who was also staying in the same dorm.

The next morning after breakfast we were internetting in the dorm room and I threw on some charm. At one point we were sitting and flirting on a bed and I was looking her in the eyes and I said to her, "All I want is to kiss you." "What are you waiting for?" she said. Of course I went straight in for the kiss and things heated up fast. I took a chair and put it under the door handle. We got in her bed and she gave me a blowjob. At that moment a cleaning lady walked in and the chair just fell to the side. I have to improve my chair under the door handle technique a bit. I don't know who was more embarrassed, the cleaning lady or Christa, but I found it quite funny. Christa wanted to stop but I convinced to go through and she did. I got my American flag but it wasn't one to be much proud of, it was just a one-noon stand.

After this, we walked over the huge defense wall in the city. I was leaving in just a few hours and my hands were almost glued to her giant breasts. Back in the hostel I tried to bone her a second time but she was afraid of people walking in again. One hour later I took the train to Shanghai and never had contact with her again.

In Shanghai I had a night out at a club with lots of Russian girls. Although I succeeded three times in Russia, I pretty much bombed out due to the fact I was a poor backpacker with close to zero pick-up skills. One of the Russian girls working at the club seemed to be into me, constantly giving me free drinking tickets but I didn't like her physically. Not all Russian girls are hot – just a lot more than other nationalities.

I went on to the city-states Hong Kong and Macau, where I had lots of fun but nothing outside the usual drinking and weed smoking backpacker fun with lots of cool people and failed attempts to pick up a few girls from several nationalities. A hundred pictures later it was time to go off the beaten track a bit by visiting Taiwan, which isn't a major tourist destination. By now I had decided to visit every country in Asia, so I couldn't skip Taiwan and had to bite the bullet on the prices of the flights.

Taiwan – Taipei

In a hostel in Taipei I met D-Lux. He was a fully tattooed Canadian bodybuilder with a strong appetite for women. We went to a big club together to pick up some Taiwanese girls. At least, that was the plan, but the club kind of sucked and I found it hard to talk with the local girls. They all seemed very childish. We tried to hook up with a few chicks but didn't get anywhere except for getting some phone numbers which were later flaked on. I had my doubts about D-Lux at first, mainly because of his foul language regarding women and crazy character. Little did I know that he would become one of my best friends on this trip.

I was getting tired of hanging around only in big cities; I needed a break from pollution and noise. So I decided to visit the Taroko Gorge nature park. I ended up getting to the Taipei train station way too early – I got there at 9:00 in the morning and the train to Shincheng didn't leave till 13.00, so I had to wait for a long time.

I arrived at 16.00 and there were no more buses to Tianchang, the small mountain village I wanted to get to. A few taxi drivers were happy to take me there but asked for prices that were pure extortion. I told them to go fuck themselves and started walking. I was determined to reach the village no matter what, but my twenty-two kilogram backpack started weighing me down, the village was twenty kilometers away and the only road up there went through some steep mountains. An unrealistic plan.

Hitchhiking there would be a smarter option, so I stood by the road for about an hour but none of the passing cars wanted to take me up the road. Out of desperation I signaled down a bus. After lots of pointing at maps and trying to pronounce the Chinese words, the guy let me in and sometime later he dropped me off at the headquarters of the park. It was already after 18:00 and near dark so the park was closed. I banged on the door but nobody came.

A few minutes later a park ranger that was doing some overtime walked up to me and asked me what I was doing there. Luckily he spoke a bit of English. He told me that the small village was still miles away. I asked him if I could wait until 6:00 in the morning so I could get the first bus to the village where there was a hostel. He said it was OK to wait in front of the door and I asked him for a chair to sit on. He brought me a chair and a few moments later a couple of office ladies brought me cookies and drinks. How nice of them. I was sitting on the chair for about an hour and the guy came back. He said I could stay in the dorm with the park rangers who were young students. A bed for the night – and free!

It was a four-bed room and the guys were friendly and spoke a bit of English. They showed me some pictures of the park on their laptops and I helped them repair a motor bike. They told me that most of the walking routes were closed because of dangerous weather. That disappointed me a lot, I was afraid I had come for nothing.

I barely slept because I had no pillow and one of the guys was snoring like a chainsaw.

The next morning I woke early and took a well-needed shower. One of the park rangers asked me to come with him and took me on his newly repaired motorbike. He drove like a madman on the wet mountain roads. It was a bit scary but I figured he did it daily. He dropped me off in the middle of nowhere and he said it was twelve kilometers back to the park headquarters. I thanked him and he drove off.

I started walking the road back and took lots of pictures. The mountains were almost vertical and a spectacle to see in the early misty morning. There were quite a few small waterfalls but no big ones. The hanging bridge was impressive too but off-limits for non-park workers because it was too slippery after the storm a couple of days before.

After a few hours of walking I was pretty much through the food I brought from Taipei. I had one snack of rice wrapped in seaweed left, which is not enough for the whole day. I guessed I had to take the next best thing: cigarettes.

After a while I reached a big open spot where a small monastery had been built on a mountain with a waterfall under it. This was a place where some tour buses stopped so people could take pictures. I was sitting on the fence when a few women walked up to me and asked me where I was from. I said I was from Holland and travelled around the world. I told them I hitchhiked up to the park and although they were Canadian/Taiwanese women who spoke good English they misunderstood me and thought I'd said I hitchhiked around the world. They offered me some food and soon other people from the bus were bringing me food too. I was kind of starving so I didn't say no to that. I got three bananas, some rice snacks, a chocolate bar, a warm cheese sandwich and a couple of bottles of water. I thanked them all and went on my way. People are friendly on this side of the world.

After another couple of hours walking I came back to the headquarters and got some food and tea again. I waited for a few hours for a bus to the train station and went on my way.

The whole trip didn't cost me much. I didn't have to pay much for the bus up to the park headquarters and I got a free night of sleep instead of paying for the hostel in the small village, which charged dearly for a dorm bed. I got free food and drinks and I saw some amazing nature and lots of waterfalls. There are worse ways to take a trip.

Taiwan – Kenting and Kaohsiung

After returning from my small adventure in the nature park, I returned to Taipei. I stayed one day in the hostel and relaxed a bit before moving on to the south of Taiwan. I was glad to escape the polluted city where it rained most days.

The bus ride to Kaohsiung only took five hours, which after some of the Russian trips I'd taken was nothing. The massive bus I took had only eighteen chairs as big as couches, along with a TV and video games. The chair had a massage function and I slept like a baby after playing some old school

Nintendo games. I arrived in Kaohsiung and met up with D-Lux, who had gone there the day before me.

We took a bus to Ken Ting, a famous Taiwanese beach town. We shared a room in a place called the RICH Hotel even though we were far from rich. The room was quite luxurious and it was on the street were all the party places and bars were. Or so we thought.

We went out later that night and it turned out there wasn't a thing to do in Ken Ting. Most bars closed down early and only a place with some ladyboys was open. No thanks!

On the streets were a lot of T-shirts shops and most of them were selling T-shirts with marijuana leaves and stoner pictures. We were happy for a moment and tried to score some weed but our happiness was only short-term. No one actually sold weed, or if they did they gave us ridiculous prices. All grumpy we bought some bags of chips and lots of beer and watched the movie channel in our room for a few hours.

We decided to go back to Kaohsiung to see what was happening there, since we both had some time to kill before flying to Vietnam. We shared a taxi with a Taiwanese couple back to Kaohsiung, which was even cheaper than the bus. Most bus and taxi drivers in Taiwan eat beetle nuts, which like chewing coca leaves gives you energy throughout the day. The problem with beetle nuts is that they makes your teeth rot away and the liquid inside the nuts and leaves is red so it looks like the buses and taxis are driven by bloodthirsty vampires. The upside of those beetle nuts is that they're sold by girls in bikini in little glass houses. When I first saw them I thought I was back in Holland in one of the several red light districts throughout Holland – not only in Amsterdam, as most tourists seem to think.

D-Lux and I stayed in a big apartment a block away from the hostel that rented it out. On Saturday we went out with an American guy.

When we walked into the club and ordered a drink, two girls approached me and said I looked like a movie star. They pulled out their phones and I had to give my number to them, which I gladly did. A second later three other girls pulled me onto the dance floor, which was still empty, and the first two girls joined us. So, there I was dancing with five girls on an empty dance floor. Other people started to dance as well and within moments the floor was packed. Everyone was checking me and the five girls out and I nearly felt like a real movie star. D-Lux was not too happy about it because nobody asked him.

At the end of the night I had five phone numbers in my phone. I tried to escalate a bit with one of the girls at the club but didn't get far. Asian girls are very shy and conservative even though they dress up sexy and come on to you sometimes. Even when they are in their early twenties they mostly act like fourteen-year-olds. Hate to say it, but it's true from a guys perspective. Over the next five days I got a lot of phone calls from them but it wasn't more than a lot of giggling and badly spoken English

Later that week we went out with a few girls I don't even remember meeting. That was a bust as well. I was going to leave the country without capturing the local flag.

D-Lux took his flight to Saigon and I followed a day later. I was about to explore the poor parts of Asia. Up till now I hadn't seen much poverty. There were some bums in Japan and South Korea but those guys didn't look like they were starving. I had seen extreme poverty in India a year before I left on my round-the-world trip. I hoped that I wouldn't have to see that again. Julia and I still had close contact and agreed to meet again somewhere. Thailand was a good option and it was not that far away from Vietnam. For now it was time to visit 'Nam, as the country was named in the many war movies I saw. I didn't know what to expect but I sure was excited

Chapter Three – South East Asia

Vietnam – Saigon (Ho Chi Minh City)

After a short flight from Taipei I arrived in Saigon, the southern capital of Vietnam. I was finally in South East Asia and ready to see what everyone was raving about. The country got off to a good start – I got a very luxurious hotel room for only fifteen dollars in one of the many alleys in the tourist area.

There were a huge number of white tourists around, something I didn't see since Xian in China. I had mixed feelings about this, since I hadn't come to Vietnam to see foreigners, but I enjoyed the western food sold in the restaurants after spending the last months eating rice and noodles. That's not to say I didn't try the local food, though. I ate Phô for the first time and loved it. It's a kind of thick spicy noodle soup with vegetables and pork meat that really fills you up for a while. When you buy it from street vendors it's always a gamble though and I don't recommend trying it if there's no toilet around.

There are literally millions of motorbikes in Vietnam and it's normal to see a mother with three small children on one bike while she's holding the groceries or a sun umbrella with one hand and using the other to steer. When people drive their bike, they don't look to the left, right or over their shoulders. They just watch right in front of them and it works surprisingly well.

D-Lux and I did go out in the hopes of finding some girls, but it was all No Money, No Honey. D-Lux even got his thousand-dollar iPhone pickpocketed while he was drunk.

Three days later we both went to Nha Trang by overnight sleeper bus, which had three small rows of beds. It was like being in a can of sardines, but still comfortable enough to have a few hours of sleep. Later I realized that Vietnam is the only country that has overnight buses like that, that actually take into consideration the fact people are going to want to sleep. I would spend many sleepless nights on countless buses in other countries fondly remembering the buses of Vietnam.

Vietnam – Nha Trang

Nha Trang is a city on the coast of Vietnam and quite a touristy one. We were there during the off-season and hotels were ridiculously cheap. I paid seven dollars for a room with marble floors, a decent bathroom, a king-sized bed, a fridge, cable television and an air–conditioning unit.

Across the street was a small bar/restaurant named Zippo. D-Lux and I went there a couple of times and had fun with the girls working there. I kind of liked one of them. Her name was Nga and she was a short twenty-two year old cutie. She barely spoke English but with the help of a small translation book we could communicate a bit. You can buy loads of knock-off Lonely Planet books for only three or four dollars there. I learned some Vietnamese but pronouncing it right was very difficult. Vietnamese is a tonal language and the same word can mean different things depending on the pitch of your voice.

I went out with D-Lux that evening, but a lot of clubs had girls who were working P4P (pay for pussy). It was quite obvious that they were hookers and D-Lux and I didn't stay long inside. Back at the Zippo restaurant I kind of picked up Nga, but not much happened with her. There was never really a chance with Nga, who was still a virgin and had never had a boyfriend before. I later heard this story many times but with Nga I still have the feeling she wasn't lying to me.

One day she took me to her parents' house in a rural area. It was fun to hang around the house with her family and lots of kids. She cooked me some food and it was delicious. We rode on her motorbike and we visited a few sites on the way there and the way back. Nga was super shy and she told she had never even kissed anyone before. After some charm talk she went to my room nonetheless and we kissed a bit but she wouldn't take her clothes off no matter what I tried. She weighed only thirty-eight kilos and I could easily throw her around the room and on the bed. We had fun but I also wanted to actually get laid. I decided to go out alone.

D-Lux had met a girl while in Saigon and she came over to see him. She wasn't my type but she was nice. At least he was banging. One night I went out with a Vietnamese girl I met in another restaurant. We went to a club together but I really didn't like the atmosphere there, it was very expensive and the hot girl I was with got kind of bitchy after a while. I cut my losses and went back to my hotel.

I later met an English couple in their forties and we went to a bar with them. Inside the bar were two hot blonde Swedish girls. There were no other foreigners around and they were eyeballing me a lot. I went over to their table and started talking my ass off. It looked like everything I said hit the spot. We were drinking quite a few beers and I couldn't figure out which one to go for. One girl was very tall and had model-like features, the other one looked like a porn star.

She told that they were leaving for Cambodia the next day and I didn't know what to do exactly. They shared a room together and bringing one of them to my room would split them up, which was unlikely to happen. Going for a threesome came to mind but seemed impossible. The problem when getting clear signals from two girls at once is that if you choose one, the other one will probably cock block you. I couldn't think of a way to bypass this problem. So I made the stupid decision to ask them to dance at another place.

We walked over to a place on the beach and danced a bit. This was the beginning of the worst cock blocking ever. There was a group of Australians lurking around but they were too scared to approach the girls. They just watched from a distance. There were about eight of them. One of them asked me if I was with the girls and I told him that they were with me there. They kept lurking around. Suddenly one of their moms (!?) asked the girls if either of them was my girlfriend and she said no. The mom called all the guys over and started introducing all of them to the girls.

I was floored by this and couldn't do a damn thing now that a few other moms were also introducing their sons to the girls. I mean: Seriously, their MOMS were picking up girls for them. What a bunch of pussies.

Of course the girls liked all the attention and the whole group sat down. The guys were on a giant family holiday and had shitloads of money to spend and they were buying expensive cocktails for the blondes. I was completely cock blocked because those asses kept talking to me while others talked to the girls. What to do when there are eight horny guys in your way and there's no way to isolate the girls now that they're getting all the attention from those buffed-up guys in their own age group? The situation was getting hopeless.

One guy wanted to go to another club and the whole group went there. I tagged along but could already tell it was a lost cause. The tall blonde was into a really tall muscular guy and they danced closely together. The other girl was also occupied. At one point I decided to call it quits and went home. I got their names for Facebook but never found them on there. I had this problem a lot with Scandinavian girls; many of them have the same or similar last names. Or yeah, they might have changed them a bit but they didn't seem the type to do that.

I felt like shit when I went home drunk and alone. The girls had to leave the next day, which was just a few hours later, but I was pretty sure they at least kissed those guys or maybe even banged them somewhere. The thought was killing me. I did all the fucking work in the first bar, they were hanging onto my lips and then I lost them to a bunch of money-throwing Aussies who needed their mothers to get talking to girls. Months later when I was getting to know more Swedish girls I started to suspect that probably nothing actually happened: they're not easy to pick up and always have cock blockers around.

Well, I still was hanging out with Nga a lot.

One day there had been a giant storm that flooded the city: in some streets the water was standing to my knees. I couldn't go to the beach for about five days. I spent the time in my room or at the bar/restaurant where Nga worked. She worked every night till midnight but couldn't spend the night with me because she shared a room and her motorbike with a coworker. In the morning she went to school. She worked twenty-eight days out of the month and earned only fifty dollars for it. I felt bad when I ordered breakfast and it cost more than her whole day's pay.

When the sun returned I went to the beach a lot and even jogged on the beach three times after a night of heavy drinking and smoking, after which I swore off booze and cigarettes because I was feeling so terrible the next day. My getting-back-in-shape mood only lasted three days before I started hammering beers again.

One night I went to the beach bar again but had to get money out of the ATM first. I took out 1.5 million Dong, the local currency. On the way to the beach bar I was stopped by some street girls looking for a customer. They pulled my arm but I refused to go with them. I was kind of drunk and one of them was feeling my nuts, which actually felt pretty good. Hands were all over my body but I pushed them all off, saying that I don't pay for sex. One of the girls hit me gently in the balls then, and like all guys know, even a small graze to the nuts will hurt. I felt them pulling on me again but managed to shake myself loose and go on to the bar. I ordered a beer, but when I wanted to pay I felt my back pocket and half a million dong was gone. I'd been pickpocketed. Luckily I had put the other million Dong in the front pocket and it was still there. I was fuming and ran back to the corner where I'd met the girls, wanting to slap them in the face to get my money back. Half a million dong isn't a fortune (about twenty-six dollars) but you can eat and drink a lot for it. I was still a very cheap bastard because I had a lot of travelling to go. Of course I never saw those girls again.

Anyway, after a while it was time to move on. D-Lux had other plans; he was going to stay there and was thinking of taking over a bar/restaurant. I gave Nga about thirty dollars to help her with her school and kissed her goodbye. I thought about what it would be like to have some short of a relationship with her. It was probably doomed to fail, with all the cultural differences between us. It would be great for a few months but wouldn't last.

I was approached by a happy Vietnamese guy who offered guided motor rides through the rural areas of the country. It's called the easy rider experience. At sixty dollars a day it wasn't that cheap but it was the only way to really see the country.

Vietnam – 8-day motor ride

This part of my story focuses more on sightseeing and less on pick–up, because it was a journey through the countryside, where there aren't really any opportunities. It was still one of the best parts of my trip.

I had booked an eight-day motor ride through the countryside with a local guide. There were several motor guides in Nha Trang and my guide's name was Eddy

Murphy. Eddy was a crazy guy who spoke good English. I've had my motor driver's license for many years (you'll remember how I used it to get into museums for cheap back in Russia) but I'm not an experienced off road rider, especially on Vietnam's dangerous dirt roads. I choose the cheapest option which was to sit on the back of his bike. We strapped my giant backpack on the back of the motor so I had something to sit against. It was quite comfortable.

The first day we took a short coastal road and then we went into Vietnam's countryside. The water at the rivers was quite low and it was strange to see people standing knee-deep in the middle of the river. They were fishing for lobster and shrimp, which were sold everywhere for next to nothing.

We stopped along the roadside and I met an indigenous family living in a straw hut. They lived very basic lives. There are fifty–four ethnic minorities in Vietnam (population 92 million), and most of them live in poverty in the rural areas. Eddy gave the man of the house some money and a few cigarettes and we rode into the mountains where the air was a lot colder. We saw many tea and coffee plantations along the way, a beautiful sight. We then arrived the medium-sized city of Da Lat, which has many temples. Most of them are beautifully decorated with thousands of colorful small tiles. After this we visited a train station housing the first steam train Vietnam ever had. It wasn't very interesting, but Eddy was making sure to stop every half-hour to show me something new, whether it was interesting or not.

The second day we visited a silkworm farm and silk factory to see how silk is made, and afterwards a temple with strange statues of Buddha. One had countless arms and a lot of heads. Outside was a giant smiling Buddha. I'm an atheist but I like the Buddhist religion. They're generally peaceful and don't try to force their religion on you.

There was an enormous waterfall close by, and if you climbed a lot of dangerous wet rocks you could get to a cave behind it. You didn't want to slip and break a leg in the middle of nowhere. I got completely soaked but it was worth it. How often do you get to look at a waterfall from inside?

We rode through a part of the country where there were a

lot of coffee plantations. You could buy a cup of coffee at roadside stalls and the taste was amazing. I never had better coffee anywhere else in the world. The plantations are small and all family-owned; the families build small palaces to live in next to their piece of land. We ate at roadside restaurants along the way and my stomach survived everything. We stopped at a school where I took a picture with a group of school kids. They were scared of me at first because I'm so tall (6.2ft) compared to rest of the people. People in the countryside are not used to tall white people and my arm got tired from waving to everyone. On one occasion a whole army platoon stopped marching and waved at me, their machine-guns dangling around their stomachs.

At the end of the second day we stopped in a native village where I met some other easy riders. One of them was a Dutch girl with beautiful red hair and two others were oversized American sisters. I met them a couple more times on my trip. Most easy riders take the same routes, but Eddy liked to get off the beaten track as much as possible.

The houses in the village were built on stilts to avoid flooding and tigers. After eating and drinking together I went to sleep and in the morning I was woken by a family of hogs sleeping under the house. I could see the mother pig and all her little ones through the large cracks in the wooden floor.

When I opened the door in the morning there was a giant elephant staring at me, his trunk just half a meter away from my face. It shocked me because I was still half asleep. I got my camera but the elephant had already started moving away.

After breakfast we got on the bike again. My bum was getting sore from sitting on the bike all day. We visited a mushroom farm and there were lots of animals around – dogs, ducks, chickens, rabbits, even a big scorpion and a giant python snake which I both held and took pictures with. We saw a lot of nature that day and visited a noodle factory and a brick factory. It seems that all the heavy labor jobs are done by women. The only man in the brick factory was a guy driving a bulldozer. The women are short and skinny but strong as a horse.

The only guy I saw working hard was a guy breaking

rocks in the hot sun. I'm guessing he fought the law and the law won? He earned even less than Nga, back in Nha Trang. The guy was breaking rocks with a hammer all month for the amount of money an average American family spends taking their kids to McDonalds. I'm not preaching socialism here but sometimes you have to take a moment and realize how good we have it our western countries.

The day after we rode almost all day to go see two waterfalls, one big one and one giant one. They were spectacular. At night we stopped in a small town and I told Eddy that my back and ass were sore from all that sitting on a bike. He said there was a massage parlor close by the hotel we were staying. We went there together. I jumped on the massage bed and a gorgeous short girl walked in. She must have been about five feet tall, had a beautiful face and sexy slim body. She had quite a special way of massaging, mainly stretching the limbs. She was pretty strong. When she was done I had her walk on my back, just like you see in the gangster movies sometimes. It felt great.

This was really the agricultural countryside, so in the days after I went to a glue plantation, a rubber plantation, a black pepper plantation. I even cut rice in the field with some local family. The children would catch rats in the field and they'd be on the dinner plates at night. It's a different world out there. You hardly see any cars because everyone is driving motor scooters, yet I didn't see any accidents with people getting hurt; in fact, the only accident I saw was a guy losing his unbelievably huge load of bananas. Quite a sight. The whole street was covered with them.

We later visited a small village where the village elder was this super happy short man. He kept laughing and cheering because of my height. He gave a long musical demonstration on his bamboo drums, which was boring but I acted as if I was enthusiastic so I wouldn't hurt his feelings and come off like some spoiled foreigner.

As we were leaving, our motor broke down and Eddy made some phone calls. He said that someone would pick us and the motor up. My western brain was thinking about a pickup truck but instead a guy on another motorbike came and pushed our motor with his foot for a few kilometers through the city we were in. No, seriously. Repairs took a few hours and we moved on. I took pictures of several war monuments and with an old (Russian) tank. After this we visited "Hamburger Hill", a famous battle zone were many soldiers died on both sides for a small piece of land. There's a very good movie about it with the same title.

What makes Vietnam beautiful is not just the amazing natural scenery but mostly the friendliness of the people in the rural areas. People were always waving and taking pictures with me and children were always cheering or running behind the bike.

The sixth day of my trip we rode to the Marble Mountains, where there are several Buddhist temples and pagodas in the mountains. I flirted a bit with a Vietnamese tourist girl and took many pictures with a school class full of teenage girls who visited the mountains. Even after visiting every country in Asia, I still say that Vietnam is the country with the best-looking girls, with have great legs and cute faces – although the Philippines is a close second.

Eddy wanted to return to Nha Trang a day earlier than planned, and had found a new customer for the ride back. I didn't mind giving up my place, because my body was very sore after sitting on the back of a motorbike for seven days. So I said goodbye to Eddy and took the bus from Hue to the DMZ, the Demilitarized Zone. It was a tour bus and I hate those buses full of fat holidaymakers, but I didn't mind this time because it rained a lot that day, and given the choice between a comfy bus stuffed with fat holidaymakers and riding on a motorbike through an endless downpour, I'll take the option with the roof.

The tour included many bunkers and a few museums. It ended with the Vinc Moc Vietcong tunnels. The tunnels were deep underground and all the work was done by women since most guys and boys were fighting the US. They dug out six hundred tons of sand using nothing but shovels and buckets. Did I mention that Vietnamese women are though? A whole village of some three hundred people lived underground for about eight years. Seventeen babies were born underground and all of them survived. The US army never found the tunnels.

After the tour I was dropped off at some restaurant where I had to wait three hours to get picked up by the bus to Hanoi. While waiting I spoke to an Iranian/American guy who was pretty cool for a guy in his forties. Anyone who reads this who ends up in Vietnam, I definitely recommend taking an easy-rider motor tour through the Vietnamese countryside. It was one of the highlights of my three-year trip.

Vietnam – Hanoi

I spent about a week in Hanoi, the capital of Vietnam. I didn't end up doing much there, because of bad luck –I ate some bad food and spent more time sitting on the toilet than going out. Hanoi does have some backpacker hostels but I found a room with bathroom for only about twelve dollars. It wasn't much but at least the Wi-Fi worked. The city has a few attractions but most visitors just stay one night and then go on to Ha Long Bay from there.

One day I went to a large indoor market to try and find some souvenirs. It was clear that not many tourists visited that place because I got lots of stares and people waving at me. It was hard to find something I liked. The clothing was too small. I'm not a giant guy but I'm tall especially compared to the very short and skinny Vietnamese, so most clothes didn't fit me. It's too bad that most people there only spoke a few words of English because there were some cute girls around.

A rickshaw driver took me all over town and dropped me off at a few museums. The traffic is insane in Hanoi, with thousands and thousands of motorbikes and people on the streets from dusk to dawn. I visited an old fortress tower from French colonial times and the military museum next door. The museum was quite interesting and had lots of exhibits. There were a few pieces of artillery and airplanes outside. Like I've said, I'm kind of a fan of military stuff and history so I visit museums and battlefields all over the world. I still dream of visiting Volgograd in Russia, formerly known as Stalingrad and site of a massive battlefield and turning point in the

European Second World War. It was the fiercest battle ever fought in history. It was from here on that the Nazis would lose the war. Why do I bring Russia up? Well…

Darya, from Vladivostok, had given me the email address of one of her Russian girlfriends who was in Hanoi. We exchanged phone numbers and met up for dinner at a Vietnamese restaurant.

We met at a square close to my hotel in the tourist area. Polina was a nice-looking girl but nothing special, I would rate her at a 6.5. She was late, of course, as most girls always are. She had a motorbike and I hopped on, grabbed her around her waist and we drove off. She had a skinny waist, so far so good. We talked for a while and I had a noodle dinner which my stomach didn't mind (for the moment). We said goodbye and agreed to meet again for a night out.

Polina and three of her Russian girlfriends, who were all studying in Hanoi for some reason I'm still not clear on, invited me for a night out. None of the girls was particularly hot but all were bangable and we went to a club on a boat.

I walked in with four white girls on my arm and heads turned. Some girls walked up to me after a while and started asking why I was there with so many girls. Then I took two of the blonde Russian girls, went to a hotel and fucked their brains out all night……

I wish I could tell a story like that but the night didn't go like this at all. After some dancing it was clear to me that the cutest of Russian girls didn't like me in that way. I decided to aim my love arrow at the other three. Surely one would bite. It didn't go anywhere; a Vietnamese ex-boyfriend of Polina's showed up and did a bit of (passive) cock blocking. Although it was an ex boyfriend, the vodka must have had her juices flowing because she was all over him. The other two girls showed little romantic interest. Our group changed venues and we ended up in another club. We met some other tourists and they tagged along. I think one of the girls liked one of the drunken guys and started dancing with him. Due to a lot of vodka, I don't remember the whole night, but one thing I know for sure:

I went home alone and feeling miserable. I know I can't

win them all but I'd already had three Russian girls before. What I should have done was build some attraction and see if one of them was interested, if not use them as pawns to pick up other (Vietnamese) girls. I already had massive pre-selection built up in the room by showing up with four girls.

The next day Polina texted me to go out again but my stomach was even more fucked up from the boozing the night before and I turned her down after initially saying yes. This must have pissed her off because I didn't hear from her again. I couldn't care less because I was about to see my Russian girlfriend from Vladivostok again in Bangkok. We had been emailing a lot since we met for the second time in Suifenhe.
I had a near accident when I almost fell of the back of a motorbike on the way to the bus station to go to the airport.

Thailand – Holiday with Julia.

The last of my BETA days is how I can best describe my vacation with Julia, the girl I met in Vladivostok. Although this took place in December 2009, it seems like a lifetime ago. In less than a month I would turn into a totally different person, but for the moment I was still a beta guy with some improved social skills thanks to travelling, socializing with people along the way and "getting lucky" with a few girls.

I had to wait two hours at the Bangkok Airport before Julia arrived. I was actually a bit nervous when meeting her because I had no idea how she would respond to seeing me again after three months. Well, she was in tears when she first saw me.

We were totally ripped off when taking a taxi to the hotel I booked online. Luckily the hotel room was not too bad; we hurried into the shower and had a bang fest afterwards. Things hadn't changed much since China. I don't remember us coming out of the room that day.

The next day was the 5th of December, a holiday both in my home country and in Thailand. In Thailand it's the King's birthday – a man worshiped by all Thai people. Insulting the King of Thailand is punished severely and could mean jail time in a country where you never want to visit the prisons. I would take a five-year sentence in Holland over a one-year sentence in Thailand. In Holland you can leave jail an educated man; in Thailand you most likely walk out a train wreck with irreparable mental damage.

We had some dinner and walked around the world-famous Khao San Road, saw some temples such as the Emerald Buddha, outside which we got fooled into a tuk tuk and did the souvenir route for twenty Baht. We didn't actually buy stuff but ended up at a travel agency and booked the rest of our trip there. The first travel agency we went was too tricky and expensive but the second one was more trustworthy, and we booked a 21-day holiday there. I remember us paying around a thousand US$ for twenty-one nights in 3- or 4-star hotel rooms, all transport all over Thailand including trains, minivans, hotel pickups, boats and even airplanes. Julia and I split the bill so I only paid about five hundred dollars for luxury hotels and not having to worry about anything. I was no longer a backpacker but transformed into a full-blown tourist.

Julia had never traveled outside Russia and was a backpacking newbie, so she didn't mind either. I don't think we could have gotten it much cheaper if travelling on our own. It saved a lot of hassle and trouble this way. The total price was less than fifty dollar a day and Thailand is not as cheap as some people think. Forget the backpacker stories of living on five or six dollars a day. They are total bullshit. The cheapest, crappiest, roach-infested room I later found on Khao San Road was hundred-eighty Baht, which is about five dollars. Maybe if you live in a remote village it's possible, but I still highly doubt it for a foreigner.

On the third day in Bangkok I got a strange request from Julia. Imagine this:

Julia (with thick Russian accent): "Neil, I want to go to Ping Pong show".

Me (laughing): "Baby, do you even know what a Ping Pong show is?"

Julia: "Yes I know, I read about it on the Internet".

Me: "Sure? What is a ping pong show, according to you?"

Julia: "Women shoot ping pong ball from vagina".

Me: "LET'S GO!!!"

And off we went, we got into a taxi and drove to a shady part of town (Pat Pong), got out of the taxi and into a tuk tuk. The driver, of course, knew the best sex show in town. "Yes Mister, I know the best".

We stopped at a place and the doorman asked for five hundred baht per person to get in. Now, five hundred baht was something like twelve dollar so it wasn't cheap but we got a free beer and could stay as long as we wanted. The stage was in the middle of the room and had tables and chairs around it.

We sat down close to the stage and a waitress brought us two large beers. The first girl walked onto the stage and inserted a small bottle of coke in her pussy and filled a couple of glasses. I looked at Julia and suprprisingly, she was having smiling. Next up was another girl doing a dance show and inserting a couple of ping pong balls in her pussy. She sat down, opened her legs and shot the balls at least 1.5 meter into a small bucket. Not an easy thing to do.

After this we saw another ten different acts including girls pulling ten meters of barbwire out of her snatch, a string of razorblades, a string of plastic roses, a girl deepthroating a long balloon, a girl smoking a cigarette with her pussy and finally a live sex show, a guy and a girl performing at least thirty different acrobatic fuck positions.

Some Chinese guys caught and pocketed the ping pong balls that missed the bucket and flew off stage. I laughed, but looking back one of them would have made an excellent souvenir for my guy friends back home. I later found out that the stage girls put a large plastic box inside their pussy, which is how they're able to pull out those long strings of razor blades, barb wire and flags.

The show repeated itself afterwards, there were some

older guys rubbing their crotch while seeing the acts. Those damn perverts, to me, at that moment, it was just a funny thing to see: it wasn't sexual at all.

When walking out, Julia and I both felt ashamed of contributing to such shameless sexual explotation. The girls on stage looked bored and sad at the same time; I'd never seen an expression on a girl's face like that before. I would see it many times again in other countries.

Julia had done some Internet research and found out that Pattaya was the place all Russians go on holiday. We went there the next day and it was the first leg of our booked holiday. In the morning the arranged taxi pickup from our hotel was late and I was sweating buckets about the guy not showing up and us losing all our money in a travel agency scam. A few minutes later we heard a honking horn and all was safe.

For those who never heard of Pattaya, it's not just the place where Russians have their holiday, it's also the prostitution capital of the world (although Angeles City in the Philippines is a close second). In Pattaya you will find the highest ratio of DOMs (dirty old man or dumb old man) compared to the general population. It's the sleaze capital, with thousands of old North American or European men looking for love or sex. I could write for ages about all the tricks girls use to trick them out of their money, but there's actually a better book on the market for that: *Money Number One*, by Neil Hutchinson. A travel buddy gave it to me when I was in Indonesia, though by then I already knew most of the tricks South East Asian girls pull on the unsuspecting tourists. Still, I recommend it.

We spent four action-packed days in Pattaya. We stayed by the Jom Tien beach, ate some (crappy) Dutch food in a Dutch-owned restaurant, went one day to the beach to meet up with a Russian girlfriend of Julia, and saw a ladyboy cabaret show. The ladyboy show, which was called Alcazar, was actually quite entertaining and funny. It's sort of a musical show in five different languages and the "girls" were hot. Such a difference with the ladyboys on Walking Street, the famous street with a hundred Go-Go bars and a thousand bar girls.

Walking street is well-worth seeing and we went there almost every night to either try out of one of the many clubs or just enjoy watching the people. I had fun walking around with a hot Russian girl on my side; she has raven-black hair and a killer body. Lots of old geezers were checking her out, because from a distance she could look Thai, and they got pretty clearly jealous at me when they found out she was actually my girlfriend, one who really loved me and not my wallet, so they couldn't peel her off me by offering more.

We got into a bus back to Bangkok and transferred at the train station. Like I said before, transport was all-included on this trip, and we had a big envelope with bus, train and plane tickets. All the tickets were dated and we had different papers for the hotel rooms. It might seem strange and really organized coming from a broke-ass backpacker like me, but this was a good deal. We took a night train down south and transferred to Ko Samui, a holiday island close to famous Ko Phag Nan.

There's not much to tell about our stay there. We had a nice room with air-conditioning, cable television and free breakfast in the morning; we did a few standard island tours and lay on the beach a lot. Needless to say we did a lot of pounding at night. We didn't go out much there, though I did have my teeth bleached with a top-notch laser treatment for only 160 dollar. By then they needed it – I hadn't brought a three-year supply of toothpaste and some of the stuff you found in the smaller places was… well, not what you'd find on the shelves back in the West.

After this my teeth stayed really sensitive for at least a week. I could only eat "white foods" the first days, such as rice and white bread. I wasn't allowed to drink coffee, tea, Coca Cola or eat ketchup or mustard. To keep your teeth white as long as possible it's better to always avoid all those things anyhow, but I like my coffee in the morning. Of course smoking was off-limits too, but I'd quit smoking already on my holiday with Julia. I can't really enjoy a cigarette when I have someone around who hates them, and I needed my oxygen for nightly sessions.

We moved on to Phuket, where we stayed in a resort-like hotel with a swimming pool and gym. By now I had heard and read about pick-up artists like Mystery, and a famous book called *The Game* by Neil Strauss. (What is it with the name Neil?)

Travelling for eight months straight in unknown countries had improved my personality and social skills but I was still kind of introverted, and I was thinking about whether there was a way I could improve more and faster. I knew where I wanted to go, and as soon as I heard about books that would improve your chances with girls and make a pick-up artist out of you, I knew I needed to study that stuff.

On a moment alone I bought a lot of books in the giant Jung Ceylon mall and made a start reading them. I was fascinated by the story of Style and Mystery, but I didn't read many pages a day.

While we were there, though, Julia and I got into a big argument. At first we were just having fun in the shower together and I sprayed some water from my mouth on her. She laughed and did the same to me, then I spit on her and she did the same to me. Of course, being the moron as I am, I took it a step further and took a piss on her leg. When she saw what I was doing she was enraged and the fun was over.

She got out of the shower and stormed off out of the room.

After a few hours she still hadn't come back and I got really worried and went looking for her. I couldn't find her. It was the only time I went out walking in the evening alone, and several Go-Go bar girls tried to pull me into the clubs. I was too worried and didn't let them distract me.

In the end I just went back to our hotel, and luckily Julia was there, swimming in the pool. I asked her if she was still mad at me and to never to leave like that again. As I said before, it was the last of my days as a beta male. Julia felt bad about it too.

We had to change hotels to another part of town and were closer to the beach now. Walking on the streets here was quite annoying. There were massage parlors everywhere and all the massage girls would sit outside and yell at you: "Hey handsom guy, want massaa, massaa?" Or they would just shout massaa massaa at you, which was funny at first but got old after fifty times or so. The massage girls were all young and hot. There was one girl/woman I really liked in the massage parlor next to our hotel. I should have sneaked out of the room and gotten a massage from her.

On the streets, people hassled you every ten meters, especially the Indian guys with clothing stores who wouldn't leave you alone even after you said no to them twenty times before. That was something I had to endure in Hong Kong as well, along with the offerings of fake drugs by Africans.

Around Christmastime Julia gave me a present for my birthday, a daytrip to Thailand's amazing southern islands. We went to the famous islands from the Leonardo di Caprio movie "The Beach", and did a short trip to Ko Phi Phi, an island I would return to later in my trip, when I'd capture a flag from a country I'd been to before but where I hadn't caught the flag.

The days flew by, and soon it was time for Julia to return home. We flew back to Bangkok and she had to take a flight back to freezing cold Russia. She cried uncontrollably the last two days of our trip and saying goodbye was hard on me too. After three weeks together on beautiful beaches and staying in fancy hotels I was actually devastated she had to leave.

This was the first girl on my trip I came very close to having an actual relationship with before giving it all up.

The days after she left I just sat in my bloody hot hotel room feeling sorry for myself. I barely ate and was very sad. The only thing I did in those five days was go to a Thai boxing event in the Lumpini stadium, which was quite spectacular. I had front row seats and was very impressed with the fights and the toughness of the very young fighters. But it didn't relieve the gloom. For the rest of my time there I killed time reading my pick-up books and trying to learn stuff and watching Prison Break episodes on my laptop.

In a few days I would go to Cambodia and everything would change for me and even my trip. But I didn't know that then.

New Years Eve 2009/2010 was probably one of the most

depressing moments in my life. I went to Khao San Road alone, got drunk on 7/11 store beer and just watched everyone else have outrageous fun. I didn't have the balls to walk up to any girl or even to have a beer with some guys. Not only did my body freeze up when I even thought about it, I was still very down and depressed from Julia leaving. I wondered if it was worth it to move on. Julia was great, and the love of my life: was going around the world for another two years really worth losing that, when I couldn't even bring myself to have a drink with someone else? What was the point of bumming around the globe if I couldn't even enjoy it? Maybe I should just move to Russia and make the best of it with her.

Well, that was pretty much hitting rock bottom so far.

Cambodia – Siem Reap

I left Bangkok early in the morning. Most backpackers buy a bus ticket at Koa San road and pay way too much for something you can easily do yourself. I hopped into a taxi to the north bus station and bought a ticket to the Thai/Cambodian border.

On the way I met a Spanish guy in the bus who was doing a short trip and we talked a lot about travelling. We took a tuk tuk from the Thai border town to the border.

I was wondering if the driver would try the Visa scam that I'd been warned about in Lonely Planet. And he did. We stopped at some "visa office" along the road. They insisted we should get our visas here. According to them, it was impossible to get a visa at the border and this was the last place you could. I told the driver that he would get no money at all if he didn't take us to the border. I also warned a few Russian tourists who were brought to the same spot not to buy the overpriced visas there. The "travel agent" saw he was losing his "customers" and told the tuk tuk driver to take us to the border.

At moments like these I feel glad that I always have a Lonely Planet guide on me, because while the prices are always wrong in the book, at least they warn you about scams like this.

Formalities at the border took one hour. That meant waiting in the sun for at least half an hour before moving indoors. They were a large group of Russian tourists around so it was a feast for the eyes but it also reminded me of my time with Julia. It took one hour to get a simple passport stamp and hawkers were busy trying to sell bus rides to Siem Reap. Some people trust anyone with a shiny laminated badge on their shirt and they paid double. The official Cambodian currency is the Riel, but pretty much everything is paid in US dollars. It's the only currency available in ATMs. A taxi costs twelve dollars and a bus nine dollars a ticket. Normally, being the travel bum that I am, I'd opt for the cheaper bus but Stefan the Spanish guy was taking a taxi and I went along.

That turned out to be a mistake. We were cramped into a car with two big Swedish guys and could barely move for hours. A bus would've been a lot better. Lesson learned the hard way.

In Siem Reap a tuk tuk driver took us to a range of expensive hotels. The Spanish guy wasn't that well-travelled and didn't put up much resistance and was fine with anything. I wanted a cheap place and after a while the driver "found" one. The cheapest place he showed us was a dollar a night, but that was just a mattress under an open roof. The guesthouse we chose was a lot better, six dollars a night for a room with bathroom. It was still a roachy place with a cold water shower, but suitable. There was a hangout place upstairs with some fitness equipment and a TV. Some girl was smoking weed and we joined her. The girl was a typical backpacker, the kind you see by the hundreds in South East Asia. Dressed like a slob in wide linen pants, a tank top and not much bothered by hygiene or looking attractive.

Cambodian girls on the other hand looked a lot nicer. Asian girls have always intrigued me and by that time I had only slept with one of them the 20 year-old Chinese girl in Dalian.

Early the next morning Stefan and I went to the famous Angkor Wat temples, the number one tourist attraction of Cambodia. It's a true spectacle. The Angkor Wat complex is not listed as one of the Seven Wonders of the World but it should be. A tuk tuk driver picked us up in the morning and off we went. First to the ticket office along the road to the complex, where we had to pay a hefty $40 entrance fee for a two-day card. The tuk tuk driver took us around the most important buildings that day but around two o'clock he came up with some of the lamest excuses I had heard in a while. He said his mother was in the hospital and we had to return early. Stefan the Spaniard believed him but I didn't and told the driver to keep driving us around till five o'clock. Although obviously it's possible to have a sick mom, and in a poor country like that there's probably no-one to look after her, it's much more likely that he wanted to return early to be able to pick up some more rides that day.

The second day, Stefan and I rented mountain bikes (only two dollars a day) and biked the whole day around the temples. I think we saw them all. It wasn't an easy thing to do and we cycled some forty kilometers in the insane hot sun and I think I drank some five liters of water that day. There were women selling water and food everywhere and as soon as you came close to them, they started yelling at you to get your attention. I heard a lot of "pretty boy" and "handsom man" that day. We ran into a few French girls at some temples and they laughed at my t-shirt, which said "Beer is the answer, what was the question?" I talked to them a bit and we agreed to meet that night.

I must say I was heavily impressed by the enormous buildings and the beautiful carvings. The temples overgrown with enormous tree roots are truly amazing. Angelina Jolie's *Tomb Raider* was filmed there. Anyone going to Cambodia or even South East Asia who doesn't visit this marvelous temple complex is a complete moron.

We never saw the French girls again but had some beers at some bars anyway. There were lots of hot Cambodian girls around in the bar street but I was warned that they were all hookers and didn't pay too much attention to them. If only I knew what would happen a few weeks later in Phnom Penh.

We ate a massive meal at one of the street restaurants; the meat is cheap and well-prepared. I had a giant meal of spare ribs, a chicken thigh and plate full of rice for less than five dollars. While eating, a poor street kid came up to me and asked for money. I told him he couldn't have money but could eat if he wanted. I never saw a little boy eat as fast as him. I felt sorry for him and the many other street kids I saw there, but it's part of the street life and you have to get used to it. But it's hard. At one point an old man walked up to another boy and took him by the hand. I immediately felt enormous rage boiling inside me. What did that old grandpa want from that boy? At the border there were warnings about child prostitution, and I'd read about drugged five-year-olds being forced to blow guys for a couple of dollars. I was furious at thinking I was seeing that in action –but the old guy and boy walked to a table and I saw an old woman next to him. They offered him a meal. My anger was unnecessary.

Cambodia – Sihanoukville

The bus ride to Sihanoukville was terrible, not the worst one on my trip but I still got a bit nauseous due to the bumpy road. I barely slept all night and was very tired when we arrived. A guesthouse a couple hundred meters from the beach was close by, but I still had to sit on a taxi motorbike to get there, fighting my sleep and nausea. When I finally fell into a dirty bed at seven in the morning I immediately fell asleep and woke up at three in the afternoon. The seven-dollar room had a bathroom, which was convenient. My nausea was still there when I woke up but I ate something anyway, and now my bowels were fucked up too. The rest of the day I relaxed a bit. Being sick doesn't bother me too much, because it's part of travelling, but it's still irritating.

The night after I met up with some Russian friends I'd met in Khabarovsk. There are quite a few Russians in Sihanoukville, and Vitaly had already told he was going to be there so I adjusted my schedule a bit to meet him again. Of course seeing Tanya again didn't hurt either. Vitaly and Tanya were having a short vacation together with another couple, Alexander and Svetlana. We went to several bars and restaurants together, including a snake and crocodile farm and restaurant owned by a Russian guy who made

Sihanoukville his hometown.

Having travelled through Russia for two months and had three Russian girlfriends, I thought I had finally understood something about Russian culture. I was wrong. Even in incredibly hot Cambodia they wanted to visit a sauna. A sauna.

The sauna was owned by another Russian couple. So off we went, with six people – another friend of Vitaly's had joined us, I think his name was Victor.

It was probably thirty-five degrees Celsius outside the sauna, but inside it was probably over fifty. And the Russians didn't want to just go in once, quickly: no, we did five rounds in it, with short beer breaks in-between going back in to sweat the beer out. Plus it turns out that the proper Russian way of taking a sauna includes beating each other on the back with bushes of eucalyptus leaves. I was "treated" by Alexander, who was a massive power lifter type of guy. He was beating the living daylights out of me, displaying his hulkish power. Luckily Tanya was a lot gentler with the leaves. It was just another crazy thing that would never have happened to me if I'd never met that crazy bum/night guard friend of Vitaly's in Khabarovsk. Sometimes you just really do have to go with the flow and see what happens after meeting people. I probably wouldn't have met Julia either.

I advise anyone planning to go to Russia to do a short visit to St Petersburg and Moscow and then take a train east, because that's where the real (and a lot cheaper) Russia is. You won't regret it, because cities there are packed with girls and there are almost no foreigners around. If I had been more skilled at picking up girls during my time there, I could have done a lot more damage than I did. Meeting Vitaly and Tanya again reminded me of just how great Russia had been, and made me think how if I'd just done the usual tourist thing, I'd never have met them, and for that matter never have ended up in a sauna in Cambodia.

The last day before I left we all went to the beach, close to a Russian nightclub. The nightclub was in an old airplane hangar including an airplane inside. For those who read this it must seem like Sihanoukville is run by Russians, but actually it's just that by then I didn't have much contact with Cambodians.

For some dumb reason, I felt I had to prove my manhood when I saw a palm tree that was growing on the beach in a forty-five degree angle, and decided to climb it. Going up the tree was quite easy, even though the stem was only twenty centimeters wide. Going down was a whole other thing, and in the end I saw no other option than to jump, which was better than to try and fall down. The landing after the four-meter jump was hard and I nearly broke my ankle. I acted like not much happened but the next day and the week after I had troubling walking straight and couldn't drive a motorbike with a shift. On the other hand I was still kind of proud that at the age of thirty-three I climbed up that crazy palm tree.

At night we went to a popular club in the middle of Sihanoukville. There were quite a lot of Cambodian girls around, and they were eye-fucking me a lot. I just assumed they were all hookers and didn't even bother talking to them. Man, was I wrong.

What follows is shameless debauchery.

And the death of a Nice Guy.

Cambodia – Phnom Penh

The use of the word Cambodian is not exactly correct, since down in Cambodia people refer to themselves as Khmer (a 3000 year old culture), but to make the stories more understandable for all readers I'll just use the word Cambodian to refer to them.

It only took five hours to reach Phnom Penh by bus. I took a motor taxi to the lakeside area, what locals call the Boeng Kak Lake. I chose the first guesthouse named by the Lonely Planet and that was probably a good choice. Otherwise, you wouldn't be reading this book.

I took a room with a big bed and simple bathroom for only four dollars a night. After freshening up and unpacking a bit I sat down in the outside television area. There were about five people watching a movie and about ten seconds after sitting down I was already flirting with a Cambodian girl named Soriya. She said that she only spoke a bit of French and not so much English. I said some French sentences I learned in high school and the famous line "Voulez-vous coucher avec moi, ce soir?" originally from Labelle but more famous because of the Christina Aguilera/pink version. I always use that line when meeting French girls, it's lame but it works. It means: "Do you want to sleep with me tonight?" Not once did a girl not smile or laugh after hearing that and it's a good way to start flirting with a girl. I watched the movie, used to the Internet café outside the guesthouse and went back to my room.

The next morning I got up early and I took a motor taxi to the Myanmar (Burma) embassy. The guard outside told me that it took six days to get a visa. I thought that was way too long, so I left. I was only planning on staying three days in Phnom Penh. Afterwards I went to Laos's embassy because that visa only took three days to arrange.

I went back to Guesthouse Number 9, which had an outside television area, a bar and restaurant area, lots of couches to sit and relax on, a large wooden deck on the water where people would sit in the evening and night on blankets and pillows.

The most popular part of the guesthouse was around the pool table, next to which were a few couches and a television. There were always some Nigerian guys around, most of them were dealing and smoking weed all day. They were friendly and never bothered or hassled me. The big boss of the Nigerians was a guy named King Kong; he was always dancing around and permanently high as a kite. I never had much contact with him but when I did he was friendly.

The staff were all Cambodian and so were a lot of the guests – or so I thought the first day. I quickly found out that none of the Nigerians or Cambodians was actually staying at the guesthouse and it was a place where everyone could just walk in and hang out. The Nigerians were not even allowed to stay in the rooms, for a variety of reasons.

At night I watched a few more movies with the rest of the backpackers, and talked to the Cambodian girl again, who smiled and admitted that she actually spoke pretty good English. There was a nice surprise when I walked back into my room. No, not a naked hottie lying on the bed waiting for me. A giant two-inch beetle lay on the bathroom floor, being eaten by ants but still alive. I ended his misery by flushing him down the hole in the floor that served as a drain for the shower. The rooms were built right above the water. A giant spider had drowned in the toilet bowl so I had to flush him away too with a bucket of water. Things like this don't exactly make for a restful night's sleep and I inspected the room like someone from CSI before going to bed. It was a one-time thing though.

I went to the "killing fields" early in the morning. For those who don't know, Cambodia lived through a five-year civil war that was supported and funded by Vietnam on the one hand and the USA on the other. The Americans dropped over 2.5 million tons of bombs on Cambodia. To put that into perspective, the total number of bombs dropped by the allies on Germany and Japan during the Second World War was under than two million. Cambodia is about 180,000 square kilometers; Japan and Germany together are around 735,000 square kilometers. For the math-inclined, that means that where on average, every square kilometer in Germany and Japan was hit by two or three bombs, in Cambodia the rate was 14. Relatively-speaking, that's up to *seven times* as much. Cambodia is generally considered to have been the heaviest-bombed country in history and yet barely anyone knows about this.

In the end, despite the bombings, the Khmer Rouge was victorious, coming to power in 1975. The dictator Pol Pot and his regime then decided to turn Cambodia into a communist farmer state and committed a massive genocide, slaughtering anyone who was considered intellectual, a minority or simply an enemy of the system. It was one of the most comprehensive genocides of the twentieth century, one not many people know of now or cared about back then. Cambodian cities were cleared of people and they were forced to work twelve to fourteen hours a day as farmers while barely being fed. Anyone who looked suspicious would be executed immediately; women and children were not spared. Owning a book or wearing glasses was reason enough for execution. Monks, teachers, doctors, musicians, writers and almost anyone with any sort of education were executed when caught, most of the times together with their just-as-innocent family. The whole world watched it happen but didn't intervene. In the end, in 1979 Vietnam invaded and ended the destructive reign of the Khmer Rouge. By that time almost half of the population of 7.7 million people had been executed, starved or died of disease. The Khmer Rouge (still supported by China, Thailand and by most Western governments at the UN) turned into a jungle guerilla and kept fighting until the early nineties. Khmer Rouge leader Pol Pot died on April 15, 1998, having never been put on trial. Despite all this, the people are very welcoming to all foreigners.

The Killings Fields consist of mass graves, a museum and a large monument filled with skulls and bones. It was small but impressive. Afterwards I went to the infamous Tuol Sleng (S21) prison, nowadays a museum, where I was horrified by the sights and many pictures of victims. It's an uncomfortable sort of visit, but it's unfair to Cambodia not to make it if you're there.

My visa for Laos was ready on Monday and I picked it up. I had no plans of staying any longer in Phnom Penh and wanted to leave the country. I had no idea that one girl would change my mind and that I'd end up staying eighteen more days and later return for another month.

I went out with Soriya to a club called Heart of Darkness, a club with a mixed selection of foreigners and Cambodians. We danced and kissed and ended up in my room where we had sex three times that night and following morning. Soriya was twenty–four at the time and a single mother.

In the afternoon she went (back) to Sihanoukville, where she stayed most of the time. I found out later that week that Soriya usually gets paid for some midnight pleasure, but she never asked me for anything, not even breakfast. I realized that I had "shored" a girl for the very first time. (Shoring is a term for having sex with a prostitute without paying for it.)

In the meanwhile I got to know a lot of other people: a guy from Lithuania who gave me a giant bag of weed because he couldn't get it across the border, a couple of English guys, I think one of them was named Matt, an cool Australian dude named Stewie and an African girl from Liberia. We smoked weed, drank beers and played pool all day. It was steaming hot and I was wearing just slippers and shorts. Every day new people arrived. Some stayed a few weeks while others went on their way in a few days.

Most Cambodian girls at Nr 9 were extremely good at pool and played me off the table all the time. I guess they spend a lot of time playing it. One of them was already getting a bit older (read 30), but she was nearly unbeatable. I ended up in bed with her one day after smoking a massive amount of weed with her. After a couple of bangs we came out of the room again in the afternoon. I found out later she was of Laotian heritage, and thus I got my Laos flag. I now had a five bang-to-flag ratio because the last four girls were also of different nationalities: China, Canada, USA, Cambodia and Laos. Nakry became a friend and we smoked many joints and played lots of rounds of pool. She became my "rolling" woman – more on that later.

The days were long in the guesthouse. I'm not a big sleeper and always woke up early. In guesthouse Nr9 that's around eleven in the morning. I spend my time smoking weed, playing pool and drinking beers.

In the meanwhile I got the attention of two 19-year-old girls, one from Cambodia named Dara and one from Vietnam named Bian. Because there was a lot of gossip, they knew that I had been with a few girls already and started to hang out with me. They used my room to freshen up or change clothes. I'm not stupid and was aware that things could get stolen so I never left them alone and of course had the chance to watch them change clothes. It's hard to steal in my room anyway, because I use certain techniques to keep my stuff safe.

I later came to trust both girls and let them alone in my room sometimes.

At night we'd sit by the water on the big wooden deck,

joking around. Bian and I smoked weed, we'd drink a few beers or rum and cokes. I slept alone that night because Dara and Bian were going out and I was too stoned to join them. I went to bed early, but in the middle of the night there was a knock on the door and the girls walked in and jumped in my bed and we slept together. When I walked out of my room with the two girls all the guests were looking at me and I felt a man, though not much had actually happened that night.

The next night they both came back to my room, but Bian left after a while and I had sex with Dara. I couldn't believe it was happening. I was having sex with the hottest nineteen year-old girl in Cambodia, a girl fourteen years younger than me. She had changed her clothes a few times at my place before but I'd never seen her without a bra before. Her big boobs were straight out of a Playboy magazine, and to this day remain the most beautiful boobs I have ever had the pleasure of sticking my head between. And that says a lot.

The next night Bian came to my room and I had sex with her too. It was my Vietnamese flag. Bian too had an amazing body and a great smile. When I saw her the next day Dara asked me if I'd had fun with Bian. I said yes, it was great, and that was that. She didn't seem to mind.

My room was close to the reception and television area, so every morning people saw me with a different girl, or sometimes two. We had breakfast together, smoked some weed and then most of the time the girls went home. The guy working at the reception was laughing his ass off every morning when I ordered some food and drinks. I was spending next to nothing per day, four dollars for a room, ten to fifteen dollars on drinks and maybe seven to fifteen dollars on food depending on whether I was alone, with a girl or with two girls. Cambodia is still one of the cheapest countries in South East Asia.

Dara had to leave to Bangkok for a few days because her "boyfriend", some American schmuck, wanted to go there because he thought Cambodia was too much of a dump. When I say "boyfriend", I really mean "money-sender from abroad", because that's what most of those guys do. They work hard in their own country but are too socially awkward or ugly to find a girlfriend. So they fly to some exotic place, in this case Cambodia, and fall in love with the first girl who smiles at them even though she's sometimes a hooker. They spend a few weeks together until it comes to a heartbreaking goodbye. The guy is usually a total white knight defender-of-all-that-is-good-and-sacred and thinks he can get the girl out of her miserable life if he sends money so she won't have to work in hooker bars anymore. A true Captain Save-a-Ho.

Of course, the girl has a couple of these guys sending money to her. The pretty ones sometimes even have five to seven foreign boyfriends visiting her from time to time. All she has to do is keep in touch with them, play the good girl and make sure the visiting times of boyfriends don't overlap. This way she can make hundreds of dollars every month without even really having to do much. The tricky and pretty ones can make a thousand dollars a month, which is a fucking fortune for a local in Cambodia.

As I said, I was starting to get some status around the guesthouse, and people were talking about me. Guys were asking me how much I was paying for those young girls and would stare at me when I told them I paid nothing.

Room 44 was becoming a famous place and people were even starting to joke about it. The room itself sucked balls: the bed was full of bedbugs, little beetle-like insects that crawl all over your body and suck the blood out of you. If I turned on the light they disappeared quickly, only to come back as soon as the lights were off. Then there were the water-pipes making a high-pitched noise from time to time. I have no clue what caused this but I was getting no sleep with the bedbugs and howling pipes – and the ladies.

During the day I would forget about it and smoke some dope. I decided to go to the Heart of Darkness club again. There were a lot of hookers out that night and even more loser white guys trying to get with some of them. Damn, those guys looked pathetic. From the look on their faces, I wondered if they ever seen pussy without pulling out their wallets first. I, on the other hand, met a short Vietnamese girl there, danced with her and went back to my room without even offering her a drink. I said upfront that I was not going to pay her money for staying with me and all she said was: "I no want your money, I like you and want be with you".

Well, this twenty-three year Vietnamese girl, let's call her Nina, was something different. She was a very energetic girl, talked a lot and was a complete freak in the bed. She didn't make it a secret that she was a pro and she fucked and sucked the living daylights out of me for the next four days. I don't think I've ever banged a girl that fanatic between the sheets. She deep-throated, talked dirty, and I made her say things from one of my 1980s favorite war movies: *Full Metal Jacket*. She had never heard of the movie but said the famous lines anyway.

O'me so horny. Me love you long time.

Nina was already number five in less than a week after my time with Soriya.

Dara texted me that she had returned early after only four days in Bangkok, and her boyfriend had come with her. I was sitting next to the pool table with Nina on my lap when Dara walked into the outside area of the guesthouse. She said she'd made an excuse to her boyfriend and come to Nr 9 to say hello to me. There was an awkward moment, but she reacted calmly and wished me a good time with Nina. They both knew each other from the Nr 9 guesthouse.

Dara's boyfriend was not a bad-looking guy but insecurity radiated from him. I saw him and Dara at Heart of Darkness but she couldn't talk to me because her dork boyfriend was extremely jealous. I remember looking at the guy and feeling sorry for him. I'd been banging his girl for the last couple of days and he was just awkwardly standing at the bar trying to get attention from a barkeep who ignored him.

Although I really liked Dara, I couldn't care too much about seeing her with her guy. Anyway, Nina stayed with me. I was on a roll but decided I'd better slow it down a bit. All that banging all day, every day, the weed smoking and beer drinking were taking a toll on my body. But I couldn't beat Nina off me with a stick. After a few days her Cambodian girlfriend Seda slept in my room too. So there I was, walking out of my room with two girls again. I had tried to do a threesome with Nina and Seda but Seda didn't feel like it. The two girls stayed with me all day, especially Nina, who was a caring girl. I didn't have to do anything anymore. She rolled my joints and when I wanted to eat I just had to open my mouth and Nina spoon-fed me the whole plate while I was watching television.

At one point during the day I was very sleepy from smoking too much weed and wanted to go to my room and sleep a bit. Nina had gone to her room a few blocks away from the guesthouse and I was sitting on a couch with Seda. I said to her that I wanted to go to sleep and asked her to join me. She agreed and when we went into the room I jumped on the bed ready to get some sleep. Seda walked straight into the shower, washed up and came out butt naked. I wasn't expecting this; I honestly wanted to get some sleep but didn't feel like lying in bed alone, and I think Seda was misunderstanding what I meant by "sleeping". But I hopped in the shower too, took a two-minute shower and had sex with Seda afterwards. It wasn't a great lay but I was kind of spoiled already at that point.

Nina came back a few hours later and laughed about the whole thing, and that night I spent with Nina and Seda together again. Seda still wasn't up for a threesome but pretended to sleep when Nina deep-throated me only half a meter away from her.

Every evening I lay down at the wooden deck with some girls around me and other girls started to show interest in me too. I felt like a fucking rock star. The power of having sex at will with a selection of girls and having some dudes say I was the King of Nr 9 gave me a powerful feeling, and this pissed off some of the other guys staying in the guesthouse. They tried to get laid with some of the girls but they were asked hefty prices or downright turned down. Soriya, my first Cambodian girl, had come back from Sihanoukville, and she wasn't too happy when she found out what had happened in the meantime. I can't name all the girls I was hanging out with, but I knew at least fifteen girls there who where always orbiting around the pool table or the lounge deck.

Now before anyone thinks I was throwing cash around, remember, I'm a poor backpacker. Well poor isn't exactly the right word – maybe budget-minded would be better. At this point I still had around 30,000 US dollars in my bank account, but throwing money around wasn't an option because I still had a few continents to conquer and a few years to go. That doesn't mean I was a tightwad, though: I'd still buy food and drinks for girls who were staying with me, but the food was only a few dollars anyway and a can of beer was only a dollar. A pack of Ara cigarettes was less than thirty cents.

One day I read an email from Dara in the Internet café close the guesthouse. She told me her boyfriend was about to leave and that she was dying to see me again on the twenty-eighth of January.

I told her I would stay in Phnom Penh a bit longer to spend some time with her again. I still had a few days left before my visa ran out. When Dara came back she was really happy to see me, telling me she hated her "boyfriend" because he was no fun at all, though she stayed with him because he paid well. But she also saw that I still was with Nina. I was in my room with Nina when Seda, Soriya and Dara knocked on my door, hung around on my bed for a while and asked me to come out to drink something and play some cards. Soon after all hell would break loose.

I was invited by five or six girls to play some drinking/card game. Room 44 had been driving me crazy, so I'd changed to a new one close to a wooden neck near the water. We all sat down on the deck and started playing. I was with Nina at the time but I couldn't keep my eyes off Dara, who looked smoking hot. We had lots of fun together, chatting and playing cards. I made a small video of it, it's still circulating somewhere on the Internet, since I wanted to show it to my friends back home.

Nina hadn't minded me sleeping with her friend Seda, so I expected her to be fine when I told her I wanted to be with Dara again. She was calm when she said okay, but looked pissed off. I should have known jealousy would take over and not to underestimate a woman's emotions. In hindsight I figured out that Nina didn't mind me sleeping with Seda once because Seda was less attractive than she was – but Dara was a smoking hot girl with Playboy boobs, and only nineteen years old.

I went over to the Internet café to make a Skype call to my Russian girlfriend Julia, who I'd neglected a bit over the past weeks. She was in tears for nearly an hour as we talked. When I returned to the deck, everything had changed. The girls were in a panic. Communication with Cambodian girls was already hard but now they were shouting and screaming at me. This is what had happened, according to eyewitnesses:

Nina and Dara got into an argument over who could stay with me, and some of the girls had badmouthed me, including Soriya who was still pissed off that I'd banged a lot of other girls when she left for Sihanoukville. Remember, these were freelance hookers who could make money every night, but they were fighting over a guy who wouldn't pay them anything for many days of company. Apparently things got heated up and Nina lost it. Suddenly, for some unknown reason, she jumped into the filthy disgusting lake and disappeared.

The girls went crazy and four Nigerian guys jumped in to search for her, but they couldn't find her. When they got out of the water, some of them had lost their jewelry, along with a mobile phone. A few minutes later I walked back into the guest house and people tried to explain what happened to me.

Then one of the girls saw that the light in my room was on and I went in, where I found Nina lying on the floor, dripping wet and not responding or saying anything to me.

I yelled to the still-panicked girls that she was in my room and closed the door behind me. She must have swum under the wooden deck and climbed into my room through the window. I tried to ask her what happened but she just stared in front of her. I reckoned she must have used some drugs stronger than just weed. She had me told that she used some "ice" sometimes, but I told her I didn't want to hear about it and told her not to use that shit. Apparently she didn't listen.

At one point while I was trying to get her to respond I

heard a knock on the door. I opened it and found Dara and a girl named Rosie there, asking about Nina. They were angry for being scared that Nina could have drowned. I went into the corridor to calm them down, closing the door behind me.

Suddenly the door opened again and Nina came out shouting something. She started arguing with Dara in Cambodian. All I could understand were the words Neil and "long hair" (I was called that there some times), and then it happened.

Nina punched Dara really hard in the face. You could hear the punch land. It could have been a knockout blow but Dara kept standing and grabbed Nina. They immediately started kicking and punching at each other. I tried to separate them but they were holding each other's hair and were all strangled up. By now the whole guesthouse was watching, including all the foreigners. Some guys working at the guesthouse ran over and violently beat both girls until they let go. I jumped in because one of the guys was really giving it to them. Dara walked off crying and Nina was crying in the corner of the room. I told the staff I would take care of it and closed the door. I dragged Nina into the bathroom, took off her clothes and tried to wash and fix her up a bit. Her face was bruised from the beating the staff gave her. It all went super fast: the whole fight took less than half a minute. The staff came back and wanted to kick her out, but I bribed them with five dollars and said she would leave in the morning.

What the hell had I got myself into? I had some thinking to do.

I told Nina to stay in the room and went outside to see what was happening there. Outside the guesthouse I found a crying Dara. Even though she had fairly dark skin I could see that her eye was blackened and bruised from the hard punch Nina had given her. She was there with her sister and some friends who were all raging and waiting for Nina to come outside. I had to talk a lot to calm things down. I told them that Nina wouldn't come out of the room because I didn't want more fighting. They finally agreed to stop hanging about after a while. I felt really bad about what had happened, because Dara truly is not only a very sexy girl but also a sweet and honest one. Most freelancers are coldhearted bitches but she truly was a sweet girl.

The following morning I had a serious talk with Nina. I was still angry with her, but mostly I was angry with myself for fucking things up so badly. She felt bad about it too and wanted me to have make-up sex with her but I didn't want to. After she kept pushing, I let her give me a blowjob and leave. She was not allowed back at the guesthouse for a while.

Things weren't exactly ideal for me either. Some guys I'd known for a while there were giving me a hard time, saying I'd gone too far. Basically they were just jealous because they didn't get any attention themselves, but it made things a bit uncomfortable. Then I went to the Internet café and saw that Dara had written me an email saying she didn't want to see me again because it caused too much trouble.

I wrote her back a long, apologetic email. I knew that if I wanted to sleep with her again, I'd have to lay it on thick, so there I was assuring her that she was the only one I loved, even if I'd done some other bad things, which I accepted were wrong. All in very simple language, of course, to make sure she'd understand what I was saying. Then I went to my room and watched a movie to kill some time and think things over. I was wondering if she'd reply and if everything I'd said would have an effect. But I also figured that if she continued not wanting to see me again, it wasn't going to be a disaster.

The last weeks had changed everything, and I wondered why the girls suddenly liked me so much. I supposed it could have come from implementing some of the things I'd read about in those pick-up books – I'd taken some of their advice on body language and inner game – but I didn't use their "routines or peacock tricks", so I couldn't be sure what it was. Something had definitely changed, though.

In the evening things had calmed down a bit, but people were still talking about it. After night fell I saw that Dara had come to sit on the deck by the water, but I felt a bit depressed and stayed in my room.

After a while Rosie came at my door and said that Dara wanted to talk with me. She had read my email and been moved by it. Things were OK again between me and her. I was happy as a clown. She stayed with me that night, and that got noticed. By the next day I was a legend around lakeside parts. I was that guy that slept with hookers for free and had them fistfight over me but still could lay them at night.

But I'd learned my lesson. I stayed with Dara and didn't go with any other girls, even though they now pushed themselves on me. More jealousy arose and some girls tried to split us apart. They didn't succeed, though they tried hard.

On one of the last nights I went out with Dara and Rosie. We hopped in a tuk tuk and went to Dara's house first so she could change clothes. She lived in a small concrete shack with her family, it must have been two by five meters at most, including a small kitchen and bathroom, and there were six people living there. I wondered where all the money went. Dara's older sister had done the same work for years and had an American boyfriend/money-sender, you'd expect that the family could live a lot more comfortably with all that money coming in. Their combined income must have been at least ten to fifteen times the avarage Cambodian salary, yet they were still crammed into that tiny building. It really is a different world out there. I'd been to Nina's place too: she lived in a small room a short bike ride away from the Nr 9 guesthouse, and it wasn't an improvement on Dara's place.

Dara stayed with me till the day my visa ran out and I had to leave the country. We said goodbye early in the morning and I went to on my way.

How the hell did I pull this off? As you can read, I didn't spend much money, I had no luxurious room with air-conditioning, I didn't take girls to classy restaurants or buy them clothes or gifts. I didn't throw money around in clubs and was stoned as fuck most of the time. The answer? I have no idea. Sometimes I still wonder myself.

Laos

On the bus to Laos I started reading a book for the first time in ages. The book, recommended to me by many people, was Paul Coelho's *The Alchemist*. Although it was an interesting read, after all I'd heard about it I expected more from it. It was not a life-changer the way many people had told me. The real life-changing happened in the weeks before when I went from a shy regular backpacker to a womanizing bastard, and had nothing to do with that book.

I spent some time at Don Det, one of the 4000 islands in the Mekong River. I needed some rest and enjoyed being on my own for a while. I spend one night with a German girl, but no bang. After five days I moved on to Vientiane, the capital of Laos.

While I was there I decided to get things in order for going to Myanmar next. Getting a visa at the Myanmar embassy was a major hassle for the girl I went to the embassy with but a piece of cake for me. Burma, or Myanmar as it now called, is a military dictatorship that's a bit afraid of researchers and journalists. Since I had already seventeen pages of stamps in my passport, it was obvious I was just a traveler, but she was a different case, and they took a really long look at her. When I say it was easy for me, though, I should mention that it still took five days, during which I was stuck in this boring city. I went to the riverside bar a couple of times but except for Russian girls and Cambodian hookers, my game was still much undeveloped. Oh, how I wish to walk into that bar now, when I'm usually fearless and have pretty tight game.

It was time to visit the big backpacker trap named Vang Vieng, a place every backpacker in South East Asia will end up at some point. When I walked off the bus I saw two English-speaking white guys walking barefoot. I don't know what their idea was; maybe they were planning to write a book named "Around the world barefoot", but it looked disgusting.

The biggest reason backpackers go to Vang Vieng is the tubing down the river. It's a debauched carnival of drunk and drugged-up 21-year-old backpackers. During the day people go tubing and get drunk at one of the many bars on the side of the river. The river and its bars have a sort of Mad Max look and when you're there for the first time it's fun to do.

When you're out on an inner tube, Laotian guys will throw ropes and pull you into the bar area, where loads of people are getting drunk on cheap cocktails. There were slides and zip lines, and everyone had paint on their body saying things like that they were sluts or took it up the ass. I felt old and not at ease there. It clearly wasn't my scene. Girls would climb up the rocks or go to the bar and scream "wooohooo!!" every two minutes for the rest of the day. After about five times you just wanted to toss a bottle at them.

At night, all the bars were open and people got drunk over many drinking games and rounds of free drinks. I tried to pick up some girls, but the girls there had an attention span of one minute until the next woohooo and I had no verbally strong game, so I didn't bother too much. When the bars closed people moved to the riverside bars and drank buckets of Vodka Red Bull. I got drunk here a few times but usually not too much because I hate hangovers.

There were shitloads of restaurants in Vang Vieng, all playing the same two television shows. No matter where you went, it was either *Family Guy* or *Friends*. If I have to choose between those two I'm more of a *Friends* person, so I usually ended up in the same place.

One day I made a lot of eye contact with a cute girl but she left soon after with her girlfriends. The next time I saw her she was wearing a long dress, but when she sat down her dress moved up and showed some disgustingly hairy legs. I lost my appetite immediately and gave her an obvious dirty look. She should learn to behave like a woman. It only convinced me even more that white backpacker girls are not for me. Most of them dress poorly and don't take care of themselves, but they still walk around thinking like they're the main prize. I ran into a similar situation in Bolivia a year later.

I killed my time with reading some pick-up info, watching movies during the day and going out at night. Some people were really fucked up on drugs and acted crazy and made complete fools of themselves in front of everyone. I took it easy with the mushroom shakes and smoked some opium instead. The drug prices were complete rip-offs and I'd say half of the stuff was fake anyway.

I can't believe I stayed ten days here but I did. Like I said before I didn't feel at ease in this scene and decided to go back to Cambodia where I would be a somebody again. Dara and

Nina had both been emailing me, asking when I'd return.

I had to go to Bangkok first, to cross the Thai/Cambodian border in the east. It was not possible to go from Laos to Cambodia without a Cambodian visa from the embassy, even though the other way around is possible. And thus began one of the worst bus rides of my trip.

The bus went from the north of Laos to Bangkok; this meant changing coaches four times and barely any sleep. The bus company in Vang Vieng promised us a sleeper bus, but the seats didn't even recline so I barely slept the whole ride. My stomach is always my biggest enemy when travelling and I thought it would be best to eat as little as possible so that I wouldn't have to take a shit on the bus. There was no good food along the way so I ended up with only a bag of chips and some candy.

And after all that, at arrival in Bangkok I was very sick. Of course I wanted to find a place to stay as soon as possible. I found a dirty shoebox of room close to Khao San Road for five dollars a night. It was a shitty place, but at least I had a place to stay after asking at several other places. Khao San Road is a horrible tourist place with far too many street hawkers and fat couples. I barely left my room because I had some serious food poisoning and nearly vomited when I walked down the street and smelled the sewage and looked at the food at the food stands. I played it "safe" and only ate at Subway and McDonalds and stayed away from street food, but I still had to run for the toilet a few times.

I bought some new T-shirts and shorts on the streets, a decent pair of (fake) Diesel Flip Flops, some cool bracelets and a brand new pair of earrings. The earrings look expensive but I only paid six dollars for them. People seem to think they're diamonds. I still wear them. According to my pick-up books I had to "gear up and look cool". Not bad advice, of course, but I wasn't exactly unpopular my last time in Cambodia when I was wearing ugly white shorts, stupid t–shirts and a pair of old worn down slippers. I still picked up a lot of girls and figured it must have been something else that attracted them.

Phnom Penh – second visit

A couple days later I headed back to Phnom Penh. I left early in the morning because I wanted to get there in a single day. It was a gruesome and bumpy fourteen-hour ride including yet more long border formalities, but when I arrived at Guesthouse Nr 9 the guy working at the reception was happy to see me again and shouted out: "The ladies' man is back!" Then he said to me, "You good guy, always many ladies in your room", and the girls working in the kitchen came out and were smiling at me. It was a major ego boost: the guards and tuk tuk drivers outside had been joking and cheering too. One guy shouted "He fuck all girls!" I can't say it didn't give me an ego boost. I was known here.

I took a room on the side of the guesthouse, showered the sweat and dirt off of me and walked out again. I couldn't wait to see the all the people again I met the last time I was there.

As I walked to the pool table area I felt great and heard Darth Vader's Imperial March playing in my mind. It's better to have some outrageous inner game than feel self-conscious the way I did in Vang Vieng among all those ultra-young backpackers.

Tina, a girl I met, my first time in Phnom Penh but haven't mentioned yet, shouted "Neilllll!!" and jumped in my arms. Her French boyfriend was looking grumpy and I didn't understand why at the time; later Tina told me he was pissed off because she only gave him a kiss on the cheek when he arrived at Phnom Penh airport.

Despite all the drama and the fight between two girls over me the last time, I had a fun time and wanted to relive those days of being a popular and wanted guy. I said to myself, *OK, take it easy this time. Both Dara and Nina have emailed you and want to be with you. Nothing to worry about – and by God, take it easy this time.* But no, the last time turned out to only be a warm-up…

I just had to fuck things up again.

The first few days it was just fun to see everyone again. I smoked some weed with Nakry and Lisa, two older girls always staying in guesthouse Nr 9's bar area. I usually gave them five dollars so they could buy weed and some mangos. They would roll the joints and cut up the mangos for me. I didn't mind them smoking my dope too because for two or three dollars they could buy a pretty big bag of weed. If I had to buy it myself I would've paid at least eight to twelve dollars for the same bag.

As I said, these days were OK and it was fun to hang out with some friends again but I didn't see Dara or Nina. I'd already texted them a few times to let them know I was back, but never heard anything in return. Some girls told me that they were angry with me but I couldn't figure out why. Everything was OK when I said goodbye to Dara.

It got me thinking of leaving to another city if things didn't change soon. One day, a young girl named Jorani was paying a lot of attention to me. Now, this girl was aiming some other dudes too, but she wasn't good in English and was pretty stupid. I played pool with her a few times and gave her a beer. The words "let's go to my room" were enough to convince her. It was early but she was already drunk. I made her take a shower and had sex with her afterwards. At the time I was completely numbed and didn't care much about anything else than myself. When I think back I tell myself I probably shouldn't have had sex with her.

It was still early in the evening and I was checking my email in the Internet café across the street. Suddenly someone tapped on my shoulder, and when I looked up it was Dara, who wanted to have a word with me. It's hard sometimes to understand those girls because of their limited knowledge of the English language, but I found out that there was a lot of bullshit being said about me. Two Vietnamese girls, Bian and another one whom I'll call Nhu, had been telling bullshit stories about something I was supposed to have said. I got angry and told Dara this was a complete lie and that I wanted to talk to those girls first. I went with Dara to the Heart of Darkness club.

I met both other girls outside the club and we talked it

out. It seemed that Nhu had told some lies to Dara. When this came out, weirdly it was Bian rather than Dara who got really angry with Nhu. She started shouting at her, and since this was all in Vietnamese I couldn't understand anything, but I heard my name "Long Hair" a few times. Bian was furious about Nhu lying to her and slapped her hard in the face. Nhu pushed her back and Bian took off her shoes and tried to swing at Nhu with her four inch heels. I had to duck for cover a few times not to get my head bashed in with a heel when I tried to separate them. At least fifty people were watching it and some stupid old fat white guys were cheering. I told the one closest to me to shut up or he would be the one eating street pavement. He ran off. He didn't even walk, no, he *ran* off, the yellow coward.

I got the girls to stop fighting by pulling them apart, and Dara took Bian inside Heart of Darkness. She was still kicking and screaming – not only was she very beautiful, she was a hot pepper too. Meanwhile I took Nhu to Guesthouse Nr 9 with a motor taxi. She grabbed me around my waist and tried to cuddle on the way there but I told her to let me go. After all, she was the one who'd been talking shit about me. I was angry because when I finally saw Dara again, she was angry with me and then there'd been another girl fight over me. Less than three days after me returning to Phnom Penh.

Arriving at Nr 9 Nhu couldn't stop crying and wanted to hold me all the time. Her face was still red from being slapped so hard by Bian. Of course all people in Nr 9 were staring at me again and asked what was wrong this time. I just said "Another fight over me", and the gossip machine started rolling again. Some backpacker guys were asking about me and of course the "crazy girl jumping in the water and fighting for me" story came up and was immediately told by some others.

But Nhu was still crying, and a girl in tears is a genuine weak spot of mine. I felt sorry for her and realized that due to all the communication problems I would probably never completely find out what all the fuss was about. I took her to my room to get the attention away from us and she wanted to have sex with me. After some refusal, I caved in. It were her massive dick-sucking lips that turned me on. I had sex with her just four hours after I had sex with Jorani.

The next day I saw Dara, but she didn't say much to me, still pissed that there was a fight again concerning me.

She had been planning on coming back to me, but the fight changed her mind. It really pissed me off because the stunningly beautiful nineteen year-old Dara was the main reason I'd come back to Phnom Penh in the first place. Bian and Nhu had already made up and everything was all right between them. The only one who got screwed was me.

In the evening I met two German guys, one of whom really seemed to like Nhu. She looked at me and whispered that she needed money to pay her twenty-dollar rent. She knew she wasn't getting money from me and asked if I'd mind if she went with the German guy for one night to get twenty or thirty dollars from him. I'd already banged her five times, so I didn't care so much.

A day later I saw Dara again. She came to Nr 9 with her little brother, the one I had seen at her house when I went to Phnom Penh the first time. We talked a bit and she said she just wanted to be friends now. Dara was the only one I cared a lot in Cambodia, about but unfortunately someone else fucked that up for me.

In the meantime, there was a girl orbiting me all day named Ary, and she was determined to get with me. She wouldn't leave my side and came on to me all the time, so I took her to Heart of Darkness and danced with her a bit. Afterwards we went back to my room and we had sex there. She was pretty good in bed but didn't have a clue about giving a blowjob. Maybe I was just spoiled because Nhu was great at it and had big dick-sucking lips.

When I woke up the next morning and Nhu saw me with Ary, they immediately started arguing about who could be with me. What a life I had back then! It's not one to be proud of, but it felt pretty damn good getting treated like a popular rock star. Ary was a jealous girl and a bit crazy, and she was soon driving me and Nhu up the wall. At one point they were yelling at each other again and I shouted out: "Hey take it easy, shut up!" They became quiet as a mouse and a lot of people laughed about it.

Some English backpacker girls were asking about me and showed some interest, but I couldn't care less about their fat white asses and ignored them. I was busy enough as it was. Nhu was desperate for my attention, massaged me in front of everyone and then pushed her half naked breasts in my face. That became so awkward that I took her to my room again.

At this point I was the fucking boss around there. There were at least four or five girls I had banged around me at any time of the day. Guys were jealous and trying to get me to leave. Nhu or the two older Cambodian girls would roll a joint for me or massage me when I complained about a sore back or neck. It's hard to imagine all this went down without paying a dime, but it did.

About seventy percent of people in the bar/restaurant and pool table area were non-guests of the guesthouse. There was a Thai girl with whom I flirted a bit, but she was always with friends. I had met her before in January but she was with an older girl who irritated the crap out of me with passive cock-blocking and annoying bad English.

For some reason I was not much attracted to Thai girls while I was in Thailand, but Areva looked more Chinese than Thai. Picking her up was a piece of cake. It just took some pool table gaming. Most guys get all serious when playing pool and don't understand it's the fun while playing that the girls like. Areva and I sat down at the waterside on the wooden deck and I made out with her. She was shy at first but I drove her crazy. An hour later I took her to my room and banged her there. Areva was already thirty-eight but had the body of a twenty year-old. Her skin felt like silk. Only thing I didn't like about her body was that she was flat-chested. Dara's massive Playboy boobs were too beautiful to easily forget and I would compare all girls to her. Dara had gone off the radar a bit and didn't visit Nr 9 much anymore. I'd hit the jackpot with Areva without knowing it. I can't say too much about it to respect her privacy but she had a good job as a manager and was in charge of some important project in Phnom Penh.

The next two days I slept at her place and we had sex all

the time. Her apartment was very fancy and had air conditioning, a gift from above in this country. She also had a king-size boxspring bed, a flatscreen TV, an iPod, two BlackBerries and a MacBook. Dara's family shack this was not. The hot shower was a warm welcome after nearly two months of cold showers.

After some talking, I found out that she'd been tricked before by a few guys who cheated on her. I asked what she saw in me, because it was pretty damn obvious I was playing around with a lot of girls.

It was already too late. She was head over heels in love with me. Some girls make the same mistakes their whole life and she was one of them. She was into bad boys. I tried to protect her from herself but it was too late. She became obsessed with me. The greatest compliment a guy can get, sure, but a damn annoying one too. She already had a whole future lined up for us. She would get me a job at the company she worked for and I could stay at her place.

I got nervous of her obsessive behavior and decided to slow things down a bit, and at night I went to a goodbye party thrown by Tina for her French boyfriend, who was going back to work to France.

It was a barbeque and most the Nr 9 personnel were there, me included. A girlfriend of Tina's who left to Germany later was there too and had invited some Australian guys. Me and the guys didn't like each other. Ever since I was massively cock-blocked by that group of Aussies in Vietnam I had disliked most of them. They were also hating on me for no reason, but I guess it was jealousy since two of the guys tried to get with some girls but didn't like the price tag that came with it, and they knew I didn't have to pay. The third one, who was quite a good-looking guy, left with one of Tina's girlfriends and had sex with her. I was too drunk to go out later that night. They all wanted to go to some expensive club but I declined and went to sleep alone for the first time since I set foot back in Phnom Penh.

I woke up with a massive hangover and could barely drag myself to the guesthouse's restaurant area to get some breakfast. Waking up took a while and I had a discussion with a girl named Wi. I had loaned her ten dollars a week before, when she had been continuously nagging me for some money. I was really stoned that day and gave it to her as a loan. A week later she had not returned the money and I said she had to pay up in cash or another way. She chose the other way and I took her into my room and actually had great sex with her. Since it was kind of paid for I didn't count her for my 80-girls challenge.

Another girl who was always orbiting around me was Devi, a thick Cambodian girl who had big boobs and massive dick-sucking lips. She was not attractive by normal standards, but I usually don't care about that. If she excites me, she's good to go. Those big boobs and lips did excite me and I had flirted with her a bit in the days before. Devi asked if she could use the shower in my room since it was nearly forty degrees that day, I said "sure" and we went to my room. She took the shower and I just hopped into the shower too. She gave me a surprised look at first but a smile followed a second later. I had great sex with her. Sometimes a thick girl feels ten times better than a skinny one. The saying "more cushion for the pushin' " is true. When I say thick, I mean Asian thick, which is a bit chubby but soft silk-like skin without cellulite or blubber. Chubby is not fat. I don't like fat girls at all.

That night Areva slept at my place. Three different girls in one day. This was getting out of hand.

Tina, who had just said goodbye to her French boyfriend, then asked me to come to Sihanoukville with her. She was going to enter the Miss Sihanoukville competition and wanted me to come with her to take some pictures and lie on the beach for a week. Three of her girlfriends would come with us too. We could share a room. I said yes for four reasons: one, I don't get asked to go to the beach with four girls every day, so this was my chance. Two, sharing a room with me? Yeah right, she wanted to get fucked by me. Third, I wanted to take some distance from Areva who was really getting obsessive; and fourth, I had no chance of getting back with Dara or with crazy sex freak Nina, who had disappeared of the radar since my return.

You might think it was going to be a nice beach holiday.

Think again. Of course it was another round of mayhem.

Cambodia – Sihanoukville

I went to Areva and told her I needed a break from Phnom Penh and would be back in a day or four. She didn't like it, but said she would go back to the main office of the company she worked for in Bangkok.

When it was time to leave, it became clear that the three girlfriends of Tina weren't going with her. I called one of them when I already was on the bus and asked her about it and she said she knew nothing about it and couldn't go anyway. She was going to move to Germany to meet her "boyfriend", who had managed to get a German passport for her and her Cambodian baby. She wanted to come with me and have sex with me – she said it straight up over the phone – but she couldn't.

Tina was sitting right next to me and heard everything. She acted pissed off, but I thought to myself, *Well, be pissed off, you little liar. I'm gonna have you anyway.*

A few hours went by and Tina, who was only 1.5 meters tall (five feet), had already crawled up against me in the bus and gone to sleep.

Just an hour before we arrived I got a phone call from Areva. I couldn't believe my ears. She told me that she was in Sihanoukville with her friends. She had taken a private car and raced ahead of me there. This was clearly stalker behavior. Tina got even grumpier when she heard the news.

Tina had brought her scooter with her in the storage compartment of the bus, and when we arrived in Sihanoukville we used it to find a hotel not far from the beach. It was a nice room with two single beds and air conditioning. Areva had called and texted me a few times already since I got her call on the bus, but I took my time because I couldn't be bothered to hurry and talk to her again. I needed a moment to let this situation sink in and come up with a solution. Tina and I went to the beach and had a massive seafood dinner.

141

My plate was filled with delicious fish. Two tiger shrimps, three sorts of grilled fish, a big grilled squid, a giant baked potato and salad – for only three dollars.

Tina and I were sitting there when Areva called again. She was looking for me on the beach and was walking past all restaurants there. I told Tina to relax and I would take care of it. She was not happy with the situation and neither was I.

Five minutes after I told Areva the address, she showed up with four other people: her older Thai girlfriend, a Cambodian girl I'd met before in Nr 9, and two Thai guys, one of whom was her brother. All four of them worked for her. My eyes nearly fell out of their sockets when I saw them and I didn't know what to do, so I said as less as possible. It was an awkward situation. Drinking a beer with the girl you ran off with to another town and the girl you're running from and four of her friends and family is not something covered in the etiquette books. I took Areva apart and gave her an angry speech about her stalking me, I said that I already paid for the hotel room with Tina and was not going to stay with her that night. She was disapointed but said she understand me. I was thinking: *You understand what? That I'm banging this other girl tonight? How naive are you?*

I went to the hotel room with Tina and she said nothing for a while. She just took a shower and lay on the bed with her head turned away from me. I explained the whole thing to her as best I could, mentioning that I couldn't help that a girl was stalking me. (In Pick Up/PUA terms a stalker must be the ultimate pre-selection.) In the end I just jumped on her bed and lay besides her. No much later I took her clothes off and started kissing her in her neck. She defrosted pretty quickly. Her face was one of the most beautiful faces I'd seen in Cambodia, not to mention her short skinny body. I'd had the hots for her ever since I saw her the first time in January. She rode me like a wild horse all night long.

Something I do nearly every time I have sex with a new girl is ask at what point they were attracted to me. She told me that she had always liked me, but that since the day Nina and Dara had fought (she was there), she absolutely wanted to have sex with me and waited for the right moment. Girls love bad boys, whether nice guys like it or not.

The next day was even more awkward. Tina and I went to the beach and the whole Thai gang joined us. Tina was boozing her grumpiness away and I had to divide my attention between her and Areva.

That night Tina had to go join the other Miss Sihanoukville contestants at the Oasis Hotel, and we left early to prepare. The contest was taking place close to our hotel. A friend of hers joined the competition too. She was deaf from childbirth and quite beautiful. It was hard communicating with her.

The election was pretty clearly rigged by the judges. The jury consisted of one Cambodian woman (whom I met before when hanging out with the Russians) and two foreigners. According to bystanders their girlfriends won. I'm not sure if this was true, but I'd believe it. The main prize was $250, which is quite a lot of money in Cambodia. While Tina is a very beautiful girl with model-like features, I couldn't keep my eyes off the other contestants too.

While the Miss Sihanoukville pageant was going on I met two Dutch guys on holiday, who praised my accomplishments so far in Cambodia. The compliments came with Jack Daniels and cokes.

After the Miss Sihanoukville thing was over, we went to a bar on Tina's motor-scooter and I saw Areva again. We played some pool and because both Areva and Tina were there I mostly talked to other people to keep the peace. I couldn't completely control myself, though, and flirted a lot with the Cambodian girl in Areva's group. After a while, I had a talk with Areva and told her this situation was getting out of hand and that she was way too obsessed with me. Her brother, who was looking angry all night, came to talk with me.

The situation became a bit dangerous because you never know with Thai guys, they might be very good at Thai boxing, one of the most effective and brutal martial arts. It's best not to mess with them. His friend was standing close by too and kept an eye on us. I had to figure out if the friend was there in case Areva's brother attacked me and was losing the fight or if he was there in case I was the attacker.

The funny thing was that Areva's brother was not angry about me going to Sihanoukville with another beautiful girl, hanging out with her all day and night, but he *was* angry because I talked a lot to the Cambodian girl in his group instead of to his sister. I said that was all a big misunderstanding and I wanted nothing from this girl. (Well, I would have banged her if I had the chance but it wasn't a priority.)

After this Tina wanted to talk me again, and then after that the Cambodian girl who was afraid of losing the job she got from Areva. I couldn't believe what I was hearing and had to talk my ass off to all of them to make it all better and not get my ass kicked by two Thai guys.

Fortunately, Areva and her friends/employees had to leave after the weekend to get back to work in Phnom Penh. Although it was a stalker move to follow me like that, I felt bad for Areva. She sent me poems and messages on a weekly basis for months after I left Cambodia. She was quite obsessed with the ole Skywalker.

I was finally alone with Tina. Tina was still grumpy about the whole thing and was drinking a lot.

The rest of the week we spent on the beach. Every day was kind of similar: we would go to the beach around noon, get a few deck chairs and eat some breakfast or lunch. After an hour she would jump on her scooter and buy a bottle of Jack Daniels whiskey in a liquor store close by. From every corner of the beach her "friends" would come by and enjoy the whiskey; as soon as the bottle was empty they all had something to do all of a sudden. I told Tina that her friends were using her to booze up for free but she waved my comment away with the words "Not true, they are my friends".

Tina's deaf friend, who unlike the others was a real friend, joined us one day with a foreign boyfriend. She got really drunk and the young foreigner got scared of her. She got really wild because of how much she drank. Tina calmed her down and they left. I don't want to say too much about her because she really was a nice girl.

During the day there would be several kids around our deckchairs. They would sell handmade bracelets for a dollar. Sometimes I paid half.

By nighttime Tina would be drunk too and would become jealous if I even looked at another girl. She'd start a fight with me and burst out in tears if she couldn't win the argument, and eventually jump on me to settle the score with sex.

This went on for days. During the day everything would be all right and we would have fun on the beach, eat lobster, shrimp and squid all the time and drink some bottles of Jack Daniels, or Dack Janiels as Tina often said, mixed with Coca Cola, but at night her jealousy would take over and she would respond angry to every situation that involved other girls.

One night we were at one of the beach bars and met a girlfriend of hers with her American boyfriend, a young guy with blond hair who owned a small jungle guesthouse on one of the islands. They got into an argument about the keys to their room that night. The girl, named Sophon, was very pretty and I exchanged a few words with her, and she told me she wanted to break up with that guy. Back in the hotel room, Tina flipped out.

I was sick and tired of her bitching about me by now. I told her I came with her to Sihanoukville to spend my time with her and away from other girls but it looked like I had traded one obsessive girl for another.

That night I slept in the other bed in the room and told Tina to shut up and go to sleep too. Early in the morning I bought a ticket back to Phnom Penh at the hotel reception. When Tina woke up and found out I was about to leave she dropped on her knees and cried her eyes out, begging me to stay with her in Sihanoukville. I said it was too late and was determined to leave on the bus. She said she would pay for my ticket if I stayed longer. A contestant of the beauty pageant on her knees begging me to stay. A situation unthinkable in Holland. After a while I promised her to stay one more day and then go back to Phnom Penh with her.

Things were all right that day, hanging out on the beach

again with the three happy beach kids and some other friends. I saw Soriya again, who was still a bit pissed off at me since she had been the first to be with me and I had sex with ten other girls since her. Both Soriya and Tina were at Nr 9 when Nina went crazy and jumped in the water. Tina had spent the 400 dollars her French boyfriend had given to her, mostly on drinks and food. I'd spent 140 dollars that week. A male factory worker in Cambodia makes a hundred dollars a month if he is lucky. Tina had spent four times that amount in little over a week. She lived off the money her boyfriend sent her and had no other income. She told me he was dumb enough to send more if she cried a bit on the phone. Man, these girls were coldhearted.

Back in Phnom Penh I rode around on Tina's scooter a bit out of boredom and stayed at her one-bedroom apartment at the lakeside area. It was a nice place to sleep at night compared to the rooms in Nr 9. Tina was happy as a clown that I was staying with her, doing my laundry and making a giant meal at night. I was eating lobster and giant gamba shrimps all night. The bottle of Jack Daniels didn't survive the night and neither did the giant bag of weed.

The following morning we had an all-day banging session and my package hurt till the next day. She invited me to her birthday but that day was just outside my visa period. Once again she begged, this time the whole day, to extend my visa. After a while I agreed to it and left my passport at Nr 9 to let them extend it for me – for a fee of course.

The same day I agreed to stay, Tina got jealous again, after a few days of calm. The problem was that we were hanging out at Nr 9 all the time and there were always at least five girls around that I have had sex with at some point. Nina had also returned to Nr 9 a few times and had openly flirted with me. I really wanted to be with her again, because I liked that crazy Vietnamese girl, but I'd made a promise to Tina that she would be the only one while I was in Phnom Penh. She had won, so to say.

The beginning of the end came when Tina and I went to a bar called Sharkey's, which is a large English pub with a lot of pool tables, a good band and lots of old guys looking for a taxi girl, as freelance hookers are called in Cambodia. I never made a secret about banging a lot of those taxi girls, but I never paid a dime for it.

Trouble started when at first Bian and Ary, who were both there, and later Dara, came to say hello. Dara flirted a bit with me and Tina's face became grumpier by the minute. We decided to go back to Nr 9 and hang out there a bit. After one hour Dara walked in. She had changed her clothes. She looked better than ever in a short mini skirt and her big boobs sticking through her shirt. Tina was talking to someone on the phone and I had to screw things up by talking to Dara in a far corner of the place so that Tina couldn't hear what we were saying. Dara told me that she wanted to be with me again but couldn't because of all drama and fighting before. Now that I was with jealous Tina it was out of the question. "I also want to be with you," I said to her and I charmed her for a full 10 minutes. She was quite emotional and suppressed her tears.

The one who was not suppressing her tears was Tina, who was crying out loud. "Let's go to your apartment and talk about it again," I said to her, which we did. We got into an argument and Tina flipped. She was shouting and kicking things in her room. She went to the bathroom and lay half naked under a cold stream of water, shouting, crying and breaking stuff. It was like a scene from a movie, and I saw no other option but to leave, so I packed my backpack and went back to Nr 9 and got a room there. It was already past midnight now and I went to sleep alone and feeling bad. I heard a girl bang at my door in the middle of the night, but when I asked who it was and the answer wasn't Dara or Nina I didn't let her in. It was actually a girl I knew and was attracted to, but I wasn't in the right headspace to be coldblooded once more and just let her in and do my thing.

When I woke up I went to the guesthouse reception and asked them for my passport back without renewing the visa. It was due in five days and I wanted to get out of Phnom Penh as soon as possible. As I sat in the Internet café I was surprised to see Tina come in and give me the laundry I had forgotten at her place. She had folded and ironed everything but didn't want to talk to me anymore. Her hand was wrapped into bandages. She'd probably hurt herself while breaking stuff in the bathroom. Later I sat down in the television area of Nr 9, and as soon some girls found out I'd had an argument with Tina they were swarming around me.

I could see Tina having fun playing pool and laughing with some people, and thought to myself that if she could have fun with others, there was no reason for me to be down, and invited Nhu to sit on my lap. Of course, when I tried to get in contact with Nina or Dara I couldn't reach them by phone. Just my luck again. All I wanted was to stay with one of them, preferably Dara. Ary and Jorani were trying to get with me too, but I told them both to get away from me.

In the afternoon I went with Nhu to her room inside the water village on Lakeside. I have never seen a poorer place than the water houses there (besides in India of course). I had to walk over several dangerous planks just to get at her place, which she shared with another girl.

Afterwards I took her to my room and had sex with her again. I couldn't resist her big lips and sexy little breasts with nipples that were always hard and poking through her shirt.

In the evening, I was sitting with Nhu on my lap when I saw someone I didn't expect in Phnom Penh. It was Sophon, Tina's girlfriend, whom I'd met in Sihanoukville. Sophon was happy to see me. I told her I broke up with Tina and she said she'd broken up with the American. I told her I was going to Battambang to get close to the Thai border and leave from there to Bangkok. She looked up and said her mother lived there. Without hesitating I asked her to join me there. She happily said yes. I told her there was a bus in the morning and asked where she slept that night. She said "At my girlfriend's house". I told her to get her stuff and move in with me in Nr 9. She declined because Tina was there too during the day and night. "I can stay with you, but then we go to a hotel in a different part of town," she said. I thought about it a bit, looked at her beautiful face and tight body and said "OK, let's go". I packed my backpack, paid the bill and said goodbye to the people in the guesthouse.

When I walked out with Sophon by my side, Tina walked in and looked furious. At the time I thought I'd had my revenge on her, but now as I'm typing this, two years later, I feel stupid for treating her like an object. But on the other hand, I promised her I wouldn't stay with other girls and still she flipped out every time I talked or looked at one. She is a beautiful girl but trouble all the way.

Sophon and I checked into a room and I tried to bang her that night but she wouldn't put out, except for some kissing. It was the first time I met some resistance from a Cambodian girl. We left in the morning and after a long ride we arrived in Battambang, where we found a nice luxurious hotel for only six dollars a night. After taking a shower and some lunch we went to see her family who lived in a forest outside Battambang.

The house was made of bricks with a sheet metal roof; there was only one big room inside. There were chickens around the house and a dog that looked very old and miserable but was only a year old. Sophon was only twenty years old and her mother only a couple of years older than me. She breastfed the youngest son all the time and took out her big breast with giant nipples right in front of me.

Sophon had two younger sisters around the age of seven and ten. There was also an uncle around who slept in a hammock most of the day. Sophon's mother invited me to stay at her place but I declined. The house had only one room and one bed. Although I didn't mind sleeping next to the mother for a bit, I decided to stay with Sophon in the hotel.

I had sex with her that night. Although gorgeous looking she wasn't very adventurous in bed and she said she had only had the American as a boyfriend. A blatant lie, of course. I saw her with quite a few foreigners on her Facebook in the years after.

The next four days I stayed in Battambang, hanging out with the family during the day and most of the evening. I must say I enjoyed staying in a rural area, and laughed when the mother was drunk at night because she was not used to drinking. Every night she cooked a nice meal with ingredients I bought at the market with Sophon. Her two little sisters were cleaning my pockets out of small change with a Cambodian card game.

In the morning I called Julia on Skype and we had a long talk and she was crying all the time. I felt bad because I just had sex with Sophon that morning, but forgot all about it as soon as I hung up.

I didn't mind buying food at the local markets and some extra soda for the kids every day but at times I thought they were taking advantage of me a bit too much. It bothered me a bit that her neighbor asked three and a half dollars every time we drove back to the hotel on his motor bike. Going back and forth twice a day it added up to fourteen dollars a day. I think I spend close to $120 for just four days on the hotel, food and drinks and motor rides. Sophon was clearly looking for a money provider/sender and didn't really care that much for me on the inside. She was begging me to stay and extend my visa just like Tina had the week before, plus she wanted to get married and have kids. She is really very beautiful but I'm not falling for that trick and I left Battambang the next day, Sophon was nagging my ears off about having a baby and I was glad to be on the bus.

She wanted to keep in touch but for the next two weeks I kept silent about my whereabouts. Now I have no contact with any girls in Cambodia anymore. I've unfriended them all. It may seem odd, but there's a reason. Some guys aren't very happy with me over there, and have started sending me more than a few threats. Point is, Cambodia's still a dangerous place, and it's worth taking threats there seriously. It wouldn't be too difficult to find someone willing to kill someone for you, especially if you told them he'd been "dishonoring" local girls, and some of those threats have been death threats. I can probably never return to Cambodia, however much I'd like to.

I came back for Dara or Nina but instead I had made another mess.

Short visit to Bangkok

I was fed up with all the drama and fighting in Cambodia and wanted to do some proper travelling again. I took a bus to the Thai border, where I met a Canadian girl named Kate while we were waiting for our passport stamps. Kate was on her way to Bangkok too and we talked the whole four-hour ride. Kate would be a seven in most guys' opinions, and her blond hair and sometimes bitchy face made her attractive to me too.

I tricked Kate into sharing a double room with me. We had walked down Khao San Road a few times already and I told her it would be better to share an air-conditioned room than to each get a cheap single one with a fan. It's a trick I came up with in Laos, though the German girl I shared the room with there wasn't up for romance, and it has the advantage of being true.

That day we went to the MBK mall to hang out and eat. At night we drank shitloads of beer on Khao San Road. I pitched some game at her and she received it well. Back in the room I jumped in her bed and we made out a bit, but she didn't want to bang on the first night. Ironically, she said she'd many one-night stands before but stopped doing that. I was thinking *Nice timing*.

The next day neither of us was not feeling too well, due to all the drinking and the Thai food, and not much happened between us after that. I don't even remember us saying goodbye. I just missed her when in Singapore and saw her again in Sidney a year later. I stayed a few more days and booked a flight to Yangon in Myanmar, formerly known as Burma.

Myanmar – Yangon

The flight there took only one hour and on arriving I was surprised at how easy it was getting through customs. I didn't notice the fact I'd entered a military dictatorship at all. The only thing I did notice was that the taxi was super old and crappy. I haven't seen that in other South East Asian countries. In Thailand most taxis are brand new and a lot cheaper than tuk tuks if you have to drive far.

The hotel was old but at least the owner was a jolly guy and spoke reasonable English. My room had no windows and only one electricity socket, so I had the choice of using either the fan or my laptop. When I used my laptop inside the room it was boiling hot in there and I was afraid my laptop would just burst into flames.

The street the hotel was on was really old and broken up. The pavement was terrible and you really had to watch out where you walked, a lesson I would learn, painfully, a week later when I totally busted my toes open on the pavement and left a small trail of blood to my hotel. There was plastic crap and paper all over the streets. In so many words, it was filthy.

The first day I stayed in and met the other people staying in this hostel/hotel. We were all sitting of the rooftop and talking a bit. I didn't seem to like anyone there. One Swiss guy was really weird, he was talking with something like five different accents and tried to be interesting but in my opinion he made a fool of himself. I think he was trying to impress the two American girls who were true hippie tree-huggers and talked about living in tree huts and growing their own food. Clearly they'd never heard of razor blades, since they had really hairy legs and armpits. I was clearly not amused.

I won't go into the whole political/moral debate of visiting the country or not. Yes, it's a military dictatorship, but people still earn money from tourists and infrastructure is developed for it. I was there in 2010 and I think it's getting better there now.

Yangon, formerly known as Rangoon, is a massive city with a population of five million. I had miscalculated the distance on the map and I walked for almost two hours in a heat of thirty-eight degrees to see the Shwedagon Pagoda. It was tiring but fun to walk around. I was a big attraction in a city that doesn't see too many western foreigners, especially around the part I walked. The pagoda was breathtaking: it consisted of one big stupa (temple) and many other smaller stupas and Buddha statues. It is all made of gold and almost blinding to look at. Because it's a temple you have to walk barefoot and the floor outside was sizzling hot – some parts I had bite my teeth and keep a straight face while getting my feet scorched. Some locals were just standing on the floor and were taking pictures, they must have asbestos feet.

After this I hung around for a few days seeing other parts of the city. One funny thing about the hotel I was staying at was its giant breakfast. Apparently the hotel was mentioned in a Lonely Planet magazine once as the one with the best breakfast in Asia and the owner had build his formula around this. There were posters and plaques everywhere referring to his breakfast and the owner mentioned it several times a day. He wasn't lying about it. The breakfast buffet was the biggest I had ever seen and you had choice of some twenty-five different dishes in the morning. Every time I ate until my belly resembled a balloon.

Myanmar – Bagan

I wanted to visit the 4000 temples in Bagan, a site matching Angkor Wat in sheer size and beauty. I hopped in a taxi and told the driver to take me to the bus station. "Where are you going?" he asked me and I told him "Bagan". Twenty minutes later I found out why he asked me this. It wasn't so much a bus station as a bus village. There must have been a thousand buses there and at least fifteen streets with bus companies and restaurants. He dropped me off at "Bagan Street" and I bought a ticket there.

In the bus a Portuguese tourist (the only other white guy) sat next to me and we talked a lot. His name was Alehandro and like me he was travelling for an unknown period of time in South East Asia.

The bus ride took only ten hours and was comfortable at first – well, as comfortable as a chicken bus can get. Of course it was a loud, stinking bus, but I always like to travel like this and immerse in the local customs. We arrived in the middle of the night in Bagan, took a bicycle taxi to a hotel and were surprised to not get ripped off at all. People are friendly and as soon as they find out you're not a dumb naive tourist, they will drop the price and treat you nice. I think they don't like the gullible money-throwing type of tourist much. They like the money but not the attitude. Alehandro and I both took a separate room with hot water bathrooms and air conditioning for only five dollars a night.

The following morning we went to look at all the temples. We took a horse-drawn cart with driver and he took us past all the major temples. The views were astonishing. I think the number of 4000 temples is a bit exaggerated, but there were at least hundreds of them. We saw the fifteen biggest ones.

There weren't many other tourists around, so it must have been the slow season. While looking at the temples we saw many young girls and a couple of Burmese school classes on a field trip. I had my picture taken at least twenty-five times that day, mostly with young high school girls. Myanmar is still a very conservative country without much contact with the outside world, especially not the West, so it was a big deal for these girls to get a picture with a tall blond guy like me.

I was planning to go south after returning to Yangon, but an old German guy (they are everywhere) who married a Burmese woman and lived there told me it was impossible due to guerilla warfare in the south. Tourists were not allowed to travel by land. Too bad, because it would have been great to (boldly) go where no-one has gone before.

Myanmar is also one of the friendliest countries I have been. Tourists are well protected and even the military and police personnel doing the many road-checks were polite.

Alehandro went to another place to do some more sightseeing. I should have gone with him to the Inle lake, but I was in hurry to leave the country. I still had so many other places to visit and had already stayed six weeks longer in Cambodia than I'd planned. I wanted to make up for lost time.

Now I feel I should have stayed in this beautiful country a lot longer and not made chasing pussy my first priority. I'm still in contact with Alehandro, who is still travelling around South East Asia while trying to earn a buck selling pictures.

Back in Yangon, I went to another and much better hotel, where I got everything included for only a few dollars more than at the first one I stayed. The owner confirmed it was impossible to go south. I wasn't travelling on a schedule, so I had only booked a flight into Myanmar, which was a big mistake. There are no ATMs in the country and you have to bring brand new hundred-dollar bills to change. The official government rate is a joke and you have to resort to the black market exchange.

The first time I changed a hundred-dollar bill, I received a hundred bills of 1000 Kyat. Now the Kyat bills come in the following denominations: K1, K5, K10, K20, K50, K100, K200, K500 and K1000. You can imagine that having a giant wad of K1000 bills gets a lot of attention in Yangon, and a woman selling nuts on the street nearly fainted when I pulled it out. The nuts were only 200 Kyat. I soon learned to get as many small notes as possible. Even weirder is the 1988 decision to abolish all currency notes not divisible by the number 9 on the advice of an astrologer, who considered it to be a lucky number. The move wiped out the savings of most Burmese and contributed to a partly successful uprising a year later.

Booking an online flight out of the country was a major hassle; my credit card didn't work at any of the airlines, even the Burmese ones. Travel agents had no tickets either, unless I was willing both to pay a fucking fortune and wait a few weeks. My plan was to fly straight to Malaysia, but I couldn't book anything so I had to rethink things. I went to the airport but couldn't get a ticket out of Yangon that day. Twelve dollars on taxi rides wasted.

On Saturday night I went alone to a night club. It was very hard to find one. The entrance fee was quite steep and so were the prices of the drinks. I was still in the same mindset as in Cambodia and so just sat down and waited for girls to walk up to me. I was the only foreigner in there. I had at least expected a few NGO workers or expats showing up on a Saturday night, but there weren't any, so I was all alone at my table. Finally some girls approached me but they were obvious hookers looking for free drinks and stupid guys. My hooker game didn't work here because I had no pre-selection or social value in this place. My club game was still underdeveloped and I didn't know how to proceed. I was so used to have girls fall into my lap in Cambodia that I didn't have a clue what to do here.

It was going to be the water festival that week, a celebration all over South East Asia where people throw water at each other in the streets. Some of the hooker girls threw some ice water on me, which wasn't funny in a club at night. I warned one of them not to do it again while I was talking to another, but at one point that bitch did it again and poured ice water down the back of my neck and I pushed her really hard away from me and she nearly fell. And I told her to fuck off. She got all angry and bouncers had to calm things down. The whole club was looking at me but I couldn't care less.

I sat down again and a group of Burmese offered me a drink and we got talking. We talked about the water throwing and they said it was a normal thing around this time but not in a club. The two girls in the group were whales and the guys were the same size, it was too bad because they spoke excellent English, unlike ninety percent of the other people inside. They were very drunk however and invited me to all sort of things. They asked me to stay for the water festival and I would be their guest of honor. Foreigners still have a lot of value here since less than a million people visit Burma annually and most stay only in the tourist areas. I got their business card but never called them. I had had it with this country and wanted to get back to Bangkok. A Burmese flag was nearly impossible to capture so I figured *Why stay longer?* On the way back to the hotel a hooker asked me for thirty dollars for a night of fun and I considered it for a moment but declined. It's not a true flag if you pay for it. Anyone can do that, even a grandpa in a wheelchair.

On Monday I went back to the airport again with my backpack and paid dearly for a ticket to Bangkok. A few hours later I landed in Bangkok again.

Thailand – Bangkok

I arrived in Bangkok for the fifth time, directly after the giant riots that killed twenty-six people. I was advised not to go there and thought *What the hell, I'm going anyway; a bit of urban survival is always fun.* On the way from the airport to Khao San Road I saw roadblocks everywhere and some tourists on the bus who arrived straight from the USA were very scared. But on Khao San Road it was business as usual and you couldn't even notice half the city was on lockdown.

When I arrived the water festival had already started and people were throwing buckets of water at each other or using super soaker guns on each other. I was pretty much soaked by the time I arrived at a guesthouse a couple of streets away from Khao San Road. Luckily my military backpack is waterproof, and honestly, it was hot enough that the soaking wasn't a bad thing. I guess that's why they invented the festival in the first place. The guesthouse was a lot better than the one I stayed the time before. I had my own room with fan and small bathroom and window for seven dollars. It was a backpackers' place and the food was better than in parts of Khao San.

The water festival lasted four days and I decided to try to join the fun a bit and bought a super soaker myself. But I'm not the type of person that can just walk out the door and act all crazy all of a sudden and enjoy the party, I'm just too serious for that. That was a problem I'd had in Vang Vieng in Laos too. Most people started drinking just after noon and that might explain why they were in a happier mood. If I start early I'll be wasted by nightfall and then not feel like doing anything anymore.

Thai kids were throwing flour at everyone or slapping some mud looking stuff made of flour in your face. The party was good but just wasn't my kind of thing. I was still too self-conscious to go all crazy with the masses. Even after my whole trip I still feel the same. I learned to live with it and frankly I don't give a fuck anymore. So what, I might have missed out on some lays this way. I still banged plenty of girls in all sizes, shapes and colors and brought home a skill set and inner game that will stay with me forever. The only thing I regret my last visit to Bangkok a bit is that I didn't go out to clubs. For some reason I really didn't like Thai girls and was too cheap to pay entrance and five dollar drinks. If only I realized how much I would spend later in South America, I would have laughed at Thai prices. I probably missed out on five or six notches there.

I bought a bus and ferry ticket at the guesthouse and wanted to move on to Ko Lanta. A small group from my guesthouse assembled and waited for the bus. The bus was going south to Suran tani, where lots of people would be separating to go to different islands or cities. An Asian girl sat next to me and when we got talking she was very enthusiastic about my round-the-world trip. The bus left in the afternoon, so after a few hours it was dark and the girl, who was of Japanese/Philippine heritage, crawled up against me and fell half-asleep. I stroked her hair a bit and we cuddled and kissed in the bus. The loud English guys who overheard us meeting and talking couldn't believe what they were seeing, I kissed an Asian girl in a bus two hours after meeting her.

I've changed her name to Kishiko, which means "child of the seashore". Kishiko was headed for Ko Phi Phi and had already booked everything there. Since my ticket also included a minibus and boat ride I had to go to Ko Lanta. We agreed to meet again on Ko Phi Phi. I found a guesthouse on Ko Lanta but didn't like the island so much; it was kind of deserted at the time and the beach was full of rocks. The guesthouse was only half-occupied and there wasn't a damn thing to do at night. At daytime I was talking to some Swedish girls but they were not interested in me in a romantic way. At night I ate dinner and drank some beer with a half-Swedish, half-Philippine girl. I didn't get far with her either.

Thailand – Ko Phi Phi

I left Ko Lanta after two nights and took a boat to Ko Phi Phi. I found a nice room with Wi-Fi and a balcony in a guesthouse and I went to the address that Kishiko had given me and waited there for her.

It took a while for her to show up and when I asked the lady working there she couldn't remember a Japanese girl checking in. I thought I'd been stood up, but then she arrived. Her room was kinda shitty compared to mine and she didn't like it either.

That night we went for dinner and later to the beach where some beach parties were going on. I kissed her there on the beach and we walked back to her place and kissed on her bed and were probably about to have sex. I was cock-blocked by, of all things, her shower that wouldn't work. She said something like, "Okay, I go to sleep then", so I had to charm her up again and we walked to my room. Back home I always used to be nervous when going to my room with a girl and even on this trip I was a bit nervous with the Russian girls and the ones in China. Now I didn't feel nervous at all and figured it must have been because of all the banging I did in Cambodia. When we walked, I literally thought *OK, going to my room now and fucking this Japanese girl.* I'd never been calmer than that moment. I'd struck out in Japan and didn't get my flag there mainly because my game/pick up skills were non-existent and everything was so fucking expensive in Japan that I didn't even bother to go to a club. I'd been more focused on true travelling and having fun with other backpackers than on the local girls.

Anyway, we went to my room, took a shower and had great sex together. She was shy at first but became wilder the longer it lasted. I think we had sex at least three times a day for four days straight. She went crazy every time I went down on her. I loved her high-pitched voice.

On one of our last days together she got a bit sick and had a bladder infection, so of course we stopped having sex, and I wondered if she fell ill because she walked around naked all the time in my room. It was by this time I had some plans for a book and learned about the concept of flagging. I captured my Japanese flag in Thailand.

In those four days we stayed on the beach, although like most Asians she was scared of getting tanned. At night we went to play pool or hang out at some beach party. The beach parties were wild with people jumping through burning hoops, me included, and drinking buckets of Vodka Red Bull.

One day we walked across the island, which was quite a steep climb up and down the hill; it was not that high but the terrain was very rough with some proper jungle climbing. The beach on the other side was nearly deserted and amazing. We stayed there a few hours and snorkeled a bit.

We said goodbye a day later, when she went to Ko Samui to meet up with a Japanese girlfriend of hers and I went on to Krabi, where I stayed one very rainy day before moving to Malaysia.

I'm still in contact with her once or twice a year.

Malaysia – Langkawi

I was ready for a new country and went to Malaysia by bus and boat. I'd chosen Langkawi as the first place to go. On the ferry to the island I met a couple of Swedish girls and we shared a taxi to find for a guesthouse together. The well-known popular guesthouse we looked at was nearly full and had only one room left. I told the Swedish girls to take that one while I looked for another room.

I found a much better one for fifty ringgit, about sixteen dollars a night at that time. It was a beach bungalow with bathroom and a small porch. I liked that one way better than the one the Swedish girls were in, which was a couple hundred meters away from the beach. It was all of an eight-meter walk to the beach from my bungalow. I think it must have been low season because all the beaches nearly empty.

I stepped out of my bungalow onto the beach the next day and saw two girls lying in the sun. I took one of the free deck chairs, lay my towel on it and walked up to the two girls and asked them the corniest line ever. "Hey girls, can you put some sun lotion on my back?" One girl was English and she jumped up from her deck chair and started rubbing my back in with oil. The "lotion" line may seem corny, but it works. It shows have the balls to walk up to half-naked girls on the beach and that you don't give a damn about their opinion about you. I've never been fat but I didn't have a beach boy body either around that time – that sort of thing isn't important. Use it: you'll separate yourself from **95%** of guys who only watch the girls from a distance – including most ripped beach boys.

Sheila was quite fanatic in her lotion rubbing, and I told her that she was giving me a massage rather than just putting some lotion on my back. She laughed. She was on holiday after doing some volunteering. Her friend was a short Malaysian girl and as I found out later, the most dangerous girl I met on my trip.

Sheila was a very enthusiastic girl and smiled a lot. She told me about which places to visit in Malaysia and I found that she was staying in the beach bungalow next to mine. I invited them into the water and we swam and flirted a bit. The Malay girl was still not saying much.

That night I ate some pizza with Sheila and went to a local beach bar called Babylon. You had to sit in the sand at a small table and there was a local reggae band playing cover songs. I'm a reggae fan and the band was not bad at all. Sheila's friend Moni wasn't anywhere around and after a few beers I asked Sheila to go for a night swim. She agreed and we quickly changed clothes and went into the water. She was very interested in my romances around the world so far and I told her a few stories, including the Cambodian girl-fight story. This may sounds like a risky story to tell a girl but lots of girls love a playa. It's the ultimate pre-selection. I invented a seducing technique at the spot which I call the shark technique. It's pretty simple, really: I made sure we were out to where the water comes up to my chest, and slowly started walking around her in circles. I kept talking with a slow seductive tone, and slowly come closer to her until I was within arms' length. As I talked, I looked at her lips, opening her mind to the idea of kissing. Do that, and the good stuff starts. If you're trying it, this is when you tell her (not ask) to give you her hand, and when she does pull her towards you and hold her close. And go in for the kiss. (It might seem that if a girl's already in the water with you she's already up for kissing, but most girls will go in with just a guy friend too and she needs to be convinced.)

My freshly-invented seduction technique worked very well and we kissed a lot in the warm water. Sheila was a passionate kisser and had a nice round booty even though she's a white girl. Although we were "dry" humping in the water, she seemed to keep control of herself and I couldn't convince her to sleep with me. We both went to sleep in our separate bungalows.

The next day we met again the beach bar, and she admitted she was married back home but that she had lost control for the first time the night before. Not much later that night we went night-swimming for the second time and I kissed her again. But her friend Moni showed up and was crying, I thought by myself, *Go away you cock-blocker.*

Moni went on crying and Sheila tried to comfort her. She had no place to stay and asked if she could sleep at Sheila's bungalow. Sheila had known her a week but didn't trust her too much yet. I knew I wasn't going to have sex with Sheila that night so I looked at Moni and her incredible big round Brazilian-style ass and thought *What the hell, easy winnings,* and invited her to stay at my place.

Well, let me tell you, it wasn't that easy with her. I had a big two-person bed in my room and tried to get it on with Moni, but didn't get any further than finger-banging her, she wouldn't do anything else. I was pissed she got her rocks off and I didn't.

Sheila left the next day and gave me ankle bracelet. I wore that bracelet until it fell off my ankle almost 1.5 years later. She is one of the few people who know about this book.

22-year-old Moni stayed with me that day and I soon found out she had no money at all. I paid for her food, which barely costs anything on Langkawi since the island's a tax-free zone in Malaysia, meaning that food, booze and cigarettes are very cheap there. I had a full day to convince her to have sex with me. At night we were in bed again and she said wasn't in the mood. I looked at her body and saw that short but a bit thick body with a big sexy booty and I just knew I had to make her mine. We kissed and I started kissing her breasts and sucking on her nipples and she got very horny after this. She touched her pussy and started moaning. I had found her weak spot. We were banging shortly after and did so at least three or four times a day, ending in doggy style nearly every time. I couldn't get enough of her big luscious lips, perky breasts and big round booty. Malaysian flag captured.

The trouble started when we went out to a nearby club. There were four English guys there and one of them was very drunk and annoying. He was forever trying to make a move on Moni, which looked ridiculous because the guy had the pick-up skills of a doorknob. He was still very annoying. I told his friends that if they didn't control him I'd use a more violent way of telling him to fuck off. They talked to him a bit and he came to apologize to me.

Moni just loved the attention, and now a Malay guy started making trouble. He was acting very weirdly and aggressively towards me and her. Maybe he was a strict Muslim or was just jealous, I don't know. He was with a group of friends and I had already pushed him back once. He looked like he was on drugs: his eyes were wide open and his movements were uncontrolled. I told Moni we had to get the hell out of there before I got my ass kicked by his group of friends, because that's the usual way of fighting in Asia – all against one, especially when if the one is a tall foreigner.

We jumped into a cab and went back to my room. We were both quite drunk and for the first time I didn't hide the key of the room. I didn't trust her a hundred percent, and always locked the door from the inside and hid the key.

I woke up in the middle of the night, still dizzy from the booze and sleep. I heard her come in to the room and she'd brought food with her. I asked her where she'd been and she said that she was hungry and gone out to buy some rice and chicken. I didn't give it any thought and went back to sleep.

The next time I woke it occurred to me that I'd never seen her with money before, but I just thought that meant she didn't want to spend her own money if it wasn't necessary. People aren't particularly rich around here, so why should a girl going with a (relatively) rich foreigner spend money when she could get him to?

But then we went out for breakfast and ate some pancakes, and when it was time to pay the money from my back pocket was gone. I knew I'd had forty ringgit on me (about $14) the night before. I had paid the taxi fare with a fifty-ringgit note and the driver had given me forty back that night. I asked Moni directly if she'd taken the cash out of my back pocket in the night and had paid for her food with it. She denied it and acted very upset. I told her that I didn't have the money for breakfast, and she paid the bill.

We went back to the beach bungalow, where the first thing I did was look in the hidden wallet in my backpack. The 100-ringgit note I had in there was gone too and I confronted her with this. I told her to give my money back and get the hell out of my room.

She got really angry and denied everything. I told her that it was possible I could have lost the money from my back pocket on the way back to the bungalow, because I was quite drunk but no fucking way had I lost the money from my backpack while my credit card and passport were still in the same place. She kept denying and got really angry, shouting at me. I got tired of her and decided to cut my losses, took her bag (which was always already packed to go) and threw it out of the room. She wouldn't leave the room and we kept arguing shouting at each other. She got really angry and started threatening me, saying that she was crazy and would hurt me. I just laughed at her and said that I'd met way crazier girls than her. She literally said she would "kick my ass" and I laughed even more. She was all of 1.50 m (five feet at most) and I'm over 1.88m (6,2), with more than ten years of martial arts under my belt.

She said she would go to the police and I said "Go ahead but just get the fuck out of my room". She tried to trick me by making a fake phone call to her "Malay friends" but I knew she was on the island alone. Sheila had told me. Then she said she would kill herself and I said "Go ahead do it, see if I care". She was obviously bluffing. She couldn't win verbally, so she got crazier and more physical. She tried to punch me but I just pushed her away. I sat down on the bed and said she couldn't win and should just go away now. I was calm. She wasn't finished yet and locked the door from the inside and put the key in her pocket. She said "I'm going to kill you". I laughed again but she wasn't kidding.

She took a mirror off the wall and threw it on the floor, picked up one of the pieces and charged at me with a sharp piece of broken mirror in her hand.

I had only a split second to think and luckily survival mode kicked in. I jerked out of the way of her weapon and hit her in the face with my forearm. She fell down and got up again even more raging, wildly swinging and stabbing.

I smashed her down again, this time not too gently. She dropped the piece of glass and got up and charged at me again, kicking and screaming. I pushed her back and she fell to the floor. I stood over her and had had enough of it. I picked her up and told her to give me the door key, she refused and I slapped her in the face, not really hard but enough to make it hurt. I did this one more time and finally she took the key from her back pocket and gave it to me. I said, "Now, get the fuck out of my room".

She dropped to the floor and cried uncontrollably – no fake tears, these were real. She sat on her knees and looked me in the eyes and cried. Her resistance was broken. She tried to hug me; I pushed her off me, which made it even worse. Her will was broken and she tried to hold on to me, grabbing my dick and trying to kiss me while saying "Please, please". She took off her clothes and started touching herself, still saying "Please, Neil, please". I had adrenaline flowing in my body and I threw her on the bed. She wanted to give me a blowjob, but no way in hell were her teeth getting close to my dick. I took her hard from behind and she seemed to enjoy it, begging for more. It was one of the weirdest and most fucked-up situations in my life.

As soon as we were finished we lay on the bed and talked a bit. I said that she still had to leave and that if she wasn't leaving I would check out of the room and leave the island the next day. She begged me to let her stay and I thought about what would happen if I threw her out at this point. What could she do? She could go to the police and accuse me of rape, or she could just go out and cry rape and point out my cabin to locals, and everyone knows a raging lynch mob is easily formed in any Muslim country. Langkawi is a tourist destination but also a fairly small island without much in the way of police. I didn't have a local phone card and barely knew anyone on the island. It seemed best to let her stay the night and leave the next day to the mainland.

The rest of the day she was sweet as a kitten and I let her pay for everything, since she still didn't want to give me back my money.

At night we watched a movie on my laptop and went to bed early. We had sex twice that night and she was desperate to please me. I felt sorry for her. I think she was shocked that I gave her so much trouble.

We left the next day to the mainland. I paid for the ferry because she said she didn't have money any more, a lie because she couldn't have spent all of my 140 ringgit.

We got into an argument again at the bus station because she wanted to go with me to the east coast of Malaysia. I said that was never going to happen. I paid her 12-dollar bus ticket to Kuala Lumpur, the capital of Malaysia and she had the nerve to ask me for more money. I told her no but eventually gave her a very small amount to make her shut up and she walked off cursing – she even slapped me. I wanted to slap her back but there were quite a few guys around and I thought it was safer if I didn't hit one of their own in front of them.

She got on the bus and I never saw her again, but a few months later she wanted to add me on Facebook and I let her. I was quite fascinated by her behavior and wanted to see how she was doing. Her big round butt and her legs had always been on the verge of being too thick and she's crossed that line now. She actually has some older Swiss guy as a boyfriend now and I can just imagine how this guy gets fucked over by her all the time. I still have her on my Facebook till this day and every once in a while she writes this:

I miss you Neil.

Malaysia – Perhentian Islands

After I finally got rid of the she-devil Moni I took a bus ride to Kota Baru, on the east coast of Malaysia, and from there took a boat to the Perhentian islands. I didn't realize there are no ATMs on the islands. My money supply was limited and I had to stay in a dorm room with other back-packers. Inside the dorm room I met one of the biggest nerds ever.

He was a true omega male, the worst kind of "man". He was so awkward that I just had to spend some time with this guy and figure him out. If you start learning about game and pick-up, you get more and more interested with the psychology behind it. The guy was so unwillingly funny that I can safely say that he was the weirdest, most awkward guy I had ever met. He was a Malaysian computer programmer (the prototype nerd) and had a weird name that I forgot. I'll just call him Jack.

The Perhentian islands are a place of unworldly beauty: the pristine clear blue water and the white coral sand beaches are amazing. I was staying on Perhentian Kecil, the smaller island. It's famous for its budget accommodations and amazing scuba diving. The island has no central power source so everything is powered by diesel generators.

My guesthouse wasn't that far from the beach and I was tanning every day. At night I would go to one of the only two beach bars and sit down at a table in the sand. There are Turkish pipes for smoking and everyone was drinking Monkey Juice rum. Beers were very expensive on the island – it wasn't a tax-free zone like the last Malaysian island I'd been on and a small can of beer cost nearly four dollars. A small bottle of Monkey Juice was sold for eight dollars and it was 25% strong liquor. Mixed with Pepsi it was delicious and a cheap way to get drunk.

I was hanging out a bit with Jack but soon found out he was too much of a passive cock-block. He had such strange habits that he would scare most girls away. I tried to teach him some pick-up skills but it was hopeless. He would screw things up and it would rub off on me.

During the day, I went to the beach to get a suntan. Jack came along and I truly was ashamed of him with his super skinny body. I advised him to do some weightlifting back home because no girl would ever like him like that. Apparently he understood my advice to get exercising the wrong way, because he started going for long beach runs. It was hilarious to see him run with his skinny body in thirty-eight degree temperatures. I felt sorry for the guy but he was headstrong and wouldn't listen when I said he'd better stop running along the beach. He looked like a Malaysian version of Butthead. Same big head and big hair.

There was a big group of hot Swedish girls on the beach and like most Swedish girls in South East Asia they were only interested in sun-tanning all day. I manned up and walked straight up to them and asked them to put some tanning oil on my back. One girl ignored me but another one, who was tanning topless, got up and put the oil on my back. I talked to her a bit and for the next few days she rubbed my back during the day but at night they were nowhere to be found.
I asked them about it and they said they didn't like to go out.

The island was full of Swedish girls though, and I met the two Swedish girls I'd seen on Langkawi again. We got talking on the beach. They were there with another Swedish girl named Johanna, who had massive tits. I had to control myself to avoid looking at them all the time since all the girls were topless. All my attempts to pick up one of them failed.

I was still in the mindset that I'd take just about anyone with me so that I didn't have to go out alone. That has changed now, and I'm more likely to go out alone these days. Just then, I asked Jack to go to the beach party with me.

Since everyone was always sitting down at tables in the sand it was kind of hard to make contact. You needed some balls to walk up to a table and ask if you could join the girls. Some attempts were more successful than others. I usually went first and introduced Jack later. I'd told him what to say and do but he screwed up everything.

I approached two girls at a table, who happened to be Swedish also. One was a very beautiful girl with a stunning body, the other one was a fat hog. The hot one laughed at everything I said and things were going well. I asked the girls to go night swimming, since I had success with that approach in Langkawi. The hot one said yes and but the fat hog was straight up cock-blocking me. I whispered to Jack to keep the fat one busy, something a good wing would do even though he is totally not interested in her. Since I was wearing shorts, a t-shirt and flip flops I was all ready to go in to the water. The hot Swedish girl, who had dyed her hair black, went into the water with me. I did my Shark technique®, and was quickly making out with her. She took her bikini top off and I was sucking on those salty titties. She had her legs wrapped around me, my hands firmly on her round butt and we were dry-humping like crazy. *Oh, dude*, I thought to myself, *after all this time, you're finally going to get a Swedish flag*. Sweden is always in any top three of lists of beautiful women. Usually it's Brazil, Sweden and Russia.

Trouble started when her swine of a girlfriend started shouting at the sea shore. "I'm cold, come out of the water, let's go," she was shouting to her friend. I tried to convince the hot one to stay in the water with me but the fat beast kept calling her friend. Jack just stood there with his hands to his side. The Swedish babe went out of the water and she promised she would walk her fat friend back to the hotel and come back. I couldn't do anything more than agree and hope she would return.

I walked back to the dorm room, took a quick shower to get the salty water off me, and went back to the beach.

The Swedish girl never returned and I was waiting on the beach for her feeling like a fool. I was still quite drunk from the rum, though, and horny as hell.

I saw a group of girls and heard that they were speaking French. I asked them if I could join their table. Only one of them spoke English, and she was the hottest one there. The girls came from Belgium, but from the French-speaking part and not the Dutch-speaking one. I just rambled some words and sentences I had learned in high school and ended with my classic "Voulez-vous coucher avec moi, ce soir?" Since when I used those same lines with the first Cambodian girl I met it ended in a fuck fest, why not try it again and see if it would work again?

They laughed and gave me some more rum and we joked around a bit. They were all kind of drunk and I asked them for a swim. Two of them declined and left, including the cute one who spoke English. The three girls who were left wanted to swim with me. Now, they weren't lookers but one of them had quite a sexy body. I started sharking her in the water but with my extremely limited French I didn't hook her.

What happened next is nothing to be proud of, but yeah, it happened. The chubbiest girl was probably turned on by my slow talking in the water because she literally grabbed my arm and pulled me towards her. Sort of a reverse Shark technique. She forced herself on me and I looked at her giant tits, which were the size of my head. I was like, *There's almost no one here, it's dark, I'm horny and she has giant knockers.*

After some kissing she grabbed my dick and tried to insert it in her snatch. I was drunk and the water wasn't helping. My dick was only half erect. My pride was in jeopardy. I took her by the hand and walked off to another part of the beach. The tide was still low and the water had cleared a spot between some rocks. She pushed her giant and very firm boobs in my face; their weight nearly crushed me, and then started blowing me there. Must have been weird with the salty water but it didn't seem to bother her. We had sex between the rocks and that's how I (shamefully) got my Belgium flag.

When we walked back to the beach her friends were still waiting for her and started yelling angrily at her. I heard the word "affaire" so I guess she had a boyfriend or husband back home. I never saw her again and it was one of the few times I didn't use a condom. I guess the salty water protected me or there's a very handsome baby in Belgium now.

I don't think she can ever find me again. The guesthouses there don't really keep records and she didn't know which one I stayed at anyway. I had captured a flag but lost my dignity with this girl. Getting laid a lot is only cool when it's with girls who look attractive, anyone can bang a whale. In my defense, yes she was chubby but no whale. She was also still very young, so there was no cellulite blubber flapping around.

The following days I stayed on the beach a bit during the day and reached my optimal tan. I could sit in the boiling hot sun for hours and not get sunburned anymore. I was pissed about it: I wasn't even that dark. I don't tan well and it always takes ages, and now I had reached my maximum.

One amazing thing I saw there was a Dutch guy drinking a special mix after finishing his diving master license. It was a rite-to-manhood kind of thing. I hope I can explain it well enough. He had to put a diving mask with a snorkel on, and the top of the snorkel was sawed off and replaced by an upside down plastic coke bottle with the bottom cut off. Because it's a snorkel you can't breathe at all and have to keep drinking until the bottle is empty. They poured in two cans of coke, half of bottle of Vodka, a small bottle of Monkey Juice, a can of beer, and a large squirt of sun-block lotion. He drank all of it at once and was drunk within ten seconds. I have never seen drinking like this in my life and can only say one thing: RESPECT! Nine out of ten guys failed this test but the

Dutch guy did it.

Malaysia – Kuala Lumpur

My time had come to move on again. I was out of money and had to take the boat back to the mainland.

I had to take my flight out of Malaysia in the capital of Kuala Lumpur. I got a virus on my laptop after using a memory stick in the hostel's Internet café. It was one of the only and toughest viruses I've ever had on one of my computers. I almost spend three whole days trying to fix it and finally gave up. In the meanwhile my credit card wouldn't work so I couldn't book a flight to the Phils. That took me another full day to fix. I think I called the credit card company at least five times before they figured out what was wrong.

The prices of clubs and drinking are very high in KL, as Kuala Lumpur is called, so I didn't bother going out and wasn't in the mood anyway with a broken laptop. I truly hate it when it's not working. I already had my Malay flag and it was trouble enough getting that one and living to tell the tale. So all I did was go up the famous Petronas towers and visit some malls before I got on an airplane and flew to the Philippines.

Philippines – Manila

The Philippines have always intrigued me. It's a South East Asian country with a heavy Spanish influence and it's partly Americanized as well. Back home my standard answer to the question "What do you want?" was always "A million dollars and a ticket to the Philippines". I've said that for years, as if the Phils were some sort of promised land. And they are: The country is fantastic, but it took a while to realize it.

I had planned a full itinerary and was going to stay seven weeks, including fifteen days with my Russian girlfriend Julia, who was going to visit me there. There's only one popular guesthouse in Manila and that's where I stayed. The place is usually packed with all kinds of backpackers, from serious hikers and bikers to the occasional girl-crazy guy like me.

One of the guys I hung out with an English guy who had traveled and worked a bit in Australia. He told me some impressive hostel stories. I always say that the amount of banging going on in hostels is truly overhyped, but that doesn't seem to apply to the guys working in a hostel. Most of them get laid regularly with a wide range of girls. It's an ideal job for picking up girls, because even though the job is shitty and pays next-to-nothing, you're still kind of an authority and girls look up to you since you're the guy pulling the strings who knows all the ins and outs in the city.

He and I went out for a couple of games of pool and sat down in the street bars in front of the guesthouse. Now, most people would hate the area: the street is full of strip clubs and there are lots of prostitutes and child beggars around. But you get used to it very quickly and I enjoyed the company of the bar girls while drinking a beer, though I never pulled out the cash to pay for any of them. The more you drink the more you have to be careful, though, because they were some ladyboys around looking for a customer too. Not that they're all bad: befriend a ladyboy and he/she will introduce you to many girls. An unusual tip but one that works very well.

Second to Warsaw in Poland, Manila was one of the most destroyed cities during World War II, but before this, it was one of the most beautiful cities in the world, having been compared with London, Paris and Prague. Nowadays, Manila is not a very interesting city. There are few places for sightseeing and most of the churches and cathedrals are worn down.

Most people hate the city and consider it poor and dirty, full of exhaust fumes. You have to look through all this, and if you have some money to spend it's not hard to stay in a nice area of the city for thirty to forty dollars a night in a nice hotel room in Makati, the financial district of Manila. I was a traveller on a budget, so I stayed in the poor but party area of Malate.

At night most people would sit at the giant table in the common area of the hostel and talk and drink a bit. There was a German girl who was taller than me and I'm a tall guy. She had a bit of a husky build but she had giant hooters.

I had ignored her and her big titties all the time since I had read in a game/pick-up book that this was a good technique. When I was making jokes with the guys about having sex with so many girls on my trip I already made sure that she heard parts of it. When I finally got talking to her she already knew I was some kind of a player and later that night when people were getting more and more drunk she kept saying "I'm not going to be your number twenty-two on your trip, oh no! That's not going to happen". It was a clear signal on the slut radar and only an idiot wouldn't see that's an invitation to pick her up.

We gathered the group together and all of us went to a sketchy place called LA café (now Manila Bay café), which is basically a giant freelance hooker bar. I had never seen so many hot girls in one spot. There must have been a hundred girls in there. It was almost overwhelming and I started ignoring Franka the German girl again. Partly as a technique, but also because I couldn't care less about her since there was so much eye candy around.

With Franka, there was only the physical attraction of her height and enormous boobs; as soon as she opened her mouth nothing more than annoying drunk bullshit came out. I normally don't like to talk bad about people but damn, she was annoying.

As always the Philippine band was amazing. The Pinoy bands are all over Asia for a reason; the Philippine people have great singing voices and love to sing. Except for the clubs it's all very romantic American music and it's not strange to see a big Philippine guy sing a Peter Cetera song. Well, it's strange, but it's not unusual.

We were all getting pretty drunk, Franka most of all, while we tried to play pool with some Pinoy guys. After eating a bit we all went back to the guesthouse. Which is where things got interesting. All of a sudden, I was having sex with Franka in the top bunk bed of the room she shared with a German guy she was travelling with but not banging. That was unexpected.

Since together we weighed quite a lot, I was afraid we were going to break the bed with our animalistic banging. I didn't expect much from her but she was wild between the sheets. That night I got my German flag. My peeking at

Franka's firm and beautifully shaped breasts all week was now rewarded, and I couldn't stop playing with them.

The next morning we had sex again and from here my memory kind of fades. Sometimes it's all a big blur thanks to the cheap and tasty San Miguel beer. I think she left the next day. She later disappeared off my Facebook.

The guesthouse is a trap: you plan to go there for a few days and you end up staying two weeks. Every night I would hang out with other travellers and the girls across the street at the three street bars. The freelance hookers there were hard to convince, it's no Cambodia where I did so much free banging that my dick nearly fell off. Now that I'm writing this I wonder why I didn't go out much those days to pick up Pinays. I guess I liked it too much in the guesthouse with the other backpackers.

I met one Philippine girl in the guesthouse. She was living in the neighborhood and visited the guesthouse a lot to meet the regulars there. I flirted with her a few times and don't even remember how I picked her up. I was sharing a dorm room with seven other people and I just took her there, hung my big beach towel around my lower bunk bed and had quiet sex with her there. She had nice breasts for an Asian girl and was twenty-six years old.

When I tried to bang her again in the dorm a day later, the personnel came into the room and she had to leave. She was all embarrassed because she knew the staff.

A few days later I went to the LA café for some shoring and met a girl there who couldn't hear or speak. She was a freelance girl showing some good cleavage. I had to communicate with her with a notepad and ballpoint. She did some magic tricks with a napkin and either they were very impressive or I was too drunk to see the trick. I took her in a taxi and we went to the bar across the street from my guesthouse. Some of the waitresses I knew there had fun looking at me struggling to talk with hand gestures and a notepad. Imagine communicating with someone who is deaf and can't speak other than some noises; she'll obviously not be highly educated if she works as a freelance hooker. Her English writing was limited. We mostly communicated through body language.

I took her up to the guesthouse and tried to sneak her into the dorm rooms. Non-guests weren't allowed in the rooms, but the night guard who saw us didn't do anything. I got her in my bed and had quickly hung the towels around my bed again. She took her clothes off and I also undressed. Suddenly I heard one of the Philippine staff walk into the room, looking for the girl.

It was dark and I put my finger on her mouth and gestured to be quiet. Since Philippine girls are very short and tiny she was easy to cover with the blanket. The guy didn't see her and left the room. We kissed some more and I was ready to go. I had my dick hard and the condom in my hand when the door opened again and the light was turned on. The guesthouse worker had returned and this time he was looking through the whole room, lifting sheets and blankets (!?). When he saw my girl, he told her something in the Tagalog language they speak there. Of course she couldn't understand because she's deaf. They guy talked louder and she was just shrugging her shoulders and put her head on the pillow. I told the guy to leave us alone and that she was deaf. The little fucker didn't want to listen and said he would make a scene if she didn't leave. The bastard was just jealous of me because he knew of me and the two other girls. He had already warned me when he saw me leave the dorm room with the first Philippine girl. It was too bad I had to let that girl go but she probably would have asked me for money afterwards. Call me freaky but I still have a deaf girl on my bang list.

Two new flags in one week was not a bad score and it was the second time I had five girls in a row from different nationalities. Not much later I freed myself from the night life and went to bed early. I had gone to bed drunk at six or seven in the morning for nearly ten days. It was time to do some actual sightseeing.

Philippines – Banaue

After ten days and with a liver bloated from the many San Miguel beers, I went to Banaue, a small city in the north of Luzon Island. Banaue is famous for its 2000 year-old rice terraces, all built by hand in the mountains and covering over ten thousand square kilometers. It's referred by locals as the Eighth Wonder of the World, which is a bit exaggerated in my opinion. Nonetheless, it's a fantastic site.

I arrived there by night bus and hadn't realized it would be freaking cold on the bus. I was wearing shorts, a thin jacket and flip flops. I froze my ass off all night and it was a very uncomfortable ride. The seats couldn't recline and I barely got some sleep. I've been on lots of chicken buses and if I can still remember this one after taking nearly a hundred buses worldwide, then it was a shitty ride for sure.

In only four days I would see Julia again and I was looking forward to it.

The next morning I went with a driver/guide and his tricycle into the mountains. The guide was high as a kite. I was wasting daylight arguing about it and in the end just decided to go with Stony Tony. I got a free tricycle massage on the dirt roads in the mountains. My bones hurt for days and I was coughing my lungs out for a day and a half from inhaling exhaust fumes for hours. But it was definitely worth it. The views of the terraces were stunning. It's hard to explain, and even when looking back at the pictures it's difficult to feel the impact of this piece of man-made nature.

We drove around all day over dirt roads and through small native villages with waving children, one of which we visited. Banaue is a tourist destination but there weren't many around that the time. The rice terraces are still used to this day and the rice has a red or purple color and tastes terrific. I ate many a plate of it. There was not much else to do there since I found no bars or other places for meeting girls.

After just three nights and some alcohol recovery I went back by night bus to Manila. This time I thought I was smart and put on a lot of clothes before getting on the bus but now the bus was steaming hot and I was sweating like a pig. Another 12-hour hell ride.

Back in Manila, I took a taxi straight to the airport and had to wait for five hours there for my flight to Cebu, where I was going to meet Julia again. I was looking forward to seeing her again. It had been over six months since we last met.

When I later looked at the pictures I took in Banaue I saw one where my face was all bloated from drinking so much in my ten days in Manila, and I swore never to become one of those fat old white guys drinking beers all day. You see a lot of them all over South East Asia and I had despised them ever since I first saw a few of them in Nha Trang in Vietnam. Now I saw how it began and how easy it would be to turn into one, and resolved to avoid it at all costs.

Philippines – Cebu and Boracay

It was the first of many times I would arrive in Cebu airport. I had gotten a Lonely Planet book of the Philippines from the owner of the guesthouse in Manila. It mentioned a guesthouse in Cebu and I went there. It had a bar and restaurant and the rooms were ok. I had to wait two nights for Julia.

I spend my days hanging around in the guesthouse and doing some stuff on the internet. During the day I'd seen a Philippine girl with enormous breasts who worked in the office attached to the guesthouse. She looked over a few times but wasn't too obvious about it.

Later that night I saw her again in the guesthouse bar. Her breasts looked amazing and when she sat a couple of bar seats away I was actually a bit nervous to approach her. An older woman and a friend of her introduced her to me; her name was Jenna. From that moment on my game was so tight that I even amazed myself. Everything I did or said seemed to work. She said she had an American boyfriend who came over every once in a while but I already knew I had to make her mine.

The knee touch

I always test the situation by doing the knee touch. It's obvious you have to sit so close to a girl so that you can touch her with your hands, but it's even better when you can touch her legs too. I let my knee rest against her leg and see what she does. There are only four scenarios possible:

• She notices the leg touch and pull her legs away and makes sure she keeps a big distance from now on – she doesn't like you. There's a 10% chance you get her. At best

177

you are in the Friend Zone.

  • She notices your touch and pulls her leg away just slightly. Nothing is lost yet but she is not yet ready for physical contact. Try it again a bit later after some more talking. There's a 50 % chance you can still pick her up, but most likely not the same night.

  • She notices the leg touch but lets you make the touch. – All right, this is good news; you can probably already kiss her that night.

  • She notices the leg touch and starts rubbing her leg up and down yours. – She is good to go, you're a fool if you don't try to kiss her and you should try to go for the Same Night Lay (SNL).

Bonus trick – The Spin Move.

A guy who knows this move already knows more about picking up girls than at least 90% of the male population on this planet. Anyone who can lift his arm, give a girl a smile and rotate this wrist can do this.

  After flirting/gaming your girl take her outside or bounce to another spot in the club and make sure you walk on the left. Grab the left hand of your date/girl/target with your right hand; this will make sure the move goes fluent. Slow down/stop and raise your arm above her head, she will now notice this and look at you and wonder what you are up to. Smile at her and spin your girl clockwise. Just make a small circle with your arm, no need for ultra short salsa moves. She will enjoy this and laugh. "What guy does this?" she's thinking. No time to waste, when finishing the turn step close to her and pull her in with your left arm on her lower back.

Now go for the kiss.

  At the end of the night Jenna and I said goodbye and I grabbed her hand, pulled her away from the outside bar, spinned her around and kissed her. She was surprised but went along with it. It wasn't a long make-out but I already got to squeeze her breasts a bit. My mission to touch those gigantic knockers was accomplished. I had no idea what the
178

future was going to bring for us, so I just took my chances for that night. And a good decision it was.

The room in the guesthouse was a shabby one and the toilets in the hallway didn't flush that well. I couldn't bring Julia to a place like that and I moved to a hotel fifty meters away from the guesthouse. This hotel room at least had a clean bathroom and an air conditioning unit. It was also twice the price, but still only seven hundred Pesos which was about sixteen dollars at that time. A lot of things are very cheap in the Philippines, but compared to other South East Asian countries hotel rooms are expensive.

Julia was going to arrive around 10pm and before that I still had time. I sat down with Jenna in the guesthouse bar again. We talked and laughed, and she showed me pictures on her laptop and Blackberry. She was totally focused on me and I knew I had her in my pocket. Somewhat later I went back to my room to freshen up when Jenna came to my hotel and asked for me at the reception. The reception called my room's phone and asked me to come downstairs, where Jenna asked me if I took her small backpack, maybe as joke or something.

I denied it and she told me someone took her small bag while she wasn't looking and she had lost her laptop, Blackberry, other phone, camera and some money. It had a total value of eight hundred dollars, she told me. I felt really bad for her because I felt it was kind of my fault. I gamed her so hard that she couldn't think straight anymore and didn't pay her attention to her bag. We looked for her bag together but soon found out it was really gone. She was crying. In the meanwhile I had to pick up Julia from the airport. Jenna and I agreed to keep in touch a bit and that I would see her after I returned from Boracay.

Julia was very happy to see me again. She cried when she saw me at the airport, the way she always did. We hugged and kissed and in the taxi to the hotel she told me I looked very different from before. I had longer hair and acted a bit differently, she said. She had probably hyped up this two-week trip over and over again in her own head, and for me it was totally different.

A lot had changed since we last met in Thailand. It had been a turbulent half-year: I had visited six other countries and banged seventeen others girls of nine nationalities in just six months. Of course after this I felt different too; I still had feelings for her, but nowhere near as strong as back in Thailand. Back then, I nearly gave everything up just to be with her and almost ended my round-the-world trip for her. My sister and my own thoughts pushed me to continue my trip. And of course my rock star-like status in Cambodia had changed me a lot too.

Julia knew something was up and told me she hated the idea of me being with someone else but knew that I had met some girl in Cambodia because I went there twice. She had no idea of how many girls I've been with and I hope she never finds out. I admitted there was another girl and when I said that I kept thinking about Dara, I still thought about her a lot. Despite all this, we had mad sex that night.

We took a trip across the city and saw the usual sights and at night we were hungry so I took a risk and walked over to the guesthouse restaurant next to where Jenna worked. I wanted her to see me with Julia, I don't know why but it was probably to establish Pre-selection, a jealousy plot and because I like to live on the edge of drama a bit. Pre-selection is a player's strongest weapon.

When she saw us she looked surprised and a bit envious. Julia has a bikini model body; she even did some modeling when she was younger. Jenna, the Filipino girl, is very short and had a small belly. Her giant boobs are her strong points, so to speak. . Physically speaking, I also liked her as a person a lot.

Julia and I left the next day by propeller plane to the island of Boracay. I thought about joining the mile-high club with Julia but banging her in the toilet would be too obvious.

It was only a fifty-seat plane and it only had two toilets without any curtains in front of it. She later told me she would have tried it, she fantasizes about those kinds of things. As always Julia paid her half of the rent so we could afford a nice air-conditioned room with a swimming pool. Our resort was only about 150 meters away from the sea and the beach road where everything was happening.

Boracay is a small island with about four kilometers of white sand beach. It's a typical tourist place and mostly visited by young couples like Julia and me. There were also lots of Asian tourists. One day I will return there and get that Korean flag. We did all sorts of activities like jet-skiing, the banana behind the speed boat and parasailing, which was an amazing experience. The Football World Cup had started and at night we went to an English bar to watch the matches with at least a hundred other people. Boracay has visitors from all over the world and it was fun to watch the matches with actual people from that country. My Holland/Netherlands team was kicking ass every match and ended in the final.

I noticed it became harder and harder to talk to Julia. Maybe it was because we spent twenty-four hours a day together but that wasn't a problem before in Thailand, where we'd gone three weeks without separating.

It was me who had changed; I just wasn't into her as much. The sex was great and she was up for anything I wanted between the sheets but outside the bed our connection was becoming weaker by the day and that bothered me.

I tried to text Jenna but didn't receive any messages back and I stopped trying. A few days later I realized her phones were in the stolen bag, so the number she had given me was useless. I had to think of another way and broke my brain over the name of the company she worked for. When I finally remembered it I gave her a call immediately.

She was very surprised to hear my voice after a week and acted a bit cold. This changed soon enough when we started texting each other on her new phone number. Julia became suspicious because Jenna wasn't the only one sending me texts. I had handed out my Philippine number to a few girls in Manila and they were texting me too. I hid my phone and had put it in silent mode but Julia saw me checking the phone a few times and of course she wasn't happy with that. She had every right to be angry about it; I would be pissed off myself if it was the other way around.

One day we went to Puka beach. It's only a fifteen-minute tricycle drive away from the main tourist strip but hardly anyone goes there. It's the perfect beach to bring a girl.

The sand is pearly white and you can snorkel and see amazing fishes just twenty meters from the beach. We also did an island boat tour which was cheap and a great day out. It included an unlimited buffet lunch and even two bottles of beer each. I ate and drank so much that I could barely stand up from behind the table and walk to the boat. The eyes were bigger as the stomach, as we say in Holland.

Two weeks past very quickly and when we arrived at Cebu airport again I made a big mistake. I wanted to grab a lighter out of my bag and the necklace and bracelet I secretly bought for Jenna fell out of the top pocket of my backpack. Julia saw it and immediately knew I had bought it for a girl.
Call it female intuition. She started crying and I made up a stupid excuse that I bought it to wear myself. I could have said that is was for my sister or mother, but I fucked up by reacting nervous and saying it was for me. She didn't say anything on the way back from the airport to the hotel where we stayed before. She cried a bit and I felt like a rotten bastard.

That evening things cleared up a bit. Julia had thrown the bracelet and necklace out of the room in the bushes. I "admitted" I'd bought it for a girl working in the Manila guesthouse who asked me to bring something for her when I returned to Manila. Julia believed my "confession" and that night everything was okay again. She was still very sad and cried because she had to leave.

We woke up the next morning and had fantastic sex for the last time and I brought her to the airport in the afternoon.

We said goodbye and she cried a lot. She didn't have the holiday she expected and she was disappointed about our relationship. Julia knew I was going to continue my trip for at least another year and she wouldn't have the chance to see me again. It would have been too expensive for her to visit me in South America but she did speak about it.

After saying goodbye to her I took a taxi back to Cebu center and texted Jenna that I was coming to see her. I went straight to the McDonalds close to her house and met her there. She even brought a gift for me. Of course I had nothing for her since Julia had thrown it away. I gamed her hard and was lying in her bed within an hour and although Jenna was very horny and wanted to fuck, but I suddenly realized what a giant scumbag I was. I had just said goodbye to a crying Julia, who had saved up her money to see me, and there I was in bed with another girl. I didn't want to have sex with Jenna anymore; I kissed her and went to sleep.

When I woke up the next morning I didn't even realize where I was, but I felt someone stroking her hand over my back. It was Jenna, who now realized I had woken up. She started rubbing other parts of my body and I soon forget about what happened the night before and boned the living daylights out of her. Jenna was very good in bed and performed miracles with her lips.

She was only twenty-three and still had to go to university in the morning before working at the office/travel agency from 5:00 PM to 11:00. I stayed another week in Cebu.

At night we would break sex records and she asked me to stay longer with her. During the day I had nothing to do and walked around the city a bit or went to the Ayala mall, which was packed with beautiful girls. I always took a jeepney bus there which was the cheapest way of getting across town. It was almost guaranteed that any time you get on a jeepney there's always a hot girl on it.

I started to fall in love with the Philippines. The friendly people, the fact that a lot of people speak English, that it was always warm and everything is quite cheap. If you look you can find delicious food for only a couple of dollars. I had to continue travelling but in my heart I didn't want to. The same feeling I had before came over me; I was getting tired of packing my bag every three or four days and wanted to relax a bit with someone who actually cared for me instead of hanging with drunken backpackers all the time.

Philippines – Palawan

I left for another island but promised Jenna she would see me again. It's a short flight from Cebu to Puerto Princessa on Palawan Island, and finding a guesthouse was easy. There were already some hawkers waiting at the airport and they took me to a place close to the water.

The guesthouse was a nice place and had all the things a guesthouse needs: a restaurant and bar, television, bar and a few young girls working there. The place was owned by a fat old Australian guy who was married to a Filipino girl he yelled at from time to time. I didn't like the guy but sometimes I could understand his anger. At times the cultural differences really show up, with some huge gaps. They probably say the same of us. Actually, they probably think we're crazy, because they have a way of taking everything literally, so our way of looking at the world must strike them as totally nuts.

Accommodation isn't as cheap in the Philippines as in other South East Asian countries, so I took the dorm room, which I shared with two young French girls. They were both good-looking and I asked them to go out with me to find a restaurant and drink some beers in the city center. The girls were both studying in Kuala Lumpur and on a short holiday in the Phils.

We choose a restaurant that also doubled as a karaoke place. It was a big outside place with a roof and a small podium in front. Filipinos are very musical and will grab any chance to sing a karaoke song. No matter what drunken state or how awfully they sing.

I had the idea that the girls sort of liked me, but not in a romantic way. It's not that easy to pick up a girl when she is travelling with a friend. So I focused more on one of the staff members back at the guesthouse, named Dana. She wasn't the prettiest girl around but I could see she liked me and was up for some romance. I had all the time in the world to talk to her since I wasn't very active in those days.

I went with the French girls to a beach close by the guesthouse, but it was kind of dirty. Later an almost two-meter tall American, Greg, and a Swiss girl joined us. The beach was nearly deserted by then but there was a group of Filipino guys doing a lot of drinking. They came over and wanted to talk. One of them was an older guy who was only wearing an old-fashioned pair of underwear; he was covered in sand, even his face. He was very drunk and a bit annoying.

He challenged me to a sparring fight. I declined, even though for sure I could kick his ass in a sparring or even a real fight, but he had at least seven friends with him. I had just met Greg, who was tall and strong, but I didn't know whether he'd help me if the all those guys ganged up on me.

Once I'd said no, the drunk guy, who looked utterly ridiculous in his underwear and with his face covered with sand, started challenging the American. It was hilarious because Greg was at least two heads taller than him, muscled, and sober. As it turned out the drunk guy didn't really mean it and all his friends apologized for him. I had forgotten that I was in the Phils, where people are super friendly. A similar situation in Europe would end up with Greg and me getting beaten up by a group of guys. Here, they just offered us the bottle of rum about forty times while the drunken guy started rolling around in the sand again. It was one of those situations where you had to be there to see how funny it was.

The World Cup was still on, and since the Dutch team had a match that evening I went to a foreigners' bar to watch it. The whole place was orange, Holland's national color, since there are quite a lot of Dutch expats living in Puerto Princessa and they were all there to cheer on the team. I met a nice Dutch girl named Kyra who worked for an NGO there, actually. I'm still in contact with her every once in a while. She always hates it when I post pictures of me kissing girls on Facebook.

Not unexpectedly, the Dutch team won.

The next day, the French girls and most of the people in the guesthouse left the city to visit other parts of the island. Clearly my flirting with Dana had worked, because I got to kiss her that night. Now I wanted to find a place to bang her.

I went to a club with her and the two other girls working there and was treated like a rock star. At this point my hair was already touching my shoulders. When I stepped in line for the toilets all the guys would let me go first and some even took pictures with me. "You look like Axl Rose," they said, and one of them even compared me to Jesus, which was pretty funny. I mean, yes, by all accounts Jesus was a bit of a bum, essentially backpacking around Judea and staying in the equivalent of hostels, but I've never heard it suggested he was gathering flags from all the cities there. Or maybe they just left that bit out of the Bible. You have to admit that "Hey baby, I'm the son of God" would be a pretty good pick-up line.

I was told I look like Kurt Cobain a lot, but I guess that's just because I had the same hairstyle. It surprised me a bit how popular I was there, because Puerto Princessa sees its share of tourists. Guys were handing me beers and it just became ridiculous at one point. I'm just a backpacker with long hair, people! Maybe it was because I rolled in with three girls on my side. Anyhow, ridiculous or not I didn't refuse the beers.

A day later one of the single rooms was freed up and I took it. Dana made a lot of last-minute resistance but I knew I was going to have sex with her. At one point when the owner and his wife were gone I finally got Dana in my room. We were-half naked when suddenly one of the other girls working there shouted "The boss is coming!" Dana didn't want to lose her job and jumped out of the bed and out of the room, pulling her clothes back on. It turned out the girls had been joking and the boss wasn't anywhere around. Needless to say, I wasn't very happy with her co-workers at that moment.

Later that day I had sex with her anyway. It was a very different experience from Jenna since Dana was quite tall, especially for a Filipina girl.

Later that week I finally got my laptop fixed. I still hadn't managed to get rid of that stubborn virus I got in Malaysia on my own and now it was eating away my hard drive. Some guys at a local computer store fixed all my drives and installed a brand new copy of Windows 7 for only six dollars. Back on track, I went to another part of the island.

Philippines – El Nido

El Nido lies in the far north of Palawan Island and I took a local bus there. It was the cheapest option and it was half the price of the tourist bus.

Always take local transport if possible; not only is it a lot cheaper but more importantly you can enjoy the local people and culture way better sitting on an old chicken bus than being surrounded by fat stupid tourists in ugly hats being herded around like a pack of overfed hogs and all taking the same photos. And for immersing yourself in the local culture, nothing beats taking an over-packed, stinking and noisy local bus ride. It's uncomfortable, there are babies crying for hours, the food in the "highway" restaurants is terrible, but most people respect you if you're not a fat money-throwing day-tripper on an air conditioned bus with an underpaid guide. They respect the fact that you're willing to see them instead of just looking at their country. Most tourists just think the poor local people are part of the scenery.Taking their buses, you know that they're real.

Nearly the whole road was a dirt road and the driver was an absolute maniac. I don't think he ever used the breaks – in fact, I'm not completely sure the bus *had* breaks – and it was more like a rally race than a bus ride. We broke down twice along the way and stopped at a roadside restaurant where the driver repaired the bus with only a screwdriver and some duct tape. The restaurant looked horrible but I had to eat, so I took the risk. It didn't taste bad but I feared my bowels were going to explode once I got back on the bus. By some miracle I was fine and had no trouble at all. Maybe it was all those young moms breastfeeding their babies on the bus that kept me distracted.

El Nido is one of the most beautiful places to go in the Philippines, comparable to South Thailand. It has beautiful beaches with lots of coral, excellent water for diving and snorkeling and it's still pretty secluded from mass tourism.

Of course when I arrived the weather was terrible and the guesthouse there sucked. Instant karma for peeping at those breast-feeding MILFs. (Actually, I'm not sure if it's fair to call them MILFs when most of them were ten years younger than me.)

The weather finally changed after a few days and I took a daytrip to the islands. I took a small fisherman's boat to the sea with two local guys and four tourists.

The sites were beautiful; we snorkeled above the coral,

saw hundreds of colorful fishes, went into a few caves and even fished at the end of the day. It was a perfect day out and only cost five dollars each. Where else in the world can you do that for prices like that?

Back to Puerto Princessa

After a day or five I took the bus back to Puerto Princessa. Just my luck – it was the same driver! Eight more hours of praying that I didn't go home in a body bag. I'm not overreacting here. The guy was insane. Sometimes you just have to close your eyes and remind yourself that he's clearly done this run many times and he's not dead yet. It's just a bit hard to trust that his luck will hold.

Once I was back in Puerto Princessa, amazingly alive, I looked up Dana and we took a hotel room in the city. I was lucky to be with her because I would never have found it on my own. The room was OK, had a bathroom and was even cheaper than the dorm bed I had in the first guesthouse. It was two hundred–fifty pesos only as they say in the Phils. Now Dana and I finally had some privacy and we banged till daybreak.

The next morning we walked around town and she introduced me to a highly addictive sort of ice cream named Halo Halo. We relaxed a bit and then went to the TomTom club to watch the World Cup Final between Holland and Spain.

I'd told people in El Nido about how this was a great place to watch football, and invited them down to watch the final. All the people I'd invited were there and so were Kyra and her friends.

Unfortunately my country lost the final from Spain. It was a very aggressive final and both teams were kicking the shit out of each other. It looked like they we're up for another 80 years of war between Holland and Spain just like in the 1600's. Unlike the Football final Spain couldn't win that one.

My last day on the island I spent with Dana and her family at the beach. It was a fun day. First we went with the whole seven-person family and all their food and drinks on one tricycle. The thing could barely drive and the family paid as much as I would normally pay for a 500-meter ride. No matter how much you haggle sometimes, if the (taxi) driver is smiling you are still paying too much. I don't mind paying a bit extra since I have way more money than the driver, but I hate getting ripped off.

The food brought by the family was delicious and I repaid the favor by bringing a bottle of Tanduay rum and a few bottles of Coca Cola. You can actually buy a bottle of rum for a dollar and a half there. We swam a bit in the water, which was filled with green goo and seaweed. I played Football with the kids a bit, and it was just a good, fun day. The next morning I said goodbye to Dana and went back to Cebu to see Jenna again.

Philippines – Cebu and Bohol

Jenna was happy to see me and quite frankly a bit surprised too. She said she never expected to see me again. Unfortunately she was on her period, but when she saw the disappointed look on my face she said the magical words,
"I will suck your dick for four days."

And she did. She works miracles with her big lips. I think she's the best I ever had, even better than the Vietnamese girl in Phnom Penh.

During the days while Jenna was working it was kind of boring for me and I flirted with Jenna's girlfriend from university. She was a typical 18-year-old virgin girl and she ate up everything I said to her. She wasn't the hottest-looking girl around but she had that cute innocent look and I liked it. I gave her my diamond ring routine and she loved it. I was playing a tricky game this way and knew she would eventually say something to Jenna about it.

The diamond ring routine

This one's a bit hard to explain because it's a push-pull routine and you need to work some facial expressions, but it works very well in less developed countries.

When I'm sitting down with a girl I always sit within reach of her. We talk a bit and suddenly I grab her hand or her fingers and look at them with a frown on my face.

Girl: "What? Why are you looking?"

Me: "Where is your diamond ring?"

Girl (smiling): "What do you mean?"

Me: "A pretty girl like you who doesn't have a diamond ring on her finger, that's just weird. You know what? Tomorrow morning I'm going to buy you the biggest diamond ring I can find and then I'm going to marry you the day after and we will make many babies together."

Say this with a smile and then keep a straight serious face. Now, the girl laughs and gives you a funny face because she also knows I'm just a poor travelling guy – but still, she has to wonder if I'm serious or not. I just might be a gullible guy and she can't risk passing up on that. And then you go:

"I saw a nice big plastic diamond ring at the toy store in the mall, is that OK with you?"

Now she laughs and probably pushes you away or something. You now had some solid touching by holding her hand, you put the image of a relationship and probably sex in her mind and you made her laugh in a way that other guys don't.

Now completely drop the subject and talk about something else from there on. If you see her again you can use it a recurring joke. Bring it back up and make some jokes with her but remember not to act the funny joker but still be seductive/flirty.

Works well when meeting the girl several times, especially with restaurant, hotel or bar staff where it's clearly not a date.

Philippines – Island of Bohol

Now there came another test of my courage after that crazy bus ride. I had to take a Philippine ferry for the first time ever.

Back in Holland the only news you ever hear from the Philippines is that Manny Pacquiau's won a boxing match or that another ferry's gone down with everyone on it. So even though objectively I knew it was safe, I couldn't help being a bit nervous when stepping on board.

The ferry ride took about four-and-a-half hours and it wasn't bad at all. I had bought the cheapest ticket and had to stay on the deck, where there were many rows of bunk beds. I got talking to a girl/woman with an amazing set of lips. Most Asian girls have big lips, but hers were phenomenal – big, luscious, sensual. I tried to game her a bit but she wasn't too receptive. We shared a tricycle ride into town but the driver tried to rip me off, asking ten times the normal amount. She translated and said it was the normal price. I got really angry with the guy and just pressed some bills into his hands.

It was still too much but at least I got rid of both of them. She probably thought I was some stupid foreigner she could rip off too, and I threw away the telephone number she had given me. Other girls had also asked for my phone number on the ferry and some of them were damn cute, but they didn't speak a word of English. It's almost no use trying anything that way.

Early in the next morning I took a local bus to see the famous Chocolate Hills, one of the main attractions on the island. The local bus was amazing, I was the only foreigner on the bus and everyone was just looking and smiling at me. Call it ego-tripping if you will but when this happens to you every day of the week, you start to feel damn special, even when you know any other foreigner would probably get the same treatment – but other foreigners aren't taking the local bus like you are. Especially children are always happy in Asia: they run along the bus, waving and shouting at you.

I saw massive green rice fields and ate the local bus food, a dry paste of rice and something else wrapped in a banana leaf. The old wrinkly grandmas who sell it along the way are not the cleanest-looking women and taking local food is always a risk, but it doesn't mean it isn't tasty. You learn how to live with it after a few weeks. I was fine this time, and it had actually been a few months since the last time it made me really sick. My stomach was finally getting used to the unhygienic situations. By now, I had forgotten the taste of bread.

The bus stopped every few minutes when people on the roadside waved the bus down. It's really interesting to experience a simple bus ride, and just one will teach you more about the culture than reading half-a-dozen travel guides.

After two hours the bus dropped me off at the road next to the Chocolate Hills. After making sure I wasn't getting ripped off by a local motorbike driver and getting driven there, there was only one more obstacle before I could finally see these hills that had been hyped up by everyone I met.

That would be the 400+ steps to the top of the hill. It's not that they were uneven or anything: they were perfectly normal concrete steps, with a railing to hold on to. There just happened to be over 400 of them. Before long I felt like the big bad wolf, huffing and puffing away. I actually had to stop in the middle and catch my breath like an old man. I was getting out of shape.

Maybe I'd already been spoiled by seeing so many beautiful things in the fourteen months I'd been on the road already, but the Chocolate Hills just didn't seem that impressive to me. It's just a series of small, brown-colored hills. I'd still recommend seeing it but only if you're going to take a local bus there, which will be a lot more interesting. The Hills are a good excuse to take that bus. Also, you get some exercise.

The motorbike guy was still waiting and took me downhill when I got back; I gave him twenty pesos for the ride back instead of the forty he'd asked for and he got all angry, but I just told him he wasn't getting more and walked out on him. He was cursing me for a few minutes before he gave up. To the inexperienced reader I may seem like a fucking cheap bastard but I figured: why would I give a guy who does nothing all day and just hangs out with some friends and occasionally rips off a tourist eighty pesos? (His first price was even two hundred for a return ride.) A girl who works in department store for ten hours a day makes little over a hundred pesos a day, and what about the people breaking their backs in the rice fields in the countryside? They make even less. Them I'd pay. They actually work.

After waiting half an hour a bus came by and took me back to Tagbilaran. The way back was even more interesting than the first trip. My teeth were playing the xylophone against each other because of the terrible roads, I was inhaling exhaust fumes, the wooden benches were so tight and crowded that I had to sit with my arm out of the window and it got sunburned really bad, and then there were the people: the guy sitting next to me trying to talk to me without speaking a word of English, the 3-year-old poking me with his little finger just because he'd probably never seen a white guy before, a guy sitting two seats away from you with a giant rooster on his lap, the teenage schoolgirls poking each other and giggling when they looking at me. I loved all of it and laughed at the people in the air conditioned bus that passed by us. What were they experiencing? Absolutely nothing! A fucking bus ride like you can get on any air-conditioned bus in the world!

Since there isn't a whole lot to do in the city center, I went to bed early and got up early. I wanted to visit the Tarsier wildlife sanctuary to see the mysterious creature that was used to model my good friend Yoda.

I took a jeepney to a small village and had to stop at the side of the road to walk a few hundred meters to the wildlife sanctuary. Jeepneys are a typical Philippine thing. It's kind of a big pick-up truck with benches that seats twelve to twenty people, depending on its size. They are always covered in religious quotations, spray-painted Jesuses and lots of chrome. Some of them are real works of art. They are almost always crowded and a tall guy like me has trouble walking between the people and finding a seat. It's not unusual to have to sit tight betweens some hot young girls.

There are two ways of paying. The bigger jeepneys have a guy standing or hanging out the back who collects the money. In the smaller ones you have to give the money to the driver. The fare is dirt cheap, usually seven or eight pesos, which is something like fifteen cents. If you sit in the middle or the back you have to give the money to the person next to you, who passes it on to the driver. Sometimes your money changes hands four times before reaching the driver. The driver gives your change back and your change returns the same way. This system would probably never work in Western countries because someone would just pocket the money, but they don't even think of that there. They all drive on the same routes and when you reach your destination (and don't speak the language), you take a coin and knock it on the metal frame of the jeepney and the driver takes the hint and stops. If you want to get on one, then you stand at the side of road and watch for the jeep with your route number on it, wave your arm and the driver stops.

A group of teenagers on this particular jeepney invited me to join them on a picnic in the park. Although there were a few cute girls I had to say no since I needed to take the ferry.

The jeepney dropped me off close to the wildlife center and I went to see the famous tarsier, a small 4 inch/10 cm creature. It's hard to describe the tarsier: it's known as the world's smallest monkey, but it isn't a monkey, just like the Koala bear isn't a bear. It had giant eyes which are actually bigger than its brain, but then I've met some people in my life that applies to as well. Their legs are very long and so are their thin, bony fingers. I was able to take some good pictures of this extremely shy creature.

As I mentioned before, this creature was the inspiration for the appearance of Yoda from *Star Wars*. The force is strong in this one!! This sanctuary is the only place in the world where you can see the Tarsier out of its natural habitat and the owners have succeeded in breeding them so that the tarsier population can grow again. The Tarsier is on the list of most endangered primates in the world. They only live in the Philippines and parts of Malaysian Borneo and Indonesia.

I recommend that anyone in the area go see the Tarsier in the Bohol sanctuary and leave to a small financial contribution

By the time I left the sanctuary I was in a hurry to get back and didn't have time to wait for a jeepney, so I stopped a teenage boy with a motorcycle, agreed on a price and got driven back to town. He was speeding like a maniac except when he passed people his own age; he was kind of parading me around and even stopped to show me off to his friends. I was just in time to catch the ferry at noon. Back in Cebu I stayed with Jenna again. I left for Manila three days later.

Philippines – Manila and Cebu

I don't have much to say about Manila. I hung around in the guesthouse for a while, drank a lot and wasn't much into picking up girls at the time. I missed Jenna and went back to Cebu again. This wasn't in my plans, but at this point I didn't care much. When a one-hour flight only costs thirty-five dollars it's easy to move around the country.

I stayed in Jenna's room for a few days again and then her landlady told her I wasn't allowed there anymore, I guess because we weren't paying double rent or maybe she just didn't like people hooking up in her building. I was quite grumpy about it because now we had to move to a hotel nearby, which cost me about $140 for two weeks. We couldn't move to the other hotel close to her office because too many people would see us there.

Jenna had lost her job because the owner of the guesthouse and office building was a friend of Jenna's American boyfriend and had told him about her and me. He had dumped her and stopped sending her money. He was a cheap bastard anyway, only sending her $150 a month even though he owned his own business. I still felt guilty about her losing all her electronics when I was picking her up, and now because of me she had lost her job and her steady money-sender. Basically I had made a mess of her life.

In the next two weeks we went out to Club Pump on the weekend and visited a few sights around the city like the San Pedro fortress and the biggest skyscraper in Cebu, which includes a sort of rollercoaster ride on the outside of the building on the thirty-seventh floor. In the morning she had to go to university and at night we would have steaming sex.

I remember her screaming so hard one day that the management was knocking on the door asking if we were all right.

The day came when I had to say goodbye to Jenna, and I hated it. She was crying her eyes out and I didn't feel like leaving, but I had to make a decision: stay with Jenna and slowly run out of money or continue my round-the-world trip. It was the same decision I had to make with Julia. I'd chosen to move on then, and it didn't seem right, or fair to Julia, if I didn't do the same this time. I was sure I would regret it afterwards if I didn't continue my trip.

Malaysian Borneo was my next destination and I had to take a plane from Angeles City, the prostitution capital of the Philippines, a city comparable to Pattaya in Thailand. I went there one night before the flight to check it out but hated the long line of bars full of bored go-go dancers and sleazy fat old men. There may be some people in the city who look like angels, but I doubt there are any who act it.

One teenage boy selling cigarettes convinced me to buy a pack of Cialis, the boner pills; they were only three dollars for four tablets so I thought *What the hell, I'll just buy them*. I had no idea it would be nearly two months before I got laid again.

The next day I flew to Kota Kinabalu and a long dry spell began.

Malaysian Borneo – Kota Kinabalu and Sabah

After four months of the Philippines I had major trouble getting used to Malaysia. It's a Muslim society, and that comes with lots of limitations. A lot of girls wear head scarves and that almost immediately rules them out as potential dates. Kota Kinabalu is the biggest city on Malaysian Borneo, but there's not much to do, either in terms of nightlife or of sightseeing.

The city was almost completely destroyed during World War II and this means there are no historical buildings whatsoever. I found some bars but hardly saw any opportunities to find a girl. The tourist girls I saw were either with a boyfriend or unattractive girls who come to a country like Malaysia purely for sightseeing and immersion in local culture. I have nothing against that, but it makes my mission a lot harder.

A small part of the Malaysian population is of Indian descent and that was good news for my stomach. I love

196

Indian cuisine, even though you end up sitting on the toilet more than usual. There were also a lot of Chinese restaurants around with big buffet meals for about four dollars.

Kota Kinabalu was also the hometown of the crazy Malaysian bitch that nearly stabbed me to death. I even considered contacting her since she was (and still is) in my Facebook friends list. She was good in bed and maybe I was up for a shot of drama and adrenaline. After thinking about it for a moment – not a very long moment – I settled the matter by considering that seeing her again would be a sign of genuine craziness and that if I did so I might as well give up my trip, fly straight back home, and check myself into the nearest insane asylum.

Since I intended to continue my trip, I didn't call her., sparing myself both psychiatric treatment and the possibility of having my throat cut. Or my balls cut off in the night, since I wouldn't put that past her, either.

After visiting the Japanese prisoner of war camp and museum in Sandakan in the north of Borneo, I took the local bus to Sepilok, a place famous for its interesting orangutan rehabilitation centre which is on every traveller's list.

It was a farce. I had to pay about a $10 entrance fee, and there was another $4 camera fee, which I didn't pay.

The park had a giant entrance and a two-meter wide wooden walking bridge through the "jungle". After barely one minute's walk I arrived at the feeding platform where there were some two hundred tourists waiting with their big cameras. And when I say tourists I mean tourists. They came straight of the air-conditioned bus and were all wearing the tourist uniform: big hiking shoes, trekking pants, temperature reducing t-shirts, small backpacks with water tubes and a jungle hat. Most of them even had the nerve to give me a strange look when I walked up the platform with my flip flops, shorts and wife-beater t-shirt. I probably looked too poor for them.

In my opinion these are the worst kind of tourists. They stay in fancy hotels where they eat western food or pay tenfold to try the local cuisine, only go on group tours. The only locals they speak to are the guides and the underpaid but still smiling staff at the hotel. They think they'll get robbed the second they leave the hotel so they never go for a walk and actually try to see something real like a poor area of town or the countryside. Wearing a fortune of North Face clothes and accessories and never using them, contributing barely anything to the local community because they spend all their money at the same place, the five-star hotel that also doubles as a restaurant, gift shop and travel agency/tour operator. And to think that most people think *I'm* the worst kind of traveller out there, because I'm just "bumming around" and don't dress prettily.

At ten in the morning a couple of bored park rangers walked up to the feeding platforms with a few baskets of bananas and watermelon. Somewhat later a couple of orangutans came swinging through the trees and sat down and ate the bananas. It was boring and I couldn't stand all the ooohs and ahhhs from the crowd while hearing a hundred cameras clicking away. This was definitely not what I'd expected and after taking a couple of pictures I left. I would not recommend anyone to visit this park and sit on chicken buses for ten hours twice to see this farce. It's just a tourist trap for fat Westerners too scared to go into the jungle. You get better views of orangutans in a zoo. Try a real jungle tour instead, one where you go into the jungle for one or two nights with a guide. At least you can be sure you'll never meet one of *them* there – and if you do, you can always live in the hope that something will eat them, though they'd probably give the poor animal indigestion.

I still had plans to climb Mount Kinabalu but after I heard it can cost up to $300 for a guide and hammock space in a mountain hut, I decided not to go through with it. I had already climbed Mount Fuji in Japan and there are other mountains you can climb for free. Besides, I'd already sent my hiking shoes from Bangkok along with other travel stuff I'd paid big money for but realized I had barely used.

Back in Kota Kinabalu I met a German guy in the hostel who was learning some pick up/gaming techniques too, and he gave me some good tips for books to read and an online forum. We went out to a club but failed horribly. A beer was already six dollars each and we were both too scared to approach the girls there who were drinking shots. I suspected they were either expensive hookers or rich girls and this way I had an excuse to myself for not doing anything.

When I think about it now I almost feel ashamed that after all the successes I'd had so far I still had some approach anxiety from time to time in Asia and even when visiting the Philippines. The German guy now lives in Thailand where he works on some software project and has some devious tricks (even by my standards) to pull in foreign girls.

This visit to the province of Sabah had been a bit disappointing and I wanted to move on to Brunei, a small oil state that is famous for its extremely rich leader, the Sultan. To get there I had to go to Labuan Island first, which is still part of Malaysia. It's the place where the Japanese surrendered to the Allied forces at the end of the Second World War, and I went to visit the monument commemorating that and a few other historical sites.

The Kingdom of Brunei

Brunei is an extremely wealthy oil state, and that comes with lots of benefits for its 400,000 inhabitants. There's free education and healthcare, no income tax, and the government can provide cheap mortgages and car loans. The downside is that you have to live by strict Islamic rules and regulations. Nightlife is non-existent, there are no bars or clubs, alcohol is strictly forbidden and even the cinema was closed down.

Behind the giant luxurious mall and mosque are people living in wooden shacks built above the river water. If you look you can find an entrance to these water villages and have a walk around and see how the poor people live in shacks while overlooking a gold-covered Mosque. The giant mosque is visible from nearly everywhere in the city. It's a beautiful mosque but for some reason I wasn't allowed inside, even though it should be possible for foreign visitors.

With some time and determination, I think it would be possible to get a Brunei flag but it might take a few months and lots of tricks. I didn't have the time or money to do that.

The mall had some girls working in the shops but it was clear to see that most were still virgins. You're welcome to try, but don't hold your breath.

After visiting several places and museums in those two days I moved on the other Malaysian province on Borneo – Sarawak.

Malaysian Borneo – Sarawak province.

On the bus from Brunei to Miri I met a Japanese girl and we travelled together for a few days. She was a typical nerdy Asian girl and unintentionally very funny. We took a bus to the Taman Negara Niah Park, a national park containing the famous Niah caves. To get to the caves we had to walk about 4 kilometers on a wooden walkway through the jungle.

The caves were massive and the biggest ones I have been in my life. The views were breathtaking. The walking bridge through the caves was two meters wide and was missing the railing here and there. In some parts it was pitch dark and we had to use the light of our phones to navigate to safety. At some points the cave was seventy meters high and the walking bridges led to a giant staircase which took us minutes to climb and catch our breaths.

When we reached the exit we had to walk a bit more to see what we'd come for: the prehistoric drawings on the wall. They were hard to see since we had to stand behind a fence at ten meters distance, which was a bit of a bummer, but I don't regret making a detour and visiting the caves. If you're ever anywhere near Sarawak, make sure to go.

When we returned to the park entrance we were quite tired from all that climbing and walking, but took a bus down south the same day to Kuching, another large city in Sarawak Province. I stayed four boring days there. The only nice things to see were a Chinese holiday being celebrated and the riverside. I tried to go out a few times there but only found empty bars during the week.

I spent most of my time doing stuff on my laptop. There's another orangutan park nearby, but after my bad experience in Sepilok I didn't go there. I also skipped the famous indigenous longhouses after seeing a few pictures of them online. They looked too modern to me and I didn't trust the "traditional showcasing of culture", which sounded like a tourist trap for the fat air-conditioned-bus folk. I had to wait my time before my flight to Singapore, where the Formula One Grand Prix was being held. I had bought a ticket for it while in the Philippines.

I lost my second cell phone, which had my Dutch Sim card in it, so I had to call my phone company back home and cancel my card before someone made thousands of Euros in phone calls on it.

Singapore and Malacca

Singapore wasn't a big success. In cities like this you'll have to be travelling with some money in your pocket, not as a budget backpacker. One day I went to the party area, Clark Key, but I hated the place. It was where middle to upper class people went for a drink. Everyone was dressed up in their best clothes and had an iPhone. A beer in a bar cost $12 and it was just San Miguel beer from the Philippines, not even some fancy imported beer from Belgium or Germany. I left the bar after one beer.

Lots of people were there for the Formula One race and

went out and smashed a lot of money. It really made you feel like a bum and I didn't feel at ease at all. The only thing you can do there as a backpacker is stand on the giant bridge over the river and drink cans of beer from the convenience store.

I also had to go alone to the Formula One race. I was supposed to go with a guy I'd met at the hostel but he just disappeared a day before. What a dick! It was the first time I went to an event like this and I would rather have enjoyed it with someone else.

The races were OK but I had to guard my seat for hours to avoid others stealing it. My bladder was nearly exploding. Prices were horribly expensive, even for Singapore, and most people were there in groups already. The Mariah Carey concert after the races was pretty good. I stayed five more days in Singapore, but mostly just because I had some serious stomach problems. I had fever at night and stayed in bed all day watching movies.

The only good thing about the hostel was the incredible speed of the Wi-Fi connection. I think I downloaded about 30 movies that week. I flirted with an Indonesian girl for a while there but never got anywhere with her. My self-esteem and courage were leaving me after nearly a month in Muslim Malaysia. Self-doubt found its way into my head.

So instead of seeking out girls I indulged my taste for military history and visited a British bunker complex from World War II, along with Fort Canning, which is where the British had surrendered to the Japanese. The story behind that defeat was quite interesting. Although the Japanese was heavily outnumbered and Singapore was considered a stronghold, they conquered Singapore in less than a week. A lot of the British POWs were sent off to work on the airport at Sandakan in Borneo, and later marched the Death March to Ranau – the same places I was in just a few weeks before. It was a strange realization.

I left Singapore and went to Malacca (a former Dutch colonized city/stronghold with typical Dutch scenery), where I stayed a day or two before taking the ferry to the island of Sumatra in Indonesia.

Indonesia – Medan and Bukit Lawang,

After Malaysian Borneo, Brunei, Singapore and Southern Malaysia, I really needed a change of scenery – and, of course, I really needed to get laid. It had been nearly a month since I last had sex.

Indonesia had always intrigued me because it's such a big part of Dutch Colonial history and one of the reasons the little country of Holland is/was quite rich.

I crossed the Strait of Malacca by ferry, and in Dumai I got a fresh new visa sticker in my passport, which by now already had twenty pages filled with stamps.

Indonesia is one of the most diverse countries in the world. It consists of over 17,000 islands and has everything you could possibly wish for in terms of scenery. There are tropical rainforests, mountains, caves, waterfalls, rivers, indigenous tribes, volcanoes, hundreds of languages, wildlife and, of course, beautiful beaches. I think the island of Sumatra already has all of these and there are thousands more islands to explore. One can easily travel around them for a year and still find new, surprising things. Sumatra is the biggest island in Indonesia and the fifth largest in the world.

I knew I was going to see beautiful things here and experience a lot of local culture. I also knew that Indonesia and especially Sumatra is over eighty percent Islamic, and therefore that it was going to be hard to pick up girls here.

On arrival at the Indonesian ferry port I had to do some brutal negotiating with a guy on a motorbike to take me to the nearest bus station. I had my backpack with me but taxi drivers were asking for ridiculous amounts of money. The first thing I noticed was how many words are similar to my own Dutch language, and there were also quite a few loan words from English.

The guy on the motorcycle explained a few things to me and was generally a helpful guy.

When arriving to a new city you have no knowledge of, you always have to be careful when negotiating a (taxi) fare. Some guys will say your destination is many kilometers away and then drive a few blocks around and drop you off just two kilometers from the point you started. In this case, the guy on the bike hadn't been lying, and also directed me to an ATM and some other places. I gave him a tip on top of the negotiated fare and he left with a big smile.

The bus station was in fact just the office of a bus company that offered trips to Medan, where I wanted to go. It was around noon and the bus left at six at night, so I had nothing to do for the next six hours. I came up with the idea of learning some Indonesian words on top of the ones I already learned in Malaysia, which has a very similar language. I asked the two young girls behind the counter to translate a few words for me and they laughed when I asked words like crazy, ugly and bossy.

The night bus to Medan was one of those typical hellish rides I'd gotten to know so well. The roads were terrible, mostly dirt roads in the mountains. We stopped at a restaurant along the way and I had a giant meal. The Sumatran custom is to fill your table with lots of dishes and only charge you for what you ate. Eating a lot and pointing at only a few dishes will save you money but in a way that's kind of shameful. I hate to admit it, but I did it a few times. Skywalker needs to save some money for beer too. I stopped doing it after someone showed and lectured me on turning to the dark force too much. I can't say she wasn't right.

I met Darren in a guesthouse in Medan. He was an overly polite guy from the Channel Island of Guernsey, part of the United Kingdom. Darren had been backpacking for only a month and had just arrived there. Since we were planning to visit the same places in Sumatra we decided to hang out together for a while.

At night we tried to find a place to go out and the hotel owner next door, who was a nice guy (but had a shitty hotel), advised us to go to a party. One of the hotel workers knew where it was and we jumped on a becak (kind of a motorized rickshaw).

It was a long ride and we were starting to worry a bit. We were already outside the city and in the countryside and it was getting dark. I'm not easily scared and try to stay rational and calm, but this looked suspicious even to me. We had been driving for nearly forty minutes in the middle of nowhere.

Was he planning to rob us with a bunch of his friends? It couldn't be – he worked at the hotel next door where we stayed. Darren, who was only twenty years old and not a very experienced traveler, was getting worried as well. He's a tall strong guy but that doesn't help much when a group of guys pulls a knife on you.

After a while, we started to hear music in the distance, and as it got louder we saw the outline of something that looked like a barn. I said to Darren that we were probably OK, but it was going to be a weird night.

Dropped off at the barn, we went in. The music was extremely loud. Lots of guys were drinking beers at big tables, there was a small stage and some people were sitting on couches close to the dance floor.

We had some beers and soon the waitresses were sitting down very close to us. We tried to talk to them but they barely spoke English. They gladly helped empty our 1-liter bottles of beer. The guy who took us there had no money, of course, and we gave him a beer too. We danced a bit to the loud Indonesian music with the girls and drank some more beer.

A few more guys came over to meet us and have some beers as well. One of them was a muscular soldier in uniform, who has to be one of the craziest dancers I've ever seen. I'm guessing he thought he had some suave moves, but he didn't. I remember him looking over from the dance floor and I bet he was thinking he was doing some pimpish dance with the girls there while showing off to the foreigners. We had seen him at the hotel too; it all looked OK so far.

Then at the end of the night, they presented us a big fat bill. I told the waitress the amount was way too high – she'd counted everything everyone had drunk when they were at our table. A bouncer was coming over to have a look and the other one was also looking our way. The guy from the hotel said we'd better pay. Darren was nearly shitting his pants and I started worrying. Was this a bar scam like they used in Estonia? The bill was a lot, but not hundreds of dollars, so it wasn't a scam like that. They'd just charged us all the drinks of all the people around our table, including four waitresses.

I talked to Darren and we agreed we'd pay for our own drinks and the few beers the waitresses had had, but not for the guys we didn't know who came to sit at our table. When I told the waitress this those guys started yelling, but I stuck to what I said. I got some of Darren's money from him, and just put it down on the table along with my share. And then we walked away.

We paid something like thirteen dollars each, which is quite a lot for just a few Indonesian beers in an out-of-town barn bar, but at least we didn't have to deal with a machete-wielding gang of thugs and buy our way out.

We rode back to Medan on another rickshaw and were glad it ended this well.

The next day Darren and I took the local coach bus to Bukit Lawang, a small mountain village on a river famous for its jungle tours. There were only a handful of tourists and the village was quite empty. It must have been off season, or else tourism is dying out the way it is in the rest of Sumatra. I took an enormous room with bathroom and balcony for fifty thousand rupiah, which is roughly five dollars. We had spoken to a guide on the bus who "by coincidence" sat on the bus with his photo book and promotion flyers.

The next morning he came to our hotel and we agreed on a price after a series of brutal negotiations. One of the details we hashed out was that the guide had to bring me a pair of hiking shoes. I hadn't worn shoes in months. I send my hiking shoes back to Holland when I was in Bangkok and had thrown away my Nike trainers on the Perhentian islands in Malaysia; I'd been in flip-flops ever since. That's five months on flip-flops; I even went to clubs in the Philippines wearing flip-flops. I admit that the sound can get pretty annoying, but they're generally fine – except that you don't want to either climb a mountain or walk a jungle in them.

We left early that morning with two guides and two German girls. The "guide" who sold us the trip said he didn't actually go with us himself and I got really angry with him. That wasn't part of the deal and maybe I overreacted a bit. The two German girls and the guides were unusually quiet for the first half-hour, so it must have made an impression.

This was real rainforest, the kind you see on television sometimes. An ocean of green with paths in-between barely wide enough to walk on.

After an hour of walking we saw our first orangutan in the wild. It was a mother with child, high up in the trees. This was already a hundred times better than the trip I made in Sepilok/Borneo and we were just starting.

Another hour later we saw the second one, and then we had lunch at a place where rampant with small, cheeky monkeys. They were trying to steal our food and drinks and weren't scared at all. We ate a lunch of rice and vegetables out of a banana leaf and honestly I was glad to be sitting down.

Darren and I had downed quite a few beers the night before, and walking in a rainforest isn't easy even if you aren't mildly hungover. Everything is wet and slippery, there's lots of climbing, and I wasn't really used to doing physical things anymore. The last time I'd really done something mildly intensive was visiting the Niah Caves in Borneo. The exercise before that was probably banging Jenna in Cebu, which was almost five weeks before. At least Darren, who claimed he'd never done any sports in his life and is a fairly big drinker, also needed to catch his breath.

It was only the start of this jungle tour and there were some challenges to face. We saw more and more wild orangutangs along the way, and then we came across a famous one named Mina, who is only half-wild. We had run into another jungle group who had shown us the way to her. One of the women in the tour group came close to Mina, and the orangutan wanted to cuddle a bit with her. The woman allowed it and Mina grabbed her – and wouldn't let go.

Orangutans have crazy long arms, are super strong and can break your neck like a twig with one hand. If one goes crazy, you need a whole group of guys to hold it down. The situation was getting a bit dangerous for the woman, and she started to look frightened. Her husband just stood there, and he was looking scared too. He didn't even try anything, and just let the guides deal with the situation. What a fucking wimp that guy was.

The three guides had trouble breaking the woman loose

from Mina without angering her, but in the end they succeeded. The mountain was almost forty-five degrees steep and I had the two German girls standing between me and the situation. The path was only half a meter wide and Darren and I couldn't do anything to help. I hope the guides think twice the next time they allow cuddling with wild animals.

A few hours and many sightings of monkeys and orangutans later, we arrived at base camp. We were exhausted. The humidity in the jungle is murderous and we were out of breath all the time. Eight hours of climbing in a wet, slippery environment.

Base camp consisted of a few canvas cloths on the floor and a small bamboo roof one meter above the ground. As night fell we ate some food the guides had cooked up and I even smoked some weed with them. The weed was of terrible quality and I didn't feel anything.

We played some cards and one of the guides told a few bullshit stories about how he had some million-dollar business plans with some environmental company. He was trying to pick up the girls and I didn't object to that. The way they looked in jungle gear, the girls were about 5.5, maybe a 6 if they got dressed up.

Apparently the environment and the food didn't agree with Darren, because he got sick and barfed his guts out only five meters away from our sleeping places. His stomach really hurt and he kept saying "I'm in agony".

A few days later I told him that I probably was the only one there knowing the meaning of the word agony. The Indonesian guys and the German girls just nodded every time he said it. We laughed pretty hard about that.

The next morning we woke up early and my back felt shattered from sleeping on the ground. The guides took us along the river and told us that we didn't need shoes. We walked barefoot on razor-sharp rocks and I'm the worst climber in the world even in boots. I would have done it with shoes but now my feet hurt so much that I went back early. I really didn't give a shit what the others thought of me: I was too insecure to climb those rocks barefoot next to an ice-cold wild river, and could already see myself falling down and breaking and busting both my legs open in the middle of the jungle. Darren later told me that they saw a waterfall which wasn't even that impressive and his feet hurt like hell too. His feet were in agony, so to say.

The next morning as we had breakfast a giant lizard came close to us. He was at least two meters long with his tail. The girls were a bit scared but the guides just carried on eating their food, not paying any more attention than we would in the West if a squirrel came by. The lizard started chomping down on something close by and we were all taking pictures. Then I realized that the lizard was eating at the place where Darren had thrown up and saw that the lizard was just scarfing down Darren's barf. Luckily I'd finished eating once I realized this.

The guides packed up the camp and burned all the trash, including the plastic bottles. In the jungle they didn't even allow us to throw away a banana skin, and the night before, that one guide had had such a big mouth about his big environmental plans, and here he was, burning plastic. That's one way not to litter, I guess, but how much good it's going to do I can't imagine.

Afterwards, they made a raft out of the inner tubes of truck tires, tying them all together, and packed up the whole camp onto it. Then we got on. It's a bit hard to explain but it was a sort of caravan downriver resembling wild-river rafting, which was really fun to do. Some parts of the river were very fast-flowing and we all got totally soaked. Who needs Disneyland? It took us forty-five minutes of rafting to return to the village of Bukit Lawang, where we had a few beers before saying goodbye to the guides and the German girls.

Darren and I stayed two more nights there to recover from the muscle pain and to look around the area a bit. Darren said he had girlfriends back home but he was still a beginner in the art of gaming. I gave myself the challenge to turn him into a player. First I had to get rid of his overly polite behavior and Alpha him up a bit.

I flirted with the girls working at the guesthouse and tried to kiss the receptionist there, Nazir; she had big luscious lips and all I wanted was to kiss them. I knew a lay was almost out of the question so I set my goal low. I did my best but didn't get further than going for a walk with her, and even than her girlfriend accompanied us. Her girlfriend looked interested in me and didn't mind me hitting her on the bum a few times.

The village of Bukit Lawang probably has no more than two thousand people living there. The whole village had been destroyed in 2003 when a flood came down the mountains and nearly washed the whole town away. Everyone knows each other since it's fairly far away from any big city, so it's a not a place to hunt for girls. Nazir did teach Darren and me a lot of Indonesian words and I wrote everything down in my phone. This was later used as an outline for one of my tips and tricks articles, which will help you enormously in having fun with local girls. I strongly advise to have a look at the article and make your own list of words for whatever country you go. Memorize the words and use them in conversation with local girls. They will be shocked that you know those words and laugh about it. I have used this technique in multiple countries and it always made me stick out from the rest.

There was an English girl named Charlotte we met there, and we went with her to the nearby bat caves and had a few drinks together. We saw our jungle guides sitting all cozy with the German girls. I guess those guys, who were both very skinny and ugly, did actually get laid from time to time. Being a tour guide always gives you status, just like any broke-ass local with a surfboard in Bali. I would do the same if I were in their position.

Indonesia – Medan

We stayed in the same guesthouse as last time. I flirted a bit with the girls working there. Sometimes I practice just a bit on less hot girls just to see their reactions to my game. I advise anyone to do the same – it gives you a really good sense of how you're doing.

At night Darren and I tried to find a place to go out. We had a becak driver take us to some bars, but they were either fucking expensive hotel bars or dumps. After we'd tried a few the driver said he knew a place for us and drove to a bar that looked like some sort of tourist bar. I looked around and saw the big Medan mosque. The same mosque that was waking us up every day at five in the morning when they start yelling their prayers over the enormous loud speakers attached to the tower. The bar was only a hundred meters around the corner from our guesthouse and we had never seen it before.

We had a few beers there and an expat told us about a street named Merdaka Walk, a street with a lot of bars. Darren and I decided to go there and walked back to the main street to get a becak. On the way there I saw two young girls walking by and called them over. After some talking they agreed to go with us to Merdaka Walk. They barely spoke English and some dude who was walking past came along to help translate. He said he was a neighbor of the girls, but he looked like he was lying.

We all sat down and ordered some drinks, though since they were Muslim, Bayian and Cinta (the Indonesian word for love) didn't drink alcohol. That saved us money on expensive drinks but also meant that they weren't "loosening up" with some booze in them. The guy translated for us and we bought him a beer too. I had already enough of the situation, since it turned out that the girl I liked at first was only seventeen and barely spoke a word of English. Darren, on the other hand, was heavily impressed by Bayian, who seemed to like him.

As we left later we had an argument with the translator guy over a few dollars. He was demanding a pack of cigarettes for the girls, who didn't actually smoke, and some money for him. The girls were very confused and didn't understand what all the fuss was about. I'm sure he badmouthed us a lot; we couldn't understand what he was saying anyway. We got rid of him but not of the girls. Darren was going crazy for cute little Bayian, but I suspected she was a gold digger looking for a money-sender. Darren was still a gullible small-town guy, and in my opinion a bit naïve to think a hot 19-year-old girl would fall for him overnight. He changed a lot over time but at moments like that I felt I had to protect him from himself.

The next morning I texted Cinta to tell her I didn't think it would work out between us. She was very disappointed, but later when I was sitting in the guesthouse bar having some breakfast she came by with Bayian to see Darren. And she had brought her older sister with her. Putri was only two years older than Cinta, and smoking hot. She looked like a model but also like a true gold-digger. Too much golden jewelry, and an expensive dress and designer shoes. I talked to her a bit but no way was she getting to spend my cash. I sat there and started eye-flirting with an older girl sitting on another table. She smiled back at me and it went back and forth a few times. Darren and the girls saw what was happening and the girls weren't too happy with it.

When the older girl stood up to leave I said to her "Hey, you forgot to give me your phone number", and just handed my phone to her. She smiled and put her number in my phone. Darren gave me an admiring look. The two sisters were not pleased.

That night I met up with Renny, the girl who gave me her phone number, and we talked a bit. Darren went out with Bayian to the cinema and had kissed her there. Renny had brought a girlfriend with big tits and they were both acting flirty.

We decided to go out together the next night to a club. That night Darren took Bayian to his room, but nothing happened there. He said she wanted to but her mom called and she left. I said he was lucky she didn't cry rape. He didn't really know anything about her and got really nervous about it. I admit, I might have misjudged the situation a bit.

We both really needed to gear up with some new accessories, so we went to the shopping mall. I finally bought a pair of dress shoes for the clubs and only paid thirty dollars for them. I wore them for nearly one-and-a-half years and went out in eighteen countries with them. One of the advantages of always being on the road is that you don't need many clothes. By the time people have seen you wearing a few different shirts you're gone again. I bought a rock-star-looking leather bracelet for four dollars which I'm still wearing today. The metal parts are rusty now but it makes it look better.

Before we went out I went over to Renny's place on the back of her motorbike. She let me touch her boobs while driving the bike but she wouldn't kiss me when she stopped. It should have been a big warning but I was blinded by a six-week dry spell and the hunt for a new and important flag. I could never return home without an Indonesian flag. One of my friends back home is half-Indonesian and used to be quite the player himself. I needed that flag no matter what.

Renny called up another friend and the five of us went out in one of their cars to the first club. We drove straight to a place that Darren and I had visited on our first night out but left because the drinks were too expensive. We had told the girls we didn't have much money and they answered that we would only spend 200K, which was like twenty dollars.

Of course those twenty bucks was gone by the time we bought the first round. To make a long story short, we had a nice night out and went to a couple of places. We posed a lot for funny pictures. I could touch the boobs of the girls all the time but couldn't get them to kiss me. How weird is that?

Clubs close early in Indonesia and on the way back we went to the Mc Drive. We talked and joked around in the car a bit while we were waiting for the food. Renny, Darren and I were sitting in the back seat and suddenly the hottest girl of the bunch leaned back from the driver's seat and had a make-out session with Darren. I couldn't believe my eyes. Me, Le Grand Skywalker, outplayed by a rookie. Renny saw that I was not happy with it and I didn't say a word to her.

Back in the guesthouse I went straight to my room while they sat down with all the McDonalds food. I'm a huge fan of that greasy stuff but had to take a shit upstairs. The Indonesian food had already been fucking with my insides for days and drinking a lot that night made me explode in the bathroom. Of course the toilets have to be flushed with buckets of water and it all took a while.

When I came down they were all silent because they thought I had been angry and left. I made up an excuse that I had to take off my new shoes because they hurt and that I brushed my teeth. What else could I say? "Oh hi girls, I just took a major crap upstairs, pass the French fries please?"

The girl with the big tits wanted to have sex with me, but only if we went to a fancy four-star hotel nearby which had a bubble bath and costs forty dollars a night. Since the girls had already lied to us about club prices, it might have really been sixty dollars. I told her I had a room upstairs where we could go directly but she declined. I wanted to fuck her bad but had the feeling it wouldn't count as a notch or a flag if it was only possible in an expensive room. It felt like prostitution to me.

Now, many of you readers will think that forty bucks for a hotel room isn't much to get laid, and I agree. It's not much if you're on a two-week holiday. But when you're on a three-year trip you have to be a bit of a penny-pincher.

The girls left and I went to bed. I wanted to move on to another place but Darren wanted to stay behind with Bayian a bit longer. We agree to meet again at Lake Toba, one of the most beautiful places in Indonesia.

Indonesia – Lake Toba

The ride to Lake Toba, also called Samosir Island, was another classic. For five hours I was trapped inside a small minivan full of locals with suitcases and plastic bags. An Indonesian woman was sleeping on my shoulder for hours.

A short ferry ride later I was on Samosir Island, in the middle of Lake Toba. The lake was formed by the biggest super-volcano ever: the Toba Caldera, Yellowstone's bigger sister. The last time this volcano blew up it resulted in a mass extinction of the human population. Only five to ten thousand breeding pairs remained and it affected the genetic inheritance of all humans today. At least, that's what happened according to the Toba catastrophe theory. It's hard to find out if it's true, since it happened millions of years ago.

What the eruptions *did* definitely do over the years was leave a stunningly beautiful volcanic lake with an island in the middle.

Samosir's main town, Tuktuk, used to be a hippie destination, and later turned into a major party place where the early backpackers came to go crazy at spring parties. All that has changed and people have moved on to Thailand for the full moon parties. Tourism in Tuktuk is nearly dead, and it's considered an off-the-beaten–track destination nowadays. Accommodation is cheap and many guesthouses are empty or barely occupied. Locals still reminisce about the days when the guesthouses were packed and business was good. I still recommend it to anyone on Sumatra or an Indonesia tour, especially if you want a few days rest. Go for three or four days. It's cheap, it's quiet and it's beautiful.

I met a few guys who went here for the sole purpose of relaxing or being lazy all day. You can live here on a budget of less than ten dollars a day if you want.

I found a room with bathroom in traditional Batak style for only six dollars. The first night I hung out with a small group of tourists, including the Charlotte I had met in Bukit Lawang a few days before. I was on fire that night, entertaining the whole group with travel stories, being the group leader and the only alpha guy there.

One of the girls was a smoking hot Norwegian girl, Maria, and she was hanging on every word I said. She was clearly admiring me and only mentioned that she was engaged hours later. That's always a good sign and I remembered how I'd heavily made out with Sheila, the English girl in Malaysia, with her not mentioning her marriage till the next day.

Maria was a 7.5 in my opinion, probably an 8.5 when dressed up for a night out. The stunning blonde had been motor-riding around the island with a mixed group, and one of the guys was passively cock-blocking me by keeping me from getting some time alone with her. Whenever there's a hot girl around there are always guys who are too afraid to do any flirting whatsoever with this girl and secretly hate the guy who has the balls to do so.

Guys like this always orbit around the girl and never give you a moment alone with her, because they know that they're going to feel even more a failure if they see anyone else succeed. I know exactly what I'm talking about because I was that guy myself for years before. I would go out, see other guys have fun with girls and think every guy who was talking to a girl was getting laid. I would go home very angry with myself and sometimes in an aggressive mood. It seems to me the world would be a better place if guys learned to pick up girls early in their lives. I suspect that lots of insecure guys get into trouble or do crazy stuff because they are so socially incapable of getting girls. The world would have a lot less crime and way fewer weirdoes if they were happily in a relationship. Now that I have more knowledge of social dynamics, I know that not every guy talking and laughing with a girl is getting laid and it's only a small percentage of guys that will pick up that night. I was too blind to see it and now feel sorry for guys in the same situation I was in before.

Did something happen with the Norwegian girl? The answer is no. Her Norwegian girlfriend, who was sick the day before, joined her and guarded her 24/7. It's always funny how the one guarding or protecting her friend from the "bad" men are always girls that are a six or lower on the scale of hotness. All that time Maria was giving me signs of liking me, but some girls do that and still put you in the friend zone. I have never figured it out and Darren, who came to the island a day later, said the same. She liked me a lot but not enough to cheat. I kept in touch with Maria for a while and saw her again five weeks later in Bali. I tried to set up a time to meet again but we always seemed to be in different places. I ran into her on the street when her boyfriend had come to join her. Actually, I was just looking at her and she was the one who recognized me. Her boyfriend was a big, strong, handsome guy, and somehow that made me feel a lot better. They got married a year later.

Darren had said goodbye to Bayian and came along a day later. We went out to the mid-weekly disco night. There was a small bar/club with a live band a few times a week. We met a couple of other tourists and most of the local girls there were working girls. I had conversations with a few of them, did some test flirting to find out if they were hookers and concluded that most of them were. Not to be overly politically correct, but by local girls I mean Indonesian girls. I don't mean local Batak tribe people – though who knows, maybe some of them were.

Darren and I sat down with a Dutch guy who was there

to blow all his money on his Indonesian girlfriend, who wasn't even that hot. There were a few other girls around and I talked and danced with one of them, named Henny. She gave me her phone number and the next morning we texted a bit.

At one point I mixed up Henny's name with Renny from Medan: I texted her something naughty about Renny's boobs and meant to send it to her, but Henny got it instead. Oops.

Renny was still texting me, as were the teenage sisters Cinta and Putri, along with Nazir from Bukit Lawang. I was getting forty to fifty texts a day from all these ladies, which sounds like a lot but was nothing compared to my later visit to the Philippines.

After fixing the mistake about the boobs message by just saying it was for another girl (a cold-hearted win or lose pre-selection move), we agreed on meeting. She said she would pick me up for a ride around Samosir Island by car.

This all sounded great, but when she arrived with the Dutch guy and his girlfriend I realized that Henny was a lot older than I had seen through my giant beer goggles the night before. I guess she was close to forty. Darren looked at me and laughed. I got into the car and we drove off to a viewing point.

The Dutch guy is best described as a raving lunatic. He talked at high speed and it was all nonsense. He kept rambling on about the weirdest things and I was left looking to Henny for answers a few times. She would just smile. Then I'd turn my head away because I didn't want to make her think I liked her too much. With a ton of beer in my system I would have captured the flag with her, but no way in hell was I going for it sober. All and all they were nice people, but clearly not my kind. The Dutch guy's girlfriend was the only person I could have something resembling an actual conversation with.

After a few hours driving we returned, and I never had much contact with Henny after. I had some beers with them on another day but that was it. The Dutch guy was just too much of a nutcase to hang with when sober.

The guesthouse where Darren and I stayed rented out

motor scooters and after hearing good things from the other group we decided to go for a trip around the island. Since there's basically only one road, we figured it shouldn't be too hard. We left early in the morning and after an hour arrived at the same viewpoint I'd been the day before. It was starting to get hot and we were only wearing shorts and t-shirts. Just an hour later our arms were totally sunburned and we still had to do six hours of riding.

Sunburns or not, Samosir Island is an amazing place to visit. It almost has more churches than houses, all Christian since the Dutch colonizers introduced that religion to local tribes on Sumatra. The Batak tribe was completely Christian and that meant I could eat pork again. It had been quite a while and it was delicious. We saw traditional Batak houses with the steep roofs and beautiful woodcarvings; the views on the blue lake and surrounding mountains were stunning and the green rice fields looked amazing with the sun reflecting on them. As always in Asia, you had a crowd of children following you everywhere you stopped. We drove through small Batak villages with names like Loembanboentoe.

For a Dutch guy Indonesian is actually very easy to pronounce: just read the word out as if it were Dutch and most people understand you. If you hang out in a country for a while you learn how people pronounce certain syllables and that makes it even easier.

We had to stop at least every twenty minutes to get into the shade. Our arms and legs were already red as boiled lobster and it started to hurt. We both started worrying now since we weren't even halfway there. The roads were in terrible condition, it's mainly dirt roads full of potholes. Our scooters were quite fast but it took a long time to drive just fifteen or twenty kilometers. The sights were beautiful and we saw coffee plantations and endless rice fields.

At one point we stopped for some lunch at a roadside restaurant and people gathered around us to look at the red lobster guys eating rice and pork. As always people were friendly and smiling at us. I asked for an apotek, which is almost the same as the Dutch word apotheek, which means pharmacy.

After driving around a bit we found a few places that resembled a pharmacy. Of course they didn't sell sun-block, since they'd never even heard of it. I had to describe the situation by pointing at my arms and saying "auw, auw" and making a painful face. It wasn't very hard to do because my skin was already screaming at that point. We were desperate to find something to lessen the damage and bought body lotion and put that on our faces and arms. I still don't know if it helped, or because lotion has oil in it it just made it worse. At least it had a cooling effect for a few minutes. I figured it was best to keep our arms hydrated. When we thought we were about halfway round the island we stopped again to eat.

The owner of the shop and restaurant was very friendly and even spoke some English. He told us about the glory days at the end of the 1990s, when he still was a younger guy himself chasing tourist girls. Darren opted to stop there and wait for it to get dark. We still had four hours of driving to do and I convinced him to keep on driving despite our severe sunburn. If we had to wait for sundown then we had to wait for hours since it was only two o'clock and the roads would be dangerous to drive in the dark. The shop owner also advised to keep on going because it turned out we weren't even halfway there. We had been driving for five hours now but the roads were so bad that it looked like nothing on the map. We lotioned up and went off again after buying a shitload of water and cookies.

Much lotion later we arrived in a town named Pangururan, which was big enough it was worth looking for long-sleeve shirts there. Of course, for some weird reason we couldn't find any long sleeve-shirts at any of the stores we passed. I know it's always above thirty degrees here, but goddamn someone has to wear them sometimes. For some odd reason, even though our faces were melting too we didn't look for caps.

Pangururan is famous for its hot springs, but that was the last thing we had on our minds. Getting out of the sun and taking a cold shower was the only thing we thought about. I was ready to steal someone's clothes if I saw a jacket or a sweater hanging to dry somewhere.

People later told me that the hot springs were old, badly maintained, and in general a waste of time and money to visit, so luckily we didn't miss much. There were a few small roads though the jungle and mountain leading to Tuktuk village, but tourists had been lost on that road and needed saving by local people to get back to civilization, so we avoided them.

Darren had had enough of it by now and turned into Valentino Rossi, the famous motorcycle racer. He didn't stop for anything anymore, even though we passed quite a few interesting places along the way. Luckily the last part of the circle around the island was mainly good road and we could hurry now. I nearly broke my hand when I drove through a pothole at seventy kilometers an hour. My rental bike survived and so did I.

By the time we made it back to the guesthouse our faces and arms were purple and I feared that I'd get an enormous blister, like the one I had in Nepal a few years before. Back then my skin had looked like wrapping foil with the air bubbles in it and I'd had to get a doctor and medical treatment to get rid of the, horrible pus-filled, one inch across and half-an-inch high blister. It was too disgusting to look at. I still have a scar from it, though it's only visible when I'm tanned.

For some reason the showers in our rooms were ice-cold and despite (or maybe because of) the severe sunburn I couldn't bring myself to stand under it. I had to just splash myself to get clean. Darren had a bathtub in his room, filled it with water and sat in it nearly two hours to cool down. He looked like a Popsicle when I saw him again.

The next days were mainly filled with us avoiding any contact with sunlight and using massive amounts of body lotion to keep our skin from falling apart. We swam a few times in the lake and watched a DVD (Machete) we been meaning to watch for a long time.

The people in the guesthouse were a special bunch. There was a Danish guy who was totally creepy. He seemed to be there for the sole purpose of doing nothing; he never had any money, never talked and gave off a disturbing vibe. Then there was a fucking hilarious German guy. With his short curly hair and the dumb hoggish expression on his face, you wouldn't give him any chance with girls. But if you asked him, then he was a real Casanova. He told us that he'd had a threesome with two extremely hot girls in Jakarta. "How did you do it?" I asked him. "I just showed them my breakdancing" he replied. Well, later on we all went out to the local bar and he showed us.

It was the most horrible breakdancing I have ever seen. People were laughing and clapping and he considered it a compliment and turned it up a notch. And if that wasn't bad enough he went on stage and asked the guitarist if he could sing a song. I have a video of it and still watch it when I need to get out of a bad mood.

He was a better guitar player than me, but not by much – and I can barely play two chords. His singing was horrendous and sounded like some kind of long stretched-out death moan. It was the worst sound humanly possible.

All the people inside the bar were loudly laughing and clapping. By the end of his "song" I'd nearly pissed my pants laughing. I usually admire people with the balls to go on stage and sing even though they can't, like you see in karaoke bars worldwide, but this guy was just too much. Anyone familiar with the Astérix comic books will remember Assurancetourix, the village musician. Well, this German guy sounded just like him.

Back in the guesthouse he told us that he had fifty thousand Euros in his bank account and travelled ultra-budget. He was planning on travelling through South America for eight months, spending only three thousand Euros. Anyone who's ever travelled there knows that's absolutely impossible. I've never seen a guy make such a fool of himself. You might think it would work in terms of getting girls: some girls will go for a guy with the guts to publicly make a total ass of himself. But not this guy.

I later found him in the Facebook friends' list of one of the girls we met there, and I checked his pictures. He never went to South America.

Indonesia – Bukit Tinggi

The next part of my trip wasn't that interesting, but it gives me an opportunity to give an insight into how a ride to an off-the-beaten track destination on an Indonesian HELL bus goes down.

In this case we were lucky to be able to buy the tickets to Bukit Tinggi directly at the guesthouse on Samosir Island, after asking around a bit what the prices were at other places. I remember that it wasn't cheap, but then again it was a twenty-hour bus ride in what we were told was a luxury bus. I would have opted to go totally local but almost everyone advised me not to, and Darren didn't feel like it. So luxury it was.

We woke up in the morning, packed our stuff and walked to the point where a wooden passenger boat could bring us back to Parapat on the mainland.

The trip across the lake took only about half-an-hour. There's a local market directly where the boats arrive in Parapat, and it's a small mayhem of fruit and vegetable vendors, scammers trying to sell you overpriced or fake bus tickets and people selling meat that's lying there in the open air, covered with flies. There's the stench of garbage and the sight, sound and smell of people butchering chickens and cleaning fish. We finally found our way through this chaos to our bus company and waited for the bus to leave.

Luxury bus my ass. It was a complete disaster. The seats didn't recline at all so we had to sit up straight the whole night. We were the only foreigners on the bus and it was packed with curious locals and their many boxes and plastic bags full of merchandise and household products. People were eating all kinds of food and even smoking was allowed, so the whole bus smelled like sweat, exotic food and cheap tobacco. The only thing missing were chickens and goats going up and down the aisle.

By nightfall the bus was filled with a fine blue cigarette mist. With the smell, the lack of sleep, the loud music and the extremely bad and bumpy roads, this had a nauseating effect. We even ended up taking strong 10mg Valium tablets, but still couldn't sleep at all. The bus was stopping in every little bumfuck village, and the worst was yet to come.

One of the two teenage boys sitting in the seats before us got sick and projectile-vomited in the walkway. He even hit the guy sitting in the other seat and didn't even apologize. Half of the guy's leg was covered in vomit and he didn't even get angry at the teenager. There was a large puddle of barf close to our feet and the stench was awful. If you covered your nose you could almost taste the vomit and if you covered your mouth then the smell was unbearable. The teenager vomited a few times and made no attempt to clean anything up.

We stopped at a roadside restaurant but neither of us was hungry any more, and we just bought a few bags of chips to get through the night. We flirted and took pictures with the local teenage girls selling the chips and soda at the roadside. It was the middle of the night and we saw Barfboy eating a giant bag of chips and smoking a cigarette. Within half an hour on the bus he vomited again and was even joking with his friend about it. I think it was the bus driver or the guy helping him who "cleaned" the walkway by covering the large puddle of vomit with newspapers.

When we arrived at five o'clock in the morning we were totally broken down. I was already used to enduring some vicious bus rides, but this was the number one hell ride so far.

Every hotel in our guide books had at least doubled their prices since the last printing, only a year before probably because they saw the book and knew everyone would go there. After a while we found one guesthouse with a German owner who still had a cheap room. His prices had also doubled, but at least they were still affordable. We both took a separate room and fell asleep. The German owner was friendly and helpful, but smelled very bad. He had terrible body odor and coffee breath. Apparently his local wife didn't mind.

The room had a bathroom but no shower. To wash yourself there was a large tub full of water and a bucket. Since I had no idea how long that water had already been in the tub, I just washed my body with it and used bottled water for my face and to brush my teeth, but I still felt dirty using the tub water. We knew one thing. We had to get the fuck out of that place and find something else. The next day we found a much better hotel and shared a room to split the costs.

Bukit Tinggi doesn't have much to offer. It's a small city and not many tourists visit it nowadays. Just like Lake Toba, tourism is dying here. It was weeks since my last lay and I was eager to find a place to go out, but good luck with that in a city that's known for banning holidays as Valentine's Day and New Year's Eve because the city's administration considers them not in line with Islamic tradition and they might lead to young couples committing immoral acts like – shock! horror! – hugging, and kissing. All we did there was a bit of flirting with sales ladies in the local mall.

There was the possibility of taking a hike in the nature parks surrounding Bukit Tinggi, but we didn't really feel like it and just walked around the city a bit.

We visited the Japanese headquarters from the World War II occupation. They consisted of an enormous tunnel and bunker network dug out by locals and POWs. It's pretty impressive when you know in how short a time it was built, and ten times more interesting than the other "famous" fortress named Fort de Kock, a remainder from Dutch colonial times but nothing more than a few cannons lying around on a hill.

Speaking of misery, I went for a wet shave with a one of those classic cutthroat straight razors. Darren and I went into a local barber shop after attempting to visit a mosque. The barbers were laughing and joking with us and the atmosphere was good. My mood changed completely when I sat down in the chair and the barber put some lotion on my face. It was a very thin layer of lotion and nothing compared to the thick shaving cream I usually use. That should have been warning enough, but I didn't start to get a really bad feeling until I saw his razor. It looked old, like it was the first razor in human history. What followed was ten minutes of pain. I hadn't shaved in four days and already had four millimeters of stubborn hair on my face. It felt like the barber was shaving me with a blunt axe. It hurt like hell, especially around the chin and under the nose. Darren had no mercy: he just stood back laughing, shooting some pictures and even a short video of my torture. When we walked out I swore never to do something like that again. I still had patches of hair everywhere and had to shave again just to get it smooth.

I'd gone for the whole straight razor torture because I thought it was an ultimate alpha male thing to do, and was always trying to "man up" Darren a bit. We joked for weeks about buying one of those straight razors and using it in hostels to show everyone what tough motherfuckers we were. As of then, every time I saw Darren do something I considered wimpy or heard him complain about something, I'd act out sharpening (stropping) a straight razor on my arm and say "Man up, Darren!"

We were running out of time on our visas and had to take a plane to the capital, Jakarta, to save time – not to mention avoid another nauseating thirty-five hour bus trip and a ferry to get to Jakarta. After a five-hour minibus drive to the neighboring city of Padang and a lot of hassles with the tickets, we were able to fly to Jakarta where I would finally bust a nut again.

Indonesia – Jakarta

It had been nearly two months since I last got laid. What had happened to me? Was I losing my dark powers? Was the Force no longer strong in me? I guess it has more to do with travelling on a budget that meant I couldn't afford to have a good time in clubs – and by good time I mean paying for the entrance fee and a few drinks for me and/or a girl without making calculating how many meals I could have bought with the same money, or how two beers equals a night in a cheap hotel room.

The other two factors in my not getting laid were that I was travelling in very conservative Muslim countries and the obstructing approach anxiety I still had sometimes. In hindsight I should probably have travelled a few months less and spend a little bit more each day.

It was already ten o'clock at night when Darren and I arrived at Jakarta airport. The taxi took nearly forty-five minutes and because we were following the guide book's advice we went straight to the backpackers' area, named Jalan

Jaksa. Of course all the guesthouses were full or too damn expensive.

We found one dirty old place with rooms full of fungus that still cost eleven dollars. We were tired of walking around with our backpacks on in a bar area and having everyone look at us so I opted to take the room, get drunk and fall asleep in the stinking room, and then get up early and find something better. The only good thing about that place was the powerful shower. I felt really clean after washing my hair and taking a good shower after weeks of shitty showerheads where it was more like the water was leaking from the ceiling than having some pressure behind it.

We went to a bar named Memories that had a live band playing and a good atmosphere. One of the staff told us that the bar also rented out rooms upstairs and we had a look. The rooms were modern and had very clean attached bathrooms. It cost only a dollar more than the other room with mold stains on the ceiling and we moved in straight away. Nowadays I wouldn't share a twelve-dollar room, but back than I was still a cheap Charlie.

The food was good and we flirted a bit with the waitresses there. They were young and a bit conservative and had probably heard it all before, given that they worked in a bar that was also frequented by freelance prostitutes. Finding a prostitute is South East Asia is never a problem, but if you're not interested in paying a girl or not able to get her for free, then it's rather annoying to have them around and it makes normal girls even more less approachable. They keep their guard up around foreigners because they see so many of them whore-mongering around them. They get used to seeing beta guys get drunk and acting stupid and submissive to anything in a skirt. Don't be that needy guy and keep it cool.

It was time to do some sightseeing again. We wanted to go to the Kota area, where there were supposedly ships from colonial times, when the city was still part of the Dutch empire and named Batavia.

We took a train to the station nearest to Kota. The tuktuk driver who took us there didn't know his own city and dropped us off at the wrong spot, in some embassy area. This was a whole other part of Jakarta and a real elite neighborhood, with clean roads and guards in front of fancy gates.

After looking around a bit we decided to just walk to Kota, since we had a general idea of where we were on the map. We walked in the general direction of the harbor and straight into a local market filled with smiling happy people. We took some photos there and kept asking directions.

After a while of walking down a street filled with massive water and mud puddles, we saw some ship masts, but they were still quite far away. It was next to a slum and at one point we walked into a terrain that looked and smelled like an open sewer. It resembled a swamp but one with garbage everywhere. Luckily we were both wearing flip-flops. At some places we were almost knee-deep in dirty-smelling water floating with crap and garbage.

When we finally got close to the ships, we had to climb on to a wall big enough to walk on to see them and discover that they were actually not that old and clearly not interesting.

We wanted to get back to civilization and had to go back through the partly-flooded slum. I think we were the first foreigners crazy or dumb enough to step foot in that extremely poor slum. Darren still had some manning up to do, because he was getting worried again. We were lost and people were giving us looks. But the looks were all friendly and we had kids running around us, posing for pictures, cheering and clapping. It was great, and the only time I was the least bit worried was when we turned around a corner and a large group of teenage guys was staring at us. They frowned at us and it took a while before they knew how to react to seeing two tall white dudes in their area. In the end they waved and smiled at us. Kids were running after us, girls were giving shy smiles and people even offered us delicious food that we gladly ate because all that walking had made us hungry. I enjoyed all of it and took quite a few pictures.

The one truly sad thing we saw was a guy with Down's Syndrome walking down the street. The kids were cheering and pointing at him and even throwing stuff at him. He just smiled like a big happy baby and walked on.

After hearing a happy "Hello mister" at least two hundred times we reached the end of the slum and took a tuktuk to the train station. I later found out that we'd been really misinformed and that Kota wasn't an area with old ships at all but one with old colonial buildings. Oops.

We took the cheapest train back we could find. It had no doors and was filled with poor people; small street kids were hanging on the outside of the speeding train while looking at us. I hoped that they weren't just showing off to us going to get in a deadly accident. I sure as hell wasn't encouraging them. The fifteen-minute train ride only cost eleven cents.

The evening found us hanging around at Memories and talking to some girls there. One of them, Annie, spoke reasonable English and tried to get me in a hotel room. I declined several times because she was clearly a freelancer, who might ask for money later. The girl she was hanging out with was a straight-up money-hungry ho and I thought Annie would be the same.

At night we went out to a bar area whose name I don't remember. Something with a capital letter. All the bars were full of prostitutes and Darren even scored us a couple of free tequila shots of one of the girls there celebrating her birthday. Well done bro, you're starting to learn. I'm not a big fan of tequila but if it's free, I'm there. Darren was on a year-long round-the-world trip and still in his second month, and sometimes he was even stingier than me.

The last night was a big success. We met a nice woman named Mona and her gay guy friend. She invited us to play pool and ordered a lot of buckets of beer. At one point I told Darren to slow down the drinking because maybe we were getting set up for a scam. She was a bit too friendly in my opinion, and we started to worry about the bill. It turns out we worried for nothing. Mona paid for everything and we found out she had quite a bit of money. Our group went back to Memories, just down the road. It was our turn to pay for some beers now and we did.

Jalan Jaksa is kind of a seedy street, with a mix of backpackers, expats, locals, hookers, gays and Africans doing "business", so you can expect anything to happen there. I saw

Annie watching me with Mona, and she walked past us a few times to make her presence known. Mona and I were flirting but I couldn't get anywhere close to a kiss with her.

I looked around and to my surprise saw Darren talking with a girl with giant tits I had noticed before.
When I say giant, I mean giant. She had the biggest tits I'd seen since I left Cebu and Jenna behind me.

I quickly said something like "just a moment" to Mona and walked over to join the conversation. The big-boobed girl, Donna, was sitting there with two gay guys and another girl. I soon found out that they were all colleagues working in a hotel. We got talking and things went very well. Almost everything I said was well-received and we joked a lot with each other. I wasn't paying attention to her boobs at all because I know that a million guys must have stared at them before and she must have had a hundred complements about them. The trick is to look like you're talking to hot girls all the time and are not even the slightest bit impressed by her appearance. Only guys who have high value do this and any girl will see this as special. You have to adjust your inner game to this, and the Force was strong in me that night. That night I knew how to hide a two-month dry spell.

Donna and I made fun of each other and joked about the World Cup Football final, because she was for the Spanish team and I of course for the Dutch team. At one point I wanted to touch her hair for some reason – I don't remember why, but I'm sure it was some pick-up trick – but instead of touching her hair I accidently touched her boobs and in a split second I said "Oh, sorry" in a very nonchalant way and just kept talking. Now don't get me wrong. My hand had bumped into her boobs from underneath when my hand went from my knee to her head and I used enough power to actually lift her heavy boob a bit. I could see on her face that she didn't know what to say or do at that moment. The sheer fact that I kept talking like I bump into massive boobs five times a day and don't even notice this anymore helped me build enough pre-selection and value to keep her interested and not come off as a creep who wants to cop a feel.

Mona had to leave and said goodbye. She was slightly

grumpy that I had kind of ditched her. I was getting a bit drunk and kept talking to Donna until her friends wanted to go home. I got her phone number and said goodbye. I was disappointed because Darren and I had agreed to leave the next day to Yogyakarta, a city in the middle of Java Island, and I might not get to see Donna again. Our visa time was running out and we still had a lot to visit.

Annie came over to talk and before I could brush her off she pushed me towards the stairs. She had been watching me the whole night talking to Mona and Donna and since pre-selection is a mighty weapon. She'd just about had it with me rejecting her. She pushed me to my room and before we went in I mumbled something about not paying for anything and she just kept pushing me.

We took a shower together and I banged her good. She was very flexible and knew exactly how to do doggy style with an arched back, something a lot of girls still have to learn. "Face down, ass up, that's the way I like to fuck", just like in the 2 live Crew song. I was so excited about banging again that when I came I shouted out "Number 27!" and celebrated my 15th flag. I said it in Dutch so I didn't have to answer any questions.

We talked a bit and said goodbye. I went downstairs and found Darren talking to the two waitresses we were hanging out with. According to him I had an enormous grin on my face and it was obvious I just done some banging. He knew it, the waitresses knew it, and even the guy down the street selling meat on a stick knew it.

Two hours later we were at the Jakarta train station where we sat on the floor and drunkenly dozed off in a half sleep while waiting for the train. Not much later we were on our way to Yogyakarta.

Indonesia – Yogyakarta

The drinking, banging and two hours of sleep didn't do me much good when we got on the train. It took seven hours to get to Yogyakarta, a small city but the second most-visited touristic place in Indonesia. I couldn't get much sleep, the food on the train tasted old and when we arrived we still had to find a hotel room. It surprised us that it was hard to find a decent and cheap room. The small alleys close to the main street were packed with guesthouses and hotels.

We split a room again and I was sick the first two days. My stomach was really fucked and for most of the day I just lay on the bed.

A day later, once I felt a bit better, Darren and I rented a scooter to visit local temples and the world-famous Borobudur temple. People in Jakarta had already warned us NOT to go to Yogyakarta because of the erupting volcano, Mount Merapi. The government had already raised the alert to its highest level on the 25th of October (2010), and we arrived at the 27th. A couple of dozen people had already died in the surrounding villages and the army had evacuated everything in a 10km radius around the volcano.

Of course two travellers named Darren and Neil didn't care about warnings and the fact that it was all over the news every day. We drove off on our rental scooters and tried to get as close as possible.

At one point we came to the 10km zone and were stopped at a military roadblock. Borobudur, or Bombadoor as Darren called it, was closed due to the ash fall: the temples were covered in about eight centimeters of it. We decided to make the best of it and drove around the volcano area and saw the evacuation of villagers and livestock. Some of the cows were badly burned and it made me feel really bad to look at them like they were a tourist sight.

I had suppressed my ever-exploding bowels with a handful of tablets I got from Darren, but the nausea, combined with heavy pollution and breathing in a lot of ash, almost made me vomit inside my helmet. We decided to turn back and relax. The whole city center was covered in a few centimeters of ash and we had to wear masks.

Yogyakarta was about twenty-eight kilometers away from the volcano, but even over that distance it covered the city in ash and we could see the glow of the magma at night. Over a one-month period the volcano erupted several times and the official death toll was 324 people by the 24th of November.

My stomach got worse again and I had to spend another two days lying on my bed. Darren had copied about forty movies off my hard drive and was watching movies most of the day. There were hardly any tourist girls around and we couldn't find a club to go to at night.

I was texting with Donna the whole day and Darren almost lost it hearing the same ringtone over and over again. Donna was still very much interested in me and I had used a couple of fantasy texts I'd come up with after listening to the MP3 files of the Mystery pick-up method on her. I had already listened to them several times by now and used some of the techniques. Sometimes a routine or technique doesn't seem right or feels outdated, but can be adapted. I don't like to use routines and would only advise you to use them if you're an absolute beginner and need to get started with something to help you approach and say something to a girl. Of course, if that something works well then you should use it again in every way possible.

Saying that she was a witch and had put a spell on me fired up a million ways to play with her and use seductive texts. I came up with the story that she appeared in my fever dreams and she should stop bothering me and just let me sleep. It's all a bit hard to explain and it's too bad I don't have all those texts anymore.

After a while I started to send more seductive and openly naughty texts about what I was going to do with her if she would be with me. This got her all horny and she started emailing me some half-naked pictures doing sexy poses. I fired it up some more and pretty soon she wanted to fly over and meet me for a few days. My thoughts went something like this; *What? Come over here by airplane at your own costs? Damn, this girl has money!!!!*

A day later she said she couldn't get off work on such short notice but we could meet in Bali if I wanted. And yeah, that's exactly what I wanted. Darren and I packed our stuff and went to the airport the next day.

We had tried to buy a ticket online but for some reason it didn't work with our credit cards. We went to several counters to bargain over ticket prices. I had already written down the online prices so they couldn't cheat us with wrong information. They all asked us the daily price, which was twice the price online. I got angry and said that we tried to book but that their website failed; I didn't even lie about it. They looked on the company website and gave us the promotion price, which was actually thirty dollars cheaper each. We'd already been arguing for four-and-a-half hours at the airport by the time our plane left.

Indonesia – Bali Kuta beach

Ah, Bali!! The beaches and the bitches, I have good memories on both of them – though some bad ones too.

It was clearly the rainy season when we arrived, because the streets in Kuta were flooded. A single room with a window already cost fourteen dollars, so we decided to share a room again, at least for the first couple of days till we found something better. My stomach was still upset so I wasn't really active the first few days.

Bali is famous for its beaches and its nightlife. Let me start with the nightlife. Most of it is concentrated close to the monument for the bombing victims. Drinking is cheap and most bars have special offers. One place had an offer of three hours unlimited Heineken beer for five-and-a-half dollars, and in another club, the Sky Garden, they even had one hour of free food (tapas) and special cocktails. I didn't even bother to eat dinner anymore and just loaded up on snacks there every night.

Sky Garden was the only place guarded by bouncers with some serious machine guns. This had to do with the many deaths caused by bombings by an Islamic organization in 2002 and in 2005. The first bombing killed 202 people, mainly Australian and European tourists. Many of the members of the fundamentalist Islamic organization were sentenced to death afterwards.

Club Bounty was another place we went to a couple of times, and I had mixed feelings about the place. It was full of wild monkeys, as I called Australian bogans tourists at the time. Most of them were stupidly drunk and dancing around, jumping and swinging their arms. It was hard to dance near to them because they would step on your feet and elbow the drinks out of your hand without giving a damn about it.

Darren needed copious amounts of alcohol to get on the dance floor and wasn't bothered much by the wild Aussies. Maybe I was the one who needed to do some "manning up" this time.

We met three girls, all around thirty though looking much younger through beer goggles. We took two of them to the beach and I was quickly making out with the one called Lenny (yes I know, first a Renny, than a Henny and now a Lenny). Darren had a better-looking girl named Lilly and made out with her a bit. Although I tried to get the girls back to our place, they declined and went home.

The following night we ran into them again and I focused on the third girl, named Harmony. She was stacked with even bigger boobs than the girl from Jakarta who was going to visit me. (For some reason girls with humongous boobs are attracted to me, poor me!)

I walked her back to her room along with Darren and Lilly. Since I had already danced and kissed with her I of course wanted to stay at her place, which would give Darren our room alone with Lilly. I stayed with Harmony and banged the living daylights out of her, twice that night and once in the morning, as I usually do. She was kind of voluptuous, but having her enormous boobs dangling in my face while she was her on top was great.

The next morning we kissed goodbye. Later at night I saw a very strange girl. She had the face of a 20-year-old but the length of an 8-year-old – and having quite a set of boobs, even though she couldn't have been taller than 1.10m. Now, before you think I'm some creepy weirdo/pedophile, she wasn't a midget with short legs and a big butt or looked like a child. Her whole body was in proportion except that it was a small version of a beautiful girl. She was always with a cute girlfriend of normal height. I knew just one thing after having banged just about every body type from skinny to fat and from short to tall: I just had to experience it.

People said she was a prostitute working together with

her girlfriend but I never saw her leave with a guy. Lots of guys approached her and so did I.

Over the next weeks I failed at every attempt to dance or even talk with her. She said I was too much of a Keong Racun, which is the term for a player/womanizer and literally means "poisonous snail". *Keong Racun* is also a famous song in Indonesia, and I saw it being performed by many live bands across the country. Everyone knows it; Donna had already sent me the link to a famous YouTube version of the song, lip-synched by two average-looking girls who became quite famous with it. (Search for Sinta and Jojo.) Darren eventually danced a bit with the short girl, but I couldn't get close to her without getting brushed off with the words "Keong Racun".

I decided to make the best of it, and made this word part of my Indonesian vocabulary. I even had a necklace made with a small wooden name tag with the letters Keong Racun. It was a great way to get some attention from girls.

I moved into a nicer room close by our hotel because I didn't want to meet Donna and stay in a dump with her. She acted a bit distant at the airport and went for the cheek kiss, but her eyes weren't lying to me. She moved in to the beautiful room which still cost only twenty-eight dollars a night. We were lying on the bed and we talked and flirted a bit. We both knew we were going to have sex with each other but I kept things exciting by playing push and pull.

After a while we started kissing and she went wild. I even told her to relax a bit because we had all the time in the world. She told me later she was ashamed of herself for being so damn horny. We went near animalistic in the following hours which was quite an accomplishment since I had been with Harmony the day before.

Twenty-nine year old Donna was very experienced between the sheets and I found out why later. I can't give too many details, but at the time I met her she had a European boyfriend who flew in every once in a while, as were two other fuck buddies doing the same. She had a good job as manager of one of the most expensive hotels in Jakarta.

She also had a girlfriend living in Kuta who hadn't been laid in four months, and we decided to hook Darren up with this girl. He had been dry since the beginning of his trip. It was time to see if my constantly being a pick-up drill sergeant had worked. Donna said that her friend had a car and we would drive around Bali a bit. So in the morning we went in the car and drove around to see all the sights and a couple of beaches.

Bonita was around the same age as Donna, about nine years older than Darren. She had a cute face and a set of thick legs with a round booty. I wouldn't say no to booty like that but Darren was hesitant.

The first night she stayed with him in his room but he didn't do anything more than watch a movie with her and sleep in separate beds. Of course when I found out, I went mental on him.

I ranted at him and asked if I had to come in his room and fuck her right in front of him to show him how it's done. I went too far and we got into an argument. We'd already been hanging out for four weeks and were starting to get on each other nerves. Still, he had sex with Bonita that night and I gave him a proud fist bump the next day.

Two days later Donna went back to work in Jakarta and I promised her I would visit her again. We had been on a bang-a-thon for three days and I needed to rest my balls a bit. I left the fancy hotel room the same day and went to another, cheaper hotel nearby, though not the same one Darren and I had stayed in at first. That one was too noisy in the morning.

I found a nice double room with bathroom and stayed there for the remainder of my time in Kuta.

Darren stayed with Bonita for several days but I had the feeling that I had pushed him too hard. He said that he was not that attracted to her and that they had didn't have much to talk about. According to him the age difference was quite annoying too.

I was a bit angry with him because he didn't really want to do much during the day. I wanted to go to the beach but not alone; it made me feel awkward to be on my own with large groups of people around me. I met Lilly again and hooked up with her, which may seem like a dick move towards Darren but he had a girlfriend now, and had only kissed Lilly twice anyway.

She said that she'd wanted to get together with me that night on the beach, but I was with her girlfriend Lenny then. I didn't know how much I could believe her, because I heard from Darren that she was still sending him texts sometimes. I of course had kissed her one friend (Lenny) and banged the other (Harmony) so I couldn't say much about it.

We had a lot of fun and went out together almost every night. Lilly was a sweet and smart girl with a great tiny body. She was quite shy and careful between the sheets but soon became much wilder when the orgasms came, something she had never experienced in her previous marriage with some local dickhead who beat her from time to time.

Lilly owned a small business so she had to go into the office every day. At night she would sleep in my room. I was bored as fuck during the day and when she couldn't go out one night I went out alone – going dolo, as it's called in pick-up terms.

In Club Bounty I saw a tall muscular blonde girl who looked Russian standing next to a pillar. I walked up to her and asked her if she indeed was Russian. Her eyes widened and she stumbled: "How do you know?" I told her about my two months travelling in Russia and she obviously liked to hear that. I went with her and her girlfriend to the beach the next day.

Vicki was muscular and when I asked about it she said she'd been arm-wrestling for many years on a student team. She had a great lean body and a firm butt. I couldn't get far with her beyond one make-out that night.

We went for some food later that night and arm-wrestled; I won but barely. "Your powers are weak, old man," she said. No, not really, but that would have been cool. I was glad I won but wouldn't have been too ashamed if I hadn't. She was strong and I was weakened from travelling and my daily diet of beer and junk food. I could see she wasn't that interested in a holiday romance, and except for going to the beach a few times I kept her at a bit of a distance. I was still texting with Donna a lot and even the girls I had met in Medan were still texting me crazy messages, but I hardly replied to them. I had to be careful that Bonita didn't see me with Lilly, and Darren had to make excuses for me too.

One day I decided to learn how to surf and went to the beach to get some lessons from local guys there – I didn't feel like paying thirty-five dollars to get a four-hour boot camp with four others at an official surf school. The guys on the beach were sitting in the shade, renting out boards and giving cheap lessons. I went into the water with the instructor and after a while I was able to stand up and surf a bit.

At one point when I fell of the board for the hundredth time, I hurt my foot and got a huge cut in it. It bled quite heavily but since I was just starting to enjoy being able to stand up and surf, and salt water sterilizes anyway, I continued the lesson until it really started to hurt. My foot was swelling a bit and the surfer dudes put some ice on it.

It kept bleeding and they said it would be better to stop now and return tomorrow to continue the lesson for free. I agreed and limped back to the hotel.

The funny thing was that my swim shorts were totally ripped up too. I had no idea how it happened but I must have looked like an idiot limping with a bloody foot and trying to hide my ripped up shorts by holding a small bag in front of it. The cut in my foot was quite nasty and the skin was damaged as well. I couldn't wear a flip-flop on that foot because the cut was just where the sandal strap was. I could walk barefoot in the streets in the evening, which isn't weird in a beach town, but during the day the pavement was too bloody hot to walk on. I let the wound dry out all day but at night I had to wear something to the bars, so I taped some bandages on my foot and used my flip flops again. This opened up the cut every night. It took nine days and a new pair of shoes to get the wound to close and heal. This was my first and only surfing experience; I wanted to surf in other countries, but found board rental prices and lessons too expensive in Australia and Brazil.

Bonita had to start working again and Darren and I started hanging out a bit more than we had been the last little while. I had to avoid Darren if he was with Bonita because I didn't want her to see me with Lilly and tell Donna about it. I really liked Donna and she had promised that I could stay at the hotel where she worked for free.

Darren and I took a boat to the nearby Gili islands and stayed there for four days. The other guests included a lot of English guys who got shitfaced and played cards every night. I, of course, was on the pussy hunt every day but didn't have much success. I really didn't like western girls anymore at that point. Most of them were overweight and didn't take good care of themselves. No need to start a rant about western girls again, but let's say I wasn't too fond of fat girls dancing like wild monkeys and being so drunk that you could hardly talk to them. When you already know you have a cute skinny girl with silky skin and beautiful black hair waiting for you and after that another cute one with giant knockers who has a free room for you in a five-star hotel, you are not too bothered to find something new.

After four days I left and Darren stayed behind one more day boozing with his English drinking buddies. I stayed in Kuta for another six days with Lilly before I said goodbye to both her and Darren. There's so much more I could tell about the time in Kuta: the hassles we had to extend our visas, both getting stomach flu, the places we visited on Bali, the shop girls and waitresses I was flirting with. The time I forgot my bank card at the convenience store and a store guy went out of his way to find me, the ladyboys riding around on scooters in the middle of the night and following you in the small alleys on the way to your hotel. I laughed when I saw stupidly drunken guys being lured into the alleys by luscious "babes" – they were in for a surprise. The look on the faces of convenience store girls when I bought lots of condoms almost three times a week, the statue of a Ronald McDonald on a surfboard, the time that…

Indonesia – Jakarta second visit

There have been only two occasions that I had someone waiting for me when I arrived somewhere. The second time was when I came home. The first time was in Jakarta.

Donna waited for me at Jakarta airport and there was even a driver with her to take me to the hotel. I had definitely hit the jackpot with Donna.

When we arrived at the hotel it was all luxury and class. This time I wouldn't stay in a dirty old room and flush a toilet with a bucket of water. This was an enormous five-star, resort-like hotel where I could jump in the pool or take a free jet-ski ride whenever I wanted. Basically everything I wanted to do, eat or drink was free. Donna had to work that day but still came to our huge room every now and then and we banged like crazy. Her E-cups were hard to resist. And of course it wasn't all about the sex. She is a genuine kind and friendly girl. Always smiling and in a happy mood, even if I wasn't. Not once have I seen her grumpy or angry.

In the evening I went to the restaurant and feasted on the massive buffet there. Tables of delicious food including lobster, shrimps, T-bone steaks and other kinds of expensive food. This was a huge difference from the rice and chicken or Big Macs I had eaten in Bali every day.

After the dessert, which included lots of delicious ice cream and fruits, I could barely stand up and walk to the elevator myself. This went on for three days. I think I gained a couple of pounds in just a few days. In the morning I would eat the breakfast buffet. I would order room service for lunch and ate $18 steak sandwiches, and in the evening it was dinner buffet time again. I was enjoying the good life.

I noticed that there were massages on the room service menu and asked Donna if I could get one. "Yeah, sure," she said and ordered a masseuse for me. The masseuses I had seen walking around the hotel were young hot girls.

I was looking forward to a hot massage from one of those girls but when I opened the door there was a 40-year-old woman with arms like a WWF wrestler. Disappointed but still looking forward to a massage I lay down on the bed and was dumb enough to say that I like a strong massage. Well, this roided-up woman massaged the living daylights out of me. She was almost breaking my ribs and spine but the worst was still to come: my legs. I don't know how she did it but I had tears in my eyes when she "massaged" my calves and feet. Saying that it was too strong didn't help much. Afterwards I could barely stand up straight, and walking hurt because of my battered calves.

Donna and I always had open talks about everything and I jokingly accused her of sending that female butcher up to my room. She laughed and said she didn't anything about it. "Can I have another one tomorrow?" I asked her. "Yeah, no problem," she said. I made the phone call to the reception myself this time and specifically asked for a young, good-looking girl and an oil massage. I even made the guy repeat a few times.

Now nothing stood in my way from a nice hot girl coming up to the room. I was wrong again. The woman who showed up wasn't a young hot girl but about 36 years old, though she had a nice big butt. She gave me an oil massage (which still hurt like hell since my body was still battered from the day before) and I tried to game her a bit but she kept asking for a big tip if I wanted something extra.

As I said before, Donna and I talked openly about sex and relationships, and it became clear to me that she considered me as a fuck buddy, or a "bed friend" as she named it. There was some feeling involved but she had a few other guys who visited her from time to time too. There was the Spanish business man who visited sometimes, an Australian one as well and an English pilot who flew around the world and came to see her when he flew to Jakarta. Hearing this hurt my ego a bit, and while I'm never actually jealous of someone this guy made me feel a bit green with envy. She showed me a picture of him and the guy was ripped and handsome. He made tons of money as an airline pilot and probably had hot girls waiting for him all over the world. I decided not to be a complete hypocrite and forgot what she had told me. She was attracted to me and that should be enough; I shouldn't show her beta behavior like jealousy and neediness.

On Saturday night Donna, some friends of her that worked in the hotel and I went to Stadium, supposedly the biggest club in South East Asia.

Since Indonesia is a Muslim country and Muslims aren't allowed to drink alcohol, the whole crowd was doing ecstasy tabs. I tried one for the first time in my life. Donna paid for the tablet, that cost twenty dollars in Jakarta. In Holland you can buy that crap for three dollars. I didn't feel so different but had trouble standing in one place. The whole crowd was dancing and raving away but it looked boring and it was very cold inside. It was a giant sausage-fest without many hot girls around. I shared half a tab more with one of Diana's friends.

One of her girlfriends who worked at the hotel was there too and she looked smoking hot. Her boyfriend was a quiet and dorky guy and I wondered how he ever landed a cute girl like her. She was wearing braces and it made me feel horny as hell. Every time Donna looked away I took a peek at her girlfriend's tight round booty that was perfectly fitted in her jeans. Sorry, Donna. I know you're reading this.

The ecstasy was making me feel extra horny and Donna and I jumped in a cab and went back to the room. We showered but I noticed that my ding dong wasn't working that well. Was it the ecstasy in combination with lots of beers? Probably. It made a good excuse for trying out the Cialis I had bought in the Philippines. I took a whole tab and for the next few hours I couldn't stop fucking. I had all this energy from the ecstasy and a raging boner from the Cialis. It was unlike everything I had ever experienced. Donna moaned and shouted out loud while I kept banging her like a machine gun with unlimited ammo. People were banging on the walls and door and yelling at her to be quiet.

I couldn't believe I had so much energy. Usually after ten or fifteen minutes my tongue was already hitting the ground and I had to stop before my heart exploded. Half my trip I had been in the worst shape ever and now I felt like a superman. Even after we stopped banging after a few hours I couldn't sleep and at 10am in the morning I was still up and writing a long email to Darren, who left Indonesia that day.

When I woke up in the afternoon I felt like shit. I was dead tired and my nose and throat were seriously hurting. I blamed the cold club and the fact that the air conditioning had been on all night while we were banging and sleeping. Donna felt fine except for the fact that she had trouble walking from being sore between the legs and having muscle pain.

242

I didn't want to eat that day and felt sick; I even threw up that night, which was embarrassing because Donna heard it.

The next morning we had to move to another hotel because we couldn't carry on too long for free in that expensive room. Donna paid for another hotel where she claimed she got a huge discount but I don't know if that was true. I feared she paid for everything and tried to pay for stuff too. She let me pay small bills like the drinking bill in Memories earlier that week or a cheap taxi ride.

This room was luxurious too and on the seventeenth floor and had a great view over the city. I was feeling worse and worse by the minute but still went out to bars with her. The thought of beer drinking strengthened me.

I saw Mona again at Memories. I had messaged her on Facebook and she came to say hello to me and give a cold hello to Donna. Mona had not forgotten the night I lost interest in her and probably blamed Donna and her enormous busty chest for this.

That night I eased my sore throat with some beers and ate a bit but during the day I was sick as a dog again. I didn't smoke anymore and barely ate. After two nights we moved to yet another hotel, the Formula One. It was a bit of a touristy place but still very nice.

I agreed to see Mona in Memories at ten at night and she drank a lot and flirted like crazy with me, asking me to come to her room and fuck her. I wanted to but I had to be back at the hotel at midnight and knew I wouldn't make it. Annie, the girl I had sex with with in Memories café the first time I visited Jakarta was there too and pulled my arm again. Choice enough but I had to be back by midnight like some Cinderella player.

The bad thing was that Donna didn't even show up until 1:15 and I could've had gone with Mona in the meanwhile. Well, you can't win them all, and I already had a rich cute girl in my bed that was a sexual freak and pleased me in many ways.

Donna dragged me to the hospital the next day where I had the doctor examine me. He said I had a vicious throat infection and had to take antibiotics. Donna paid the $50 hospital bill but I insisted I give her the money back, which I did. The antibiotics were doing miracles and after the first round of pills my appetite came back. Donna went off to work and I invited Mona to visit me in my room. She agreed to come and see me there at eight in the evening. I had worked out an evil and cunning plan to smuggle her in through the escape exit doors so that the guards or reception workers couldn't see her and rat me out to Donna.

Mona chickened out and never showed up that night.
My extended visa ran out and I had to say goodbye to Donna. We checked out of the hotel and I went to her room in a clearly poorer area of Jakarta. She gave me an amazing goodbye blowjob and we made some naughty pictures and videos together. I sure do miss her.

Two hours later we said goodbye at the airport and I took a plane to Singapore.

Philippines – Cebu again

I had been very successful with the ladies over the last couple of weeks and it felt damn good. I flew to Singapore airport, waited there a while and flew back to the Philippines again. It almost felt like flying home. By now, Cebu especially was familiar ground for me.

Jenna was at work when I arrived at her new small room with bathroom at four in the morning. She worked at a call center serving the American market and because of the time difference she worked night shifts. The security guard gave me the key to her room and I fell asleep on her small bed.

I woke when I felt her big fleshy lips kiss my cheek. There she was: the only girl I had very strong feelings for other than Julia. I looked up to her and after my eyes made it past her enormous cleavage I saw her smiling eyes. I made love to her and we fell asleep again.

When we woke up we were both hungry and decided to visit a place we had been to a hundred times before, the McDonalds at Escario street. It was like seeing old friends again. The tall pretty girl working behind the counter, the cleaner who looked like a monkey with his facial structure and hairy arms, the bald security guard who always cleaned tables, and of course the girl with the enormous round ass. Not a hot-looking girl, but one with the biggest bubble butt in the Phils. I always joked to Jenna that I would take over a local strip club and would have this girl shake her ass to some reageaton beats. For sure I'd make a ton of money since big round bubble butts are unusual over there.

I had promised to stay a while with Jenna but I wanted to go to the South soon. Jenna had met a Swedish guy after I left. It was my own fault, I had made a very stupid post on Facebook while I was in Malaysia and she got all mad over it and went out that night. The guy had picked her up and she had been dating him for a while. I was not happy to hear about but I couldn't blame her. She probably thought she'd never see me again.

My original plan was to move on to Australia after Indonesia, just like Darren, but I found out that prices were horrible there: for the ten-day period from before Christmas till after New Year's Eve the prices would go up to maybe seventy dollars a night for a dorm bed in some hostel. Since my Canadian friend D-Lux was now living in the Phils and had told me I could stay with him for free for a while, I'd changed my plans and flown to the Phils first. The fact that I would see Jenna again and that D-Lux was promising me a fuckfest in his city made it an easy decision, though I think that Jenna was the main reason I went back. I really liked her. It was no news to Jenna that I had banged a lot in Indonesia, no matter how many albums I blocked on my Facebook. I had forgotten one mutual girl in our friends list and she had seen my Indonesia pictures.

This changed our relationship a bit but she had been with someone else too in the meantime, so we both decided not to talk about it too much.

Time flew by and there were only a few hours a day when we could see each other. Donna from Jakarta called me a few times and we agreed to meet in Manila. She would fly there and we would spend some time together there.

Instead of learning Spanish on my laptop I just downloaded a shitload of movies and watched the whole *Star*

Wars series again, which helped me come up with the pseudonym Neil Skywalker. Though I'm not some nerdy fan boy, I like the movies, and especially the idea of using the Force. The idea for some sort of book was already there and making a website came to mind, but I didn't have a clue where to start. I knew nothing of designing and programming. My friend D-Lux had promised me to help me out and since he used to design (porn) sites I wanted to visit him, sooner rather than later.

I had lived at Jenna's place for two weeks and all we did was hang out in the mall, visit the cinema and bang twice a day. It was time to leave again and the goodbye was less emotional than last time. I promised to come back and see her one more time for a few days before flying to Australia. I didn't know what to expect in D-Lux's city but I knew it was going to be good.

Philippines – The south

I hammered at the big red gate and slowly D-Lux came out. It was the afternoon and he was wiping the sleep out of his eyes. D-Lux rented a massive crib in the suburbs in a city whose name I won't give since I might want to go back there someday.

D-Lux's crib had three bedrooms, all with bathrooms, a giant kitchen, an office space, a bar and a giant living room. There was a garden around the house and a maid's bedroom and bathroom in the back. He only paid about $450 rent a month for this including utilities and a fast Wi-Fi connection. D-Lux has a passive income and was basically already retired.

The house was way too big for one person alone, and personally I would have chosen a smaller place closer to the center for a similar price. Then again, I'm not used to big American houses. I got a bedroom in his house and this would be my new room for a while. The house didn't have much furniture yet since D-Lux had only moved in a few months ago but I had a small one-person bed. I was happy to see a familiar face again, and though D-Lux isn't the type to show a whole lot of emotion, I could see he was happy to have a buddy there too. The city barely has any foreigners and the ones who are there are old geezers, dirty grampas as D-Lux called them.

Some girl stayed over in my bed the night I arrived but I couldn't get a bang out of her. I kept in touch with her for a while but never convinced her to change her mind.

The second night we went out and D-Lux brought a girlfriend with him. We met a few friends of hers and I talked to two of them. I flirted a bit with the younger-looker girl and later found out that she was only seventeen years old. That's very young, so that was out of the question. I noticed the older sister telling the younger girl to go home because it was getting late. I told her that she was being a bit harsh on her little sister and that's when she told me that it was her daughter. It would be my first real MILF and it was game on!

An hour or so later I took her back to the house. Veronica was already forty–two and had four kids, She looked like she was around thirty and in some pictures we took together she looks even younger than that.

She had all her children by C-section, so she was still very tight down there. I enjoyed being with her and she stayed almost four days with me. D-Lux and his current girlfriend didn't mind because she was a friend of theirs.

Veronica didn't mind taking it up the bum and at one point that was the only thing I did with her. Later I told her I needed some time for myself and she left.

This gave me a chance to go out with D-Lux again, and we soon sat down in a bar in a part of town with lots of bars and clubs in one small spot. It was my thirty-fourth birthday that day. He told me to approach some girls walking by. I still had some approach anxiety and declined. "Let the Grandmaster Pimp show you how it's done," he said, and stood up and walked over to two young girls walking past the terrace we were on. They sat down with us and we ordered a bucket of Tanduay Ice, a bucket of five bottles of rum-based drinks that only costs around three and a half dollar.

We had some drinks and the hottest of two was really interested in me. Prices are so low that even a backpacker like me can order a few rounds.

We invited them to go to D-Lux's house to sing some

videoke and drink some more. I ended up having steamy sex.

She had model-like features. I even tried to videotape our sex, but she was on to me and closed the closet I had my camera in. We showered afterwards and she let me take a few pictures of her. Her body was amazing and I will always remember her silk-like skin and extremely beautiful face. I thought it was the best present I could wish for. A moment later I realized I had been with Julia the year before and remembered our island trip together. It made me feel sad.

The next morning we went for a few more rounds of pounding and had breakfast afterwards. D-Lux came out of his room with his usual grumpy smile. He'd done his thing too with the other girl.

He lived in the suburbs so the mall was far away. There was a restaurant within a few hundred meters and it was a typical Philippine street restaurant: a couple of young girls selling rice and ten different side dishes. A nice meal for less than a dollar. In backpacker terms I had hit the jackpot: living at D-Lux's house was free and I could eat three meals for under four dollars. On days when I did nothing I rarely spent more than five or six dollars on food and drinks.

The birthday girl was looking for a boyfriend and I told her I wasn't looking for the same thing yet. We exchanged numbers and she left.

D-Lux and I went out again and this time I did the approaching. I walked up to some girls and asked if they would sit with us. Normally this wouldn't be a strong line but here it doesn't matter much. We talked a bit and had a few drinks in a club. D-Lux didn't like the girls and went home while I walked the two girls back.

One of them was named Carry and lived in a poor area of town where foreigners usually never go. It wasn't a straw hut slum but it was definitely a poor area. Carry had a very small room there. The mattress just fitted between the walls lengthwise. It was that small.

We bought a few beers at the convenience store and I was out of condoms again. I actually stole a pack from the store because I didn't want them to know I was buying rubbers right in front of them.

We went back to the room and the three of us went to sleep on a mattress one meter wide. It was kind of crowded and I started making out with the thicker one, Carry, and was feeling her under her skirt. She got horny but the other girl, who had a far hotter body, hesitated. I soldiered on and got her half-naked too. I was lying in the middle of the mattress and holding a big boob with my left hand and a small boob with my right. This went on for a while but I couldn't get a threesome out of it. We went back to sleep again.

When we woke up somewhere past noon, the skinnier girl left and I was having sex with Carry within ten minutes. It felt good; we had good chemistry together and knew how to please each other. So what if she wasn't the hottest girl around, she was nice and even cooked me breakfast while I was hanging out with her friends.

The room she rented was in a building with several other people where all the cooking was done in a central corridor. Most people spent the day sitting there talking and watching some television on a small fifteen-inch screen. People were friendly without wanting anything from you. Carry and I said goodbye and I took a jeepney back to the suburbs.

Why spend four dollars on a taxi if I can get the same ride for twelve cents? If I saved some money here I figured I could spend a bit more elsewhere. This way I can also actually see something of the city and interact with its residents.

A couple of days later another girlfriend of D-Lux came by, and she stayed with him for a long time. In fact she became his regular girlfriend. Her name was Rachel and she was a really good-looking and friendly girl. She was quite the cook, too, and made some delicious pork adobo, probably the best meal I had in all the time I stayed in the Phils. It even made me a bit jealous of D-Lux for having a girl who could cook like that.

I was walking over to the convenience store daily, where I'd buy some iced coffee and a whole roasted chicken every day of the week. I'm a simple eater – fancy stuff is nice, but I can live on the same food for a long time. Sometimes I ate the chicken at once and poured it down with some beer. A whole delicious chicken for 140 pesos, which is like three-and-a-half dollars, is dirt cheap. I never saw cheaper chicken anywhere; even in poor Bolivia it was more expensive.

Rachel brought a girlfriend over to D Lux's house and I slept with her too. Candy was very short, just like most Philippine girls, and also quite fanatic between the sheets.

I had to go out by myself for a while now, since D-Lux was staying with his girlfriend all the time and blowing his money on drugs, something I had a few discussions with him about. I met two very young girls and I took one of them home, which was always easy to do since my friend had a videoke installation and a cute little Chihuahua dog. I loved that little over-excited dog. Whenever I tried to pick a girl up, this was one of the things that really helped me out.

After talking to them for a while I would ask them if they wanted to go to my place and have a drink or two, quite a few girls would say no since my buddies house was far away from the center. Showing a picture of the dog and letting them know I had a videoke machine usually hooked them in.

So this girl went home with me and spent the night, but when we started to make out and things got heated up, she shouted out "Yours is too big and too strong!!" She was very skinny, almost too skinny; she still had a nice rack, though, and I wondered what she would look like if she gained a few kilos. She said she only had a few Korean boyfriends before and they didn't pack much of a punch. She wouldn't even let me try and all I got that night was a blowjob. She said I had to warn her when I came. I didn't and still remember the betrayed look on her face.

In the meantime I was getting at least a hundred texts a day. This was even worse than Indonesia. I still had the same phone number from my first time in the Phils, when I stayed four months. Girls I met during that time were texting me, Jenna was texting me, Donna from Indonesia was texting, it drove me crazy. Girls in the Philippines will give your number to other girls and they want to "practice their English with you", in other words this means hang out with you but usually just to chat. Sometimes they even actually want to practice English. I was going crazy from the endlessly ringing phone and having to charge it every night.

I stopped doing dates with girls I met online after a while because the results were horrendous. Girls would show up with two other girls so you'd always have to pay for three people when having a coffee in a Starbucks rip-off in the mall. And of course the dates went nowhere this way. I tackled this problem by making girls promise that they would show up at a place alone. I would tell them that we'd be meeting in a mall and that they didn't need bodyguards for that. It's a good method to weed out the shy girls and the ones who even show up with their mom – yes, really, this happens.

Having a free room at D-Lux's place saved me a lot of money and I helped him out by buying a couple of dozens of beers a few times and fixing a few minor things in and around the house. I paid some money for the electric and water bill and shared the costs of the Internet bill. Although I now shamefully admit it was reluctantly.

I wanted to work out my idea for a website and D-Lux agreed to help me with it. He had designed websites before but we couldn't agree on which software to use. He started designing with Dreamweaver but I was afraid if something went wrong it would take ages to fix. I found out about Wordpress , where I could do things myself, though I had no clue how to build a website and had to start from scratch.

D-Lux said he didn't know how to work with my software and withdrew from the whole thing. Still, he made a few awesome headers for me and even designed a business card while I was in Ecuador.

I wasn't allowed to bring girls to the house all the time anymore; I suspected that D-Lux's girlfriend, who also lived in the house now, had complained about it. Also, D-Lux was careful with his belongings. Can't blame him really. He had had a few break-ins in Vietnam, and in the Phils some girls had taken stuff from his house while partying there.

One night out I met Selma, a friend of the skinny ´´ too big, too strong´´ girl that had stayed with me. She was short, had nice legs and an amazing set of big lips. I couldn't stop staring at them. After a few drinks I went with her to a cheap ten-dollar hotel and spend the night with her there.

Taking a jeepney back to the suburbs the next day, I met a girl. I was lucky to be alone with her on there because normally jeepneys are packed with people. I flirted and talked with her and within a few minutes I had her phone number. I had just said goodbye to Selma a few minutes before and I was already picking up another girl.

We rode the jeepney till we both were close to D-Lux's house and parted there.

We met for coffee that night and she went home with me. I was very attracted to her and was giving myself mental high fives. Her big luscious lips were even more beautiful than Selma's. She stayed with me a few days but soon enough I got bored even of banging this cute girl up the bum. She was asking me to impregnate her all the time and I was wondering if I needed a secretary to answer all my texts and an accountant to keep track of all the banging I did.

It became one big blur of girls. Veronica was coming over every once in a while, I met new girls and went on dates all the time, a couple of times a week I went out the bars and clubs in the center. If I didn't score I could always call Carry and take a taxi there and sleep, shower and fuck at her place. I wanted to see the birthday girl again and we met in a club down town. Her younger sister came with her too and their first names differed in only one letter, so it was hard to tell them apart.

They went home with me and the three of us ended up in my small bed. There was barely room to move around but I started kissing the birthday girl and went for her younger, 17-year-old sister too. This was my chance of scoring a threesome with two sisters, but it remained a fantasy. There was no way that was going to happen because her younger sister was already reluctant to share the bed. She had already had a baby at sixteen, so she wasn't exactly new to sex.

The next morning we played some darts in the living room and I introduced them to D-Lux, who always said he was my pimping teacher but was starting to wonder how I pulled all the talent.

That night I had an argument with him when I wanted to bring over two other girls. At one point he agreed to it and I brought them there; nothing happened that night but they had already left when he woke up in the afternoon. I later met one of them again and smuggled her in, telling D-Lux it was Veronica who had been with me the night before. D-Lux was in a daze all the time from doing a lot of dope.

We had a few words again about it and I tried to talk some sense into him, because he was blowing all his money on drugs at that point. We had quite an argument for the rest of the night.

We talked it out after he told me that I had to get the fuck out of his house when he suspected I was after one of the club girls he really liked. I wasn't after her, but someone who is all aggressive and dazed from drug use is hard to talk to. I had already been staying for four weeks at his place and it was time to move on.

On one of the last nights I went out, I met an Australian guy in his late thirties.

This guy was stone cold crazy and lived there in the city. When we talked in the bar, he had a girl with him and I thought it was his regular girlfriend, but he had just met her the day before. We talked about girls for a bit.

The Aussie wanted to go to the beach at night, and now I was the one who did a pimp-style move like the one D-Lux had shown me on my birthday. I walked straight up to two girls, talked to them a bit, and convinced them to come to the beach with us.

The five of us got into his sports car and this guy was driving like a maniac. I'm not easily scared, and as you know I'd been on some crazy rides before, but that still doesn't mean I wanted to return home in a body bag. We ended up (alive) at some karaoke place close to the beach and had a few drinks there while the three girls were singing and dancing.

At the end the Aussie wanted to go to a love motel with his girl and I had to choose between the other two. It felt stupid because until that point I hadn't made a choice yet. When I chose a girl, she said she was ok with it, but I had the feeling the other one wouldn't have said no either.

The guys working at the motel tried to cheat me out of a lot of money by changing the rates. They kept making problems and I said that in that case we'd only stay a few hours.

The room was luxurious and had a beautiful bathroom. We did our thing there and slept a few hours afterwards. In the morning we took a taxi to the mall and she bumped her head really hard on the front seat when the driver made a sudden stop. She was lucky not to have broken her nose.

Two nights before I left I went out with the Australian guy again but I think he was all fucked up on pills or something. He was super hyper and ruining all our chances with chicks. I called up the girl I'd smuggled into D-Lux's house before and took her home with me. The Aussie was pissed off and drove off like an insane racecar driver, almost running over a small group of people. I was glad to get rid of that maniac.

He texted me again the next morning and asked me to go out again. I declined and spend the afternoon with my girl.

Veronica was planning to say goodbye to me and before she showed up I had to ditch my current girl, who was the tallest Philippine girl I had been with. Veronica came by to say goodbye but couldn't stay. She massaged me like she always did and we had sex for the very last time. She walked out of the gate and had to walk fifteen minutes back to the main street just to get a jeepney and sit on it for another hour before she could get home to her children. When I saw her walking away I truly felt like a miserable bastard for having used her like this. She knew damn well I was banging lots of other girls but still wanted to see me all the time even though I never spend a dime on her except for a bit of food from the street restaurant sometimes. We still have contact.

I sat down in my room and packed my bag. I thought about Jenna back in Cebu. It had been five weeks since I last saw her but it felt like a lifetime.

In the last five weeks I had sex with only six girls and had gotten blowjobs and make outs from a lot of others. Six girls isn't even that much but I had been switching back and forth between them and treated some of them really badly and now I had to face Jenna again. I had had at least nine or ten other dates, some of which were hilarious; I had been texting and chatting with girls online all the time and had wasted much valuable time that I could have spent learning Spanish or building my website. I was about to go to South America in a few months and didn't speak a word of Spanish yet.

I said goodbye to D-Lux and his girlfriend and promised to visit again someday. I intend to keep that promise. Afterwards I took yet another airplane in the Philippines. I almost knew the stewardesses by now.

I still have minor Facebook contact with most of the girls I met in D-Lux's city.

Back in Cebu and Manila

Jenna didn't look too happy when she saw me coming to her door. Of course she knew I was coming but she also knew was that I'd been with a lot of other girls. She's a clever girl and can do the math when a guy like me stays away for five weeks. She was disappointed that I had left a week before Christmas and not stayed with her during Christmas and my birthday. Being the biggest hypocrite in the world and hating myself for it, I accused her of seeing the Swedish guy again.

We had arguments all the time and I was being a dick to her. Deep down I knew it was all my own fault and that I'd been chasing meaningless sex while I had a girl who loved me.

At night we would make up and have great sex but it couldn't be the same as before. My mind was like a raging tornado; I told myself to keep on banging girls all over the world one moment and told myself to settle down the next. If I settled down what would become of my round-the-world trip, my book and my life in the future? Staying with Jenna wouldn't be fair to Julia, who I think loved me twice as much as Jenna and would almost catch a bullet for me. She has a better job, an athletic model-like body and lived in a second-world country instead of a third-world one. I knew she was almost thirty and wanted to have kids but so did Jenna even though she was only twenty-three at the time.

When I looked in Jenna's eyes I melted, but I couldn't get this raging storm out of my head. I stayed in her room and had nothing to do all day but think and worry. Donna had changed her mind on coming to meet me in Manila; I had fucked it up by not keeping in touch enough with her in the last weeks.

If I'd just emailed or texted her every two or three days I wouldn't have fucked things up so much. I talked to her on the phone and she said she might be able to meet me in Singapore when I had to stay there a few nights before I finally flew to Australia. But that wasn't the same.

The last night I spent with Jenna I tried to keep things cool and make it a nice night together. She had taken a day off to stay with me and I had to mess it up again with some jealousy shit. We fought again and I hated myself...

The three Julias in Russia, all those girls in Cambodia, several one-night stands in other countries, Donna and Lilly in Indonesia and all those girls I banged at my buddy's house, it became a blur in my mind. Girls who had good jobs, girls who barely had anything, girls who loved me, girls who hated me, the drama and the fights in Cambodia, my phone that kept ringing all day. Jealousy, rage, why am I here? Why do I not have a wife and family back home? What idiot travels around the world for this long? Am I a winner or a loser? What am I running from? I felt angry, I felt powerless.... I felt exactly like I did years before on the weekends when I always went out and couldn't get a girlfriend. I was too scared to approach or talk to any girls, stood around awkwardly trying to be cool, walked home and kicked garbage cans out of frustration and self-hatred, telling myself I would be better the next week, only to do the same thing all over again.

After picking up all these girls, I still felt bad for myself. Tears rolled down my cheeks, Jenna cried too. We fell asleep in each others' arms.

We said goodbye the next morning and I went back to Manila to stay a few days, meet some friends and hang out in the guesthouse. I relaxed a bit and started thinking about my trip. I felt better about myself after letting go of all my emotions the days before, but felt very uneasy being alone at night. For the last couple of months I had not been alone much. In fact since Bali I had only slept alone a couple of times in D-Lux's house; most of the nights I had a girl staying over, either a fuckbuddy or a new one.

One girl who always stayed in the guesthouse was interested in me. She was in her thirties and I knew her from the times I'd stayed in this guesthouse before. Picking her up was a piece of cake and we went to a love hotel nearby, had sex and that was it. A day later I ran into my first Filipina girl in the guesthouse again and banged her too.

On one of the last days I met a friend of Carry's, the girl who lived in the poor area in the city in the south. I had met Yhana there and the three of us had some chicken dinner in a nearby street restaurant. She was pretty and had a nice set of boobs and nicely shaped lips. She wanted to see me in Manila and I agreed to it. She flaked on me the first night and the day later I noticed her sitting in the bar across the street from the guesthouse. I walked over, said what I had to say about her flaking on me and sat down with her. She was there with her "sister", who was a ladyboy, and another girl. Yhana went for my charms.

We walked along the Manila Bay waterfront and started kissing. She bit me in the lip a couple of times and it really hurt. I told her to stop or I would leave. She stopped doing it for but started biting me again a few minutes later. I gave her a short soft slap in the face, pointed my finger at her and told her again not to do it anymore. She actually got excited by that and we went to a love hotel nearby. She was only nineteen years old but when she dropped her towel after the shower her body looked and felt very saggy, her breasts looked big before but felt like deflated balloons now. Her skin was soft but her legs and arms were flabby.
She had done a good job hiding all this in her tight dress before. She had probably gained a lot of weight when she was pregnant before and lost it all afterwards. It felt weird.

After a short blowjob she mounted me and I felt absolutely nothing. It was like she was riding me without me being inside. We switched to missionary and again I felt nothing, she was wider than the room we were doing it in.

Finishing was nearly impossible like this. I'd already had trouble with it since I had so much sex with so many girls I didn't feel much for. Doggy style always worked but this time I had to bang so hard that my heart rate went through the roof and I needed to catch my breath for several minutes afterwards. It surprised me that she had actually enjoyed all of it and asked for more.

How the hell could she have liked it? I felt like I was fucking air when I was inside her, she couldn't have felt much either. She started getting wild again but my dick was out of service. She jumped on me and began biting me again, telling me to rape her. Wow, this girl was a freak.

I slapped her around a bit and choked her, and she became wilder and wilder and fought back like a lioness. I was not in the mood to have sex again but wanted to please her anyway; I used my fingers and kept putting more of them inside her all the time until nearly my whole hand disappeared inside her. WTF! When she was finally satisfied, we slept a bit and left the room later. The only thing she said was not to tell her girlfriend what happened. Yhana was beautiful to look at but the worst lay ever. Another mindless fuck with someone I barely knew. I still have most girls on my Facebook but except for Jenna I don't have much contact with them.

I had forgotten all the guilt, regret and self-pity I felt in Cebu.

Nr 40.

Half way there....

Chapter Four – Oceania

Oceania – Australia

My plan was to go from the Philippines to Australia, then visit New Zealand and carry on to South America. Looking into things, I found that single flights were horribly expensive, especially the one from New Zealand to Argentina or Chile ($2-3,000). It turned out to actually be cheaper to buy a round-the-world ticket. A lot cheaper. I paid $1,700 for this: Singapore to Sydney, Sydney to Auckland, Auckland to Buenos Aires –and even an extra flight include from Buenos Aires to Santiago de Chile. Four flights for less money than just one.

The only problem was that I had to decide how long I was going to stay in Australia and New Zealand. I figured twenty-five days each would be enough. The countries were horribly expensive anyway and I didn't want to spend much money in a western country. South America and hot Latinas were waiting on the other side.

I flew from Manila to Singapore, stayed there two days, and flew to Sidney. Donna told me that she couldn't meet me there. This was the second time she'd promised something and called it off later. She then said she'd try to meet up in Sydney and spend some time with me again. It never happened and I lost contact with her not much later, when she told me she was going to move to Perth and stay with one of her boyfriends, and probably marry him. She's too wild to ever be a long-term relationship option for me, but still I had such a good time with her that she is still on my mind from time to time. But so are many other girls too.

The Brisbane customs had it in for me: I had to make a short stop there before I flew to Sydney. After a long interview, a study of my passport and ongoing tickets, I was able to convince them I was only planning on doing some sightseeing and would then be moving on to New Zealand. Non-Australians over thirty aren't allowed to work in Australia, so customs are worried when they see rogue backpackers coming into the country who might take on an illegal job there.

Everything in Sidney, and I mean everything, was

expensive. I stayed in a hostel that looked like a backpacker factory.

There must have been at least four hundred people there so everything was really impersonal. The ten-person dorm cost twenty–six dollars a night and I spend about ten to fifteen dollars a day on food. The cheapest pack of cigarettes was twelve dollars and a pack of Marlboros cost eighteen dollars.

Except for the sightseeing I didn't like the city at all. Sure, the Sydney Opera and the famous bridge are beautiful, and so are a few other things, but it's just a big city like I'd seen many times before in Europe. The girls there weren't really lookers and I wasn't interested in backpackers at all. After all, I'd just come from South East Asia, where life was dirt cheap and girls were very welcoming and caring.

One of the first nights I went to a club where I had to pay eleven dollars for a small bottle of beer. In the Philippines I could buy almost ten beers in a club for that money. I couldn't help calculating everything and seeing how impossibly expensive it was for a traveler who didn't have a job there.

One night I pulled some Australian girls into the movie room of the hostel. I kissed and finger-banged a 17-year-old Australian girl there and when I went out to the hallway with her and made out some more, trying to find a place to bang, a drunk English guy just stood there watching us make out. The fucker just stopped walking and looked at us from no more than three meters away. We asked him to leave us alone and he asked why. I told him that he was being creepy and bothering us and he got all aggressive. The girl told him to go away too, and I told him to fuck off and he started shouting and cursing. The girl rolled her eyes and said something like "men" and walked off. I went after her but all this aggressive behavior had turned her off and she went to bed. When I walked back to punch the fucker in the face now that the girl wasn't there to witness it, he was gone.

Let me be frank about Australia, I didn't like it much. Can't say I had a good time. Maybe I had outgrown staying in a hostel full of twenty-two year olds. Everything cost too much to have a fun time. Staying in a hostel , eating a couple of fast food meals, smoking a few cigarettes and having a beer already busted my budget, let alone going out to a club, paying the entrance fee and having an expensive beer, or taking a taxi or even the damn bus. There were some places with cheaper beer and it wasn't all bad but I wasn't in the mood for gaming. For the last one-and-a-half years I had been in Second- or Third-World countries (except Japan and South Korea) and returning to the stressed Western world was hard on me.

The Blue Mountains were something different. It's a nature park close to Sydney and it takes a few hours by train to go there. The natural scenery is beautiful and some sights gave stunning views over forests and canyons. It's a must-do if you're around Sydney. I did a few hiking trips around the area and met some interesting people along the way.

I moved on to Melbourne afterwards and met a German guy in the bus on the way there. He was a bit nerdy but I could have good talks and fun with him. There was a guy we called The Schwein on the bus. You kind of had to be there, but this was a huge guy in an old suit with his fingers full of paint, who had some disgusting habits. He would put his seat down and lie half-over his chair so that I, being unfortunate enough to sit right behind, almost got crushed. He was snoring, burping and even farting a few times. He even rinsed his mouth with water and then spit it out on the floor. The guy was a swine.

I talked a lot with the German guy, and it turned he had even published a book himself, so I told him about my plans to write one. He was enthusiastic about the idea and tried to push me towards it a bit, but I was depressed about my current situation. The whole no-money thing, the unattractiveness of the backpacker girls and the longing for the good times I had living well in South East Asia on little to no money combined to get me down. I despised the western world and hated the thought I had to go back to Europe one day.

After visiting Melbourne I did a one-day tour with the German guy to the Twelve Apostles, a natural landmark along the Great Ocean Road. We also saw some of the famous koalas from up close. Melbourne is a nice city but it gets boring real fast once you've seen the sights. The only thing I really liked there was the AC/DC lane, an alley dedicated to one of my all-time favorite bands. I tried to get with one of the friendly girls from Singapore I'd met on the one day trip but that failed.

I was running out of time and enthusiasm for exploring Australia anymore, and I just went back to Sydney and stayed in a different area of the city, Kings Cross, the seedy part of town with a few small hostels and lots of strip clubs and bars. I stayed in a small hostel there and felt way more at ease but still suffered from some major bouts of depression and approach anxiety. I just couldn't wait to go to South America and experience some real travelling again.

The hostel wasn't an impersonal four-hundred-person backpacker factory like the others in the centre. This was a rowdy place with maybe forty beds and small common areas where people knew each other. We were smashing the bags of Goon every night and had atrocious hangovers the next morning. Goon is a surrogate for wine but it doesn't even have grapes it in. It's sold in ten-dollar plastic bags with a tap on them. The plastic bag goes in a carton but as soon as the bag of Goon is half empty people rip the carton apart and take the bag out. A four-liter bag of Goon will get two to three people very shitfaced and I have seen people using the half-full goon bags as pillows.

The hostel wasn't very quiet, let's say, but it was fun and I could easily have stayed there a while. The only problem was that there weren't too many good-looking chicks around. There were two (English) twin sisters who had reasonable bodies and could pass the boner test but they had very such bad habits, like getting wasted beyond belief, falling down all the time and once even drunkenly eating everything they could get their hands on, even food that had been lying on the floor for a while. The thought of kissing a girl like that disgusted me.

By this time I was doing some preparations for my blog and it was at this point that I starting translating my Dutch stories to English ones. Of course the Dutch blog was written for family and friends so I couldn't write everything down.

This made translating difficult and I had to dig deep in my mind to remember all the details. Luckily I have an excellent long-term memory.

When I got to writing about Australia, though, I had just received some angry comments from ashamed family members about my Cambodia stories, so I only wrote down a ten-sentence story about what happened in Australia. That's why you are reading a short version of a nearly a month there. I had not written everything down about Australia at the time and the Goon was eating my brain cells away, so my memory fails me here just a bit.

From Kings Cross I moved to Bondi Beach, a beach famous all over the world. I was staying in a hostel close to the beach and met some people there. I went out with them a few times and watched the rugby games. I even attempted to get myself out of my rut by trying to pick up some local girls, but the thoughts of not having a place to stay and no money for a hotel unconsciously blocked my vibe, and I sucked at both the approach and the following chitchat.

On one of the last nights I went out with the Canadian girl I'd met at the Cambodian border, who happened to be in Sydney too. Back then I had spent a few days with her but didn't get further than some making-out and sleeping in the same bed together. She made it clear that it was not going to happen again and said I was a kind of a man-whore for sleeping with so many girls everywhere. Facebook's a bitch sometimes. I laughed it away, remembering that Jenna sometimes called me a man-whore too.

We had a crazy but fun night out anyway, together with a Filipino guy and a drunken annoying Irish guy who we managed to ditch later on.

New Zealand – Auckland & Pahia

Moment of Dutch pride to set the record straight: just like Australia, New Zealand was discovered by a Dutch captain and not by the English, who didn't arrive until nearly two hundred years later. His name was Abel Tasman and both the island Tasmania and the Abel Tasman Sea are named after him. For those who have been curious has to how an English colony caught a weird, un-English name like New Zealand, well, it's not English. Tasman named it after the Dutch province Zeeland.

Australia, in the meantime, was originally New Holland, but the Dutch didn't see much use for a huge country bereft of spices, unlike Indonesia, and left it alone.

I decided to only visit the North Island because I arrived just after Christchurch, in the south, was hit by a major earthquake. Many people died, and others were left homeless. Not exactly a tourist attraction.

Auckland was just another big capital to me and didn't have much in the way of special attractions, other than the Sky Tower and the beautiful skyline in the harbor.

The first hostel I stayed in pretty much sucked; the eight-bed dorm was occupied by foreigners working in town and everybody went to bed early every day. One funny thing worth mentioning was this giant guy who asked me how long I was staying in the dorm. "A few days," I said – and he gave me a new pair of earplugs. The guy snored like a fucking chainsaw – but at least he was aware of it.

One of the girls staying in the dorm was quite fat and had massive boobs. She was friendly but way below my standards for even thinking about having sex with her. I think she mistake my looking at her big boobs for interest because she came on to me a bit. When that didn't work she changed her bra right in front of me and a few others, possibly in a last attempt to get my interest. It didn't work. A similar situation had happened in Hong Kong when I shared a small dorm with a Finnish girl.

There were quite a few Argentineans around since New Zealand is a popular place for the middle-class tourists to go. What I should have done was practice my barely-existent Spanish with them a bit.

I booked a package tour from one of the famous bus lines there. They were supposed to be party buses, but the vibe wasn't really there.

The bus went up north and we first stopped in Pahia, the Bay of Islands as it's also called. I stayed in another hostel and it was fun there. I was playing cards/drinking games with a small group of people.

A day later I went for a skydive. It was time to man up again and face some fears, so I thought I'd give it a try. The American instructor named Dean was a really cool guy. He looked a bit like James Hetfield, the lead singer of Metallica.

We got into the small airplane and it was a bumpy ride to gain height. It was quite windy that day and the small propeller plane was shaking from side to side. It was a tandem skydive, and I wasn't scared at all until Dean opened the door and we shuffled towards the exit. I looked down and at that moment I got a bit nervous. It was too late: we jumped.

The first thing that surprised me was the enormous air pressure. It was like getting hit in the face by air. The freefall lasted about a minute, since it was a 12,000-foot jump. The view was amazing: you could see all the little islands, the forests and the fields. Still, one minute of freefall was more than enough for me and I was a bit worried that I was going to be sick. I have a weak stomach for everything that involves spinning around quickly. The parachute opened and Dean started doing tricks while yelling some woohooos and wahaaaas. It was fun but I was glad when we landed and took a few more pictures. The adrenaline was still pumping through my veins when we got back to Pahia. I was proud to have ticked another thing of my list. Skydive… Check!

The tour I'd booked consisted of open tickets where you could hop on and off a daily bus whenever you pleased. I was short on time so I took the bus even further up north and we stopped for several interesting things along the way. We exited the bus at the most northern point of New Zealand and went to try something called Dune riding.

How it works is that you take half a surfboard and slide down the enormous sand dunes with your belly on the board, using your legs to brake a bit. After a quick instruction we all got our board and hurried up the dune. Running up a sand dune is not easy and about halfway there I heard something that only happens in my travelling nightmares. A sound I was scared to death off. Krk! The sound of my lower back almost breaking in half.

I almost fell to my knees in pain and didn't know what to

do; in my mind I was even starting to panic a bit. People were shouting out "Come on Neil, let's go!" I pulled myself together but already knew this was going to be some serious badass pain. *Come on, man up!* I told myself. *Maybe it isn't so bad.*

I stood there like a statue for half a minute while the others had already started going down the dune and having fun. I pulled myself together and painfully walked to the top. Sometimes you know when you're being a stupid idiot and go along with it anyway. This was one of those moments. I "surfed" down the dune and hit a few bumps, which just made it worse. When I was down I could barely get back on my feet, but a few people were watching me and I gathered some strength. I got back on the bus and sat down. Others were still having fun but I was cramping up.

We still had to ride back, which took four hours with a lot of photographing stops. I was in some serious pain during this ride and the ibroprufen I got from others didn't help anything. Once I got back to the hostel, I limped over to the convenience store, bought four bags of chips and some bottles of water. I lay down on my bed, took two 10mg valium pills I'd bought in Cambodia without a prescription, and slept for hours.

Every time I woke up, I ate something, took another valium and dozed off. I had always had back problems when I was younger and even had a small hernia when I was working in construction. Back then, I had to walk around in a corset for two months and could barely take a dump without being in pain. I'd had back problems in the Philippines too and at one point needed a massage to loosen up before I could even think of sex. I laughed it off as luxury problems since it was caused by the banging of young girls.

Surprisingly, this time my back problems weren't as bad as in my younger years, but it scared the hell out of me all the same.

What would have happened if my back had gone the same way as before? Barely being able to walk, in a country where nobody cares for you and your homeland is a twenty-four hour flight away? Especially since I already had a nonrefundable ticket to Argentina.

The pain eased a bit after a while and I went out with some Irish girls to a local disco, but I still had to be really careful and didn't even try to pick up some local girls there who definitely looked interested in me.

Anyway to make a long story short, nothing happened that night except for lots of drinking and valium-taking afterwards. I went back to Auckland the day after.

New Zealand – Back to Auckland

I went to the Nomads hostel, which turned out to be a lot more fun than the first one I'd been to. It had its own bar and I even met up with Greg, the American guy I'd met in the guesthouse in Puerto Princessa a whole seven months earlier. He's a fanatic skydiver and had done hundreds of jumps. We had a beer and talked about our trips and laughed about the crazy sandman in Puerto Princessa.

Later that week I hung out with two Swedish girls in the hostel. We were getting drunk off the cans of beer we smuggled into the hostels and playing cards in the dorm. The next day I went with them to an island nearby and the three of us spent a day on the beach together. Neither was a stunner and I had a hard time choosing one.

At night we went out together and I decided to focus on the short one, but she wasn't interested in me. Drunk as I was, I took aim at the other girl, but though she was interested at first she told me she didn't want to be second choice or even third choice. I remember her saying something about being third choice, and I think there must have been yet another Scandinavian girl who I went after first, before the short one.

There was a lot of drinking that night, so my memory fails. I do remember that I still convinced the Swedish girl about something because we ended up in bed together, but she was still a bit pissed with me so we didn't have sex. It was in her dorm bed anyway. She had some ugly tattoos, and I don't even feel bad about not scoring a flag with her. It was surprising I got that far considering the lousy state I was in and my depressing moods about picking up girls. I needed a change of scenery, and quick.

I had posted a message about a meetup on a pick-up artist forum, and one guy replied to me. We met up a few times and we went out together. We were both having major bouts of approach anxiety. Australia had ruined all my build-up confidence and it wasn't much better in New Zealand either. We had a couple of small successes with talking to a few "sets", as it's called in pick-up terms, but got nowhere with "escalating towards the lay". I slept in a dorm and security was too strict to smuggle in any girls. I approached some girls in the clubs and I saw him run after a girl in the streets and approach her there.

Though we didn't score any successes we did have some fun, and sided with a wingman I even felt a spark of the dark force coming back to me. But it wasn't enough to get me out of my depressing state.

Once a year, usually around Christmastime, I watch all three extended editions of the *Lord of the Rings* saga. I love movies like that and used to watch them all in one day, locking myself up in my home cinema room with some bottles of water and five bags of chips. A lot of the movies was shot in New Zealand and I wanted to see the real locations. There are some tours but I didn't want to see fake stuff at a really high price.

I planned a trip from Auckland to Turangi, a small place in the middle of the northern island next to a massive nature park. I booked a hostel online and got on the bus.

You'll meet the most interesting people of walks of life when taking buses around the world, although you need a thick skin if you're a realist and skeptic like me. I've met too many naïve tree huggers who were all for the environment but apparently didn't mind that their iPhone was built by 15-year-old Chinese girls in horrible near-slavery conditions. Follow your principles all the way through or accept the fact that the world revolves on greed and other basic principles imbedded in our genes during caveman times.

People want green energy but seem to forget that an island like Sumatra with beautiful rainforests full of irreplaceable wildlife was 2/3 deforested because of the high demand for "green" palm oil.

The hostel in Turangi looked more like a campsite, with lots of rooms and bungalows. I was the only resident at the time and the friendly and helpful lady working there gave me a room for myself instead of an eight-bed dorm room. I asked about the Tongariro Alpine crossing and she arranged for me to get picked up the next morning.

At a quarter to five in the morning a minivan picked me up along with some other people. Around seven o'clock we arrived at the start and it was still dark.

The Tongariro Alpine crossing is 19.4 kilometers long, and I can't remember a day in my life before then when I'd walked anything even close to that distance, let alone in the mountains and in the horrible shape I was in. I knew it was going to be hell that day, but I was motivated to push myself.

My back was still sensitive but not painful anymore. The first six kilometers I walked with a Swiss girl whose name I've forgotten. The sunrise amongst the misty mountains was amazing.

We arrived at the spot where the climb to Mount Ngauruhoe started, the volcanic mountain used as a model of Mount Doom, the mountain where our little hobbit friend had to toss the ring in to destroy the evil powers of Sauron. The Swiss girl looked at the mountain and said she was already too tired to climb it. I tried to convince her but she chickened out. Now I had to climb it myself. There weren't many other climbers around, just a few small groups of friends and some couples climbing together. I literally told the Swiss girl that I would climb Mount Doom or die trying.

At 2200 meters, the mountain isn't even that high, but the sides are nearly sixty degrees steep and the loose volcanic ash makes every step a chore. There isn't really a path up and you have to climb over some parts made of rock, and sometimes use your arms as well. I kept thinking about my sister, who had gone through a rough period with her health and is known for her toughness. She used to travel a lot as well and is an even bigger fan of the *Lord of the Rings* trilogy than I am.

After two hours of climbing I reached the top. It was

covered in clouds and despite all the exercise I was soon feeling pretty cold since I was only wearing shorts and sneakers. I was really proud of myself and thought about how proud my sister would have been and how much she would give to be there with me.

At this point my legs were already tired and I would have called it a day if possible, but I still had thirteen kilometers more to walk. I crossed two more mountains which were also steep climbs, only resting a bit to eat and then moving on.

The mountains were very colorful and the way the sun lit up the different sides of the mountains was amazing. There was a whole palette of colors ranging from dark red to pitch black.

Suddenly the smell of rotten eggs hit my nose and when I went over yet another mountain I saw the deep blue sulphur lakes in front of me. It smells terrible but they are truly stunning when viewed upon from the top of a hill.

After taking some photos I kept walking. My legs felt like rubber already. I reached a mountain cabin and resting point. I had been continuously walking and climbing for nearly seven hours. Well, I was in the worst shape of my life, having smoked and drank a lot in the months before and living only on junk food or street food. Some people passed me by a few times but they were at least ten years younger than me and who knows how fit they were. I met a couple there who had hiked all over the world and even they said it was hard to do in seven hours.

The last minivan left at four-thirty and it was already three o'clock. I had to keep on walking and it was still about six kilometers. Luckily it was mostly downhill on a nice paved road now, it wasn't really climbing anymore, but I'd already climbed so much while being so unprepared that my legs were really starting to go.

The last hour of walking was mostly through a forest with lots of tree roots and small steps along the way and I was dead tired. My whole life I'd never had knee problems, not even when I worked as a tiler and sat on my knees all day, but now it felt like people were sticking hot needles in them.

Luckily I was smart enough to have brought lots of food and some candy with me so I could keep my energy going. I learned to do this the hard way when climbing Mount Fuji in Japan and in Nepal, where I almost had a heart attack due to an extremely low blood sugar level after being sick for weeks there. I remember eating some chocolate afterwards and feeling like new in just a couple of minutes.

My back was hurting more and more with every step I took and I nearly passed out towards the end. I had to keep myself going by listening to inspiring music on my phone like the *Eye of the Tiger* song and the *Rocky* tune I use as my alarm clock ring to get a motivating start to the day. I thought of my family and it seemed like there was no end to this hellish ordeal.

I thought about one of my favorite books by Stephen King, *The Long Walk* (written under pseudonym Richard Bachman), about a seven-hundred kilometer life or death walk in a future fascist America. It's the first book I'm going to read again as soon as I finish this book and I recommend others to do so also

Coughing my lungs out and more dead than alive, I finally made it to the rendezvous point. The last minivans were about to leave and I hopped on one.

All the other climbers complained about how hard it was to do everything in one day. Some had only done the official 19.4km mountain walk and not also climbed Mount Doom. I took off my shoes and longed for a hot shower. I had walked and climbed for twenty kilometers and had only rested maybe five times five minutes. By the time we were back in town my legs started cramping up and I stumbled into the massive supermarket and bought a liter bottle of Steinlager beer and four bags of that delicious chips they sold in New Zealand. I took a hot shower and locked myself up in my room with my beer and groceries, knocked down a couple of valiums and slept a long time.

A few days later I went back to Auckland and spent a couple of nights there in a hostel, desperately trying to learn some Latin Spanish on my laptop before I left to yet another fascinating continent: South America.

Chapter Five – South America

Argentina – Buenos Aires

The flight to Argentina took twelve hours and I had flown back in time. The route description to the hostel I had written on my phone sucked; as soon as I got off at the metro stop close to the hostel I was lost, and it was my first chance to speak some Spanish.

"Donde esta calle…?" I asked, and surprisingly it worked. I found the hostel, which was kind of a rock hostel. It was my second choice: my first had been the Millhouse hostel. I had heard the wildest stories about it. Some described it as total debauchery with sex everywhere. Others were very mild about the place. Either way, I figured it was one place where I'd have the chance to get my mojo back and score some flags. Well, unfortunately that hostel was already all booked up when I looked online even two weeks before. I guess it's a popular place.

The one I did get into was a hostel in the Palermo neighborhood, an area where all the bars and clubs were. I took a dorm room and went out alone the first night. I had to see for myself what all this talk about Palermo was about.

I left the hostel around eleven and started walking, and kept walking because I couldn't find any bars with people who were out drinking. I saw a lot of restaurants that looked like bars but people were still sitting in big groups and eating at tables. How the hell could I meet a girl in a place like this if they were all sitting down?

I kept walking and walked into a dark street with no-one around except a large group of teenagers and I was walking towards them. They were sitting there smoking and drinking and there were at least fifteen of them. They had seen me too and stopped talking and just looked at me. I'm no pussy but this scared me a bit.

I had met an Argentinean guy on the plane from New Zealand to Argentina and he had told me some scary stories about kids walking around with guns at night. I thought he acted like a pussy at that time and didn't really pay much attention to it. Now I was wondering if he was right. What could I do? If I stopped and turned around they would know I was worried about it and maybe had valuables to hide. It seemed best to Man Up™ and just keep walking like I always did in situations like this. I kept walking straight at them, looked over to them, stopped and lit up a cigarette and walked past them with the meanest cigarette smoking face I had, looking a few of them in the eyes. I heard them say something with gringo and laugh but they didn't do anything. I'm not saying I scared them because they could easily have robbed me blind and beat me to death that night and no one would even see. But by walking straight at them with my chest out and looking at them while taking a few deep puffs of my cigarette with a mean face and giving them a small head nod, I had probably gained their respect for showing no fear whatsoever. Spitting on the street while keeping an eye on them is also making a manly "I don't give a shit" impression. Just don't do that right in front of them. I'm not saying that these techniques will always keep you out of trouble but it worked for me on several occasions in Russia, South East Asia, and now South America too.

I never did find a good bar to go to that night and walked back to the hostel. There they told me that people in Buenos Aires don't go out before two at night and that I probably past a lot of bars that would be booming later that night. I stayed in, lazy from walking at least thirty blocks that night.

The following night was a Saturday night and I met some people in the hostel bar. Most were just regular backpackers but there was also a couple from Australia. She was actually from New Zealand and since I just came from there it was easy to start a conversation. The guy was a straight-up alpha natural. Good looks, muscular build and naturally charming. The girl was freaking hot, not to put too fine a point on it.

The guy told me he got lots of sex when he worked on surf beaches all over Australia. He didn't seem like a bullshitting type of guy to me and it was the first time I was actually a bit jealous of a guy.

He was obviously naturally popular with girls and traveled around the world with a truly hot girl at his side. It strengthened my own goals.

We stood in line for the club and Argentiniean girls approached him and started conversations. I was like, *this guy is the real deal.* A born natural who didn't care about talking to girls in front of his hot girlfriend. I have seen so many guys who show real beta behavior when their girlfriends are around. This guy wasn't bothered at all and neither was she.

I made some approaches inside the club but the language barrier hit me hard and the girls who spoke English were kind of looking for free drinks. I was halfway through my 80-girls challenge and was positive that South America would be some sort of South East Asia all over again where I'd rack up the notches quickly.

Having no idea how long my money would last I didn't know the timeframe I had and thought I'd better start quick, I had a lot to making up to do after the bad time I had in Australia and New Zealand. Little did I know that Argentina was considered the hardest country in South America for picking up girls, and a long struggle had begun.

On Sunday a new guest arrived in the dorm and I didn't pay much attention to her when she walked in. She looked a bit thick from the other side of the room. My eyesight has been a cock-block to me sometimes because I have minus two on both sides but refuse to wear glasses in public and only tried contacts for a short while back in 2006. Making eye contact is hard when you can barely see someone's eyes, especially in badly lighted clubs.

I probably lost some bangs not noticing that girls were checking me out or trying to make eye contact with me. As I said before, I can be a pretty smart guy but with some things I'm dead stupid.

Anyway, I was lying on my bed with my laptop when she walked in and I thought she wasn't that good-looking. She said hi and asked me where I was from, the standard way of saying hello in backpacker land. I said Holland, and then she asked me if I had a pair of scissors – or "seizors" as she said with her exotic accent. "Yeah sure, I have some," I said.

She walked over and said she was from Brazil. She had taken off her jacket and as she turned around I saw she wasn't a bit thick at all. She just had a big round Brazilian ass, a Bunda grande as they call it, a flat belly and a big pair of C-cups. I watched her walk away and talk to me and I felt something I hadn't felt in a long time. My heart rate nearly doubled and I had instant movement in my pants. I had been with so many girls already that I wasn't turned on anymore by merely seeing a girl, but not her. I wouldn't say it was love at first sight, I was too numbed already by my previous experiences on my trip, but this girl brought back the fire in me. Her name was Charlize and she was on a ten-day holiday in Buenos Aires. She worked in a store in Sau Paulo and she was an obvious (hard) rocker type.

Over the next few days we talked a lot and even did some sightseeing together.

At night we sat on the floor in the hallway closely together with our backs against the wall. I showed her some YouTube vids and I put my leg and shoulder against her. This is always a good test to see if and how much a girl is in to you. She didn't pull back and I felt excited like a teenage boy again. What the hell was wrong with me? Was I the stone cold womanizer banging his way around the world or a guy looking for true love?

At that moment it looked like it was the latter, and the approach anxiety and minor depression I suffered in Australia and New Zealand had thrown me back to my old beta self.

We went to see the movie *Suckerpunch* in the cinema. We sat closely together and twenty minutes into the movie I grabbed her hand and she immediately starting rubbing her thumb on my fingers. This was the go signal for me.

We turned our heads and for the next hour we kissed and barely saw anything of the movie.

We had to walk a long way back to the hostel and stopped everywhere to kiss. I used an old trick of mine, the "Look at this move".

The "Look at this move"
When you walk down the street with a girl, act seriously

and point at something in a store's window and say, "Wow, look at this". It doesn't have to be special, anything will do. She's curious and goes to look what you are pointing at.

At this point you use the spin-move on her, grab her and kiss her. Girls LOVE this and I have used this trick dozens of times. You can also do this when walking around with a girl but you're not sure if she likes you yet. It's an excellent way of getting close to her and doing some touching. You can use it whether you're just dating or have been married for over forty years like my parents. It doesn't matter. It makes you unpredictable and more exciting than the average guy who just holds her hand and tries to act interesting with some boring old story or bragging about his accomplishments in life. I'm probably not the inventor of the "Look at this move" but it always works very well.

Or just say something like this: "O my god, look there" and point at some dark corner or alley. "Come here, I want to show you something" also works, push the girl into the dark where no one can see her or will judge her and make out there.

Girls are self-conscious, especially in countries that are on the conservative and/or religious side. It's the element of surprise and her being naughty that excites them. She has to trust you for this, don't do it with a stranger or someone who is clearly not interested in you. I always make a lot of fun when walking down the street with a girl.

For example: I ask the girl to tell me something about some boring statue and they start explaining stuff and I just make fun of them. They start hitting me on the shoulder and say that I'm such a mean guy. Once they say that, you are already an attractive guy in their opinion. Do not underestimate the element of surprise when picking up girls.

When Charlize and I returned to the hostel it was already past midnight and a lot of people were already sleeping. We sat on the couch in the internet room and kept making out. She turned off the lights and sat towards me on my lap and my hands went over her big round bunda. She took her shirt off and was sitting in front of me in only her bra. It was late but people could still walk in. My hands went up to her boobs and massaged them, and she took her bra off too. I couldn't believe my eyes and hands. Her breasts were absolutely perfect. My first thought was that they were fake, but I was afraid to ask since the last time I did that gave me a funny reaction. We had no place to have sex but talked about going to a motel the next time. The dorm was out of the question for her.

The next day I met an American girl named Elizabeth, who had traveled South America a bit but had now decided to stay in Buenos Aires for a while. She was a nice-looking girl and was running a nice blog about her travels and her stay in Buenos Aires. We got talking about blogging and I showed her my blog. She was surprised when she saw the title but interested at the same time.

Girls are ALWAYS intrigued if a man is doing well with the ladies. I was already with Charlize and I'm pretty sure Elizabeth was interested too, especially when Charlize acted a bit jealous around her. Pre-selection is the light saber in the hands of the love-Jedi.

We went to the La Boca neighborhood the next morning, a very famous part of town where there a lot of small bars, lots of tango dancing, and the home of the Boca Juniors Football stadium. We visited everything and had a nice day.

At night Charlize and I went to a love motel in the same street as the hostel. We took the room for only three hours because it was quite expensive. It was a room full of mirrors and had some romantic Spanish music playing in the background.

After showering I waited for her and she looked magical when coming out of the bathroom. We were both only wearing a towel and started kissing. She was a bit shy at first but once I started using my tongue on all her body parts she became very horny.

A funny thing happened when I finished her with my tongue. She nearly exploded in orgasm, coming so hard she was knocked out and for a moment I thought she'd gone to sleep. Now I felt exactly how millions of women must feel after having sex with their lousy boyfriend who finishes and rolls over to sleep. It was no surprise I didn't like this feeling. I said "Hey, wake up!" to her and she replied "Ow, Neil, wait one minute, it still feels so good". I asked if she wanted me to do it again but she said no because she would have no energy left afterwards. She took away my towel and was pleasantly surprised. "You… you are so clean," she said in her thick Brazilian accent. Apparently her last boyfriend had never heard of shaving or trimming down there.

She ferociously attacked me and I felt her heartbeat through her warm lips. I had already trouble controlling myself after all this built-up pressure over the last months and her slow way of pleasuring me almost got the better of me. She said she never liked giving blowjobs that much but with me she loved it.

A bigger compliment is hardly possible. Ten minutes later she stopped and mounted me, riding me hard while rotating her hips, her perfect boobs bouncing in my face and her big round ass visible everywhere in the mirrors.

I couldn't hold it anymore and busted a nut really quick. I moaned a bit but I did it in such a way she didn't notice I'd already come. "Let's change positions," I said, and she didn't notice I came after only five minutes. I took her from behind and looked at myself in the mirror while hearing her breathing heavily and softly moaning a bit. "I'm back in business, capturing the Brazilian flag after only four days in South America," I said to myself. I looked down at her big round butt and felt proud. I lasted a lot longer now and blamed the first quick one on the long dry spell and the very strong feelings I had for her. She never noticed that it was twice, and it was actually very risky to continue fucking with a loaded condom.

I was crazy about Charlize; she was a true rock chick and always wore tight black pants and a t-shirt with a print of Iron Maiden, Testament or some band I had never heard of.

That week we went to several places in and around Buenos Aires. We went to San Telmo, the Hard Rock café, a cemetery for prominent Argentineans where we saw the grave of Eva Peron, the famous first lady.

We had a picnic in the park; we went to Tigre, a small

town close to Buenos Aires which lies in a sort of river delta.

Around midnight we would go to a love hotel and make love all night. The early busting was a one-time only thing and we couldn't get enough of each other.

On one night she wanted to stay in the dorm but was very shy about sleeping in my bed while others were around. I slept in a lower bunk bed and used the sheet of the upper bed to cover the side so no one could peek in. She came into my bed and we started kissing, I used my fingers to get her off and afterwards she gave me a blowjob. I was lying very unconformable and asked her to move a bit. The bed was squeaky and made a lot of noise and she wouldn't move. I asked her again, she said no and we got into an argument and she left the bed without finishing the job. We both went to sleep in our own bed and the next day she left early to do some sightseeing on her own.

I thought I had fucked everything up and wrote her a private message on Facebook. It was a pretty beta letter where I explained the situation and said I was sorry for being a rude dick to her.

I don't believe in being strictly alpha or beta. Being a strict alpha means being an asshole most of the time and never admitting a mistake. I think it's better and wiser to act with a mix of both. This trip for me was more about alpha-ing up than totally eliminating the beta in me. It's better to think smart and keep things going than to be stubborn and miss out on opportunities. I call this being Bepha.

After she read my letter everything was ok again and we went to a hard rock bar called The Red Bell, and to Luján Zoo the next morning.

Normally I don't like going to a zoo in poor countries but this one was well-kept. A woman with enormous cleavage sold bags of bread and corn to feed the animals and I went to buy some twice just to have a look at those gigantic knockers. She wasn't much to look at but man, would I enjoy motorboating those babies for a while.

The last evening we went back to the big metallic flower, a giant flower made of shiny metal in a park. We brought some food and drinks and it was supposed to be romantic picnic, but after a few minutes we were kicked out by the guards who were closing the park for the night.

We walked around a bit, with me doing the "Look at this move" all the time, and we started making out heavier and heavier. She was wearing a jean skirt and when I felt under it her panties were soaking wet. She said she fantasized about outside sex a lot and we went looking for a quiet spot.

It can be just a bit difficult to find a quiet spot to get naked in a big city like Buenos Aires. There's traffic and people walking around at all hours of the day and we had to look for a good spot.

We finally found a place in the bushes next to the train tracks. She pulled my pants down and freed my boner who was gasping for air the last hour.

Charlize was so impatient and horny that she almost seemed aggressive. I pulled down her skirt and really gave it to her from behind. A long train came past and made lots of noise and she screamed loud. I swear to this day people in the train saw us fucking even though we were kind of standing hidden in the bushes. We came at the same time and it was perfect, Charlize mentioned this moment for ages after we had said goodbye to each other later.

It was time for me to fly to Santiago in Chile. My plan was to go there, see the Chilean guys I hung out with in Russia and travel south from there, crossing the Argentinean border and going up again from. I kissed Charlize goodbye and promised her I would see her again in Sau Paulo, where she lived. She was about to leave too, on a flight to Foz de Iguazu, a Brazilian city close to Puerto de Iguazu.

I had to really hurry up in the morning because I was late and the international airport was at least one-and-a-half hour by metro and bus. When I got there I couldn't find my flight on the boards anywhere.

I went to the information counter and showed my E-ticket. They told me I was at the wrong airport! I had to go to the small airport close to where I lived. I couldn't believe it. It was a flight to a different country; by definition, it was an international flight. So of course I presumed it would leave from the big international airport I had arrived eleven days before. It was too late already and I went back to the hostel. I felt no disappointment, though. This meant that I could spend more time with Charlize and could even go with her to her next destination: Puerto de Iguazu.

Argentina – Puerto de Iguazu

The Argentinean bus was luxurious but expensive. Eighty-five dollars is a whole lot of money for a bus ride and I didn't think it was justified even though it was eighteen hours and you got some food and drinks on the bus.

Jeremy, a guy I had met in the hostel who was going in the same direction and I arrived in Puerto de Iguazu and went looking for the guesthouse where Charlize was staying. On the way there we saw a hot waitress and noted down the place to eat there later.

Charlize had booked a dorm room at the hostel but changed that to a normal room as soon as she knew I was coming there too. We shared the costs and for the first time we could enjoy each other company without having to stay in a dorm or going to an overpriced love hotel.

The town of Iguazu is built on the triple border of Argentina, Brazil and Paraguay. The Iguazu waterfalls are the biggest in the world and make Niagara look like a small stream – at least, according to a few American tourists there. Jeremy was a really nice guy and I invited him to come with us to the famous waterfalls of Iguazu. The waterfalls are gigantic and really amazing.

We decided to have dinner in that evening and bought groceries. Charlize is a vegetarian and I don't mind eating a vegetarian meal every once in a while as long as I can eat my manly meat too. But we got into an argument anyway. An argument about onions. Onions, of all things. She wanted to cook pasta but chop up two whole onions in it along with a whole lot of other vegetables. I said one was enough because I didn't want to stink and we got into a fight over it. We didn't speak for several hours, we're both that headstrong. I was so angry that I almost packed up my bags and moved to a dorm room. Later I figured I'd acted childishly and should keep the peace, because I did want to stay with her. I was damn hungry too, and I didn't want to go out and spend extra money on a restaurant, so I told her that I didn't want to have a silly argument over food. She must have thought she'd overreacted too, because she only put in one onion and even cooked some meat for me.

Was I a pussy for giving in to her? I don't think so; it gave me an excellent view into what the future would be like if I was ever became serious with her. That doesn't mean a guy should act like a mangina or listen to the feminist crap you hear on television or see in the movies all day. A man should be a man but a man also needs to eat.

Charlize and I went to Foz de Iguazu the next day, and it was my first short visit to Brazil. I already liked the country after passing the border. Loads of hot girls with big bundas and I liked the typical rice and beans meals we bought there. The bus didn't even stop at the Brazil border and I didn't get a stamp in my passport.

We went back the next day and passed on through to Ciudad del Este in Paraguay. We had to cross the big bridge to Paraguay by motorbike because according to the Lonely Planet book it was too dangerous to walk across. We did some shopping there and Charlize said that everything was dirt cheap there and that many Brazilians living in the south go there to buy cheap electronics and consumer stuff. She bought so many bottles of lotion and perfume that she needed to buy an extra small backpack to carry it all.

On the way back we were stopped by border control and they checked our bags. I was sweating because I didn't stamp my passport at both the Brazilian and the Paraguayan border. Luckily he didn't check my passport, just the bag.

We went back once more to Paraguay to hang around and do shopping. We went over the bridge again by motorbike taxi.

When we returned I said to Charlize that I wanted to have the stamps in my passport and I walked across the big bridge back to Paraguay. Got a nice entry stamp in my passport, crossed the road and walked back again to get my exit stamp. Nothing happened at all on the bridge, no robberies or hassles like described in the Lonely Planet. Yet another myth had been busted, although I won't advise to try it after dark.

Charlize and I said goodbye the following morning when she had to fly back to Sau Paulo. I promised to visit her once I reached Sau Paulo and she said I could stay at her place. I was happy to hear that because Brazil isn't a cheap destination.

I went back to Brazil the same day by myself and visited the Itapu dam. It wasn't easy to get there on my own. Except for the people at the dam I didn't meet anyone who spoke a bit of English and even my Spanish was misunderstood all the time. But that was probably my own fault since I barely spoke any.

The Itapu dam is the world's second largest hydro dam and it's interesting to see how they harnessed the awesome power of water. I battled myself a way back through local buses and the Brazilian and Argentina border and met a nice guy back in the hostel in Puerto de Iguazu. His name was Larry and he was an American from San Francisco. He was on a short trip of a few months through South America. A fun guy to hang out with but also up for a real conversation.

My little romance with Charlize had brought back my fighting spirit out regarding girls but I felt guilty about going out that night and going hunting for local poon. We stayed in and played Gran Turisimo 3 half the night on the Playstation in the guesthouse.

Larry was on his way down south and we decided to go there together. We took a bus to Rosario, the place where the hottest girls in Argentina come from. I had read on the Internet that it had a five-to-one girl-guy ratio. Larry and I talked about picking up girls and I mentioned my site.

We met the hottest girl cop ever at a road block. We were almost the only guys in the bus and she checked our passports. To this day I regret not acting like a damn tourist and coming up with a silly story so I could take a picture with her. She was an eight in looks and probably one of the cutest girls I had ever seen in my life. She looked sexy in her uniform and I daydreamed about her arresting me. This girl was marriage material.

Argentina – Rosario

Larry and I stayed in a shitty hostel in Rosario and talked about girls. I had just read a booklet about picking up Argentinean girls written by Roosh. This booklet however had scared the living daylights out of me. It described a sort of girl I had not yet encountered on my trip: the coldhearted Latina chick, nearly impossible to pick up, with a bitch shield up to the roof and who would not reply to your texts or calls.

A large amount of time, a social circle and even lots of money was needed to get with one of these girls. They were considered the hardest of the hard to pick up and I feared that my plans of picking one up were out the door. I had no money or a social circle there; I don't have a great style in clothes. Hell, I look like what I am, a travelling backpacker bum.

We went out that night and couldn't find any place to go. We were there during the week and pretty much all bars were closed down or there was little to do inside. We changed hostels the next day and found a livelier one.

During the day we walked around the city a bit, looked at some sights and took pictures. We tried to day game a bit but were too scared to even approach some girls. We walked around the city and every time we saw a cute girl we tried to push each other to open her. I made one half-assed attempt to talk to a girl but her English was very bad. Larry helped out a bit since his Spanish was a lot better than mine. It led nowhere but it gave me a little boost.

Day-gaming is only for the strong and I had almost never done it. It is damn hard to just walk up to a girl in the street and start talking; it is hard in your own country but when you're in a country where not many people speak English it really makes you self-conscious and you feel like an instant moron sometimes. My approach anxiety went through the roof.

The stories were true, though: we saw an unbelievable number of hotties and not that many guys around. We even asked a taxi driver and the hostel owner about the girl ratio and they both confirmed that there were way more girls than guys.

In the afternoon Larry came up with the idea of using the

Internet to find some girls. He logged on and sent out about thirty messages to girls on a website called Couchsurfing. I told him that I thought it was only for staying at their houses but Larry said you could also use this website to meet people for coffee.

A few hours later a couple of girls replied to his email and they came to meet us. They were two sisters and one of them was good–looking, but no stunner.

We went out to an Irish pub and ate a pizza and drank some beers. I tried to game the younger sister but failed. She went home while her older sister stayed with us.

We went to play some pool and later went bowling at the same place. The three of us had a lot of fun that night and I noted down that I had to start using this website myself.

It was time to move on and we went to Cordoba.

Argentina – Cordoba

Cordoba was supposed the ultimate place to score girls, according to most Argentineans.

The city is a lot cheaper than Buenos Aires, girls have better attitudes and the city has eight universities, all full of hot young girls. All the ingredients for a successful time.

But fear had struck in my heart and I was getting scared of approaching girls in clubs. The fact that Larry was scared too didn't help much.

Charlize contacted me daily and messaged me how much she missed me. I began wondering if it was all worth it. Should I just give up on my challenge to bang 80 girls? I had already had lost so much precious time in the beginning of my trip and again in Australia and New Zealand. I would never make it. I wondered if what I did with Charlize actually counted as picking up. Maybe it was a romance, like so many people have on a holiday. The pressure of scoring got to me and maybe I should go back to just travelling with the occasional bang, just like all other travelers. But that idea was scary too.

We were sitting with a small group of people in the hostel kitchen when two girls mentioned that they were from

Greenland. Larry nearly choked on his drink when he heard me ask if Greenland had its own passports. He knew why I asked that question. The answer was no, Greenland is still part of Denmark. I already knew that but wanted to make sure. I decided that if I could get with one of them I would make an exception to the flagging rules. Normally I treat any country that has its own passport as a separate flag, but Greenland was just too special with its 58,000 inhabitants. I wanted that flag and I wanted it badly. So much for self-doubt.

The whole hostel group went out that night and we went to a club somewhere not too far from the center. The two Greenland girls were cute but no stunners. They also weren't interested in me, except for having me in the friend zone. They were interested in two uninteresting and ugly Argentinean guys. One even had braces and a stupid expression on his face. What made them get the girls? Probably being Latino and having the balls to approach.

Argentinean guys have aggressive game, not as aggressive as the Brazilian caveman game but still pretty hostile. They will just grab a girl and start dancing, there's no asking involved. Larry said I should do the same but I was too chicken to just grab a girl. We both got frustrated with girls and with each other.

Half-drunk, we left the club and jumped in a taxicab. Larry and I slept in the same dorm room and nobody else was there. We had a massive discussion about our approach fears. I was bitching and complaining and quite frankly overreacting. Larry was less worried about picking up girls and said he just wanted to enjoy his trip. We almost got into an argument over it and I felt like I had hit rock bottom. I was back to square one, couldn't pull any confidence out of earlier conquests.

I slept off my hangover the next morning, when I realized that I had forgotten my jacket at the club the night before, the one I had just bought ten days before. I grumped myself through the day, had a short talk with Larry and felt ashamed for my bitching and self-pity the night before.

The same day, a major breakthrough happened. I got in

touch with Darren, the buddy I traveled with for six weeks in Indonesia. He was already in South America for a while and was visiting Cordoba again. We agreed to meet in a club that night.

I went over to the massive club by myself. I couldn't find Darren and he didn't answer the phone. All disappointed I drank some beer, which came in one-liter glasses.

It was dark inside with only the strobe flashing and was standing against some pillar and looked around a bit. I looked at some guy standing close to me and he looked at me at exactly the same moment. We both looked away and then I realized it: it was Darren! He realized it the same moment and we jumped up and hugged each other. Man, was I happy to see him, and he was even happier to see me.

He introduced me to a Danish girl who he was hanging out with but I barely noticed her. I was glowing and felt strong. It was so good to see someone again I had spent six full weeks with, travelling through a third world country, having all kinds of adventures together and me being some sort of a mentor to him for picking up girls and other stuff. We had gone out many times and even kissed the same girl.

While we were downing another liter of beer I felt my balls grow to epic proportions. I was on fucking fire and walked straight to two girls passing us by and started talking.

"Hey, where are you going?" I said to them when I saw that they were heading for the stairs to the second dance floor. They started talking Spanish and knew only a few words of English. I soldiered on with some horrible Spanish and didn't care what they thought about it. I remembered the words my friends from Chile had taught me in Moscow: "Te quiero dar un beso" (I want to kiss you). I whispered it in her ear and she turned her head and kissed me. I pushed her against the wall and made out with her. We danced a bit and had a drink.

Darren tried to get with the other girl but it looked she wasn't that much in to him and he went to look for the Danish girl.

My girl was ready to go and I couldn't find Darren anymore to say goodbye. We had only talked 10 minutes at most.

We walked over to the girls' apartment and we tried to talk a bit. No need: we were banging within minutes of entering her apartment. She was average-looking but had a good body.

The sex wasn't even that good, and when we went for a second round she was even on the phone with her girlfriend while riding me. I grabbed the phone out of her hand, threw it of the bed and told her to stopping messing around with it. She had been texting with her friend before when I was taking her from behind. I didn't like her at all but I fucked away all the frustration I'd built up over the last week feeling sorry for myself. Skywalker was back in business again, Return of the Jedi!! Argentinean flag captured!

I slept over and we said goodbye in the morning and exchanged phone numbers but we both knew it was just a formality. She knew I was not going to call her again.

Everyone was having breakfast in the hostel kitchen when I returned and Larry looked up when I came in with a big grin on my face. I fistbumped Larry and he knew enough and so did the others. I was fired up and full of energy.

I worked on the website that day and Larry, who did something in software for a social network company, helped me out. Till this day I don't know what exactly happened in my mind but after meeting Darren and hate-fucking that girl,

I became nearly fearless in nightly club game. My theory is that because I was kind of a mentor of Darren in Indonesia and taught him a lot about girls there, I just couldn't bear to face the shame of failing in front of him. Well, whatever it was, it worked and I was going to take as much advantage of it as possible.

I went out most nights during the week to a place called Maria Maria. It was a good place to go, with a live band on most days and always enough girls. It was a twenty-minute walk away from my hostel and it saved me on cab fare every night.

I got shot down by a lot of girls that week, probably for being too fanatic, but I didn't care about it. I went on with the plowing and was convinced I would get another bang soon.

The hostel were I was staying was great. It's called the

288

Baluch Backpackers Hostel, and it's pretty well-known. It has everything you needed to have a good time. It's small, so it's very easy to make contacts with others. There are weekly asados (barbeques) where you can eat as much steak as you want for forty pesos, about ten dollars. Argentina was living up to its name as the country with the best steaks in the world. The friendly owner noticed I was a big eater and didn't stop throwing big, juicy, four-centimeter thick steaks on my plate. I normally don't promote places but this one I can really recommend it if you want to have a great time in Cordoba.

I went out at least three times during the week to Maria Maria, and on the weekend to a club close by Cordoba's main square, called Studio Theater. I did loads of approaches but had trouble with the language barrier. I was so fired up that I would approach every girl no matter how much she was out of my league. I walked up to them and started talking, girls would ask how long I'd been travelling and saying almost two years always made one hell of an impression.

Anyway, one night I met three Brazilian girls who studied in Cordoba, chatted a bit with them and walked back to the apartment they were staying. Two of them walked straight upstairs and I was left behind with the girl I had been talking to for a while. This girl was smoking hot. She had a nice light brown skin, beautiful straight hair, a nice pair of perky tits and a nice big round booty. Her lips were big and sexy and she had a lip piercing. I kissed her and felt that her lips were super soft, I couldn't stop holding and kissing her, she wanted to take it slow a bit but I grabbed that big booty with both hands. She pulled away my hands but five seconds later I would put them back there. You have to be persistent sometimes. Those big soft lips just kept me busy and it was the best kissing I had ever done up until then. Another Brazilian girl would take over her position as world's best kisser a few months later.

We met up again the next day and I ran the best game I could, but now that she was sober she wouldn't kiss me anymore and confessed that she'd had an Argentinean boyfriend for a week. We met up once more that week to eat an ice cream and I tried again, but no success. I dreamed about her big soft lips around my dick that night.

Cordoba is Argentina's second largest city and a nice place to walk around. It was also the city where I've seen the most breastfeeding ever; you couldn't walk down the street without seeing a mother with a boob hanging out. It surprised me because I not noticed this in other Argentinean cities so far.

The ice cream in Argentina is very cheap and tastes amazing; I took several girls from the hostel to get an ice cream during the day and was fine-tuning my game this way. Backpacker girls were still on the bottom of my bang list but sometimes a cute girl came by. I loved walking around in the city center during the day. There were lots of hotties around and great music came from every shop I passed. I had always liked reggeaton but now I started loving it. I also heard a new kind of music: the music of the poor people, known as Cumbia Villeria. There were a couple of other songs I liked and downloaded. I used them later to pick up girls.

The weekly barbeques were great but for the rest of the week I was eating empanadas or chorizos on the street or heading over to Subway or McDonalds. Larry called me McDonalds' biggest fan. He'd left after a week in Cordoba because he was on a tight schedule for his trip.

I went out alone a lot and actually started enjoying it. Before, I would just take about just anyone from a hostel to go out with, no matter how beta or how much of a passive cock-block it was. Now, I didn't need the help.

The Brazilian girl still contacted me on Facebook but wouldn't go on a date with me because of her boyfriend. One night I ran into some of her friends, and since I was very drunk I tried to pick one of them up. It didn't work and the next day I got an angry email from the hottie and she unfriended me. I couldn't care less anymore. I knew that with my new-found powers I would ravish my way through South America. I planned to visit every country and capture every flag.

One night I went home with a really hot girl, but she barely spoke any English. Her girlfriend did but she was picked up by an Argentinean guy, and once we were at her apartment we had to sleep on a lounge sofa. This girl was at least a seven and a half in looks but I had a hard time connecting with her since my Spanish was almost non-existent and so was her English. We made out a bit and both fell asleep spooning, knocked out by the booze.

The famous Argentinean drink Fernet is an instant hangover, and I hated the stuff, but one of those girls brought me a half-liter of it mixed with Coca Cola. Mixed drinks are very strong in Argentinean clubs, it's like ¾ booze and ¼ cola, and it's relatively cheap too.

When we woke up together the next morning we barely knew what had happened the night before. We exchanged numbers and said goodbye. She flaked on me a couple of times when I tried to set up a daytime date, but two weeks later she sent me a message. I didn't reply to it. I had been celebrating my two-year anniversary of my trip with three German guys who were regulars in the hostel. The bottle of scotch I had bought for the occasion was already empty before we went out. I was very drunk that night and got an insane cold the day after. I stayed in bed for four days only watching movies all day instead of doing some writing to catch up with my website.

I had been nearly a month in Cordoba and would stay a month more if I could but I had to move on. I took a bus to Mendoza and trouble started.

Argentina – Mendoza

By this time I was in love with Argentina. I liked everything: the music, the food, the people. Instead of staying a week in Cordoba I stayed nearly a month. Now it was time to hurry up again and just pay Mendoza a short visit.

Since private rooms were still too expensive for my liking I stayed in another hostel. It looked like an OK place and the girls working there were OK-looking, but nothing special so far. I had been approaching like crazy in Cordoba but had only been with one girl and kissed a few others. Not results to go bragging about, but at least I conquered my fear to approach. It was all restricted to night game, though, and I had not been day-gaming at all. At night alcohol fueled my fearlessness but during the day the approach anxiety came back a little. Just walk up to a girl in the street? What the hell was I going to say to her? And what if she doesn't speak any English? In a club you can just turn around and walk back to the bar and approach another girl, but in the street I was afraid to look like a fool. I thought about Rosario and the girls Larry and I had met when using the Couchsurfing website.

A new plan was born, a plan that I should have executed in Cordoba where I was not doing much during the day and gambled everything on night game. *New city, new chances*, I thought, and send out about twenty emails in the next hour.

One girl answered very quickly and wanted to meet the same night. I agreed and went out to buy a shirt. I had been freezing my ass off all the time in Cordoba and needed a long-sleeve shirt instead of the t-shirts I was wearing. It took me a lot of shopping and walking before I found a shirt that would work in a club. It cost two hundred pesos, which was about fifty dollars. I'm ashamed to say it was the only dress shirt I owned for the rest of my trip.

The hostel combines all the partying with three other hostels owned by the same guy, and every night there's something to do in one of them. That night was a pizza night and when I was chatting with some people and eating the greasiest, cheesiest pizza ever, a girl from Panama joined our table. She seemed very interested and Panama is a pretty rare flag.

I was wearing jeans, nice black shoes and a brand new shirt and felt like a million dollars. I looked totally different from the other backpackers and I got noticed a lot more. I had to meet the girl I met online around ten at night so when I left the table I asked for the Panamanian girl's phone number; she didn't have a phone but wanted to see me again. She said I should come to see her the next day in another hostel. I felt like it was already a sure flag and bang and walked off with confidence.

The girl I was meeting at ten o'clock was working in another hostel not connected to the party hostels. As soon as she opened the door she was undressing me with her eyes.

The hostel was deserted and had no guests around. It had seen better days and most people were staying in one of the four party hostels now. We sat down in the kitchen and started to talk. I sat real close to her and start flirting after only a few minutes. She was definitely interested. I kissed her after half an hour and less than ten minutes later I had my dick inside of her.

Jewel was a bit thick but had giant tits and that will make me forget about a small belly. She was only twenty-three and quite a fanatic in bed. After a couple more rounds of sex, she asked me how long I was staying. I said "A day or five" and she wanted me to be her fuckbuddy for that time, no strings attached. I was OK with this and thought *Wow, my first solo online meet-up, and banging within forty-five minutes.* I went home early in the morning.

Later that day I met a second online girl for a drink; she was a tiny and skinny girl with a kind of happy girlish behavior. Let's name her Veronica. Her profile said that she was twenty-seven, but she soon admitted she was thirty-four but changed her age because everyone thought she was younger. She did look a lot younger and I started to regret using my real age instead of making myself five or six years younger since I can get away with it.

I kissed her after a while and although she was a bit shy about it in public, she went along with it.

That night I banged Jewel again in the hostel. The following day I met up with Veronica again and we walked around a park while I kissed her everywhere. She was playful but didn't want to bang. I met up with her a few times more but couldn't seal the deal.

In the meanwhile I was flirting with the girl who worked at my own hostel, but Jewel had to quit her job and started working at one of the other party hostels. This was bad news for me because now she would be at all the parties and could see everything I did.

That night Jewel and I checked into another unknown hostel to shag all night. I had the chance to practice my Spanish with her and brush up on my dancing skills but I didn't. Something I regretted many times later.

The Panamanian girl had seen me with Jewel and her interest cooled down. Jewel was getting more suspicious by the minute and tried to follow my every move.

I went out with a third online girl and we had a drink in a lounge bar. At first it wasn't going so well and we just had a pretty superficial conversation.

We went to another place and Jewel started texting me all the time, asking where I was. I texted her back that I was seeing an online date and that I wasn't available that night.

The third girl, whose name I think was Bea, got more interested and I did some of my coffee date game on her. Jewel called me and I pressed her call away. She kept calling and finally I picked up and she was asking me where I was but I didn't tell her.

By now Bea and I were drinking at some bowling bar and Jewel must have heard the sounds of bowling because fifteen minutes later she showed up there. I saw her and her big boobs bouncing down the stairs and I was afraid she was going make a big scene. I left the table and went over to talk to her. I told her that we weren't in a relationship and that I could meet other girls if I wanted. She accepted it but was pissed.

When I got back at the table, Bea was suddenly a lot more interested in me; I decided to play the player card and told about how the Vietnamese girls in Cambodia beat the crap out of each other over me. She ate up every word of the story and kept saying "You are a special guy". She invited me to her house to "drink a few shots of Jägermeister" together. Code talk for "I want to have sex".

At that moment Jewel showed up AGAIN and that really pissed me off. I told her I didn't want to see her again because she was way too clingy and obsessive. She didn't want to hear about it and cried and begged me to go with her that night. Stupidly I agreed, just to get rid of her. I told her to wait like twenty minutes and I said I needed to say goodbye to my date. Bea and I walked up the stairs and at the door I grabbed her hand, spinned her around and kissed her.

I was dumb as fuck for not manning up and going home with her and leaving Jewel behind. We agreed to do the

Jägermeisters the following day but she flaked after a few texts in the morning. I had lost momentum and she had probably talked it over with friends who advised her not to meet me anymore. Never heard from her again.

It reminded me to never to let go of a sure thing and that I had to stand up for myself more. I get soft when girls stir up drama and start crying.

Jewel kept growing more and more jealous, but she never stopped acting slutty around all the drunken hostel guys who all wanted to be with her and her giant tits. She was trying to make me jealous or something. I still had a chance with the Panamanian girl but Jewel kept cock-blocking me every opportunity she had. Since all the hostel parties were combined, she was always around. She pissed me off more and more but it was my own fault.

One night I saw her kissing some ex-boyfriend and got really angry with her, told her to fuck off but she started crying and begging me not dump her. She stayed in my dorm bed that night. I was weak again.

I did get a break from her when I took a winery tour, which was nice. It's the reason most people go to Mendoza anyway. Our small group from the hostel visited a few wineries where we could sample quite a lot of wines and even some absinthe. Absinthe, nicknamed the green fairy, is forbidden in a few countries because of its hallucinating effects and an alcohol percentage of 75%. It felt like drinking liquid fire.

There was a Canadian girl on the tour with whom I was flirting a lot.

At night one of the hostels had a barbeque night and off course I ate loads of steak again. After dinner people started dancing and the Canadian girl and I came close to a kiss, but surprise-surprise, cock-blocking Jewel and her big tits showed up. She was wearing a low cut dress and her enormous tits were almost falling out of her dress.

Lots of guys looked at her and a few made a drunken attempt to talk to her. The hostel was giving free tequila shots for guests and everyone was getting shitfaced real quick.

Jewel first started trying to make me jealous by dancing

with some other guys and when she saw I was a bit pissed off about it she jumped on my lap and almost rubbed her big tits in my face in front of the Canadian girl, who lost interest after that. One of two Chilean sisters was also interested in me but the damn language barrier made that fail big time. Body language and the worst Spanish ever only goes so far.

I decided it was hopeless to try to get away from Jewel and decided to stay with her one more day, bang her a few times and get the hell out of there. I made the best of the night and danced a lot with Jewel.

We fucked like wild animals later that night in some hotel. Making each other jealous, stirring up drama and being frustrated with each other sure brings out a lot of raw passion. She had to work during the day and I met up with two girls I met online and also once more with Veronica.

I left Mendoza after ten days instead of the planned five. At the time I was a bit disappointed with myself for not being more coldblooded with Jewel, the way I'd been with girls in Asia. The truth was that despite all the drama I actually enjoyed her company a lot. She taught me a lot about Argentina, the music, some dancing, and we generally had fun, but our agreement to be just fuck buddies was a bad one.

I learned a lot that week and had tried out different techniques while meeting online girls for a drink.

Techniques that would be helpful in securing my next flag in Chile.

Chile – Santiago

The trip from Mendoza to Santiago takes about six hours and is more like a sightseeing tour than just a bus ride. The bus swirls through the snowy Andes and the views are spectacular.

Since Chile was known to be more expensive than Argentina, which already wasn't cheap, I went to a hostel again. I went sightseeing a bit and went to the hill nearby the Bellavista neighborhood where I was staying.

I climbed it with two American guys I had met in the hostel. The climb was quite steep and it took about an hour to get to the top, where there's a massive Maria statue on top.

Well, what can I say? Bellavista means "Beautiful view", but the whole city was covered in a thick cloud of smog. I hadn't seen so much smog since Almaty, in Kazakhstan. Santiago is closed in by mountains on all sides so the smog can't really go anywhere. Combine this with a city full of cars and the result is a big brown blanket smothering the city.

On the way down we saw a few young girls and we started talking to them. Their English was reasonable and I invited them to go for a beer since we were already in Bellavista, which is the bar area of Santiago. We sat down and I started gaming straight away. The girls must have liked us, because they invited us over to their apartment at night. The Americans were from some farmer state in America and a little rough around the edges. I had an eye on the hot girl who seemed to like me, the one who invited us to her apartment. The two other girls were OK-looking which was quite normal to see around Santiago.

At night we bought a bottle of Pisco, Chile's local alcoholic drink – though there's a huge dispute with Peru over who actually came up with it first. I like the drink so I'm not taking sides on this one. We drank lots of Piscolas (Pisco mixed with Coca Cola) at the girls' place and I was already looking around where to sleep that night. Unfortunately there was only one bedroom.

One of the Americans had very foul language and I was afraid he was going to screw things up. Foul language and inappropriate subjects like violence and religious/political views are best avoided when talking to girls, especially in countries where violent political coups aren't even ancient history.

We went dancing in a club in Bellavista and I made a move on the hot one. She didn't want to kiss and to my surprise the two Americans were making out with the two other girls. I tried again with the hot girl and but she didn't want to. We danced a bit more and I saw that a couple of girls were eyeballing me from a few meters away.

I had noticed them before but didn't pay too much attention to it since I already had a date. I walked away from our dates and headed over to the bar for a beer. There was a corridor leading to the toilets which had some lounge seats, I sat down and saw the other girls walk by. I tapped one on the shoulder and started rambling away when she turned around. About half a minute later I found out that neither of them spoke a word of English. I grabbed the cutest one by the hand and said "Bailar!" which is Spanish for dancing. We danced and I was making out with this girl within two minutes, making damn sure the other three girls saw me kissing her. They walked off with angry looks on their faces, and the Americans followed.

When the club closed I got the number of the Chilean girl and walked back to the hostel. As far as I understood she wanted to meet me again the next day.

When I saw the Americans again in the morning I asked them what had gone on. They told that the girls were very upset and bitched about me for the rest of the night. I think the rude guy said he got laid, but I had strong doubts with his story since he was very drunk that night, had zero game, and no place to bang. I didn't ask too much about it since I had kind of ruined their night by revenge-kissing the other girl and pissing the first three off this way. Well, she had it coming for leading me on and flirting all the time with me. Maybe if I invested a little bit more time in her, she would be my Chilean flag.

That night I met up with a girl I'd connected with on Couchsurfing.com. By the looks of her profile she was at least a seven, highly educated with a big government job and had lots of interesting, out-of-the-ordinary hobbies which I can't mention without revealing too much of her identity.

Paula and I met up at a subway station after a lot of hassle finding the right location. I was very impressed with her appearance, which was very classy and sophisticated.

We had a few drinks and I did my date game on her, which is basically being totally different from everyone she had ever met before. I have perfected this over many dates and it's a good way to get into girls' pants. The conversation with Paula went very well, and after we bounced to a few different locations. We went dancing at the same club I'd been to with the three girls. I'm blind as a bat in clubs but I think I saw one of the girls there, looking all angry at me while I was giving Paula an extra spin around smiling like a big happy baby.

At one point I was out of money even though we had been splitting the bill all night. This is another advantage of meeting a girl on Couchsurfing. You meet as equals without any intent to date, so it's normal to split the bill. Meeting as equals is where it gets sneaky. The girl is a local who is willing to show you around the city or meet you for a drink and you turn it in to a seduction without her noticing it at first.

All you have to do is create an attractive profile with a good background story and lots of pictures. Make sure you have some pictures of you with girls around. Use pictures which give a reasonable doubt about whether the girl's a girlfriend, but nothing too obvious. I have about a hundred pictures on there, about twenty of which are of me with a girl. Girls who see your profile will read between the lines and see that you are popular with girls, and this way you establish the most powerful tool of a womanizer: pre-selection.

The rest of the pictures should be of you in all kinds of interesting and exciting places, some landscapes, a few bro pictures of you hanging out with friends, a few mixed pictures and pictures of scary stuff like the ones I have holding snakes and scorpions and doing a skydive. The whole profile should say Fun. After a while you will have lots of reviews of girls saying how much they enjoyed ~~fucking~~ meeting you.

Have a few (fake) reviews of dudes also. Now compare this to the profile of all the regular dudes on there with boring stories and pictures. You will already stand out and have lots of dates lined up before you even arrive in the city.

Anyway, back to the story. Paula bought me a few drinks and I asked her to come with me to my hostel. We went there some minutes later and I sneaked her in past the reception.

The dorm room was still empty and we went to my bed and once I lay down it was obvious that all that booze had hit me like a hammer. I had whiskey dick and didn't perform well between the sheets. Paula was very drunk too and said it was OK but things like this barely ever happen to me and it bothered me a lot.

A guest walked into the room and we decided to stop fucking. I remembered how much I hated having sex in hostels and not having money enough for a decent room.

We were both very hungover the next morning and I walked her back to the metro station. She complemented me on my interesting, funny and dreamy questions the night before. In other words, you're not boring like the rest. I had to walk her past the reception and the breakfast area and so the whole hostel saw me walking around with this hot Chilean chick.

The personnel was not amused when I returned and tried to lecture me in front of the guests, saying it was not allowed to bring girls in the middle of the night. I just shrugged my shoulders, put a big smile on my face, and said "I didn't know that". This situation shouted out Pre-selection, and suddenly some of the foreign girls in the hostel were interested in me.

But I had other plans. My whiskey dick had hurt my pride and I wanted a rematch with Paula – I really liked her too. She was everything I never had back in Holland. A hot girl with brains, a well-paying job, interesting hobbies and a classy appearance. I couldn't get the Tom Jones song out of my head and was singing "She a lady" all day. I downloaded the song to my phone and showed it to her. "It's our song", I said to her, and now she will think of me whenever she hears it. A thing I did with quite a few girls all over the world. With different songs of course.

On Friday night I saw the Chilean friends again I'd met in Lithuania, Estonia and Moscow. They had been asking me to come over to Chile for one-and-a-half years now and I was finally there.

At Gustavo's house I met his wife and my other friend Nico. Gustavo is a big hard rock fan and showed me his immense collection of CDs, DVDs, and countless pictures of him with famous rock stars. He even had his own room for it. They prepared a delicious barbeque and we drank lots of wine, beer and the bottle of Pisco I had brought with me.

I had barely recovered from the drunken state I was in

the night before and had to hit the bottle again. Nico was very excited to see me again and the two of us went out that night to some club. Gustavo had had way too much to drink and didn't join us. Nico had already branded me as a legendary pick-up artist but I was way too drunk to even stumble out some full sentences in the club. It was a fun night anyway; we talked to some girls and I ran into a girl I'd been hanging out with in the hostel in Cordoba.

The next day, I went out with yet another girl from the Couchsurfing website while having a hangover for the third day in a row. We visited a local fish market and witnessed a demonstration against the government plans to build a hydro dam and ruin the natural beauty of the south of Chile. I was warned not to join the demonstration, because the week before half the city got tear-gassed and demonstrators got beat up. There was a big police force on their feet, but things kept quiet that day. It disappointed me a bit because I wanted to see some old school rioting like I'd seen and briefly joined at Football matches in my hometown.

That night I went with Gustavo to a football match with his favorite team, Universidad de Chile or La U. It was the quarter final of some cup and they won seven-to-one against a team named O'Higgins. It was a great match and we had lots of fun there. Afterwards we had some drinks and a barbeque with his friends.

One of the last days I was in Santiago I went to the cinema with Paula and had some drinks afterwards, but not too much this time.

Later that night we went to a love hotel and banged a few times. The sex wasn't really good and although I really liked her it was kind of a deal-breaker for the both of us.

Despite the fact that she had a beautiful body with fake boobs and the most sensual big lips ever, I wasn't that turned on by her and she noticed that, and we even argued a bit. The chemistry of our first couple of dates was gone. It just didn't click for the both of us.

You can't always win – but the Chilean flag had been captured. She called off a date the next day with some excuse. I texted her that I was going to Valparaiso, a two-hour bus ride away, for a few days and would return to Santiago again later that week.

Chile – Valparaiso

I was hammering at the door of the hostel: despite having made reservations, there was no-one there. The other hostels were further away from the city center and on top of a hill.

Most of the harbor city of Valparaiso is built on hills and this gives splendid views over the city. The houses are colorful and there's lots of artsy graffiti on walls throughout the city. This is the main reason that lots of tourists and backpackers visit this small coastal city.

After smoking a cigarette and waiting for half an hour, someone finally showed up and let me in. The hostel was a big one-floor apartment and I was the only guest. I took a bed in the big dorm room since that was the cheapest option.

That night I met up with a girl through the travel website. Marisol was a good-looking girl and she smiled a lot. We went uphill to a small coffee place and I started throwing my coffee date game her way. I had my doubts if it would go as easily as it had with Paula in Santiago. I was now fully relying on my own rules about having a drinking date with an unknown girl.

Marisol was a bit hard to figure out: she responded well to my game but I wasn't sure where I was with her. I might have been in the dreaded friend zone. She invited me to meet some girlfriends and we had a few drinks in a small bar. It was there that I had the best Pisco-Sour ever.

We said goodbye at night but I didn't go for the kiss with her. I thought it might be too early for that. She wanted to meet again the night after.

The next morning I wasn't alone in the hostel anymore and met an Austrian guy with whom I went to walk around the city.

The first thing we did was look for a map and some food. We had a big and rather expensive breakfast in one of the cafes in the center. I wanted to eat well because since I'd been there I had only eaten sopaipillas in Valpo, as Valparaiso is nicknamed. Sopaipillas are a sort of pancakes made from pumpkin that you eat with mustard sauce. I loved them and two of them would fill you up for a while for only twenty cents each. The meal at the café went straight through my stomach and what went in as chicken came out looking like coffee. I almost had to run back to the hostel.

Half-an-hour later we went back to the city and walked around all day, seeing all the sites, taking one of the famous hillside lifts and visiting the Maritime museum.

The museum also displayed the capsule that freed those miners who had been stuck underground for over six weeks. The Austrian dude wanted to go out at night but I had other plans.

Marisol was half-an-hour late and it was freezing cold outside. I waited for her at a square and looked around a bit. There were street artists, lots and lots of stray dogs and students making some extra money by selling paintings and/or sandwiches. There were some bums around, but not many.

Marisol showed up and I made fun of her for being a typical woman, late all the time. Someone later told me that South Americans don't see time as a line as most punctual westerners do, but more like a cloud. This made a lot of sense to me, because I almost never met anyone who arrived in time on this side of the planet.

Marisol and I went to a coffee bar, where we talked and laughed a lot, then we bounced to a street with bars and drank Pisco Sours while joking some more. I remember us crossing the street at the wrong moment and nearly getting run over. She was the one who said "go", so I made fun of her a lot for trying to kill me.

Afterwards we went to a club that was playing all kinds of music in three different rooms. Here I saw some other foreigners but I stayed in the Latin music part most of the time, dancing with Marisol and her girlfriends.

At the end of the night, we kissed and we went to my hostel and had sex in the dorm. She's a beautiful girl but was a bit shy between the sheets. I also remember really bumping my head on the top bunk bed and Marisols feminine, motherly instinct kicked in and rubbed the hurt spot like I was a small child.

The next morning I smuggled her out the dorm without the owner knowing it.

One of the things I always ask a girl is the exact moment she was attracted to me and the moment she decided to have sex with me. This is a good way to fine tune your game and quite interesting to know. She told me that she was attracted to me from the moment we had coffee that night before, which meant that my café date game had worked. She said she thought about having sex with me after we said goodbye the first night, the night when I didn't go for the kiss.

We said goodbye but I told her I would come back to visit her again.

Chile – Santiago

I found another hostel in Santiago, named the Bellavista hostel, and it was a lot more fun there. The building is a bit old but at least the personnel were very friendly and they had heaters everywhere.

I met loads of cool people, including three Brazilian girls. I tried to game one a bit but was friend-zoned that night. They invited me to come visit them in Brazil. I tried to get a date again with Paula, who was still on my mind, but she flaked. After this I never tried again.

Gustavo and his wife invited me for dinner at one of the best burger places in the country. It was the biggest and most expensive hamburger I ever ate in my life. My belly was growing an inch that night and the next day I went up the hill with the Maria statue again to get in shape a bit.

A few days later I went up there again and noticed my stamina had already improved a bit because I was walking a lot those days and had cut back on the smoking a bit. I needed my power because I was going back to Valparaiso a few days later.

Chile – Valparaiso again.

I was planning on going north to La Serena and thought that I might as well go through Valparaiso to see Marisol again. When I arrived at the bus station in Valparaiso two hours later I saw that they also sold tickets to go south. I had

304

skipped the south when I was in Argentina because of the high bus prices. I didn't feel like paying over $400 on a return bus ticket and then have to whop out a shitload of money on accommodation there.

Chile was supposed to be more expensive than Argentina, but I saw a ticket all the way down south for only $110. Punta Arenas was nearly as far down south as its Argentinean counterpart, Ushuaia, where half the backpacker population in Latin America goes.

I wanted to go to a different place, one less crowded and more pristine, and told Marisol my plans when I met her again. She said that she'd thought she'd never see me again. She was truly happy I was back and stayed with me in the hostel again, I had rented a private room now and we couldn't stop making love that night. She has a beautiful face and body and a way of attracting me that was more than just physical.

The next three days we stayed together and went out several times, to the cinema, to do some shopping including a hunt for the coolest sweater ever except that we couldn't find the right size, even after visiting three shops of the same branch. There was none around and I had to be cold for a few more months. Marisol is a very sweet girl, very smart and has a good job, a bit shy and definitely marriage material. I might visit her again someday.

The route to Punta Arena was closed due to an earthquake that had destroyed the only road there. Marisol called almost fifteen bus companies and tried everything but alas, the road was closed for at least a week and I was running out of time. I had to move on despite having such a great time with her.

When she waved goodbye to me at the bus station I wondered if I'd ever meet a sweet and beautiful girl like her again and if I was a fool for letting go yet another beautiful girl who was crazy about me.

Chile – Calama – San Pedro

I stopped for half a day in the city of Calama, which has the world's biggest open copper mine. It was one of those giant mines you see on the Discovery channel sometimes, absolutely huge. It was an interesting experience to walk around there.

After the tour I took a bus to San Pedro de Atacama, the place every tourist in Chile goes to, that I wanted to skip it for that very reason, but there was one reason that made me go there anyway. It made a good stopover on my way to Bolivia and Marisol had told me about her younger sister living there.

For the second time on my trip I had a chance to do a double whammy: the two-sister bang. I was close to it in the Philippines and I got another chance now. I'd thought it through on the bus and decided to go for it. I would feel like a rotten bastard later.

I met Marisol's younger sister a few days later and we went out. The sister thing turned out to be just another dream. She had a boring boyfriend who was a nice guy but totally unable to stand up to her. He was friendly though.

Marisol's sister was a lot wilder than her and got really drunk. We smoked some weed afterwards with a bunch of people. The weed was really bad and we only had one spliff for a whole group of people.

Later on in my stay I went on a tour with two Dutch girls. One of them was even taller than me and we went to a salt lake where you could float in the water. I didn't go in the water all the way, it was really cold and I'd already had a runny nose for four weeks by then and didn't feel like another four weeks of snottering and sniffing.

It was freezing cold while I was in Chile. Just because it's South America doesn't mean it's automatically going to be warm – a lot of it is in the mountains, after all.

Even in the hostel it was freezing again and I had to sleep with a beanie on. It was time to move to warmer places and I took the bus to La Paz.

Bolivia – La Paz

After taking another endless bus ride I arrived in La Paz, the capital of Bolivia. The Loki hostel was recommended by everyone I had met in the South, so I went there.

Within the first hour of arriving, I met a Portuguese guy

and his friend I'd met in La Serena and San Pedro, saw a Dutch girl I met in Cordoba, and also caught sight of Chrystal, the Australian girl I had met in Cordoba and Santiago.

The Loki hostels are a chain of party hostels. It's all about parties at night and mostly aimed for the very young backpackers travelling on Mommy and Daddy's money in their gap year. It was also a hangout for hipster backpackers.

The facilities were great, with nice big beds with fluffy blankets, nice bathrooms with piping hot water and powerful showers. I needed a good scrubbing after the horrible cold outside bathrooms in San Pedro.

At night there were parties where people would dress up and get stupidly drunk. Afterwards the whole group would go to local clubs, which were shitty at best. Since I couldn't really connect with the backpackers and was looking for a Bolivian flag, I only joined the parties the first few days.

I got to know two people working at the hostel, Judith who was German and Hench a massive and ripped black guy from England.

One morning I was talking with him and told something about my website, and he said: "Oh shit, is that you? I've heard about a Dutch guy travelling and banging his way around the world." I was like, "Yeah, that's me." Hench started shaking my hand and introduced me to another staff member, saying "This is that Dutch guy we talked about".

I can't say that I wasn't a bit proud of being "that Dutch guy" and having my reputation precede me. It reminded me of the time when I heard some English guys in Bali talk about a tall Dutch guy raising hell in Cambodia.
I was pretty sure they were talking about me at the time. The group was devided into guys hyping it up and others saying things like "That bloke's a cunt".

One night I went out with the Portuguese guys and five young English girls. The girls gave off a party vibe but turned into a boring group when they started to play cards at a bar all the Loki backpackers went to. I still thought the two Portuguese guys had a chance with them but they didn't capitalize on their chances. There were Bolivian girls around but most of them were not very attractive.

At the end of the night some hot girls came to the Blue house discoteca (an underground dump). They looked like they were richer, but were also very stuck-up when approached. Those who didn't came with an overprotective boyfriend or orbiter shot me down or didn't speak English. I went three times to this dreadful place and swore never to return to this dump no matter how many free drinks they gave away.

I signed up for private Spanish lessons and went to a small office five times a week for two hours a day. The Bolivian girl teaching wasn't that good at it and I should have asked for another teacher but since she had massive blowjob lips and responded well to my flirting I stayed with her. I pretty much fucked up my Spanish lessons by not having a really skilled teacher with only limited English skills and not doing my homework or any extra learning during the day. I had to sleep off hangovers.

One night I went out to a place called Traffic, which is the only decent place to go out in La Paz, and saw a couple of Bolivian girls. Two of them looked like giant sluts and the other looked more decent. I approached the decent one, had a short talk and kissed her there. She was not bad-looking for a Bolivian girl, who are considered the least attractive girls in South America. Her name was Maria and I went out with her a few times. She was quite smart but in an annoying know-it-all way.

I moved out of the Loki hostel and went to a two-star hotel, close to the city center but far away enough to be on real Bolivian territory so I wouldn't see those damn tourists all day. The two-bed hotel room was almost the same price as a hostel bed at the Loki. I found it ridiculous to stay in a noisy dorm in the poorest country in South America.

The only difference was the shared bathroom, which was a mess but had a good hot shower. It had one of those dangerous electric showerheads which were common in a lot of South American and Asian countries. You learn a great deal about how much you're willing to take your life in your hands when you're continually taking showers in places where there are live wires just hanging out of the showerhead.

Maria and I went and saw *Transformers 3* in a local cinema. It was even more childish than the first two.

We got into an argument while making out. Although good-looking she was a bad kisser and didn't excite me much, plus it was freezing cold in the cinema, so when she touched my dick nothing happened there and she said it was small. The movie stopped twenty minutes before the end and the personnel couldn't fix the problem. Welcome to Bolivia!

When we walked out on the street I was not happy with her for saying I had a small one while she had never even seen the damn thing. It's possibly the worst thing a girl can say on a date. She didn't see the harm in it and that made me even angrier with her. I said I didn't want to see her again for insulting me this way, said goodbye and walked off.

When I woke up the next morning, I found she had send me a text message saying how sorry she was and that she had asked her girlfriends about the comment she made and they'd told her she was an dumb idiot for saying a thing like that.

We met again and I took her to my room and banged the crap out of her. Maria wasn't experienced at all and at one point I went extra deep. She asked me to stop because I was too big and she told about her Bolivian ex–boyfriend, who had a small one. I had made my point that night but wasn't in a hurry to do it again.

One night we went to a typical Bolivian disco party and that was fun. I was offered lots of free drinks and even had a funny dance with a young cholita. A cholita is a Bolivian woman dressed in traditional clothing, including a bowler hat. You will see them everywhere in Bolivia. They even have their own wrestling league, in the style of WWF.

For some reason my Bolivian phone card stopped working and I never made an effort to call Maria again on a street phone or to buy another phone card.

I was on a constant diet of rice and chicken that I bought in the neighborhood I was staying. Every night for at least two weeks I bought half a roasted chicken with potatoes, vegetables and a big bag of steamed rice for only four dollars. Enough for two meals. Although it was Bolivian street food, it was the only thing my stomach could hold without crapping my guts out all the time.

The Spanish lessons were improving a bit but I hadn't reached the level I'd expected after eight days of two-hour private lessons.

I went out on a date with my teacher to a different cinema. I couldn't wait to make a move on her and kiss those huge lips, but she kept giving me a head turn and saying no to it. She confessed she'd never been out with a foreigner and she was probably very conservative about kissing. Well, it was worth trying it anyway.

Banging a school teacher had been on my list ever since I was a spotty teenager with a boner for his long-haired substitute math teacher.

During the day I walked around the city a bit, did some writing for my websites or went to the Loki to eat lunch and use the free internet Wi-Fi there.

At one night I went out with a French guy and we went looking for the local Hard Rock Café.

When we finally found a taxi driver to take us there and stepped out of the cab I saw two girls walking out the door, planning on getting in our taxi.

I said with a loud voice "Where do you girls think you're going? Let's get back inside". They looked at each other, smiled and went back in.

They were playing reggeaton inside, and I saw Judith with a group of Israelis I knew from the Loki hostel. I turned my back on the girls I'd just lured back in to go talk to her. I saw them looking over to me from the corner of my eye and just when I thought they were about to leave again, I walked over to them and started talking. They were dressed up quite slutty and at first sight I wasn't sure if they were hookers or not. We talked a bit and I started dancing with one of the girls, named Sierra.

A few minutes later we kissed and she went wild on me. Lots of people in the hostel were looking over and I saw a bit of a disappointed look on Judith's face.

Sierra wasn't Bolivian but Spanish, and she was a real rocker girl. We went to her apartment and some Swedish dude who was stupidly drunk tagged along with the other girl. Barely ten minutes after we got to the apartment, Sierra and I went to the bedroom and banged.

The drunken Swedish guy left in the middle of the night, and the other girl said nothing happened but I had heard her moan a bit when I visited the toilet. I captured my Spanish flag that night and stayed five days at Sierra's apartment. She had a big appetite for sex. We banged so much that I was physically exhausted all the time.

La Paz happens to be the highest capital in the world, sitting at a 3600-meter altitude, and it's hard to breathe in the center, where pollution is high, the streets are steep, you're hit by thirty-five degrees sunshine, and the air is thin in the first place.

One night Sierra and I went out to a rock bar having already had a bottle of wine before with a gay friend of hers. At the bar we drank some giant bottle of blue stuff.

When we returned to her apartment I was quite drunk. I woke up in the middle of the night and went to the toilet because I felt sick. I threw up really bad and got a nice surprise afterwards. The toilet didn't flush. There was no water whatsoever and there I was in a girl's apartment with a barfed-up toilet bowl. I didn't know what to do so I just put the toilet seat down and went back to sleep. Luckily I woke up first and when I checked the water it worked again. I praised all the gods that morning for protecting me from huge embarrassment.

That day we didn't do much because I was hungover, though Sierra felt fine. It was probably because she's used to living at a high altitude. A high altitude is killing for your alcohol tolerance and gets you drunk quickly.

Sierra, who was only twenty-one years old, was into very rough sex and wanted to get beat up and fake-raped by me. I'm not really into that but I'm open for all kinds of things. The more I beat and choked her the wilder she became. I even made a video of it. One time she came so hard that her legs were still lightly shaking almost fifteen minutes afterwards.

During the day I went out to walk around a bit and rode a lot of local minibuses, which is quite an experience. My health was at an all-time low and I quit smoking to improve my breathing a bit. It took a long time for me to get used to the altitude, but at least I didn't get really sick from it like some others. I was thinking about Brazilian Charlize who I was going to visit again a few months later. I needed to get my health back to be able to have a few wild nights with her.

After two-and-a-half weeks of La Paz I needed to move on to Peru. I had gone out almost every night in six or seven different places all over town, including the infamous Route 36 bar where you can buy overpriced cocaine from the barkeep. The French guy tried some but said the quality was bad. I'm not interested in drugs besides weed anyway.

La Paz was almost the last place I could relax a bit. The rest of South America would be on a strict time schedule, a way of travelling I really hated, but I had already booked flights to get me back to Holland just before Christmas. Money was running out, and though I wasn't exactly homesick, I was starting to long just a bit for some stability and First World easy living. Backpacking takes a toll on you. And I had now set myself up to really let it hit me as I rushed around getting in as much as I could. I was going to earn that First World rest, and it was going to be great.

I stayed over at Sierra's before leaving for Lake Titicaca. Let's just say she wasn't happy about me leaving.

Bolivia – Lake Titicaca

Lake Titicaca was a short stopover where I stayed for four days to relax before I started the rushed part of my trip. I had a nice room for three and half dollars, including a big bed, a desk, a television with cable and a bathroom.

The one-day boat tour, also three and half dollars, took us to the island that according to Incan culture was the birthplace of the sun. It was great – I even ran in to the Panamanian girl I had met in Mendoza, the one who seemed interested in me but got cock-blocked by Jewel. I went in full-on pick-up mode but she didn't respond much to it. She was with one of the guys who were with her on the boat.

Over the next days I saw quite a few football matches of the Copa America and did some writing for my websites.

312

Lake Titicaca is a very small beach town with loads of regular tourists and backpacking couples. I lived on eight dollars a day there, just eating a trout with rice for breakfast at the local fish market, one tourists had barely discovered, since they'd rather eat overprized spaghetti or pizza in one of the many rip-off tourist restaurants than sit between local Bolivians guys and cholitas with their bowlers hats and heavy one-meter pigtails. The fish was delicious and was freshly caught every morning. A big plate of food for only $2.20. I'd eat a can of Pringles for lunch and street food consisting of potatoes and some pieces of cow's heart at night.

After 4 days I was totally refreshed and moved on to Peru.

Peru – Cuzco

The bus ride from Lake Titicaca to Cuzco was really something else. The bus was full of Bolivian cholitas, all carrying loads of blankets with them. They use one blanket to fold some kind of backpack and put like twenty-five other blankets in there. The number of blankets in the bus was ridiculous and the women were fighting over headspaces with other women and tourists, me included. I'm still not sure why they brought so many. Perhaps they sold them somewhere.

Cuzco is famous for being one of the first cities in Peru and has a rich history. The discovery of Machu Picchu, the ancient lost city high in the mountains, had turbo-boosted the town into a tourist Mecca.

I checked into a Loki hostel where I met Judith again, the German girl who worked in the Loki in La Paz. When you stay in a Loki hostel you can be sure you'll have good beds and showers, but also that you'll have to put up with lots of loud music. I really started to dislike drunkenly backpackers at this point and couldn't wait to have my own room again.

I had read on the internet that Peru would be a piece of cake and girls would nearly jump on your dick once you entered a club. This put some pressure in my mind because when I looked on the street I hadn't noticed any extra attention from girls. How could I? The city was totally packed with hundreds of tourists.

The first time I went out I had a few drinks at the Loki first and then went to a KFC at the Plaza des Armas afterwards to get some food.

Next up was Mama Africas, a place recommended to me by many. I walked in and ordered a beer. After just two sips of the beer I felt a weird feeling in my stomach. *What the hell? Is this what I think it is?* I felt my bowels jumping around in my body. It was time to get the hell out of there and into a bathroom. I paid the cab driver double to step on it back to the hostel and released hell into that poor toilet bowl. This night was ruined and I had to wait it out.

The next night I went back to Mama Africas and walked into the lounge bar on the first floor. There weren't many people around but I was advised to get there early and pick up the early gringo–hunters. A few backpackers and some Peruvian couples were the only ones there. I turned around and saw two girls at a table. I went straight in and started talking. They gave me the "who the hell are you?" look but I usually don't give in to shit tests and just keep talking.

My inner game was strong that night. I locked myself in by standing between the small space between the wall and table so it looked the girls were standing around me instead of me trying to pick them up. They ate up my gaming like candy, but not much later I found out that they were sisters. I called bullshit for a while, but they were actually two sisters from Lima on a short holiday. This put me in a difficult situation. They didn't seem like the type for a mystical sister threesome (if such a thing even exists) and if I gamed one I was sure that the other would cock-block me.

We went to the clubbing area on the top floor and sat down and drank some beers. I sat in between the girls and had fun with them and looked like a total pimp. They weren't superhot but OK-looking for their age, late twenties.
I was making constant eye contact with a black girl who looked like she came from some Caribbean island. Her skin was light brown, she had big curly hair and the biggest, juiciest round ass I had ever seen in my life. Her eyes were big and looked very sensual; her lips were massive and seductive.

I wanted her so bad. She was very drunk and with some guy with Rasta hair but I'm sure it wasn't her boyfriend. Even the two sisters started asking me if I liked her and said I should maybe talk to her. I wasn't sure if they were shit-testing me again or already decided not to do anything with me anyway.

The decision to stay with the two sisters and try something with them is one of the dumbest decisions I made on my entire trip. Deep down I knew that nothing was going to happen with them, but I didn't want to walk out on them since we were having a good time together anyway and it was the pre-selection I got from them that got me the hot Caribbean girl's attention in the first place. I should have tested the waters with the drunken Caribbean girl a bit. She had an ass to die for, the kind you normally only see in rap or reggeaton videos. I could have gone to the toilet and walk passed her and said a few words to test her out. I might have missed out on one hell of a good lay with this big-assed girl, and I never saw her again in Cuzco. It gave me the feeling that I was getting soft. Back in places like Cambodia and the Philippines I had no troubling walking out on girls and being a total asshole. Over there its': "easy come, easy go", but in South America it's "hard to get and easy to lose".

Although I had a good night with the two sisters and got lots of looks from everyone, I felt I had failed that night. But then, what would I have done if I'd scored one of those girls? I stayed in a fucking hostel with a strict no-guest policy at the door. The night guard wouldn't let you in if you were not wearing a colorful Loki bracelet.

After looking around for a few hours the next day I found a cheap hotel very close to Plaza des Armas, where all the nightly action was. I got a two-bed room for only a little bit more than the dorm bed price, just like in La Paz. The room was OK but had shared showers which were horribly cold.

From then on I stayed in that hotel but took my laptop and some bathing stuff to the Loki and showered and used the Wi-Fi there. They didn't take the bracelet when I checked out and I could walk in whenever I wanted. I had some lunch and drinks there so they actually made some money off me.

Judith told me a story about a guy who checked out of

the Loki after one night but left his backpack lying in some dorm. Every night he went looking for an empty bed and slept there. That's another way to save money.

I went out again and felt better and more self-assured knowing I had a place to take a girl in the middle of the night. Having to worry about a place is really bad for your inner game and can really make you fuck things up.

During the day I took some private Salsa lessons from a Dutch girl living in Cuzco, who having her own salsa school there. She was a very cute girl. I'm not the greatest dancer and it took me a while to learn the basics. Dancing in a high altitude and hot city isn't really easy and I was out of breath a lot. She taught me well and in my mind I could see myself dancing with some Colombian hotties in Cali, the Salsa capital of South America.

Well, I hadn't come to Cuzco to go out or take salsa lessons. I came there for the same reason everyone goes there: the world-famous Macchu Picchu temples.

Judith and I decided to go together and looked for tours. The tours cost a minimum of $190, and we were both careful with our cash. We wanted to go as cheaply as possible and decided to do the do-it-yourself route. We went to buy tickets at the ticket office outside the center.

Judith didn't get out of bed till two in the afternoon and was slow and had to eat first. I told her to hurry up because I had salsa lessons at four o'clock.

When we finally arrived at the office it was already past three and there was a massive lineup. I was really grumpy at that moment and the girl right in front of me in the line noticed and gave me a strange look while I was ranting away to Judith. I could hear that she was American. She was even taller than I am and had a big ass but everything was in proportion. She was built and that kinda attracted me at that moment. I thought about what it would be like to have sex with her. This girl might even be stronger than me. Only once before had I been with a girl taller than me, and that was the German girl with massive tits I had a one night stand with in Manila.

The line started moving and I bought a ticket and took a

taxi and rushed to my salsa lesson.

The next morning Judith and I left early and took a local bus to a small village named Santa Maria. The bus ride took five-and–a-half hours and was a real local experience, including me getting a suitcase dropped on my stomach while sleeping in a reclined seat. The moron on the right side of the bus hadn't properly stored his suitcase so it came down from the overhead space and smashed hard onto my stomach.

In Santa Maria we shared a taxi to the hydro station and it was an insane ride. Think high speeds in an old station car next to 200-meter deep cliffs with no railings on the sides. I knew the driver probably drove here every day and knew the road like the back of his hand but it still felt dangerous. Judith was really scared and asked the guy to slow down, which he did for about two minutes before putting the pedal to the metal again. When we arrived we still had to walk on the train tracks for over two hours before reaching Aqua Calientes, the small tourist town next to Machu Picchu.

We were totally beat after finally arriving and still had to find a room. We found one that wasn't too overpriced and shared a two-bed room.

We woke up at five and tried to get tickets for the bus up the mountain to Machu Picchu. The tickets were about eighteen dollars for a return trip and the line was massive. I opted to walk up there to save that money, and our long journey up the steps began. It took us exactly one hour to walk up the old Inca steps and my legs burned from taking the two thousand steps, some of which were knee-high. We only met two other people up the stairs who didn't take the lazy bus ride up there. I felt strong for yet another accomplishment at high altitudes. This old mountain goat was stronger than I'd thought.

We went through the ticket gates and finally stood eye-to-eye with the most famous attraction in South America.

Machu Picchu is very impressive but not really detailed; it's all big pieces of rocks but there aren't any carvings or small bits of work. We also went up Waynu Picchu, a very steep mountain that's very difficult to climb, especially if you've just walked up a couple of thousand steps.

Here you had to use both hands and feet. I was proud when I stood on the highest top possible and looked down on a very small Machu Picchu. We climbed back down the mountain and the steps to Aqua Calientes.

After one more night we walked back the train tracks for three hours the next day to the hydro station. There we found a minivan going straight back to Cuzco.

We bargained a cheap price and sat in the minivan with a group of annoying Spaniards for seven hours. Judith and I celebrated our exhausting trip with some giant kebabs.

We had only paid $110 each, including all transport, the $50 entrance tickets, two nights in a hotel room, and all our food and drinks; but more importantly we did it all by ourselves. It required some giant struggles, but those things always leave me feeling proud and make me mock those wimpy regular tourists with their guided tours and train and bus rides straight to the complex.

It might not have been a good idea to go learn how to dance after all that climbing, though. My legs felt like rubber when I took the last salsa lesson the next afternoon.

I got a haircut and looked sharp again, except for my cheap jeans with a missing button that meant I had to pull up my pants all the time. I had been looking around for a tailor to fix it but couldn't find one anywhere. I figured I'd only wear the jeans at night so that girls wouldn't notice how broken and dirty they were. At the end of my trip I was still wearing the same jeans and I must be known as South America's dirtiest and poorest player. These kinds of things I regret the most when I look back at my trip. I should have spent a bit more money on my appearance.

It was time to get my Peruvian flag and I went out again that night. A short Peruvian girl with large breasts approached me. She was with a Colombian girlfriend there, but unfortunately their brothers were too. The Colombian girl had a butterface (hot body but-her-face) but had a happy vibe and was a very sexy dancer.

We went to a couple of clubs together and then ended up at Mama Africas again. By this time I was making out with the Peruvian girl and constantly touching her boobs. Her brother didn't seem to mind.

A tall blond guy walked up to me and said he recognized me from a hostel in Mendoza. I had to think for a minute and then it hit me. I had talked to him and his friend for a while on the night I had an argument with Jewel when she cock-blocked me on the Canadian girl.

He was Australian and a pretty cool guy, and when the two girls left we went on a hunt for girls. I introduced some girls to him but he got nowhere with them. He asked me about my website and I didn't remember talking to him about it. It turned out he had heard it from someone else later. My reputation had preceded me again.

At the end of the night I approached a Peruvian girl and started gaming her. It seemed to work a bit but then she asked me for a cocktail. I had to make a decision. Would I break my own rule and buy her a seven-dollar cocktail or move away? The drink it was, because I saw a potential lay here. Well, I was right and she went home with me after some talking and kissing in some lounge seats at the club.

On arriving at my room I had to crap like crazy, and I left her in my room while I said I was going to "fresh up". I took forever and she asked where I had been so long. The best thing you can do at moments like this is just play dumb, so I said "fresh up" and gave her a dumb look. She went to wash up herself and I pointed her towards a different bathroom. She was average-looking but she had a great appetite for sex.

We banged four times that night and the following morning. I was setting new records and think I nearly broke my dick that day. Peruvian flag captured.

I texted the girl with the big tits when the other one left but she flaked on me that day. By then it was time to keep on moving, because I had overstayed my travelling schedule by a few days already. Lima, the capital of Peru, was waiting…

Peru – Lima

From Cuzco it was on to the next tourist attraction: the mysterious Nazca lines. The Nazca lines are giant sculptures in the sand only visible from the air. They are shrouded in mystery, as no one really knows who made them and how.

Some scientists like Erik von Däniken even believed they were runways for alien spaceships. Because sure, why not?

I took the bus to Nazca and arrived early in the morning. It was a very cloudy day and that worried me a bit.

A taxi driver took me to the small airport, where I asked about the weather conditions. They told me the clouds should clear up later that day but I thought they were bullshitting me. They tried to sell me a flight anyway, but they cost between $115-$140, so I didn't want to take the risk and hopped back into the taxi and drove back to the bus station. The cab driver was very friendly and even chased the bus to Lima down the street, honking his horn and cutting the bus off to try to get the driver's attention so I could get on, but it was too late. I was forced to wait for the next one. The cabbie dropped me off at the bus station and I gave him a big tip for all the effort he had made. It took me two buses and two more taxis to get to Lima and find the Lima Loki hostel.

The first thing I did when I arrived (besides flirting with one of the hot Peruvian girls working there) was take a long hot shower. Carrying around a backpack in the hot Peruvian sun and taking three different buses over almost thirty hours usually make you stink like a bum.

At night I was sitting in the hostel bar and just minding my own business with my laptop. I had some writing to do and was really focused for once. I had seen a girl look over a few times and I smiled at her.

At the end of the night she came over and almost jumped on my lap. She was a bit drunk and asked me what I was busy writing. I told her I was writing a book about my three-year trip but was wise enough not to name the title of it. She was named after a famous Simon and Garfunkel song, but let's just call her Christina from now on. I did my thing and she crawled up on me; not much later I was kissing her.

Christina was a beautiful twenty-three year-old Norwegian girl with long blond hair and piercing blue eyes. She stayed the night in my bed and we went pretty far, but no sex.

We fell asleep and the next day I checked out and went looking for a hotel room with her.

We found a decent one not far away from the Parque Kennedy area in Miraflores. She said she had to leave the same day and wanted to spend some time with me. I was going to get my first Scandinavian flag, after so much trying in South East Asia.

We spent the whole afternoon in bed but she wouldn't let me fuck her, no matter what I tried. She was naked for hours and after I went down on her, she gave me a very good deep-throat blowjob, and two more in the next few hours. I normally don't count a blowjob as a notch but with three of them in a few hours and deep-throat ejaculations; let me claim the Norwegian flag and notch.

A few hours later we said goodbye and she said we could have sex the next time we met while travelling, which never happened due to different routes. But who knows, Oslo is not that far from Holland and my friend Jonathan lives there too.

The room cost about twenty dollars a night, which was quite cheap for a big room in Miraflores, one of Lima's more uptown neighborhoods, with double bed, cable TV and a bathroom. Finding a better place for that money was going to be hard so I decided to stay there.

Only a few hours after saying goodbye to Christina, I met a girl through the Couchsurfing website. This girl was a little hottie, at least a seven and a half in my opinion; she was short and skinny and had a very cute face, light brown skin and the thickest hair I had ever seen.

We had some Pisco sours (happy hour, two for the price of one), I did my date game and she ate it all up. This was the perfect game to run on local girls, I thought.

Later that night we went out to a party at someone's house and danced a bit.

At one point when I was getting a bit tired and sat down, Evita sat on my lap and kissed me. We kept kissing all night and at the end of the night we went to my room and had steamy sex there. I can barely remember how I pulled that of so shortly after the Norwegian girl left the same room. I had landed myself a cute Peruvian girl and upgraded my flag this way.

It was great having a tiny girl in bed again; it seemed like an eternity since I left Asia with its fine short skinny girls. I spend four more days with her and she was a little sex addict.

She couldn't stop playing with my dick and constantly revived it by putting it in her mouth. Those four days were great, but on the fourth she got some stomach pains and said it was from all the fucking we did.

I was wondering why it hadn't happen before because she was as tight as a glove and I had to contantly muffle her moaning by putting the television on loud volume.

Evita had to work during the day in some office job and I had a few more dates with other girls. I kissed one of them but couldn't bring her back to the hotel since Evita was coming over every night.

We had a lot of fun together and visited a lot of places in old and new Lima.

I had the crazy plan of visiting Holland's most famous criminal: Joran van der Sloot, a charismatic sociopath guy who had already sort of confessed to murdering an American girl named Natalie Holloway. He was a prisoner in the high-security Castro Castro prison, where he was imprisoned after confessing to murdering a Peruvian girl as well.

This young guy is famous in Peru and always in the news there. Evita and I asked around but couldn't get enough information on how to visit the prison, which was a two-hour bus ride away.

I really liked Evita and hated saying goodbye to her. She wasn't a complete gringo–hunter like the girl in Cuzco, but I think she's looking for a foreigner. We agreed to meet again once I came back from Ecuador and Colombia.

Ecuador – Quito

After a short visit in Peru's number one beach town, Mancora, and a few long, boring rides on the bus I arrived in Ecuador. Since I was on a tight schedule and had already stayed too long in places like Cuzco and Lima, I wanted to skip Ecuador's biggest city, Guayaquil, and go straight to the capital, Quito.

I bought a ticket at Guayaquil's bus station and to my

surprise I saw two girls I had seen before in Cuzco. It was the tall girl who'd been waiting in line for the Machu Picchu tickets. I approached them and asked them if they were taking the same bus as me. They confirmed it, and I asked the tall girl if she remembered me and she said yes. I told her why I'd been so grumpy and they laughed about it. The two girls were Texans and on a two-month trip.

We sat down in the bus and I talked a bit to them. I was damn lucky again to have a super-hot young Ecuadorian girl sitting next to me in a bus full of locals and lots of old people. She didn't speak a word of English and we used a translator app on her phone and my Spanish pocket book to talk.

The tall American girl saw me having fun with the Ecuadorian girl and pre-selection had been achieved, especially after exchanging Facebook and phone numbers. Unfortunately the hottie got off a few hours before reaching Quito.

We arrived in the evening and looked for a guesthouse together. Everything in the La Mariscal area, also known as Gringolandia, was full, but after a while we found a small hotel where there was a bedroom with four massive beds available. We took the room and went out for dinner and drinks.

At eleven at night the bars and restaurants stopped pouring alcoholic drinks. The president has forbidden drinking at night because of all the drunken people and rioting on the streets after midnight.

Ecuador is still considered a dangerous country and is famous for its robbers and tourist scams. We didn't know about this rule and Casey, the tall girl, and her girlfriend Alice wanted to buy a bottle of booze before returning to the hotel room.

We went looking for a liquor store and found one with the help of a drunken bum to whom we gave a dollar. The liquor store was a small shop which was already closed but when you knocked on the door, a small window opened big enough to put a bottle through. We had to be careful because police cars were patrolling around and had already yelled at us through the speakers on top of their car when standing in front of the liquor store. We quickly bought a cheap bottle of vodka and a bottle of Pepsi and hurried back to the hotel. The receptionist opened the door just in time, because the police car was coming for us.

I mixed the drinks in one of those outdoor water bottles I'd bought a week before. The three of us fooled around on one of the beds. I took pictures and Casey hit the bottle pretty hard. Half an hour later Alice was fiddling around with her iPhone in the corner of the room, which was at least seven meters long, and Casey and I smoked a cigarette. I kissed her and she immediately became very wild and horny.

In the next hour I tried to get a threesome going, but couldn't convince Alice, who had a big pair of knockers. She was a little bit husky but it was all muscle since she was a Football player. (She insisted on calling it soccer until I corrected her.)

The lights went out and Casey came to sleep in my bed. It had only been days after I left Lima and I went from one extreme to the other. Evita was a short and very skinny girl and Casey was even taller and probably stronger than me. We had a lot of sex that night. I asked Alice to come over too but she pretended to sleep. I remember Casey moaning and saying "Ooh, it's been so long. I love it".

The following morning I needed to check out because I wanted a room for myself and the girls said they were going to meet some travelling friends later. We were all hungover and when I kissed Casey and felt between her legs she became so horny that she was wet through her jeans. But unfortunately it was already ten in the morning and there was no time to fool around anymore.

I checked out and moved to a hotel in the old part of town. The hotel was listed in the Lonely Planet and was situated at Plaza San Blas. I had my own room with TV for seven dollars, that's even cheaper than a dorm room close to La Mariscal. There were some other tourists around but not many. The street restaurant a couple of blocks away served basic but cheap and good food. A meal consisting of soup, rice, vegetables, a quarter-chicken, fresh fruit juice and dessert cost one-and-a-half dollars. That's really cheap and it filled me up for hours every time I went there.

That night I met a girl named Gabrielle off the travel website, and we went for a few drinks. We found a place where you could get two caiperinhas cocktails for four dollars. The date game worked and I kissed her big lips, but she was very shy and a really bad kisser. I didn't see something happening that night but went for a walk with her anyway. I was holding her hand, ready to do the spin-move when we suddenly ran into the two American girls. I'm not sure if they saw me holding her hand but I could see that they were not pleased to see me with another girl. That screwed up my chance with Casey that night, and they left the next day. I still have contact with them sometimes on Facebook. Gabrielle went home around 10:30 at night and I went home also.

The next day I went sightseeing around the city a bit and in the evening I met a cute Colombian girl for drinks. She worked in Quito as a dentist and I saw it as my chance to get the Colombian flag. I went to the same place I had brought Gabrielle, downed some caiperinhas with her and had a fun conversation with her. That night I swore that I would always use my (coffee) date techniques from that moment on. She ate up my questions like candy and it worked perfectly. We met two girlfriends of hers in a fancy bar, had some drinks on her and went to a club called Bungalow 6.

I soon found out that the no-drinking rule was only for restaurants and not for clubs. They were pouring drinks all night. We danced a bit, took some pictures and her friends went home but I convinced the Colombian hottie to stay a bit more. I kissed her soft beautiful lips on the dance floor, but she left later on. I couldn't get a second date with her and felt that I maybe escalated too fast with her. It was my first but not last contact with the famous Colombian flakiness I had read about.

Ecuadorian girls are no stranger to flaking either, judging by the twelve girls I had met online and agreed to meet, only two of whom actually went out with me.

Every night I went out, either to club Bungalow 6 or Club Nobar. Going out is dirt cheap in Quito, on weekends you only pay five dollars to get in and a beer or rum-and-coke is included. The only slow day is Monday, but the rest of the week it's no problem to find girls to dance or talk with.

I missed out with a drunken Israeli girl. I talked to her a bit and probably could have flagged her if I pushed a bit harder, but my eye fell on an Ecuadorian girl who was way more exotic-looking.

I bounced from Nobar to Bungalow 6 with her and did some dancing there. We tried to dance salsa but I completely sucked. Her style was very different and I hadn't practiced any salsa in the last weeks. Besides, that girl was a total gold digger and I let her go.

Another night I met a super tall and skinny black girl. She had a hot body with a big round booty, I approached her and found out she only spoke Spanish. I manned up and tried the worst Spanish ever to pick her up, but didn't succeed.

Every time I went in for the kiss she turned her cheek or forehead towards me. I laughed in her face and remembered the Spanish word for grandma. I said something like "Por que no beso por sus labias? tu eres mi abuela?" This terrible grammar translates to something like "why not kiss your lips? You are my grandma?" This made her laugh and from this moment on I've successfully used this line every time a girl gives me the cheek turn. She kept fighting my kisses off the whole night but kept close to me and grinding her big round booty on me all night.

After a bounce to another bar and multiple tries to get the tall black girl back to my room I just said I wanted to leave and said goodbye. She was not happy with it and I think surprised at my reaction.

Over the next week we said hi when we ran into each other but never danced or talked again. I'm still not sure what her thoughts about me were. She wasn't leeching drinks of me or anything.

Scoring girls in nightclubs wasn't easy and perhaps this was because every night the clubs were full of foreigners. There were too many options for girls and they might choose some beta idiot over me because the beta idiot would keep the drinks coming all night. Ecuador is very cheap but it was still easy to smash forty dollars if you buy girls drinks all night.

At the end of a fruitless night I met a woman named Lupe who only spoke Spanish, which made it hard to communicate. Because it was the end of the night and she was quite flirty I asked her if she was a prostitute and she became very angry with me.

I still managed to take her back to my place, which was a two-dollar taxi ride away. We had a drink at my room and I started kissing her. She was shy at first but once we were banging she turned wilder and wilder. When we banged in the morning she almost ripped the skin of my back. I guess it had been a while for her too. She had to work the next day and left her email and phone number in the morning, but I never called her again. I had too many dates set up or other nightly options.

I went for a long walk to the old center that day and even climbed to the giant Virgin Mary statue at the top of the hill. It was possible to take a taxi there but then I'd be like any other tourist, and anyway, I wanted to save that taxi money and see something of the neighborhood build on the hills.

The climb was pretty steep, with lots of steps and some deep pits at the parts where construction work was still being done. I won't recommend doing this after dark but during the day it should be OK. By the time this book goes to print, the new concrete steps will probably be ready.

One of my last nights out I met a Canadian guy who wanted to tag along with me. He and I ran into four girls on a night out, along with some German guys. (They are seriously everywhere.)

At the end of the night we were standing on the street looking for another place to go out. The police had closed down a bar known for illegal after-hour parties, and I told my companions about the illegal liquor shop. We went over and bought some rum there.

We all went back to one of the girls' apartment, except one girl who went off with the Canadian guy. I was a bit jealous about this because she was quite pretty and he was a shy guy. That girl later came back to the apartment when I was cuddling a bit with the girl owning the apartment.

The other two girls were sisters and the oldest one was making out with one of the German guys, who spoke reasonable Spanish. The girl I was with didn't want to kiss and it looked like I was the only one not getting some.

The German guys went home and the four girls offered me to stay and do something with them the next day. What? Was I getting friend-zoned here? It sure seemed like it.

If I wanted to stay I had to sleep on the couch while the four girls slept in the only bedroom. I asked if the girl I was with would stay with me on the couch and she answered no. "Then I'm going back home," I said, and walked back to my hotel room at eight in the morning.

The fact that I was friend-zoned was obvious when they asked me to go out with them again.

I went with the four girls and two kids to a pizza restaurant for dinner. The two oldest girls were around thirty and both had children from previous relationships.

Afterwards the kids went home to a nanny and the four girls and I went to Bungalow 6. If I couldn't score one of them, at least I had massive pre selection walking around with four girls. I felt out the situation with three of the girls but not the one from the night before. The two of us almost didn't speak that night.

The younger of the two sisters barely spoke English, but when I showed her my pictures on the phone I could make myself clear with my bits of Spanish.

We cuddled up a bit and I showed her pictures of my round-the-world trip so far. In-between all the pictures of me doing cool stuff were some pictures of me with girls. I tried to make it seem like I didn't want her to see them and she got all excited and punched my arm and said "Show me!" I would sigh and say okay to it. She was falling right into my DHV trap.

Afterwards she didn't leave my side and the five of us went dancing in Nobar. The tall black girl saw me come in with four girls and so did the hot gold digger. *Right back at ya*, I thought.

The youngest sister and I danced all night to the reggeaton beats. This twenty-two year old girl had so much energy that I could barely keep up. We kissed all the time while I touched her all over her body.

At the end of the night I tried to get her back to my place but of course the other girls wouldn't let her leave with me. I went home DIH, dick in hand.

I had gone out almost every night and only pulled one local girl who had seen better days in the mirror. Still, I loved Quito and will probably return here the next time I'm travelling.

In my nine days in Quito I had not taken any extra private Spanish or salsa lessons as I planned to do. I had done quite some of writing for my Dutch website and translated some stories into English.

The Adderal tablets Cassie had given me worked miracles and I had never been so focused in my life.

I also had a major email battle with Lilly, the girl I was with for two weeks in Bali/Indonesia. She had found out about my site and threatened me with lawsuits and having my website taken down if I didn't remove her pictures. The fact that her face was completely blurred out and she had her clothes on didn't seem to matter, and she stirred up so much drama it was almost an email bombardment. She said she would get someone to take my whole site down, and since she had some money and might actually manage to do it I finally caved in and removed the pictures. She said goodbye to me with some religious stuff like "my hope and prayers will be with you", and broke contact forever. Well almost forever. I got an "I miss you" email many months later.

Colombia – Cali

The trip to Colombia went well. I had heard horror stories about the border between Ecuador and Colombia. It was supposed to be crawling with FARC terrorists, paramilitary gangs and corrupt cops.

A young English student I met on the bus to the border told me he had done this ride before, from Colombia to Ecuador, and got robbed at seven in the evening.

John was ganged up on by eight or nine guys and they told him his papers were not in order. He was all alone there and got scared, which doesn't surprise me. I would be too. He paid twenty dollars to get out of the situation and I think he was lucky to get away with such a small bride.

The two of us stayed in a hotel at the border town, and the next morning we crossed the border to Colombia without too much hassle and continued our trip. John and I sat in the front of the bus and behind us sat a mom and her daughter. The mom kept smiling at me. I tried to talk to them a bit to kill time on this twelve-hour ride and quickly found out they only spoke Spanish, but it was easy to find out that her name was Juliana. The daughter was only sixteen years old and the mom looked like she was about thirty-six. A MILF, so to say. She kept touching my hair and liked it because it was blond.

The scenery of Colombia was great. We saw lots of green hills, a few mountains and lots of poor but seemingly happy people along the road and the villages. Juliana's daughter gave me a small bracelet, just like the one Evita had given me in Lima. I often thought about her and was looking forward to seeing her again.

After a long ride we finally got off the bus. Juliana invited me to her house, but I wasn't planning on going there with my backpack, laptop and passport. It was still Cali, one of South America's most dangerous cities. We agreed to meet the next day.

As with Argentina I had read horror stories about Colombian women. They were supposed to be beautiful but very flaky and the gringo factor had already died out. Foreigners actually had a bad name now because of all the whoremongers who visit Colombia to bang hookers and/or to take girls on fancy dinners and spoiling them with lots of presents which is almost the same in my opinion. Both times you basically pay for sex. Guys like this spoil the goodies for people like me. It's getting harder and harder to find places where old foreigners or loser guys haven't spoiled local girls by making them think all "whities" from western countries are dumb guys who throw around money and buy their girls.

There are still exotic places where being a foreigner gives you high status, but that world is getting smaller by the day.

The owner of the hostel was a Danish guy who had

married an average-looking Colombian girl. There were a couple of older guys in the hostel, one 70-year-old English guy with rude and quite racist humor and a skinny American guy in his fifties. The American had lived in Mexico for a long time and spoke good Spanish. As soon as he found out that I was hunting for poon, he started following me around like a dog. Probably trying to get some action himself. Both were telling me to move to Medellin, where the hottest girls were.

I had only time for one city in Colombia so I focused on Cali. Both of them oldies had a screw loose and talked about weed and booze quite a few times. I hope I don't end up like them when I'm old.

The American and his Spanish skills helped me out with buying a Sim card and sending a text to Juliana. She replied immediately by calling me, but I couldn't understand what she was saying and handed the phone over to the American who arranged a date with Juliana for me.

I was going to meet her at night at a corner of the main street, where there were a few bars.

That night I waited for her and wondered how I was going to succeed with only Spanish. She showed up twenty minutes late, with her daughter and another girlfriend. I wasn't expecting three people and she caught me a bit off-guard. Juliana had done a full makeover from slouchy mom to hot vamp.

She looked amazing wearing a sexy black dress, high heels and with beautiful makeup and hair. I had seen some potential in her looks when I met her at the bus but this exceeded my wildest expectations. Not knowing how to entertain three people in Spanish and not being willing to pay for three people all night I didn't really know how to handle the situation, and used the help of a giant bald guy who sold cigarettes and other small stuff on the street corner. He was a friendly guy who spoke some English and helped me talk with the three ladies.

The older American from the hostel also "accidently" showed up. I let him translate for me and he made it clear to her that I wasn't expecting three people.

We made another date, but she flaked on me. Never

heard from her again. The weird thing was that she always called me instead of sending me texts, even though I could translate those.

My Spanish stills sucked ass and there was no way I could use it to do day game. This made me worry about capturing the flag and I had to depend on night game only.

Cali is the salsa capital of South America and after my seven hours of private lessons in Peru I felt like I should use this to my advantage.

The hostel recommended a famous salsa bar to me and I hopped into a cab and drove all the way to the other side of the city. I sat down at the bar, which was crowded with many foreign couples. It surprised me to see so many foreigners in one place because during the day I didn't see them at all. They were good dancers and when I saw the Colombian guys dancing almost like professionals all my hopes and dreams of using salsa as a pick-up crutch went out the door.

How the hell could I be so stupid and think I could compete with locals? I had already forgotten most salsa moves and it was already weeks since I had my salsa lessons. I quickly downed a few beers and went back to the hostel.

I needed another strategy if I wanted my flag. I had flagged five countries in a row and didn't want to fail in Colombia, even though I knew it was a hard place to get laid with little money and no place of your own. I'd arranged at the hostel that I could take a private room if I brought someone there. I would only be allowed to once, but that's enough for me.

The following evening I met up with a girl from the Couchsurfing website. We went for a few drinks and drank a small bottle of Aguardiente, a local alcoholic drink.

For a long time I thought the drink was called Aqua Calientes (hot water) just like the place I had been in Peru and it reminded me of old cowboy movies where native American Indians would refer to alcohol as hot water. It wasn't until after I wrote this book and a reader pointed out the mistake that I understood why the girl laughed so hard when I said Aqua caliente. As usual my convo techniques worked and I had her in my pocket. She said we could go out with her friends that night and met them at a nightclub. They were very nice people and we had lots of drinks together.

At one point the two of us went out for a smoke and looked for some food. I saw a park and walked over there with her. I kissed her there and she seemed to be into me. She was a little hottie, twenty years old and at least a seven in looks. We kissed all night and at the end of the night we took a taxi. I tried everything to get her back to my place but she didn't want to.

Over the next few days she would flake on me.

I met two other girls from the same website but it didn't work out. The first one was a case of misleading profile pictures. She was a six and chubby instead of the slim seven she probably was five years ago in her profile picture. One thing I noticed when I went out with her was the extremely hot girl and her boyfriend/date that came with her. The girl had big fake boobs and maybe a fake butt too but looked at least like an 8. The guy who was with her was big and strong, dressed sharp as a knife and was handsome. He acted like a total beta though. I'd been told that Colombian guys were supplicating betas but this was extreme. Had I seen this guy in my own beta days I would probably have thought he was some smooth player, but when you are focused on pick-up and become somewhat good at it, you will start noticing other men's mistakes. This guy was making them all. He started off by sitting in front of the girl at a small table instead of sitting on the couches the way I did with my date. The whole date he tried to touch the girl who kept him at a distance, leaning in to the maximum trying to get closer to her. He gave her a love stare but she kept cold. I couldn't make out his words and I'm sure he could bang a lot of foreign girls with his Latin player romantic approach, but he failed badly with her. Hell, she even gave me a wink when the dude went to the toilet.

On Saturday night I had another meeting with an online girl early in the evening. I had asked the girl working at the hostel reception for a place to go out. All the places I had been exploring in the days before were sit-down places with mixed groups or salsa joints. I asked the receptionist about a big discoteca where all kinds of music were played and people would stand up and dance. I specifically said American pop music, or even better reggeaton. She gave me the name of a discoteca, and I decided to go on the date and ditch the girl if it wasn't working out so I could go to the club.

The girl I met for a date brought her younger sister with her boyfriend.

We watched a football match in a bar in the mall close to my hostel. The girl I was meeting was mestizo (half native/half white) and had a great head of fine curly hair. It felt great when I touched it but I was slightly bothered by her sister and brother-in-law being there and didn't want to go into full pick-up mode. I noticed that she had already friend-zoned me and it was time to say goodbye. I asked them directions to the club and they even brought me there with their car. They were very friendly and had even paid my drinks before and I felt a bit bad about making up an excuse and leaving them.

They dropped me off at the club and I walked up to the counter. I had to pay ten dollars just to get in. I had big money in my pocket because it was a Saturday night and I might end up in a love motel, but as soon as I walked in I could see it would be a total bust. There was a large dance floor in the middle of the giant hall and only tables around it. Groups of people were sitting at tables and there wasn't a bar to stand on.

The waitress put me on a bar stool next to a small dancing stage. Then she tried to sell me a bottle of aguardiente. I objected because why would I want a thirty-dollar bottle of strong liquor? It was already hard to talk to her in Spanish and when I asked for a beer she said they didn't sell beer. I pointed out the refrigerator with beer they had in the back and some manager guy showed up.

After some struggling they finally agreed to give me a beer. I was like "What the fuck? A guy can't even get a beer here?" The beer was served in a small glass and cost eight dollars. What a rip-off.

The place filled up after a while and people sat down at their tables. Almost all tables were filled with mixed groups and I understood later that Colombian girls would bring guys

334

to pay for drinks. Whenever I looked over at a table, the dudes at it, who were mostly big muscular guys with golden chains around their necks, looked at me with a pissed-off look. I caught on that if I didn't want my ass beaten I'd better not look at their girls.

The dance show was cool, with a big-ass girl dancing one meter away from me on the stage I was sitting on. But I hadn't come there to look at professional dancers. I came there to pick up girls. My glass was empty and I saw no options whatsoever to talk to any girls standing by themselves.

I walked out the door to smoke a cigarette and saw two girls doing the same. One of them was a nine in looks and stood close to me. She made a hand movement saying she needed a light and I slowly walked over there to give her one. Don't let them know they're hot is my motto, so never hurry up for a girl. I asked her if she spoke English and tried to make conversation but she just gave me a quick no.

I'd had enough of it, got a taxi back to the hostel and looked around in the streets close to the hostel if I could find a reasonable bar. It was pointless and I went to bed all grumpy.

I complained to the receptionist the next morning that she had sent me to the wrong place but she didn't know what she'd done wrong. I realized that this was all she knew and that she'd probably never seen a regular disco from inside.

I tried to day game a bit at the supermarket but failed and gave up after a couple of tries. The language barrier kept blocking me and everywhere I went was Spanish only.

The girls at the mall weren't that hot and I wanted to check out some other places and parks. Since I could only ask the receptionist girl for directions, I was stuck asking her. I asked her for a large park with lots of people. She said she knew one and gave me directions for the buses.

After a few buses and lots of walking I finally arrived at the park she'd recommended. It was small and there weren't any girls around. The malls I hadn't been to yet were on the other side of the city and I went back again. This sucked badly and I was losing hope of getting a flag. I had gone out every night, visited the mall a couple of times, visited a "park", met three girls from the travel website and all I had done was some kissing. I got really nervous, smoked a lot and started drinking early. I had eleven girls who mailed me back to meet them but it was a big flake fest. Girls at the mall and supermarket didn't give me the light of day and made no eye contact whatsoever. I was ready to give up.

There was a Guatemalan woman in the hostel with giant fake tits, who responded well to my flirting and said she would go on a date with me soon if I stayed a bit longer. I ran into her a couple of times but I only heard excuses when I texted her for a date. Apparently Guatemalans is no stranger to flaking either.

Two Australians had arrived at the hostel. Both were pilots in their early forties. I didn't like them much because they always seemed to talk a lot but without saying much.

One of them said he'd got laid the night before and showed me a picture of a hot girl on his phone. He didn't speak a word of Spanish but his friend did. He had translated for him and they had met her in an English pub nearby the hostel. My first thought was *Why didn't that stupid bitch receptionist tell me about that bar?*

The old English guy said to the Aussie that I'd been trying to get laid all week. The Aussie laughed and said it had happened on his first night there. I asked him lots of questions to find out how he did it. He had met her in the bar, spent quite a lot of money on drinks, took a taxi to a club outside the city, paid entrance and cocktails again and then went to a hotel with her. He said that the hotel was "only" sixty dollars. That guy had spent way over a hundred dollars on that lay, and such amounts are too much for me. It made me feel a bit better and who knows, he might have paid her something in the room. Nobody would ever know.

I was totally fed up with Cali and had no time left to go to Bogota or Medellin anymore. My mission of visiting and flagging every country in South America had failed.
My 80-girls challenge, of course, a challenge I was losing since the clock was ticking and the date I went home was already set. I was at 51; getting 29 in just a few months would be impossible, even for me. That didn't mean, of course, that I wasn't determined to get as damn close to 80 as I could. I had

set the bar high by refusing to get to the 80 by only being with Asian girls. I felt that after Cambodia, I needed a short break to let everything sink in. I could have easily gotten 20 notches in Thailand too but wasn't too bothered with it. Of course I the Phils I went overboard again to an extent.

The last day in Cali I talked with yet another German guy, who rode around in a camper van and sometimes banged girls in it. He said he knew a good place to go out and we drove off in his camper. I thought the van was a great idea. It looked like a normal bus and he told me some interesting stories. It's a great way to see places off the beaten track. We went to a place to play pool.

When we walked in I saw a pool table and some buck-naked girls walking around. They were completely naked and obvious entertainment girls. We didn't use their services but one of the black girls had a crazy attractive body and I sure thought about it.

The radio played Inner Circle's *Sweat* and I felt bad because that had been "our song" for Peruvian Evita and me. I missed her and felt ashamed for lowering myself to paying for a hooker.

I missed Evita and thought about how I was going to meet her again a week later. I had a long ride ahead of me all the way back down to Bolivia.

Epilogue Colombia - Cali

It was a big mistake to visit Cali instead of Bogota or Medellin. I heard from my buddy Darren that he had gone out quite a few times there and most of the places were good clubs with girls dancing to reggeaton beats. He was sure that I would have succeeded there. I told myself that I would have my revenge by going back to Colombia, but not before I learned how to dance some decent salsa and speak excellent Spanish.

Colombia is a beautiful country and I had barely seen it outside the nightlife. People were friendly and it made me think about back when I was travelling through Russia. Over there I wasn't worried about picking up girls at all and was meeting new and friendly people all time. It gave me a 'What the hell I'm doing with my trip?" feeling, and I was afraid I would hate myself later for not enjoying the scenery and local people more. This feeling would go away in a few days, once I was back in Quito.

8-day bus trip

My plan was to take a bus all the way down to Bolivia again, with a few stops along the way. It would take about eight days and anyone else would take a plane, but this way was cheaper and probably more fun, since I planned to see a few people again.

The trip started back in Cali and after another rip-off taxi ride I arrived at the bus station and rode for another twelve hours to the Ecuadorian border. I couldn't cross the border because it was too dangerous after dark. I stayed one night in some hotel and crossed the border without any trouble the next morning.

Six more hours of bus later, I was back in Quito, where I tried to get a date with the Colombian girl I had kissed before. No luck.

I set up a date with two of the four girls I had met in Quito before. The two sisters were back in their hometown, but I had my eyes on Jane, the one who left with the Canadian guy the last time. She had warned me already not to come on to her because I had already kissed one of her girlfriends and cuddled with another one. I ignored all she said and thought I would convince her anyway. I was way too late at Bungalow 6 and couldn't find them in the crowd of people.

After a while of looking for them I went to the other club, the one I liked best: Club Nobar. The last time I was in Ecuador I had printed out a thousand business cards that D-Lux had designed for me, promoting my website. With a little translation help from the girl working in the hostel I got a pack of photo-quality, full color business cards for thirty dollars. I handed them out to people I met along the way or left them in hostels. I also left them in places like Nobar or Bungalow 6 for a little promotion.

Inside Club Nobar a girl walked up and wanted to dance

with me. Her name was Katy and she was a short mestizo girl, a mix of black and white. She spoke good English and we got along just fine. Then she introduced me to two guys, one of whom she said was her half-brother. She danced quite sexy with him. I didn't trust the situation at hand, turned around and danced with two other girls. It was hard to talk to them only in Spanish and Katy was clearly pissed off about me turning my back on her.

I later approached her again and asked if she was angry with me but said it in a funny way. We danced again and she started grinding her little booty on my crotch like crazy. I grabbed her head and kissed her right in front of her (half) brother. He laughed and it didn't seem to bother him.

Katy and I went outside a couple of times to smoke a cigarette and kissed there. Then she told me that I couldn't fuck her and if I was looking for a girl to fuck I should talk to other girls. I was thinking *My god, what does a foreign guy have to do to get laid around here?* I thought it might just be some LMR (last minute resistance) and walked with her to the other club because I'd left my jacket there.

We ran into Jane and her girlfriend there; she had some foreign guy with her and I thought to myself *Dammit, this girl is up for it but has friend zoned me knowing I'm a player.* She seemed to like the dorky kind of guy. They saw me with Katy and we said goodbye.

Even though Katy had said she wouldn't have sex I took her to my room and we drank some rum and coke there. We were both quite drunk and started making out a bit.

One would think that a girl who goes home with a strange guy after three o'clock at night is DTF (down to fuck), but she made a stand and wouldn't take her clothes off no matter what I tried. After a while I just went to sleep and was none too happy with her next to me.

I had to get up early the next morning to keep to my schedule. We kissed a bit in the morning and her shirt came off but no way in hell was she taking off her jeans. I took a shower, packed my bags and we took a taxi to the bus station she had told me about.

Maybe if I stayed one or two nights longer she would

have had sex with me, but I don't like "maybes". I couldn't risk it; I was already behind on my schedule and wanted to get going to see Evita again. I was thinking of her more and more and wanted to be with my little cutie again.

The buses in Ecuador are probably the cheapest on the continent; they cost about a dollar an hour and there's always a lot to see on them. Most buses stop a lot along the way, though, so if you're in a hurry, take an airplane. People will try to talk to you and lots of guys come on the bus and give a loud twenty-minute sales pitch for whatever they are selling. Then they hand out samples of their product to everyone in the bus, talk about it a few minutes more and then pick it up again from those who don't want to buy it. It's a fairly unique system I haven't seen anywhere else in the world.

What's more entertaining is that sometimes young guys will get on the bus with a boombox and do some freestyle rapping, mostly making harmless fun of its passengers. Afterwards they collect money.

After a few transfers I arrived at the Peruvian border. The bus wasn't going any further and dropped me off there in the middle of the night. I got my passport stamped and there I stood alongside the empty road, with no bus in sight. I was lucky because half an hour later a bus came by and I bribed the bus driver to take me into the cabin with him. He would drive me to Piura, a Peruvian city, for ten dollars, and I agreed. I sat in the cabin with him and we talked a bit. He was very impressed with my story of travelling the world and later put me in the air conditioned bus when a space freed up. That was a lot better than sitting in a stinking cabin which was packed with bananas(!?).

On arriving in Piura I took another bus straight away and fell asleep again. On trips like this your whole day and night rhythm is gone and you kill time by sleeping a lot. I survived on chips, cookies and Inca cola, a local Peruvian soda brand. Maybe once a day I took some warm food but never took too big a chance with it since I knew I would get sick quickly in Peru.

Arriving in Trujillo I was surprised not to find a connecting bus to Lima and had to stay the night there. I found a cheap hotel with the help of a taxi driver and went out later. It was a Friday night, so that should be good.

Evita had texted me that she couldn't see me anymore because she didn't want her feelings to get hurt. I was quite devastated by that message and thought that I had probably screwed it up by not staying in touch daily.

That night I went out in Trujillo, but the night was a bust. I couldn't find a good place. The one I went to was half-empty and I went to a corner store to get a beer and wait a while. Two guys were sitting on the sidewalk and starting talking to me. They seemed quite drunk and I ignored them at first but after a while I found out they were quite nice guys. One of them was a cop and he showed me his gun. He unloaded it and we took some drunken pictures with it. I was hitting the half-a-liter beer cans pretty hard, and after a while I got some barbequed street food and then I went back to the "club". It sucked balls and was a sit-down place with only salsa and other dancing styles. I barely saw any approachable girls and I was not in the mood anyway. Another night alone.

I went on to Lima early in the morning and took an excellent bus to get there. The weird thing was that the staff took the fingerprints of everyone boarding the bus. I was grumpy the whole day because I had been looking forward to spending time with Evita again.

Taxi drivers in Lima had a bad day with me, I would bargain the shit out of them and slam doors in their faces if I didn't like the price. The small hotel I'd stayed in last time only had one room available and it was the same one I'd banged Evita and the Norwegian girl in. This didn't improve my mood and I tried to psych up for the Saturday night.

I went to a street with many clubs close to the old square but I was in a totally bad mood and didn't even feel like going out. I had forced myself once more to go out alone but this time my inner game was messed up and it probably showed. Basically, it was one of the worst nights out ever for me and I was glad to get the fuck out of Lima the next day.

My next destination was Nazca again, and on arriving early in the morning I found out that I had no more money in my bank account. I forgot to transfer money from my savings account to my regular account and had to stay one extra night to wait for money.

I took the flight over the Nazca lines and puked my guts out inside the small plane. I had booked the best flight with the most turns over the landscape so I could see all the ancient figures twice. I hadn't entered into my calculations the fact that my stomach has always been weak if I'm doing anything that spins around and that a lot of turns meant a lot of spinning. Luckily the small propeller plane had barf bags but I felt like shit.

The night before I'd some beers and a few Pisco sours with a Danish girl I met in the hotel. I had a nice room there and tried to get her in there but she wasn't up for it. Nazca has a few places to go out and I think we had seen them all. I felt like a try-hard and thought about how I was going to stay at Sierra's house in La Paz in a few days. Sierra wasn't a hot girl but she was young, really horny and longed to see me. How could one resist?

I went to Areaquipa and from there straight to Puno, close to the Bolivian border. I was getting used to sitting on buses for hours every day but cursed for half an hour when there wasn't a connecting bus to La Paz that day. I had missed it by forty-five minutes. I had to stay in a city I didn't want to be in again.

I decided to make the best of it and when I walked around that afternoon I saw a few bars I could visit that night. I ate some food and went to the Internet café.

An hour later I was barfing and shitting out my guts back in my room. I was never happier to have my own bathroom than in those hours. It was clearly food poisoning and I felt terrible.

I stayed in bed all evening and woke up bathing in my own sweat around two o'clock. I was out of water and had already drunk two liters that evening. I was burning up with fever and I really needed to hydrate myself.

The only places open now were bars and I literally broke out of the guesthouse, busting open the door from the inside in the middle of the night.

It was a clear case of Murphy's Law when I entered the

bar and saw girls sitting everywhere. All alone, all looking at me, all giving me little smiles and waiting for me to approach. I had had bad luck before but this topped everything. First not getting some in Quito despite having a cute girl in my bed, then taking long hell rides on old buses, those shitty nights out in Trujillo and Lima, Evita refusing to see me again, the extra night in Nazca and now have to stay longer in Puno and coming down with food poisoning. I wondered what I'd done to deserve all this bad luck.

It must have been karma for all the bad things I had done on my trip so far.

When I stumbled out of the bar with some bottles of water I was sick and sweating and wanted to kick myself.

I felt surprisingly well in the morning and got on the bus to La Paz. Eight hours on the bus with a short stopover at Lake Titicaca and I was back in La Paz again.

Bolivia – La Paz, Second time

La Paz, a city I despised after my two-and-a-half week stay there. The only reason I went back there was that I needed some decent sleep and to see Sierra again.

I checked in the Loki hostel again, had a long hot shower (which was needed) and brought my clothes to a laundry shop (which was even more needed), spent some time on the Internet and went to see Sierra in the afternoon. She had been writing to me a lot on Facebook and couldn't wait to see me.

Sierra and I talked a bit and she joked about how I must have had sex with a dozen other girls while I was gone. I told her it wasn't that easy, but she didn't believe me. She was obviously getting turned on and I knew she liked to play rape-game and waited weeks to do it. I decided to give it (another) try just to make her happy. I stood up, grabbed her throat, squeezed it and she looked surprised. I said: "So you want to be raped?" Her eyes, crazy. She looked happily in mine and I slapped her in the face and dragged her in to the bedroom. I threw her on the bed and forced myself on her, she struggled when I took her clothes off. I choked her and slapped her hard in the face while she was trying to fight me

343

of. She enjoyed it. I banged her as hard I could and she was screaming, shouting "No, No, No" and other things so loud that I was afraid that the neighbors would call the police on us. I finished doggy-style and she said it was the best sex she ever had in her life.

Truth be told, it was a lot harder than I thought. She fought back hard and even though I'm at least twice as strong as her, I had major trouble getting her clothes off while fighting her off. I sometimes had to ask her to relax a bit because I wasn't going to succeed with her fighting that much.

Rape play or beating a girl is not really my thing. When I was twenty-seven I had a 19-year-old Dutch girlfriend who was all into S&M. She was quite beautiful, with long white-blonde hair and blue eyes. She also wanted me to beat and dominate her. I did for a few weeks but soon stopped liking it and cheated on her with a girl I knew from my work as a taxi driver. My blonde girlfriend dumped me a week later after I showed up way too late for her birthday.

At that moment I couldn't care less, but had my doubts when I hit a dry spell in the following months.

Anyway, back in La Paz, I was quickly annoyed by Sierra and her passive behavior outside the bedroom, and her body didn't appeal to me that much. I liked her for her craziness but that was it.

I spent some time in the Loki hostel and in the evening I went back to Sierra's place. I met some friends of her and after they left she wanted to go to the rock bar we had been before (the night I vomited and the toilet didn't flush). I didn't like the place because it was boring for me to hang out with Bolivian rockers I didn't have much in common with and could barely understand anyway since they were all speaking Spanish in a loud bar.

Sierra went out alone and I watched a movie and later went to sleep in her bed. She came back in the middle of the night; she was quite drunk, woke me up and wouldn't leave me alone until I had sex with her. Her breath smelled of beer and she was very pushy. I finally caved in after a while and had sex with her again. It felt a lot better slapping her around

344

this time, but it was also a clear sign I had to get the hell out of there.

The next morning I wasn't interested in anything and just watched the whole first season of *Game of Thrones* on her television. The series was pretty good but I didn't like the fact that one of my favorite actors, Sean Bean, died in yet another movie or series. He *never* makes it to the end of a movie.

We argued more and more and Sierra's high sex drive was wearing me down. The city was boring me and I wanted to move on to explore the rest of Bolivia in the little time I had left. I spent two more nights with Sierra and she begged me to stay longer.

When I kissed her goodbye she got angry for me leaving her and bit me on my lip hard. Sierra knew I hated that.
She was a sneaky girl: she did it at the exact moment the elevator doors at her apartment building closed and I was trapped inside.
Sierra later found out about my website, left an angry comment and unfriended me on Facebook. I can't blame her.

Bolivia – Salar de Uyuni

I had slept every night at Sierra's place but stayed in the Loki hostel, where I spent my afternoons and early evenings. Hench had returned from Peru and was working in the Loki La Paz again. When I told him about my plans to visit the famous Bolivian salt flats he told me about two Brazilian girls going there too. I'd actually spoken with one of them before and the other one I had some eye contact with, but she was with some backpacker dude. We got to talking and in the end decided to travel to Uyuni together. Another guy, a Colombian, joined us as well, and the four of us took an overnight bus to Uyuni.

The night was very cold and everyone was packed in hats and blankets. But weirdly I wasn't cold at all and I wondered why. I can't stand the cold but that night I was so warm that I took clothes off in the bus. I wondered if I was coming down with a fever or if it was the thought of being with one of the Brazilian girls that warmed me that night.

We arrived early that morning, had some breakfast and

booked a tour. We paid about eighty dollars each for a three-day jeep tour, including food and accommodation.

The jeep tour is a given because it's very unsafe to head into the salt flats on your own. It may sound like a few patches of white ground, but it's still a desert the size of a small country where you can get lost and perhaps die.

Two Spanish women joined us and the six of us plus the guide/driver took off. We were in one of those enormous jeeps and I was sitting in the middle with the two Brazilian girls. The Colombian guy was sitting in front and the two Spanish women in the back. I sat right where I wanted to sit, next to the Brazilian babe with the big ass, long black hair, soft brown skin, a nice pair of boobs and full lips.
The other Brazilian girl was skinny but not too skinny, with a small but round butt.

Both were very friendly and that made it hard to figure out what my position was. Was I getting friend-zoned here, or was one of them interested, and if so which one was it?
Choosing the wrong one might destroy my options with the other. After some consideration I chose the mestizo girl with the big bunda and massive lips; she was the one I'd be sitting next to for three days, but it would be hard to game here inside a tight, quiet jeep with seven people in it.

The first day we went to see a train graveyard where we took lots of pictures together. We drove over the blinding salt flats, took the usual funny pictures and visited a salt museum.

Around lunchtime we stopped at a place named Isla del sol or something similar. It was like an oasis in the salt desert, except that instead of palm trees this one had some rocky hills and lots of cactuses.

The cactuses were massive and it reminded me of my childhood. Whenever I visited my grandparents I would always have a look at my grandfather's greenhouse, which was filled with thousands of cactuses. He died when I was in India in the summer of 2008. It was near the end of my group trip and I made it back to Holland in time for the funeral but was so incredibly sick that I couldn't even make the two hour car ride there. It was one of the saddest days in my life. During this trip my grandmother had died too, and of course

346

I couldn't attend her funeral either. Travelling is great but at moments like these it really sucks to be away from home.

At night we stayed in a small village and I asked the hot Brazilian girl to watch a movie with me. She agreed, but although we'd been kind of cozy all day, she gave me the cheek turn when I wanted to kiss her. That kind of sucked, because I was left wondering why she would be a bit cuddly during the day, agree to see a movie with me while everyone was in their rooms and then not have kissing in mind. I was right; she was just being very friendly with me.

On the second day we visited several places, like giant lakes flashing all kinds of colors, a viewpoint and some special natural landmarks. We spent the night on the high plains of Bolivia, where the temperature gets below minus twenty degrees Celsius. There was some kind of a "guesthouse" there with a couple of dorm rooms. There was one other group and after dinner we all sat around the stove. It was freezing and I went out to find some firewood and when I came back everyone was applauding me for finding something to heat up the room with. I had given up on spending the night with the Brazil girl and we went to bed. Everyone was sleeping with their clothes on and even gloves and hats. I just slept in my underwear because I still really wasn't that cold.

The morning after, we visited some lakes with lots of pink flamingos and the famous geysers in the south. We took a bath in a natural hot tub heated by geysers. It was really cold when undressing but it felt like paradise when in the water. The Brazilian girls had super sexy bodies and I had to be careful not to let my tongue hang out and drool too much. I couldn't wait to go to Brazil and slap asses like that all day.

The girls went across the border to Chile that morning and we said goodbye and promised to meet again in Rio de Janeiro.

The Uyuni salt flats were one of the highlights of my journey and a truly beautiful place to visit. I recommend them highly to anyone reading this.

A couple of hellish and backbreaking bus rides later I ended up in Santa Cruz, Bolivia's second biggest city and home to the most beautiful Bolivian girls. There's no great secret as to why: it's close to the Brazilian border and most of the hot girls there were Brazilian students. I went out two nights in a row to a club but had massive trouble with the language barrier and cursed myself for not having studied Spanish more before arriving in South America and while being there. The hotel I was staying in was a cheap dump, not really fit to bring a girl over. However, I did bring one Bolivian girl over and had sex with her, but there's not much to say about that. After a few days there I moved to yet another country that had always interested me: Paraguay.

Paraguay – Asunción

The ride from Santa Cruz to Asunción took almost twenty–five hours and wasn't cheap at all. It was clear that gasoline costs a fortune in Paraguay, which is weird because that didn't seem to be the case in other countries just next door.

There was a large group of Football supporters on the bus. They came all the way from Ecuador and were on a five-day bus ride to see just one match. Those were some truly dedicated Football fans. Most of them were really nice guys and they behaved pretty well for a bunch of hooligans. They invited me to see the match with them, but I had already set up a date for that night through the Couchsurfing website and she looked pretty hot in her profile pictures.

Paraguay was supposed to be the second-poorest South American country, but with the local prices that wasn't really noticeable. I paid fifteen dollars for a bed in sixteen-people dorm room in one of the only hostels in the city. It was a nice place in the center, but pricy. Still, so long as you're warned, I recommend the Black Cat hostel to anyone going to Asunción.

One of my eyes was fucked up and I was scared that I'd got pink-eye, which can be a STD. Maybe that Bolivian slut in Santa Cruz had given me some disease or I got some bacteria in my eye during the long bus ride I took to get here.

For the next week I was walking around with a thick red eyelid that slowly went down. I wasn't the only one in the hostel with that problem. One of the English guys I met there had the same thing for months and even had to have it operated on in Argentina.

That night I went out with Rosie, the girl I'd met online. We met in an Irish pub in the Paseo Carmelitas area, a street full of (lounge) bars and discotecas.

Unfortunately she brought two other travellers who slept at her small apartment with her. One girl was from the Czech Republic, but contrary to what's generally assumed about all Czech girls she wasn't hot. The other girl was from Venezuela and she was a looker. I had a choice of three different flags to conquer. The girl from Czech Republic had a skinny but reasonable body, but also a boyish face with short feminist hair so she was dropped first out of the selection.
The Venezuelan girl was hot but on her period or something, couldn't get many words out of her and she seemed grumpy.

So, there I was sitting with three girls around a small table. I got the usual question about how I got the money to travel for such a long period of time without working.

The Czech girl was especially curious about it. I've been asked this question a million times before and already had a whole array of evasive but funny answers.

At that time I used to say I was a bank robber.
The conversation went something like this:

Girl: "So, how did you get the money to travel for so long?"

Me: "I'm a bank robber." (said with a smile)

Girl: "Haha. No, seriously, how did you earn your money?"

Me: "I told you, I rob banks."

Girl: "No, that's not true, you are not a bank robber. Why won't you answer me?" (persistent bitch)

Me: "Do you know what a bank robber looks like?"

Girl: "Eh, no, but eh, you didn't rob a bank."

Me: "So if you don't know what a bank robber looks like, how can you say that I'm not one?"

Girl: "Hmmpf." (Starts talking to her grumpy friend.)

The actual conversation was a bit longer but this sums it up pretty well. I didn't give a damn about her opinion or that she was grumpy: the Paraguayan girl found it very amusing. Normally I answer this question with "bank robber" or "Bandido" (which has a double meaning in South America – it means bandit, but also player). Sometimes I say "pirate", or in Brazil I'd go "Vagebundo de Holanda" – which means something like wanderer/tramp/hobo from Holland – which makes for instant laughs.

If I get the money question from a guy or girl I don't like, I normally say, "You know, in my country it's very impolite to ask someone about his money after just meeting him." (It actually is and people in Holland don't like to talk about money in general.) This embarrasses them and shuts them up most of the time.

When I use the whole bank robber, bandido or vagabundo answer, it usually makes for a laugh and creates some mystery around me because I'm not giving some boring answer straight away.

Anyway, back to the story. After a few rounds of drinks the cock-blocking began.

The Czech and Venezuelan girl started complaining about being tired and how they wanted to go to sleep. I thought this would be the end but Rosie gave them the keys to her house and said "Ok, just take a taxi to this address". I was really surprised by it but now realize that I'd built some attraction between me and Rosie.

I was helped by a woman in the pub who danced and acted really crazy. She was insane. Most of the people in the bar were laughing – they weren't even looking at the band anymore, just watching her dance up the stairs, walk around and give smoldering looks. She must have been on drugs.

She gave me a flirty look and Rosie noticed. I made some jokes about her but secretly I wanted to fuck the shit out of this woman. She must have been around thirty-six years old, was dressed in a very short and tight dress that showed lots of cleavage and you could see her panties many times when she danced on the stairs. She had high heels on and nice firm legs. Damn, I wanted her, and so did all the rest of the guys in the bar pretending to just find her funny.

After a while I said to Rosie, "Let's go to a club", and we walked over to a dance club very close by. Rosie drank some more Caiperinhas and I went easy on the beer. We danced to reggeaton beats and I kissed her on the dance floor.

Rosie was a short girl of Paraguayan/Arabian descent. What a mix! She had very long thick curly hair and a very attractive body type with all the right curves.

We left the club and went looking for a hotel to sleep at because she didn't want to go to her apartment. The other two girls were there and it would make her look bad to take a guy home on the first night – especially since they'd met me and couldn't stand me, and had even said I was crazy. She said she knew some place but after a lot of banging at the door and ringing the bell, still no reaction. It was already daylight and the fact that Rosie was quite drunk became a bit annoying.

We found a cheap hotel, I think it was called Hotel Miami, but even though the sun was coming up they still asked a full thirty-five dollars for the night. Since we were only going to spend a few hours there and had already spent quite a lot of money on drinks and taxis, I didn't want to stay there and we got into a small argument.

At one point I was willing to go home alone and ditch her, but I thought about that rare Paraguayan/Arabian flag and pushed her to take me to her place. Her not knowing where the fuck-hotels were kind of made me feel better about her.

We took a taxi to her place and quietly walked in; the two girls were sleeping on a mattress on the floor and the Venezuelan girl's beautiful legs were showing. They woke up and gave me a death stare.

We went into Rosie's bedroom and Rosie was super-afraid of making a noise. We took our clothes off and I saw that Rosie had an amazing body. She was only twenty-two years old and had fantastic breasts and one of the firmest, roundest asses I had seen in my life. The sex was pretty good even though we had to be so quiet.

The two girls left the next day and I stayed with Rosie. She invited me to stay with her for the next five days but in the short time I was at her house I had already noticed that she was very particular about a lot of things. She was very precise about where things went and about keeping things clean.

I would still have stayed with her, but the pressure of scoring more girls to get to my goal of eighty was too great.

We exchanged numbers and I went back to the hostel. Over the next few nights I made up excuses to her about how I was going out with hostel friends, but actually I was going out alone, though I couldn't score a local girl in those nights. The language barrier was quite high here.

At the end of the night I would call Rosie to see if I could stay with her and she always said yes. This happened a few times and Rosie started to become annoyed about it (can't blame her), saying that I only came to her house to fuck her – which was just partly true. I also liked her quite a lot, despite the over-protectiveness of her things (like I would break stuff at other people's houses) and how she was afraid of making noises for the neighbors.

I went to meet up with another girl from the travel website and was horribly late because I kept getting lost on the buses. I met the girl (name forgotten) who took me to a nearby bar-restaurant, where I met her five girlfriends.

Keeping six girls entertained wasn't easy but I managed to do it. A few spoke decent English and even had Dutch (ex) boyfriends.

After a few drinks some went home and the three girls who were left and I went dancing. I could see that the shortest of the bunch liked me and I got her phone number. She was part-owner of a liquor store and I picked her up there a few times, I even got a free bottle of the local booze.

We went for drinks and I kissed her on the first date. I went out with her about four times and we had some heavy make-out sessions in her brand new car. Her clothes came partly off but no matter how much I tried, I couldn't seal the deal with her. She was obviously looking for a serious boyfriend, because that's all she'd ever had before. She said she'd been a virgin till the age of twenty-seven and had only had two boyfriends, who were both foreign. She was thirty now and getting pretty desperate to land a serious boyfriend, especially with so much younger competition around. She had a very good body with a small but killer ass and a smiley face.

Unlike most of what I'd read about Paraguayan girls I found them very attractive, but those were mostly the whiter ones from European (mostly German) descent.

I'm pretty good at sniffing out a liar, but I had the feeling she was telling the truth. We talked quite a lot about sex and I got her very horny, but her strong principles kept me from banging her. No need to worry about blue balls, though, because I could always see cute Rosie after.

One funny thing about Paraguay, at least for me, is their national flag. It's a red, white and blue striped flag with a round symbol in the middle of the white stripe. But half of the time the symbol isn't on the flag, which makes it 100% identical to the flag of my country.

Paraguay was celebrating their bicentennial anniversary and there were flags everywhere. It almost looked like I was walking around in Holland. Even the governmental buildings had the Dutch flag on them.

Asunción's a strange, mixed-up sort of city. For example, close by the government palace there was a small slum I was warned was dangerous after dark. Another strange thing I saw was a park in one of the big city streets with people sleeping in tents and self-made shelters. Rosie told me they were a kind of gypsy.

I had stayed over a week in Asunción and really enjoyed it there. It's definitely not a cheap city but it won't break the bank either. I'd also gone out with several girls besides the two I mentioned and flirted a bit with a Brazilian girl in the hostel.

There was a cute German girl in the hostel. I first saw her

when I went for some food in the kitchen and she was sitting there reading a book. She was wearing a low-cut black dress and, obviously, the first thing I noticed were her giant breasts and her big red lips. It was hard to miss either of them, and they looked spectacular. Her body was full of tattoos just like the Brazilian girl. Her name was the same as a German pin-up girl/woman who happened to share the same qualities, but let's name her Mylo for now. She always saw me running around the hostel being busy setting up dates and when she found out I was planning to write a book about my naughty adventures she became very excited about the idea.

One time I was walked out of the shower and saw her bra hanging to dry on a drying frame and it was so big I just had to make a joke about it. I mean you could almost house a complete village under there. Mylo laughed and I flirted a bit with her. I could see she liked me but I couldn't figure out in what way.

On one of the sparse nights I actually slept in the hostel after going out yet another time, I walked into the dorm and saw she was still awake and already in her bed. We exchanged a few words and said goodnight. As I was getting ready for bed and undressed I saw her peek over to me and wondered what to do. I sat down and gave it one final thought: should I walk over and just ask her if I could stay over in her bed or should I just go to sleep? I decided against it to avoid awkwardness if things didn't work out, lay down and closed my eyes.

For the next half hour I twisted and turned and thought about cuddling up with her and to warm each up a bit. Of course, warming up starts with kissing. It was too late now and I regretted not pushing through my last doubts. I'm pretty sure she would have said yes.

There were only a few bus rides a week to Montevideo in Uruguay. I finally left on a Friday, staying three days longer then I'd planned.

Uruguay – Montevideo
The trip to Montevideo should have been a nice one. The ticket for the 26-hour ride was really expensive but it was the

most luxurious bus I had ever been in. Instead of having 2 rows of 2 seats with an aisle in between, it had a row of 2 seats and a row with just one, each as big as a couch. I was looking forward to relax a bit after all that banging, drinking and going out in Asunción.

But after just one hour the brand-new bus broke down and we had to wait nearly two hours for a mechanic to show up. He replaced the v-snare and we moved on.

Half an hour later it broke down again and after another hour wait we had to change bus to a really shitty one. Luckily there weren't that many people on board. Normally I wouldn't give a rat's ass about a delay in a bus ride, but this time I wanted to be in Montevideo on time. I would arrive on a Saturday afternoon and I wanted to buy a local SIM card and look for info on places to go out.

I was visiting Uruguay for the sole reason that I'd decided to visit every country in South America, and had no specific interest in it. I had heard it was a boring country and in many ways just a clone of Argentina. It would have saved me at least a few hundred dollars if I'd gone straight to Florianopolis in Brazil, but since I'm hard-headed I went to Uruguay anyway.

It was already nine-thirty in the evening when I arrived there after taking a local bus, and I spent a long time looking for the first hostel. They turned me down there, but gave me directions to the RED hostel and I walked over there.

I ran into a group of French people in the hostel's kitchen who studied in Buenos Aires and had taken the ferry across to see Uruguay a bit. They were all very friendly and the two girls in the group were average-looking but bang-worthy. We drank some liquor in the kitchen and later went out to find a place to party. They had been looking for a club the night before but didn't find anything good. Most of the places were restaurant/bars and not dance clubs/discotheques.

The Frenchies were already boozed up before we left and got tired after riding around in a taxi trying to find a place to dance. We soon went back to the hostel.

It was a Saturday night; there must be a place to go in the

center. The Uruguayan guy working behind the counter wasn't any help and gave me a stupid look when I asked him for a club in the center. If I owned that hostel I would fire a guy like that on the spot. How can you not give advice on a place to go to on a Saturday night? You work in a hostel, do your job! I looked on the Internet and found something that resembled a club that was within walking distance.

The importance of doing your homework before arriving in a new city became very clear and I had learned a lesson that night. I had no SIM card so I couldn't call or text any of the girls who had already given me their phone numbers online. I refuse to make a call with a regular phone because I sometimes barely understand what people are saying if they have a heavy accent or are trying to explain me how to get there. There's always noise and I can't understand directions and addresses. If I can't text to set up dates, times and directions how to get there I don't even bother with the phone number.

I walked over to the bar I found online and was surprised to see how many poor and drunk people were hanging around on the street. This city is known as an unsafe place and I stood out with my long blond hair. The club was a bit hidden and I couldn't find it, but there was another club was in the same area and I went in.

It was a Cumbia club. You either love or hate this music. It's a popular music style and Jewel had told me in Mendoza it was a typical music for poor people. If you hate Cumbia you are shit out of luck travelling through South America, because you will hear it everywhere.

All the Spanish countries in South America listen to Cumbia, and every country has its own style. The most famous are the Colombian and Argentinean styles. The Argentineans also invented Cumbia Villeria, which is a faster style more for young people. Look for "Mc caco - No es culpa mia" on YouTube if you want to hear real Cumbia Villeria. Singing a few lines of this song will help you out with Argentinean girls. They will be very surprised you know this song and it will get you a big smile.

I happen to be one of the few tourists who actually likes

this music. It was clear as soon as I walked in that this was a real Cumbia Villeria club. Guys were dressed in sneakers and training suits. There weren't many attractive girls around, even though most of them were in their late teens or early twenties.

Of course I was the only foreigner there and judging by the looks I got from most people it didn't look like I was very welcome. I walked over to the bar and ordered a beer. The barkeep gave me one of those liter bottles people usually shared with a group.

After taking a few sips I put the bottle on the bar and looked at the people dancing, trying to spot if any girls were checking me out. There were a few waitresses dancing on the bar and some reggeaton was played too. When I turned around I saw that my bottle was gone. After one fucking minute! I had paid six dollars for that bottle so it really angered me. Maybe the barkeeper had taken it away, or the people standing next to me. Half the people in the club were standing around with a bottle of beer so I couldn't tell.

I went upstairs and looked around a bit. I didn't get approached or manage to make much eye contact. I bought another bottle and kept an eye on it.

After downing that beer fast I tried some approaches but bombed out because absolutely no-one spoke English in there. I had wasted a few hours and some money. I needed a proper dance club with people who actually had some sort of education beyond high school, or even elementary school. This is why I'd rather go through online trouble to find good-looking girls on the travel website. They have similar interests, look up to foreigners and speak at least some decent English.

When I walked back home, I found a hundred-peso note on the street and thought, *Yep, that's my beer refund.* A few meters further I saw a five-hundred pesos note and was really happy about it and looked for more but didn't find anything. I had spent about twenty dollars on that club visit and had found about thirty dollars on the way back. Not a total loss then.

The guy working the nightshift was a lot nicer than the

previous guy and told me about a different club in the suburbs and how lucky I was to stay in the Cumbia place for hours and not get beat up or stabbed.

During the day I tried to find a SIM card at the mall close to the water, but for some reason the Claro phone stores had a problem activating SIM cards that day and the Tigo cards were too expensive for a three-day stay. I walked around the city a bit and took some pictures.

Montevideo isn't a very exciting city and everything is very similar to Argentinean cities. The people look similar too. Lots of people were walking around with a thermos can under their arm – another country where people were addicted to the stimulating Maté tea. I had tried it in Rosario and Cordoba a few times but didn't really like its strong herbal taste.

That night I tried to motivate the Frenchies to join me to the club in the suburbs, because I didn't want to pay the taxi back and forth to the club. Taxis weren't cheap in Montevideo: though they drive on the meter they use strange methods to calculate the actual price, which is always more than the meter says. The Frenchies were lame again and stayed in that night, even when I asked them to join me at the nearby club I'd looked for the night before. It was just around the corner but I had walked past it. This time I found it, paying about eight dollars to get in.

It was another Cumbia-salsa-merenque place but it looked like there was more action going on. After a few beers and having built up some liquid courage I started approaching. The fact that I didn't have a place to bring a girl was in my head constantly and it threw me off my game a bit. The girl working at the hostel had looked at me funny when I asked her where to find a love hotel, and so did the guy working there after she left. They didn't even know where a love hotel was, which is weird because South Americans use them a lot since they tend to live at home with their parents for ages. It's similar to Asia and totally different from Holland and other Western European countries (except countries like Spain, Italy and Greece where staying with La Mamma is considered normal until kids are in their thirties) where people move out of the parental house as early as possible.

After some more beers I forgot about not having a place to bring a girl and just hoped for the best. The language barrier hit me hard again and I found the perfect solution only as I was about to leave.

Four deaf girls – yes, deaf – approached me while I was smoking outside. It was obvious they were on their night out and asked me to take a few pictures of them with their camera. Three of the girls were downright unattractive but one of them was quite cute and up for some dancing. I kissed her not much later and she didn't mind me touching her ass. Her lips were soft and wet and she was a quite passionate kisser. I tried to get her to leave with me to a love motel or something. Once I had her in a taxi I would make it clear to the taxi driver to take me to a love hotel.

I slowly lipsynched the Spanish word "vamos" which means "let's go" to her and pointed to the door with my head. Her eyes were sparkling and I could clearly see she was considering it. Yes! I was finally going to get my deaf girl experience after the debacle in Manila and capture a Uruguayan flag in the process. All I needed to do then was find a Colombian girl somewhere in South America and I would be back on flagging schedule.

The girl was ready to say yes, but then the cock-blocking started. Her friends convinced her in sign language to stay put and forget me. They must have been pretty convincing because it worked. I left them not much later but ran into them again in the club later that night. It didn't work out, and although I had some actual talks with some people who knew some English I had to return to the hostel dick in hand again. This is a country you need to speak Spanish.

My only chance was to get a girl through the couchsurfing website because my day game is non-existent and the chance I would find a good-looking girl on the streets who happened to speak English and who would be into me was very small, so I didn't even bother with it.

One of the girls in a phone store helped me get a SIM card and activate it but it was already too late to set up dates with online girls. The cute girl in the phone store didn't bite either.

The weekend had passed and girls were busy with studying and whatnot during the week. One girl showed a lot of interest in meeting me but didn't have the time for it. She asked me to wait a few days, but I decided against it. I was already a week behind on my travel schedule and needed to move on. I gave up on the Uruguayan flag.

She emailed me a lot even after I left Uruguay. Maybe I missed out here but I will probably never know, since I won't return to Uruguay unless I have good Spanish skills and some more money in my pocket, as the country isn't that cheap if you want a private room and take a few taxis. I guess seventy-five dollars a day would be a good minimum budget.

What did I do wrong here? First, I had made the stupid mistake of fucking up my bus ride from Asunción to Montevideo. I wanted to arrive on Thursday and get ready for the weekend but arrived as late as Saturday evening. The hostel wasn't the greatest either; the one I looked at first seemed a lot nicer but was already fully booked. Not having a working SIM card fucked up my chances to meet girls through the travel website and my limited Spanish and money cock-blocked me as well. I think if I had spoken some basic conversational-level Spanish I would have scored in that club. Club gaming is mostly a numbers game. Approach enough girls and you'll find one who is into you. Not speaking the local language rules out 95% of the approachable girls.

I had lost my jacket the night before and had no time to wait for the club to open again. It was the third jacket I'd either had stolen or lost on my trip and I bought a twenty-dollar hooded sweater at some local market. I wouldn't need it much since I was going up north, where temperatures would be better and the winter would finally be over.

Brazil was waiting

Brazil – Florianopolis
After another terribly long and expensive bus ride and a

short stop in Porto Alegre I arrived in Florianopolis.

According to all the Brazilian guys I had met on my trip this was the city in Brazil with the most beautiful beaches and bitches. They were right about the beautiful women; I saw loads of them on the streets in the center, but I didn't see the beaches at all.

All four days I was in Floripa it was either cloudy or windy. It was still early in the season and I was coming out of the South American winter. The weather would only get better with every new destination since I was headed north and for the Caribbean islands. It had been mostly cold ever since I had arrived in Argentina in late March. During the days it would be ok but after sundown the temperatures would drop fast. All of this would be over now that I was in Brazil.

Brazil is always portrayed as a country full of beautiful light-skinned girls with huge bundas walking around in G-strings all day. Could this be true? Well, lots of beautiful girls with big bundas were definitely true and Brazilian girls know how to dress and impress with their feminine and sexy appearance. Florianopolis would be the perfect place to start.

I had been told that the rich Brazilian elite visits Floripa during the summer and literally bring ships with extremely hot girls into the harbor. By the looks of the girls I had seen in the street Floripa was a place I could live forever. Girls here are light-skinned because most of them have European, mostly German roots.

Many Germans immigrated here in the last hundred years and I had basically planned much of my trip to coincide with the dates for the Octoberfest, the largest one outside Germany. I was told by at least five separate Brazilian guys and even some girls that the Octoberfest was a debauchery of beer drinking and hot girls.

I had started to learn some Portuguese and was naïve enough to think I would learn it pretty quick because I already knew a lot of Spanish, which is kind of similar to Portuguese. In my mind I had big plans to study very hard this time, but as usual I lacked the motivation to cram in a few hours of language learning every day. I had met quite a few guys who had really picked up the local language and spoke it pretty well. One thing I noticed, though, is that most of them sucked with girls.

Most guys like that are more interested in local culture and interaction with all kinds of people than in picking up girls. It takes a certain kind of person to give up the fun stuff and learn a language while travelling. Finding a balance between going out all the time and learning a foreign language is very difficult at times.

Floripa marked the beginning of lots of cell-phone trouble which would drive me mad at times.

Once again I would become my own cock-block by being too cheap with my budget. I bought a local SIM card in a store and tried to activate it, but nothing seemed to work.

I went to the store and no one spoke English. A friendly guy in the hostel went to the main phone store with me to help me out. We found out I needed a CPF number to activate my card.

A CPF number is Brazilian social security number and it takes weeks to get one the official way. I was flabbergasted by this communist-like system which kept me from texting local girls I met online. I had bought SIM cards in almost thirty countries up to that point. Usually you buy the SIM card on the street or in a store. Sometimes registration with a passport is necessary or even a local person has to come with you to the store (Cambodia) but the SIM card ALWAYS works as soon as you put it in your phone. Obviously not in Brazil.

At one point I emailed Charlize, who lived in São Paulo and whom I was going to visit in a week. She immediately sent me her CPF number and after some struggling my phone finally worked. I had now already lost two valuable days but still I was happy as a clown with a useable phone number.

On Friday night I went to a bar recommended by a cool guy working at the hostel. It's called Scuna and it was a MILF fest in there. When I walked in a lot of heads turned, which was the first time that happened to me in all of South America but was quite normal in South East Asia. I got a beer at the bar and looked around a bit. It was still too early for dancing but things got started ten minutes later.

A tall beautiful black girl with an ass to kill for gave me some eye contact and I opened her with the question "Fala inglais?" which means "Do you speak English?" Well she didn't speak any English or Spanish. Or Dutch. It was very difficult to communicate because she only understood Spanish words that were similar to Portuguese and my Spanish skills were good enough for uber-simple conversation but still sucked balls.

I could see she was interested anyway and we went out to the smoking section. As we walked out she grabbed my hand and held it as we went through the crowd.

We were sitting shoulder to shoulder and things got a bit flirty. I looked at her shoes and pointed out she was cheating with her high heels. I took her hand; we stood up and measured each other standing face to face. (a trick I like to use a lot.) Then I tried to talk again but got nowhere with the language.

As an all-or-nothing try I started talking fast in English saying how I wanted to talk her ears off but couldn't. I kept my head tilted a bit and kept looking in her eyes. She looked at me and said she didn't understand me and gave me the "I don't understand you" look. Our faces were six inches apart. I just looked her straight in the eyes, smiled and calmly said "Voce e linda" (you are beautiful). The look on her face changed and she grabbed me and started kissing me.

I immediately grabbed her ass with my left hand and started squeezing it while massaging the back of her neck with the other hand. Her ass was big, round and super firm. I kissed her more and grabbed her ass with both hands. Seeing all those big Brazilian butts all day in the center streets had made me want to touch one ever since I set foot in Floripa, so I didn't waste my chances. In fact I think it was the first time ever I kissed a black girl.

After a while the kissing moments kind of died and we went back inside. Her friends had some argument with a drunken guy and the four of them left after a while. As far as I could figure out he was the (ex) boyfriend of one of the girls. I was back at the bar.

A forty-five year old ugly hag started talking to me and of course I didn't understand shit of what she said, and wasn't interested in it either. Suddenly she grabbed my hand and pulled me through the crowd, which was embarrassing and a big de-selection. I had to ditch her quick before I embarrassed myself more with her. She wanted to kiss and dance and I just shook my head like a child until she left.

I kissed another woman when I was talking to some old dude, who spoke four words of English. He just pushed her on me and she immediately started kissing me.

The black hottie came back with her friends but kissed some bald guy who was chasing her all night. I had already read about the easy kissing culture in Brazil so I didn't really care about it. It wasn't going anywhere anyway.

I had another make-out with a MILF at the bar. She only spoke a few words of English, was around thirty-eight and I was wearing beer goggles – though, I must say she looked quite sexy in her black dress. She gave me her phone number and I told her I'd text her. Overall I had a good time at Scuna, approached a lot of girls and had three make-outs.

I lived in a hostel just a stone's throw away from Club El Divino, apparently the most expensive club in town and where all the hot girls go. It's at least twenty-five dollars just to get in so I just went there to see what was happening on the street outside.

A guy was selling hotdogs from the modified back of his car and I bought one. I sat down next to a hot girl and asked her if she spoke English and she actually spoke it very well. We had a fun conversation and things were going well until some drunken Brazilian guys start cock-blocking me, first by trying to talk to me and being annoying, later by shouting to the girl: "Are you going to fuck him?" "Fuck fuck fuck" and other stuff like that. This totally ruined the fun mood and she called the guys imbeciles and they left. I couldn't do much because they were a group of five and I'm not getting my ass kicked over this.

The girl actually lived straight across my hostel and we walked back there and had some fun and jokes along the way.

A guy tried to pick her up, saying he wanted to practice

his English with me; I tried to ignore him as much as possible and the asswipe just asked the girl for her phone number, which she gave him easily. Guys were straight-up direct about approaching girls while they were with another dude. I had never seen this before in any country.

I got her phone number two minutes later in front of the gate of her building. It didn't mean much to me, since she'd given her number so easily to the cock-block. She said she had to work till late in the evening the next day and that I should call her. I wanted to kiss her but she kept a distance. After this she said I could call her but shouldn't expect a kiss or a fuck if we meet up. I remembered the girl in Quito who said the same and assumed that if she can only meet at ten in the evening and already says stuff like "don't expect to kiss or fuck", it's a waste of time to even call her.

The next night I was planning to go to a place recommended by the guy working in the hostel. The club was called Mara Alta and it was kind of Brazilian country music club. He said I would be the only foreigner there and he would come with me, translate for me with the girls and take care of transport with his mom's car. Erik was a nice guy to talk to but by that evening he had some excuse not to come anymore. I took my losses and returned to the MILF club.

I texted the MILF from the day before who spoke a bit of English and she agreed to meet me there. I guessed that on a Saturday night out this would be my chance for my first Brazilian lay inside the country.

Boy, was I wrong; the long hard struggle for Brazilian notches only got started. I didn't see the MILF inside club Scuna and the first hour was kind of boring.

Then I met three MILFs at the bar. One was super-fat so no way I was going to be with her. The other two were different but attractive in their own way. One had a few pounds too many but they were all at the right places, a giant round ass and a nice pair of knockers. The third was tiny and skinny, around forty judging by her face, but she had a workout stomach and a small but round and super-firm ass.

To make a long story short, I kissed the short one and

couldn't stop squeezing her ass, which felt like it belonged to a teenager. She tried to stop me from doing it but I just kept on going. She stayed, so she was interested.

The MILF from the day before finally showed up, very late. She saw me talking to the three others and walked over to talk to me. I had to make a split-second decision on which woman to stay with.

I choose the tiny MILF with the round butt and brushed the other one off, saying she was an hour late and that I'd been waiting for her. She was clearly disappointed and I saw her alone the rest of the night.

Of course, it turns out I made the wrong choice, because at the end of the night the tiny MILF went home with her friends and I probably could have banged the one from the night before. I didn't care much, though, because the only reason I went to the MILF club was because it was cheaper and easier than going to El Divino, a high-end club with stunning hot but very snobby girls. My predictions for that place were that I would talk to young hot girls there but that as soon as they found out I was a poor backpacker, they would ditch me. As I said, it costs around twenty-five to forty dollars just to get in depending on the night and drinks are expensive. I didn't go there, but maybe I should have given it a shot.

I texted the tiny MILF the next day that I had to leave but would be back in a few days for the Blumenau Oktoberfest. She wanted to see me. I never went back but that's another story.

Brazil – São Paulo

In São Paulo I stayed in a hostel called Limetime or something similar. If you ever stay there, look for my writing on the wall. One of the other guests was an Italian guy who was going around the world without flying and was planning on doing South America on a moped, breaking a world record.

I cleaned myself up from the long bus ride and went to have lunch with Charlize. It was great to see her again. It had been almost half a year and I was looking forward to seeing her again for a while. When we'd said goodbye, I had promised she would see me again and she said I could stay in her house during my stay in São Paulo.

For all those months of travelling through several countries my mind had been set on that. Not only would it save me money but most important, I really liked to be with her.

A month or two before I met her again she told me she had a boyfriend in São Paulo, and I couldn't stay with her. I couldn't blame her, it's not like I'd been sitting on my hands in the past months and she knew that. I was highly disappointed nonetheless.

During lunch we reminisced about our time together in Argentina, but when I tried some subtle flirting she said that she was serious with her boyfriend and couldn't do anything with me.

In the evening she invited me over to her place to have dinner and watch some TV. I thought I would "get lucky" this time but she stayed loyal to her boyfriend (some hard rock dude). I could see she was struggling with it though, and she was nearly crying after the bombardment of sweet-talking and charming I fired upon her. A bit of cuddling was all I get out of it.

The next weekdays I saw her three times again for lunch but couldn't manage to get a grip on her. In the meanwhile I was going out with people from the hostel and did some sightseeing during the day.

Most nights I went out to Augusta Street, which was full of clubs. I still had a hard time with Brazilian girls. I managed to kiss quite a few but couldn't pull them to a motel.

On Tuesday I went to a Couchsurfing meeting, which was boring as hell. At one time when I was smoking outside the bar with a few people from the meeting a small group of Brazilians got talking with us. One girl was very young and attractive. She had pinkish-blonde hair and a small body with good curves. Unfortunately she didn't speak a word of English.

The whole group of travellers and connected locals went

to a nearby club called Vegas. The good thing about going out with a large group of people is that when the group spreads out over the club, you constantly run into people you barely know, but to an outsider you look like the guy who knows everyone inside. I met a hard rock guy inside the club who spoke excellent English and that was just what I needed. I'd already made contact with several girls but wanted to keep my options open.

I took the English-speaking guy to the pink/blonde girl and asked him to translate literally for me. The next few sentences were incredible romantic nonsense and the guy asked if I was serious. I told him just to translate. Once he was finished the girl looked at me and said to him in Portuguese, "I want to go to a dark spot and kiss him". I took her by the hand and that's just what I did, kiss her. To my surprise she was a really good kisser, I even dare to say she was the best kisser ever. Her lips were big and very wet. She made all the right movements and I loved it. I had kissed a ton of girls on my trip but this girl was prize-winning at it.

When the club closed I tried to get her to a motel but she declined and gave me her phone number. I texted her the next evening in Portuguese but never got a reply. Flakiness is top notch in Brazil.

Side note: This girl kissed so well that half a year later, when I was already back home, I tried to get in touch with her again. I gave her name, phone number and picture to eight people I knew in São Paulo and they tried to get in touch with her, but I never heard anything back. Maybe she doesn't have the same number anymore. I still think about her sometimes.

Later in the week I met another online girl, a Russian/Finnish girl who studied and worked as a translator in São Paulo and was a rock and roll girl.

I met her for a few beers in a bar close to Augusta Street and did some of my best date game. I could see that she was attracted to me. She sat really close to me and my touching was warmly welcomed. We went out for a smoke and that's when I kissed her. She couldn't stop smiling at me.

We walked back to her apartment but I couldn't get up to her room. *Damn, better luck next time,* I thought. I told her that I was going home but went straight to a club where I met a few girls, but nothing happened that night besides kissing.

The next night I went out for drinks with Rock and Roll Girl again. We kissed more heavily and this time I could kiss her perfectly shaped boobs, but nothing more. She was about to go on a one-month trip through South America and I had one more chance to bone her and get my Finnish flag. She was damn hot and I wanted to go for it.

The last night out with her was terrible. I packed my backpack and dropped it off at her apartment so I could leave the next day for the Oktoberfest in Blumenau. The plan was to go out all night and that I'd would leave in the morning and sleep all day on the bus back to Florianopolis. My real plan of course was to stay in her bed for a few hours, do my thing and then leave.

So before we went out I put my bag in her room, took a shower and we kissed a bit. When I was kissing her and went for her boobs, she became a bit distant and said she wasn't an easy girl who had sex on the third date. I might as well have gone back to the hostel because what followed sucked balls.

We took a bus to a hard rock bar where an Iron Maiden cover band was playing. The band was good but Rock and Roll Girl was distant and drank a lot. We smoked some cigarettes outside the bar and spoke to a few old dudes who were in a Kiss cover band. They obviously liked this pretty girl; twenty-three years old, she had big boobs for her slim body type and great legs. She liked all the attention she got.
I had already figured out this was bad news for me.

A friend of hers showed up, a young Brazilian guy playing in some band. They said they'd been friends for two months now. The guy was all over her and every time I tried some subtle cock-blocking, she just ignored me more.

I got pissed off with it and let her know that. She gave me a speech about how she was just friends with the guy and knew he wanted her, but that she was not interested in him. She smiled the same way at him as she did with me on the night I met her. I thought I was maybe paranoid or too focused on banging her.

At one point the band stopped playing and they wanted to go drink more beer in Augusta Street, where she lived. We argued and I was sick of her. I said I would get my bag and leave. She asked me to stay longer but I couldn't be around that cock-blocking dickhead anymore. We got in his crappy old car and drove back to her apartment with him still drinking behind the wheel.

I went to the apartment alone with her and tried to convince her to stay with me up there. The cock-block was waiting downstairs. I kept her up the apartment as long as possible and we agreed to see each other in Prague for New Year's. She still invited me to drink some more beers with the other guy but I had had enough. I thought, *for you, ten others* but I was disappointed inside all the same.

When we walked back downstairs we didn't see the guy but his car was still there. I walked to the metro station, which was already open, and went to the bus station, still quite drunk. She would start her South America trip the next day.

I was stupid to let her convince me that I could take a bus to Florianopolis really early in the morning without checking, because there was actually only one bus, which didn't leave till noon and would arrive late in the evening. This meant I didn't have time to go to the hostel and then take a three-hour bus to the Oktoberfest.

I hung around the bus station for two hours, not knowing what to do; I had based most of my travel schedule on the Oktoberfest dates. I already missed the Friday night and I would miss the Saturday night too. I decided not to go there at all and was disappointed about it all. If I'd decided that earlier I could have stayed longer in Colombia and Uruguay to keep my flag chase going, or see some of the natural beauty there.

I sent a message to Rock and Roll Girl and went back to the hostel. I looked up as much as I could about the Octoberfest in Blumenau, something I should have done before I based half my travel schedule on it. I found out that the reason most Brazilian guys like it is because they go there with large groups of friends to drink beer and have bro-fun, not to chase girls. Sure, there will be some guys getting laid or making out, but it will be hard to pick a girl up there while having not even a place to stay nearby. I was glad I didn't go after all and stayed for a few extra days in São Paulo.

In the late afternoon, she still hadn't replied to my message or added me on Facebook like she said she would. It pissed me off because it filled me with thoughts of her being with that other guy. I never heard from her again, so I'll never know. I didn't know I still had so much jealousy in me.

I met an American/Filipino guy named Andrei in the hostel and we went out with a group to Club Vegas that Saturday night. There was an annoying English guy in the hostel group who tried to get with some girls there but got nowhere. He was such an annoying beta dork; I couldn't stand him and his stupid snobby English accent. Seeing him humiliating himself in front of girls made me vomit.

That night I took a Brazilian girl named Leia, a hot Mary-Kate Olsen lookalike, all the way from the other floor to the spot where he and the hostel people were at, just to kiss her right in front of him. Suffer, dude!
We kissed all night and I couldn't stop touching her ass, which was to die for. But it stayed with kissing and I couldn't get her outside and away from her girlfriends.

There was a cute Slovakian girl in the hostel group; the dork had tried everything to get with her. Talking for hours with her about travelling, school, work and avoiding all flirting and being the listening ear and gentleman.

That Monday night, we got into three taxis to go the D-Edge club, and I was in the taxi with Andrei, the Slovakian girl and the English beta.

The beta was cock-blocking me, he knew everything better than me and kept interrupting the conversations.

Although he was young, he was bald as a cue ball. I suddenly asked the girl which shampoo she used and we talked about our long hair. Saying "I love my long hair" and stroking my fingers through it shut him up for a while.

Now, the Slovakian girl was cute but also a bore. I saw soon that no-one would get her in the end. Well, on to the

Brazilian girls. I kissed a cute 19-year-old girl in the Edge club and approached several others.

D-Edge is a place with a giant roof where everyone comes to smoke or hang out. An ideal place to meet girls. I hardly saw the dance floor or the others from the hostel.

I was hanging out with Andrei and we met Miss Brazil 2001 at the end of the night. She was there with her boyfriend, who was stupidly drunk. Although she won the title ten years ago, you could still see she used to be very hot. We took some pictures together. I looked her up on the Internet the next day and it was really her: Juliana Borges. She was quite controversial those days due to false rumors about seventeen plastic surgery operations before taking the title of Miss Brazil.

Charlize had asked me to go to the cinema with her. At first I agreed to go with her but sent a text later that it would bring back too many memories of the cinema where I kissed her for the first time. She was disappointed.

I planned to leave on Wednesday night and Charlize wanted to say goodbye.

We met in a dining place close to her house and she drank some Smirnoff ice, the only alcoholic drink she likes.

She was dressed up all sexy and looked hotter than ever. Her big boobs almost bursting out of her shirt, her firm ass perfectly round, always a smile on her face. I knew I wasn't going anywhere with her but sweet- talked anyway. I kept staring her deep in her eyes and she was very emotional, saying she wanted to be with me but had to stay loyal.

When we walked back from the dining place, she couldn't take it anymore and suddenly grabbed me and kissed me. I pulled her into an alley and we had a steamy make-out session. I was looking for a place to have sex but there was nothing around and she said she was already very late because she had to meet her boyfriend. I hated the thought when she said that.

We kissed some more and my hands felt over her body. Damn, it felt so good. I had been with many girls in the meanwhile but Charlize had always been on my mind. It felt good, it felt pure. The only girls who came close to her were sweet Marisol from Valparaiso in Chile and that little cutie Evita in Lima.

Ironically a week after I left she sent a text meant for me to her boyfriend by accident and he dumped her. I thought of going back to São Paulo and would have if I'd had more time but I was already so behind on my schedule that I had to skip cities, including the cities the three Brazilian girls in Chile had invited me to, so I decided not to.

I went out so many times and experienced so much stuff that I have to skip parts of the story. I went out with a tall, cute black girl to an all-black club in São Paulo, which was great. I never saw so many hot black Brazilian girls in one place. I was the only white guy but that didn't give me much in the way of bonus points. Language barriers were high and the approach anxiety came back, but not for long.

I also went out with a beautiful half Japanese/Brazilian girl. On that date a beaten-up, blood-covered girl came into the bar, needing medical attention. Talk about some serious cock-blocking. She was in a bit of a shock and two sketchy-looking guys took her to the hospital on a motorbike. I can't say I really trusted the look of those guys; it might have been one of them who did it.

The girl and I had a few more drinks later but she had to get up early in the morning and needed to go.

When she dropped me off at Augusta Street later that night, she told me that she sometimes went to kinky parties all dressed up in leather. My jaw dropped when she told me that because she didn't look the part at all: she was quite the artsy girl and looked classy. I tried to escalate immediately but it was too late.

Setting up a second date was hard. She wanted to and texted me a lot but had a hard time getting off from her two jobs. I guess I'll just have to get back to Brazil one day and catch up.

I was starting to dislike Brazilian girls a little bit. Since I arrived in Brazil I'd gone out almost ten times and got nothing but kisses and touching tits and ass. It was time to get my dick wet. Brazil was not living up its reputation.

On the internet I read about a lot of guys who were also

struggling in Brazil, even they had a way bigger living budget and nicer clothes than me. Some even spoke Portuguese and had problems with it. It made me feel better.

At this point I was so bored with sightseeing and doing "local" things that I was only interested in going out. Can you blame me? I was sightseeing for two years already.

Brazil – Rio de Janeiro

Rio de Janeiro is the only city in Brazil you absolutely have to visit. My hostel was perfectly situated right between the Ipenema and Copacabana beaches.

The hostel was partly owned by a friendly American guy and he told me a dorm bed was only fifteen Reals a night. That's about eight dollars a night and dirt-cheap compared to the forty reals prices I paid in Florianopolis and São Paulo.

The Pirates de Ipenema hostel was a messy place, but so much fun to stay at. The owners were nice guys and there were all kinds of characters around. There was the Turkish guy sleeping in a hammock every night, another guy sleeping a lot on the couch, and in the hostel's open "living room" stood a tent with a couple sleeping in it.

Another guy was tattooing people to make some money and when there was no one around he would tattoo himself.

The hostel dorm was old with broken beds and lots of noise. There were always dogs around, even in the kitchen and dorm rooms. The showers were a mess too, but instead of moving to a better hostel I decided to stay there and save some money. I was running out of money fast with all those seventy-dollar bus rides and going out nearly every night. I'm not a big spender on drinks and always stick to beer but entrance fees, drinks and sometimes a taxi will all add up.

Although it's not the cleanest place to stay in Rio I would still recommend this hostel if you're looking for a cheap place and want to meet some strange characters and have some fun.

One of the guests was a black guy named Paul from South Africa, who would sometimes worked the night shift and tried to pick up the drunken girls returning to the hostel.

According to fellow long-term guests he would try to

fuck just about anything with two arms and two legs. Even the 120kg beasts. Not my kind of style.

I never saw him approach any girls outside the hostel but he always had big talk about getting pussy. He was a funny guy though, but unfortunately I found out too late he was full of shit. I based too many decisions on his info because he had lived there for over half-a-year all ready and partied five times a week.

If you think about Rio de Janeiro you think of sun and full beaches, but I was really unlucky with the weather. The whole ten days I was there I barely saw the sun. If you can't spend any time on the beach then there's not much else to do other than going out every day of the week and sleeping in.

Eating out in the morning was cheaper than I expected. For breakfast, here was a small diner on the corner where every morning I ate an acai shake. The acai berries are quite healthy and delicious but the added sugar makes it a calorie bomb – one that keeps you filled for hours.

A couple of nights I went to the Emporio bar in Ipenema – a gringo bar, but that's where you find the gringo hunters. I reckoned it would be easier to get laid there.

A glass of beer cost three dollars, but outside the bar there was a guy selling cans of beer for only a dollar-and-a-half, so you could get one glass inside and fill it up outside the rest of the night since the bar was small and lots of people stood outside. That may sound stupid and the bar may lose money on the beer sellers outside, but Paul's theory about it wasn't that bad. He thought that the beer sellers and the bar worked together so that people would definitely come to this place and they would still make lots of money on selling cocktails to girls or beer to guys who wouldn't go outside for one.

One night a working girl convinced me to do a line of coke and I did. She also gave me some beers and took me by the hand to go outside the club. We walked down the street and stopped between the cars, I thought at least something was going to happen when she lifted up her skirt. Something did happen,: she crouched down, showing her big juicy ass, and took a piss between the cars. The fuck? It was the first time I saw that so I just watched the whole thing. It was fucking weird. Later she asked me a hundred dollars for a fuck and I asked her if her pussy was made of gold. She gave me an insulted look and left a bit later. I wasn't planning on paying for a bang anyway.

On Friday some guests of the hostel and I went to the Lapa street party. There are thousands of people in the streets all partying and drinking around beer stands and outside clubs and bars. Lots of samba music and dancing everywhere. The beer was even cheaper here and I drank a lot that night. It's not the safest area so I wouldn't go there and flash cash or expensive jewelry around. I saw a few pickpockets at work that night, robbing a few tourists.

At the end of the night I was alone and a pretty girl was on her way home with her girlfriend. I grabbed her arm and asked her where she was going. "Let's go dancing," I said, and pulled her close to my body. "Ok, but only kissing, no more," she replied. That was kind of weird but it was the end of the night and I agreed to it. She had big fuzzy hair and a small posture with a little but of course round butt. We danced some samba but I couldn't keep up with her. My hips couldn't follow the extremely fast dancing. Besides, it was the first time I ever danced samba.

We stopped and I pulled her towards me and said "Time for beijos" (kisses), and she looked me in the eyes and kissed me with her big fleshy lips. It felt good but I wanted more.

I had been kissing a lot of girls in Floripa and São Paulo already and was getting tired of it. I asked her if she wanted to go with me but she just said: "I told you, just kissing". She went home a little bit later and I didn't bother asking her number. Maybe I should have done it anyway, since she spoke some English and I could do a date with her.

On Sunday I went to a Favela funk part in Rocinha, one of the hillside slums in Rio. It sucked. It was hyped up by Paul all week as a pussy heaven where girls would be easy. I had high expectations because I looked at some YouTube videos and they looked amazing. Lots of half-naked girls shaking their butts. We were taken in a minibus to a giant dancehall.

376

Beer was cheap and they even gave away free beers in the beginning of the party. The music was eardrum-destroying loud. I could feel the bass in the fillings of my teeth and at some points through my whole body. The beer in my glass looked like the scene from the first Jurassic Park movie where the T–Rex is stamping around. The bass I could take but the rest of the music was way too loud. My ears were still ringing at five in the afternoon the next day.

The music is basically one guy screaming into the microphone all night with techno/funky beats. I like most kinds of Latin music but this was terrible.

We were there with three guys and four girls. We were the only foreigners among a thousand people. There were tons of hot girls around, all standing in pairs or triplets; I was advised not to approach any girl there because according to my mate Paul they all had boyfriends lurking around who would beat my ass with eight guys if I started talking to their girlfriends.

Since Brazil is mostly about kissing anyway I decided not to take a chance. It was frustrating to see so many hot girls around and not be able to do a damn thing. Paul said that the free girls would approach us. Well, guess what. No girl ever did. Not me, not Paul, not the other guy from the hostel. Nothing. The dancing was lame, with lots of guys doing a synced dance. The girls mostly stood around and danced a bit. It was plain boring. I would have more fun just watching a movie in the hostel that night.

Other guys who have been to these kind of parties later told me I had been cock-blocked by Paul saying it was too dangerous, because according to them it was definitely possible to pick up girls there.

The morning after I got myself together out of a hangover and went to the Christ the Redeemer statue by local bus. I got bad directions from hostel folk and it took a while before I made it there.

When I finally arrived it was cloudy and the statue was barely visible at times. Just my luck. I took some pictures of the city views and the statue at clear moments anyway and went back disappointed. I had put this trip off for a couple of days because I had a massive eye infection and they told me it was a common thing in this hostel. My eyes were tearing up all the time and were very red. I was dating a local black girl at this time and at one moment we bought medicine and eye cleanser and things literally started to clear up for me.

If the eye infection and not getting laid wasn't bad luck enough I also had problems with my phone. The touch screen of my phone stopped working at the dumbest times so that I couldn't use my phone to text and set up dates. A repair shop charged fifty-five dollars just to replace the touch screen but I didn't trust those guys. Besides, maybe it wasn't even a touch screen problem. The simplest solution would be buying a brand new phone but despite living in a cheap hostel, drinking cheap beers and eating cheap food, I was still spending five hundred dollars a week in Brazil.

Phones are extremely expensive there and I only had two months of travelling left before heading to Holland, where phones are cheap. I bought a cheap China phone with full options but the most important things like texting and calling barely worked.

I had to go back three times to the market store where I bought that fucker and was constantly pissed off because I had at least twelve phone numbers of good-looking English-speaking girls from the Couchsurfing website and I couldn't do a damn thing with them. Calling over Skype was a hassle because of some of the girls' heavy accents and the difficulty of meeting up on certain streets or addresses. I was arriving late on dates or couldn't find the address sometimes.

No matter how experienced you are travelling around the world, taking local buses and finding addresses in countries where you don't speak the language is insanely difficult sometimes.

I met with one of the girls I did the Salt flats tour with in Bolivia and she showed me around the city a bit. I had been friend-zoned by her already and I liked the fact that I had someone I already knew well who could guide me trough the city. She went with me to the phone shop and made it clear that my China phone didn't work properly and she got me a new one. They gave her a new one immediately, while I had to point with my fingers or use my ten words of Portuguese to do that the times I went there before.

At night I met up with Patty, a beautiful black girl from the Couchsurfing website, and I was horribly late because we agreed upon a time but I couldn't find the address. She had already left when I finally arrived there. I had my shit China phone with me and gave it a shot. The damn thing actually worked for once and I got network reception. She said to meet at Copacabana beach a bit later, and it was already after midnight.

I met her there and we went to an all-night juice/beer bar close by. Patty was pretty hot, a short but cheating with high heels girl with a small round butt and nice B-cup breasts, maybe a bit bigger than that. She said she didn't have much time that night but once we started talking the hours went by quickly. I got her to smoke some cigarettes with me and we had to stand outside the bar to smoke them. I tried to kiss her but she gave me the cheek turn. I kept on trying and she gave in not much later. From then on my hands were all over her and I kissed her all the time.

Although she said that she didn't have much time, she stayed with me in the bar till six-thirty in the morning. I use this excuse myself too; I always say that I don't have much time so I can ditch the girl if I don't like her. We guys can use those girl excuses too. My date game went flawlessly. I got her fantasizing about things and we never ran out of fun subjects to talk about. We met a few times and I wondered if she would be my first-ever black girl.

On Wednesday night the hostel group went out to a place called Club Melt. It was twenty-five Reals for people from the hostel to get in, forty Reals for others, which is a bit over twenty dollars. It was a typical gringo place and with the salsa music I didn't like it at first. I did some approaches on the tourist girls but got nowhere. I had some beers and talked to some guys and was generally bored. Luckily the top floor opened and played better music. You can't go wrong with the Black Eyed Peas for getting a place started up.

I saw a black Brazilian girl and approached her. She

wasn't extremely dark, just similar skin color to Beyoncé, and spoke a quite bit of English. I started gaming her.

After talking for a while I went in for the kiss and she declined, saying she wasn't that easy. We kept talking and I kept on going for the kiss another ten times before she finally gave in. I used player game and told her I wasn't easy either. I gave her lines like "I know you want me, I can see it in your eyes, your eyes don't lie to me". I have a whole arsenal of bullshit lines I come up with when I'm in gaming mode. The trick is using the right tone and talking speed, something you just have to get experienced at. We danced a bit and had a beer.

At one point she gave me some resistance and I said I needed to go to the toilet. When I came back, two blonde English girls I'd met before grabbed me and starting taking pictures with me. Sandra, the black girl, saw it and instantly showed more interest when I returned to her. I was pretty sure she was a working girl because she was there by herself and just had that vibe and bullshit story about her working on some boat.

Not soon after we left for a love hotel close to the favela. I paid thirty-five dollars for twelve hours and the large room had lots of mirrors and a nice bathroom with sauna.

Sandra had on a sexy red dress showing some deep cleavage. When she took it off, I realized her boobs were not just big but massive. We both took a shower and started kissing on the bed. Well, long story short, we had sex three times and did pretty much everything; I'm a boob man and couldn't get enough of her firm boobs. Banging my first black girl doggy style with full views in the ceiling mirror was amazing. She was a generally sweet girl too and we laughed a lot.

The next morning we said goodbye after a shower blowjob and I never saw her again. She was probably a prostitute but never asked me for any money.

It had been nearly three weeks since I last had sex and I had struggled a lot during those weeks in which I sometimes went out five times a week. I finally got it over with and no longer felt like a failure. Anyone who says it's really easy to get laid in Brazil is either getting very lucky, spending a lot of money or a very skilled player. Or probably just one of those liars I had met plenty of while travelling.

The next night I was supposed to see Patty again. We agreed to go to a Latin party organized by another hostel. I was going there with the group from my hostel anyway. She didn't show up at the agreed time and place and I found the Latin Party on my own after walking around a lot. Luckily it wasn't that far from the hostel.

I walked in to the small but crowded club and didn't see her there. Nor was I on the guest list as she promised, so I had to pay fifteen Reals to get in. Later I realized she used my Facebook name which, for obvious reasons, is different from my real name on my ID card.

I saw Paul and walked over to him. As I started talking to him I felt someone pinch my butt, I turned around and saw a thick girl with a very cute face laughing. I gave her some cocky/funny lines and turned back to Paul.

A minute later I went looking for Patty again but didn't see her. Pinchy Girl was still on the lookout for me and I began flirting heavily with her. I took her to the dark smoking room and kissed her there after she tried to evade it just once.

The old saying: "When in Rome, do as Romans do" worked well here. Brazilian guys have an aggressive way of flirting and kissing. They move in for the kiss very quickly, sometimes just grabbing a girl and holding her tight and forcing themselves on them.

In the western world that would be sexual assault, but here it's an everyday thing. Brazilian guys make it a sport to kiss a lot of girls and feel like quite the heroes about it among friends, but don't get laid much. I kissed tons of Brazilian girls in the first few weeks, especially in São Paulo, but got nowhere near a lay with them. Very frustrating, because usually kissing a girl is half the work done on getting the lay.

After talking and kissing a bit more to pinchy girl she sat on my lap and my fingers went under her skirt. She was quite drunk and getting her horny was very easy when I felt her up and told her what I was going to do to her.

We left for a love hotel only 45 minutes after I first met her. She walked out of the smoking room to give her apartment key to a friend and when I walked out as well I saw Patty. I pretended I didn't see her and rushed for the door, even though I heard her call my name.

Pinchy girl who now introduced herself as Marcela had her own apartment but her girlfriend was staying over that night and it was a studio with just one bed. I tried to go there anyway because I didn't want to whop out another thirty to forty dollars for a room. She said no and we took a taxi to a love hotel nearby her apartment.

When we arrived at the hotel the prices were very different from the ones the night before. A room was 165 reals, which is over eighty dollars. I told her I didn't have that kind of money and she paid half after some initial grumping.

The room was excellent, with an enormous bubble bath and a separate dining area. After the shower we started fucking straight away. As I said before, she had a thick body but a very beautiful face and giant hooters came with the package.

She was fanatical in the bed and we had sex at least three times over the next six hours.

We woke up and were served a small complimentary breakfast and coffee.

We walked over to her tiny but cozy apartment and she made some more breakfast for me. Marcela was Brazilian/Lebanese, which is a rare mix. I asked her where she grew up and she said Brazil, so I couldn't claim the Lebanese flag which would have been awesome.

We exchanged Facebook names and said goodbye. She wanted to meet me again that night but I already had other plans. I tried to go for a three-in-a-row one-night-stand record but didn't succeed that night.

I met up with Patty again and she helped me out at the phone store again. I told her to act angrily with the sales guy and tell him that she had been waiting for me a few times because my shit phone didn't work – which had the advantage of actually being true. I got my money back and since I was really sick of the shitty phone situation I went over to a real Nokia store and bought a decent cell phone there, costing 200something dollars.

It never worked out with Patty. We kissed all the time but she was not up for sex with me. Looking for a boyfriend probably.

I was happy with my new phone and tried to arrange a last-minute date with a beautiful girl. We met in a mall and had lots of fun. I seemed to push the right buttons but I was cock-blocked by her parents, of all people, who came by the mall later.

After saying goodbye to everyone in the hostel and feeling bad for leaving Rio, a city where I would gladly spend a year I took an early bus to Salvador.

Brazil – Salvador

Salvador, a place where, according to many Brazilians, I'd have to beat the local girls off with a stick. Being tall and blond was the magic formula to get laid here. I had already stopped believing any pick-up "advice" from locals.

I stayed in a hostel in Pelinrinho, which many guide books pointed to as the tourist area of Salvador. The backpacker trail is a small world: I met a Japanese woman I had talked to before in Rio.

There were also two Swedish girls and a Swedish guy travelling together. They were supposed to just be friends, but the guy and one of the girls were making out a few times.

There were a couple of Japanese guys in the hostel too and I talked to them a bit. They were much exited that I had climbed Mount Fuji back in Japan, since it is the dream and almost the duty of every Japanese person to do that at least once in their life. Or so I was told by a Japanese girl.

On Tuesday there was a street party in Pelinrinho, which is right next to some favelas and quite dangerous after dark. The Tuesday night street party is famous and a must-see for foreign visitors.

I went there with the three Swedes, one Japanese guy and one super-annoying guy from New Zealand everyone disliked but who kept inviting himself along.

The street party was very nice, lots of bands playing and thousands of people in the streets dancing and partying. I was being pretty cautious with my valuables, because Salvador is known as one of the most dangerous cities in Brazil and probably South America except maybe Caracas in Venezuela. The New Zealand guy got pick-pocketed and left early.

I felt bad for him losing a brand new camera but kind of thought he wasn't being careful enough. I had my phone with me, a camera and quite a lot of money in case I picked up a girl and needed money for a love hotel.

We went to a big square to see a wild reggae concert and that's where trouble started.

Some 14-year-old boy started dancing up to me and made indecent movements, grabbing his crotch and trying to ride up against me. I thought I was getting setup for being pick-pocketed and pushed him off. He did it again and I felt him touch my pockets so I pushed him off again while trying to protect my back pockets which I'd divided my money between.

The boy was lighting fast and grabbed the camera out of the front pocket of my shorts. I immediately grabbed him by the throat and said "Give me my camera" to him. He looked shocked by my action and pretended he wanted to give it back to me. I let him loose and he quickly ran off. But this old dog is fast too and I chased after him through the thick crowd, grabbed him again and threw him to the pavement. I choked him quite hard and felt his pockets. My camera wasn't there anymore and I wanted to give him an interrogation beating but then I realized half the ghetto was watching me. Lots of big muscular black dudes were staring at me while I was choking the life out of this drugged-up boy. I always act before I think and live by the ancient old rule of nature: An eye for an eye, but I realized that I was alone in the Salvadorian ghetto, surrounded by people who will protect their own and don't have much to lose anyway. A three-year-old camera is not worth getting my ass beaten for, and I let the boy go.

During the whole scuffle I was still holding a half-liter can of beer in my hand, even when I searched the pockets of the thief. I smashed the beer can on the ground and was furious. I was going home in two months and had protected my camera for two-and-a-half years and *now* it got stolen. All my pictures of Rio de Janeiro were gone and so were the last pictures I took in São Paulo. My pictures of me and Miss Brazil 2001 and lots of pictures I took for some business idea were gone too.

Most favela people were shocked by my brutal action, though one actually complimented me for not taking shit. The little boy, who was obviously already drugged up on glue or something, kept around us, teasing us, even snatching a cigarette out of my mouth. The boy had nuts the size of bowling balls to keep teasing us like that. He probably had a whole gang with him. He surely wasn't alone, because he'd handed my camera to someone while I was busy with him.

The small group from the hostel I was with got scared of losing their stuff too and we left.

For the rest of the night I was a bit down. I now had to buy a new camera in a country where electronics are super-expensive. Buying a new camera would set me back at least $250 for a regular Sony Cybershot camera and I would be protecting a brand-new camera again. I had just paid over $200 for a new phone and I was running out of money fast. I was expecting a lecture from one of the hostel people about beating that poor little third-world country boy who probably had to steal to survive but nobody dared to say anything to me. That was just as well for them, because I was definitely not in the mood for a hypocritical leftist lecture.

I think one of the Swedish girls was turned off by it but she didn't say anything. The Swedes were nice though. They were going to the holiday island Morro de São Paulo and I told them I would go there a day later.

I went to look for a camera in one of Salvador's biggest malls. It was hell taking the local buses there and once inside I didn't see that many hot girls around, and the cameras were horribly expensive, so I didn't actually buy one. I left to the island Morro de São Paulo the next day.

Brazil – Morro de São Paulo

By high speed ferry the boat ride took two hours and the Swedes had already sent me the name of the guesthouse where they were staying. Morro de São Paulo is a holiday island recommended by many Brazilians. I first heard of it from the Brazilian girl I kissed in Cordoba and many others I met along my trip had mentioned it.

There were lots of couples on the island. There were so many of them it quickly became clear that this was a romantic getaway island. There were hardly any girls around without a boyfriend and I thought to myself *Ok, I will try something with the Swedish girl and just lay on the beautiful beach a lot.* It was actually only the second beach I had visited in all my months in South America. I had been inland most of the time.

The first night there was nothing to do on the island and I stayed in the guesthouse. The guesthouse had dorms for twenty-five reals and after all the money I'd had to shell out in the last couple of days I thought it would be better to stay there and keep it cheap.

That night the blonde skinny Swedish girl and I went out for a few drinks but since it was a small beach island there wasn't much open and most beach bars closed at eleven.

There was a small beach party going on and we drank some caiperinhas made of different fresh fruits, which were delicious and quite cheap.

I saw two hot Brazilian girls dancing at the beach party but didn't bother talking to them because one of them looked like an obvious prostitute. She was an average-height dark-skinned girl and had an incredible round and tight ass. I saw her talking to some old guys and assume the other shorter girl was the same.

I decided to take a shot at the Swedish girl I knew from the hostel. She came to the party with me because the Swedish guy had the shits and the other girl stayed with him.

The Swedish girl had a nice body but was a bitchy butterface. I had seen her ass in the hostel dorm when she was sleeping with her blanket off, and it looked great. But her attitude didn't match her body and I couldn't exactly figure out her position on me. I could see she was a bit jealous when she saw me talking to other girls. She kissed the gayest-looking guy ever and was boasting about it. The guy made a really gay comment about my rock star bracelet to me, I'm sure he at least liked both sides. (Not that there's anything wrong with being gay.)

I think she just enjoyed pissing me off, especially after she found out about my website when I talked about it with some tourist guys. She tried to make me jealous, saying things like "Oh, I've been with like thirty guys this year but you can't have me". Like I cared about her, I was just interested in fucking her and getting a Swedish flag. I was very close in Malaysia and New Zealand. Got them (semi)naked but couldn't seal the deal. Her saying "I think I have to throw up" and kissing an ugly gay-looking guy didn't exactly gave me a raging hard boner for her.

The shortest one of the two hot girls who were dancing at the beach walked up to me and began dancing with me. The Swedish girl looked pissed and walked back to the hostel.

The Brazilian hottie and I took a walk down the beach and kissed a bit. She didn't speak any English at all. I had to talk my broken Spanish to her and hoped she understand what I was saying. When she spoke slowly I could follow most of her Portuguese. She spoke slowly but quite a lot. She was hardly quiet for even a moment and God knows what she was blabbering about all the time. She was real cute though.

I took her back to my dorm room, which I shared with a guy from Switzerland. I was sleeping in the lower bunk of one bed and he was in the top bunk of the other. I hung the sheet from the top bed over the side and we had some privacy.
Jessica was only eighteen years old, maybe even a year younger but she said eighteen, some sixteen years younger than me. Her skin was dark and very soft. She had a rock-hard body with small but firm tits and a little round booty. Despite her young age she really knew how to fuck and was really into it. I made love to her three times in the hostel bed and banged my head again on the top bunk which instantly reminded me of sweet Marisol in Chile.

In the morning the Swiss guy walked in on us and I kindly asked him to leave the room for ten more minutes, which he did. He was a typical nice-guy, despite his large body full of tattoos – or insecurity hiders, as I call tattoos sometimes.

Jessica and I went to her small village by bus later that day and she showed me around a bit. In the afternoon we said goodbye and agreed to meet again later.

The owners told me not to bring guests into the dorm room anymore, and I played dumb. Of course I knew about the guesthouse's rules but there was no night guard so I'd decided to bring the girl in anyway. If I got kicked out I could always go to another place. I wasn't going to risk a lay out of fear of having to change guesthouses in the morning.

We agreed to meet again in the morning at my hostel but she didn't show up. I bought a ticket at the guesthouse reception for the boat back to Salvador and just as I was about to leave, Jessica showed up, over an hour late.

I felt awkward because I was about to ditch her but I turned it around, pointing out that she didn't show up in time. (I used Google Translate on my laptop to get the hard parts across.) I canceled the boat ticket and I got a room in the same guesthouse for about thirty dollars. We went in the room and had sex for ages.

Having a big bed instead of a small lower bunk bed improved the sex a lot. Her body was amazing, with perfect proportions, and she fucked like a teenage porn star.

We took a shower and walked out the room past the Swedish girl, who was sitting in the lobby. Jessica was wearing next to nothing, just a small sexy top and skintight shorts wedged really deep in her delicious ass and crotch. A camel-toe was showing pretty clearly. The Swedish girl tried to look indifferent but I could see she was not happy about it. I enjoyed the moment.

That day I spent with Jessica in her small village. We walked on a deserted beach, which was really enjoyable because this was the part regular tourists never visit. People were friendly and helpful. A guy friend of her tagged along and after a while I let her ask him to leave because I was horny as fuck. We couldn't do it on the beach but I took some naked pictures of her.

Later at night we went to a local discoteca, where no white man had ever gone before. Lots of girls shaking it to the beats. The only downside was that it was in the middle of nowhere and I had to pay a lot for a taxi there and even more to get back. The barkeep asked me six dollars just to call a cab and then the taxi guy asked nine dollars for a three-kilometer ride.

We came back to the guesthouse and had sex again, and I also took some naked pictures of her again. I could beat myself up for having my camera stolen. She was up for a fuck video, but all I had was the camera on my phone, which wasn't good enough.

That morning we me love for the last time, but I had a hard time finishing because I'd overused my dick. She ripped off the condom and I did her raw. I'd only ever done that a couple of times but since she was very young I decided to risk it. Afterwards she worried she might get pregnant and asked what to do if she was. I thought *OK, here we go, that's the catch, she wants money*, but she didn't ask for that. She just wanted to know if I would want to keep the baby. I said that in the unlikely circumstance that a baby was born, then I would take care of it. No blood of mine will grow up poor. I gave her one of my email addresses to write to me if she became pregnant. Jessica never asked me for anything else and was a really sweet and happy girl. I also never received an email saying she was pregnant.

The Argentine owners of the guesthouse were friendly, even after I brought that girl to the dorm and when they had to do some translating to help us out with the pregnancy questions.

The guesthouse's name is Pousada Pura Vida, and has both dorms and private rooms. If someone goes to Pura Vida, look for the messages I left on the sides of the fridge.

Jessica and I said goodbye and I took the boat back to Salvador.

Pelinrinho was definitely not seeing me again, so I went to a hostel close to the beach in Barra. I had set up a date already with a black girl from the couchsurfing website but since I flaked on her the day before, she now flaked on me.

That day I walked around the beach a bit and walked past two girls who started giggling. One of them had a big ass but in a way you'd like it.

I walked back and approached them. Up close I could see they were still in their late teens, but I tried anyway.

The language barrier brought my attempt to a sudden stop and smiles and giggles were all I got before they went into ignore mode when I was out of words.

That night I went out with an Austrian guy but we couldn't find a good place to go out and some bars were already closing down early.

I took a bus in the morning to Belem, where I would start my river boat experience.

Brazil – Belem and the Amazon boat ride

The bus ride from Salvador to Belem took forty hours and there weren't too many people on the bus, so it was easy to get talking with my fellow travellers.

There were some cool Brazilian guys and one Colombian girl. The Colombian girl was a big black girl with huge boobs. Her shirt was quite tight and her nips were always pointing through it.

After a while I asked her if I could sit down next to her and she said yes. We talked a bit in Spanish, the only language she knew.

I could manage a half-decent conversation and by nightfall we both fell asleep. I turned my body towards her and rested my hand on her side. The five-second test had begun. She didn't move my hand or say anything about it, so my hand went exploring her body a bit. She pulled a big blanket over so no-one could see it. I was holding and squeezing those big black boobs all night but didn't want to move my hand lower since she didn't shower the night before and we were sweating in the bus all day.

I kissed her a bit and rubbed over her jeans. She was obviously horny. I asked her if she wanted share a room with me and she said yes.

We got off the bus in the middle of the night and me, her and a few Brazilian guys waited for daylight and running buses.

Some cigarettes, a few coffees and a dump later it was daylight and we were almost on our way to a guesthouse when a girlfriend from Belem called her and she decided to stay with her. We agreed to meet again later but she pulled a Colombian flake on me. Still no flag.

At the Belem hostel I met the Japanese woman from Salvador again. I stayed there two days. I went out once with the girl working in the hostel and some dudes and played some pool, but it was a very slow night.

My plan was to take the riverboat down the Amazon River to Manaus. I went to the harbor and found the boats after lots of walking around in 38-degree sun.

There were guys around selling boat tickets but I didn't trust them much. Anyone can show me a laminated plastic card and say they represent the boat company, and the girl at the hostel had made me expect much higher prices than they were offering. Actually she was the one trying to con me, since she just wanted to sell me some tickets herself.

Since the ticket offices were closed, I decided to buy a ticket from these guys anyway; a lot of people were. I bargained hard and got a good price. A hammock space would cost 180 reals and a little shared cabin 340 reals (starting price 600rs), food not included. I feared that my back wouldn't survive five days bent like a banana in a hammock and chose the cabin. The ticket man showed me around the boat and I saw it had reasonable beds, air–conditioning and a wall socket for power. That last one was just what I needed for my laptop so I wouldn't get bored and could do some writing.

I texted the Colombian girl, who was also going to take a riverboat to get back to Colombia, but she texted that she was leaving on Monday. I sure as hell wasn't waiting for her, but I still wanted to "rock the boat". That song was on my mind.

The departure time for the boat was 6:00 PM but I was already there at 3:00 to see all the things happening on and around the boat. The lower deck got packed with two truckloads of tomatoes. This was all manual labor and five guys packed for hours while one giant fat guy sat on a chair and counted every box that was put inside. He was sitting on his ass in the shade and still sweating like a dog.

The middle deck had about a hundred hammock spaces and people were busy hanging their hammocks and fighting over space.

In the back of the boat were eight cabins for two. I shared my cabin with Manu, a short but insanely ripped French guy. He was a bit crazy but a very nice guy to hang out with. I saw a couple of young girls and approached them. There were two German/Russian sisters. One of them was too skinny and the other one was a lot hotter but grumpy and quiet all the time. Then there were David, a giant Canadian guy and the biggest vegetarian I ever saw, and Kathleen, a Canadian girl.

There was an older English guy whose name I forgot and the Japanese woman I'd met in Rio, Salvador and Belem. None of them are people I'd look up normally, but once on a boat you tend to stick together.

The top deck of the ship was a sundeck with a bar and some more cabins.

Life on a riverboat is very boring and our small group of tourists sat on the top deck drinking beer and having some fun every night. I got really sunburned in just one hour and had to stay below decks during the day.

Most people on the boat were just hanging around or sleeping all day. I did quite a lot of writing for my blogs those days and watched some movies and *Simpsons* episodes.

The first few days the riverside views were very beautiful and I tried to take some pictures with my phone but results were weak. At some points the river was narrow: still a couple of hundred meters wide but close enough to see the river houses and the people who lived in them.

On the second day we saw lots of children in canoes around our fast-moving boat. They used ropes with hooks to clamp their wooden canoes to our boat and pull themselves in. They sold shrimps and other food. I bought a bag and they tasted salty but good. The ideal beer snack at night.

At other times I saw lots of children in small boats begging for food. Some Brazilians would throw plastic bags with food towards them, which is good, or give them candy, which is bad because those kids rarely see a dentist or keep good dental hygiene.

It was meal time three times a day but I always skipped the first one since it was at six in the morning when everyone outside was already up. The meals were simple, just some rice and chicken, but they were quite large. I had trouble with chewing at the time because I had a problem with the nerve endings in my teeth or something. It was the second time I had severe pain in my teeth. The first time was in Bolivia, where Sierra had advised me to go to a dentist but no way in hell was I going to a Bolivian dentist.

After Bolivia the pain gradually went away and I thought I'd left the worst behind me. By the way my eyes teared up in pain now, I was wrong. A few days later the pain stopped again and didn't come back on my trip.

There were no hot Brazilian girls on the boat, but there was "Boat Slut", as Manu and I named her. A Brazilian girl with a very sexy body but the manners of a pig. She ate like one and drank like one. She started drinking early and was completely drunk all the time. I saw her go into the cabin of some ugly guy who wasn't her boyfriend, and Manu and I wondered if they actually had sex since she wasn't in there very long. The ugly guy had been giving her beer for two days and maybe he got his reward now.

Manu was one crazy guy; he was on a strict diet back home and exercised a lot. He was very ripped even though he was forty-two years old.

At night he would take some drugs and never stop talking. It was annoying sometimes but I liked the guy. We decided that one of us should fuck Boat Slut. I tried to talk with her but it was no use, she didn't speak English and made no attempt to try and understand my horrible Portuguese.

When I spoke to her I saw that she had very bad skin and her teeth weren't that great either. I had my doubts about her, but like Manu said, "Just look at the body and pump and dump, don't even kiss her."

I could see that the German girls were grumpy because of the attention Boat Slut was getting and started badmouthing her a lot. A typical jealousy thing. Of course Boat Slut was no dating material but she did have a damn sexy body and.

The whole bunch of tourists got off the boat in Santarem to do some jungle exploring there. Me and the Japanese woman were the only ones that stayed on the boat till Manaus.

Those last two nights were quite boring and I hardly left "the fridge", as we nicknamed our cabin. The air conditioning in there was freezing since the space was very small inside. I was glad I had taken the cabin for those five days and not a sweaty old hammock.

Boat Slut had also left the boat in Santarem, and there were no other bangable girls on the boat. Maybe it was better that Boat Slut left, she looked like a girl with STDs.

The Japanese woman barely spoke any English and just a little Spanish. I admired her for travelling around South America without knowing the language. Then I realized that I had been doing the same in dozens of countries myself where I didn't speak the local language and just used my hands and feet to make myself understood.

It was strange to get off the boat and realize that you'd been disconnected from the outside world for five whole days. I don't think I'd been without Internet for longer than two days since I first started using it early in the year 2000. Luckily there had been no zombie apocalypse or, even worse, a hostile takeover by feminists.

Brazil – Manaus

I found a hostel together with the Japanese woman (I think her name was Manami) and checked in there. It was a bit of a dump but I didn't care. As long as they had Wi-Fi I was fine with it.

I went to a big mall that day and after visiting every electronics shop at least three times and bargaining everywhere I bought a Sony Cybershot camera. The camera was really expensive and I knew it would be almost half the price in Holland, or that I could get a ten times better model for the same money there. $250 lost on a camera with almost the same quality as my old one. I just really needed a camera to finish my trip. I couldn't carry on taking crappy pictures with my phone.

The Japanese woman and I left on a jungle tour the next day. It was raining very heavily and we weren't sure if we could go but according to the guide the weather was pretty changeable and should be fine later.

It took about two hours to drive to a lake, which was a pretty nice ride through some small villages and on jungle dirt roads.

We packed our stuff plus lots of provision and a bag of ice on a small wooden canoe and were brought to a large guesthouse built above the water.

There was a nice-looking girl living in the lake house. She didn't speak much English, so I quickly changed my mind from my immediate thought and decided to enjoy this jungle experience.

A couple of other guests arrived; they were dorky but nice. One Indian/English couple and some Danish people.

We were supposed to go piranha fishing on the lake, but because of the rain that part was canceled. We had to fish from the lake house.

I was the only one who caught a piranha that day and it was scary to take him off the hook, those teeth were razor-sharp. Apparently the piranhas weren't aggressive in this lake and you could even swim between them, but I didn't like that idea. There were also some pink and grey dolphins in the lake, and every once in while you could spot one.

In the evening it stopped raining and we went on an "alligator hunt". The guide, the Brazilian girl, the Japanese woman and I went in a small canoe and found some baby alligators and could hold them before we released them again. This was interesting but not very spectacular.

I shared a room with the Japanese woman and the next morning it was time for the jungle tour, which was a three-hour jungle walk where the guide explained everything about the plants and the trees, but we saw no animals whatsoever except for a couple of big blue butterflies and some killer ants who could paralyze or even kill you.

An old Amazon Indian rite to manhood was making a

boy stick his hands in a nest of already angry ants and suffer the bites. He would be paralyzed and in terrible pain for a few hours, and very sick. Once the pain was over he had to do the same thing again and once more in the evening. After this he was considered a man and he could marry if he wanted. After marriage the real suffering would start, I thought.

We were offered to stay for a night in the jungle, but we both declined. It was probably not worth the money. We had already paid about $125 for this short and boring trip. The lunches and dinner were great, with a lot of fish and tasty vegetables, but the rest of the jungle tour was overrated. We went back to Manaus and checked into a different hostel. I think it was a HI hostel and it had all the luxuries.

As soon as I walked into the hostel I saw all the people I'd met on the Amazon boat again. The German sisters were still distant and too lame to go out that night, so it was just me, Manu the crazy Frenchie and David the giant Canadian guy. I was aiming for a nightclub but they said they knew something better. We ended up in a strip club.

For me it was paradise. It was one of those strip clubs you see in the movies with a couple of stages with guys around it, a few poles the girls danced on, a couple of muscular bouncers and a big bar. I had never been to a place like that anywhere in the world. The strip clubs in South East Asia are pathetic, with lots of bored-looking girls, but these girls had big ole asses to die for. There were of course lots of hookers around trying to score a guy. They were walking around in sexy dresses, or even just a G-string.

A couple of girls were dancing buck-naked on small round tables and were getting touched by drunken horny guys all the time. The girl would crouch down and a guy would put his head face up on the table and she would ride his face without any underwear on. That's just disgusting. No matter how beautiful the girl is, she had probably been touched by many guys that night. I wondered if the guy thought about that. He was dead drunk and his friends were slapping him on the back like he was some sort of hero.

I downed lots of beers and tried to hook up with the girls there. My plan was to shore a pro, of course, but those girls were too battle-hardened already and kept asking me for drinks and money. I went pretty far with one of them but in the end she started talking about money again and I dumped her straight away.

At one point I was standing around with David, the big shy guy, and I told him that I was about to leave Brazil the next day and I would make it a point to slap as many Brazilian asses as possible before I left. And I did. I slapped at least fifteen girls before one started making trouble. I just shrugged my shoulders, but then I noticed the bouncer looking over and thought it was time to quit. Manu had disappeared somewhere and David and I went back. I slapped a few more of those big round jiggling asses on the way to the taxi. Man, I was having some drunken fun there. I use the slow slap which means that your hand rests for a second on her butt after the slap and you feel the butt jiggling. It's the king of slaps.

Waking up with a massive hangover the next morning was less fun. I had decided to go to Boa Vista and then Venezuela. I quickly bought a ticket and hurried back to the hostel to get my backpack before getting back on the bus to the station and then on the one to Boa Vista. The buying of the ticket is a whole story itself involving getting lost on the bus and ending up in some dead end small town and a beautiful blue-eyed girl selling bus tickets but this book is already long enough.

Chapter Six – The Guyanas

Guyana – Georgetown

I sat on the bus and thought about my travel schedule and my already-booked flights back to Holland that I couldn't alter as easily as a boat-ride from Morro to Salvador. I decided not to go to Venezuela. I'd heard from several people it's not safe there and though I wanted to see the world's highest waterfall you have to take planes to get there. It seemed like I'd only manage a few days there and I decided it wasn't worth the bother. I was quite disappointed about wasting all that time in cities and now needing to skip one country and not complete my plan of setting foot in every South American country.

Venezuela was only a six-hour bus ride away but I refused to go there to just hop over the border and be able to say I'd been there without any chance of seeing something of the country and its girls.

I met a Guyanese man on the bus; Guyana is an English-speaking country so we had no trouble communicating. Paul was a school teacher in Brazil and a very nice guy, but a bit too nice so I didn't know if I could trust him too much at first. It could be some scam.

When we reached Boa Vista, Paul and I were approached by a young hot girl who arranged trips for us to Georgetown, the capital of Guyana. It was a lot of hassle to get across the border and I soon realized this was some serious third world country we'd ended up in. Paul and I got on a minivan and our epic trip through the jungle started.

The driver was a maniac, not braking for anything. The minivan was packed and I was the only white guy.

At night the driver almost lost control of the van when we drove through a massive pothole in the dirt road. We went off the road and nearly smashed into a tree. My head hit the ceiling and my knee the side of the door. It hurt like hell but I pretended not much happened.

For the next few days I had a bump on my head the size of a bowling ball but luckily not visible with my long hair.

Around midnight we stopped at some overnight stop and slept in rental hammocks for about four hours. We drove on early in the morning and in the afternoon we arrived in Georgetown.

I don't have to explain that my body was broken after sitting cramped up in a minivan for that long. It was the first time I'd ever slept in a hammock and my back didn't agree with it at all. I was so happy I hadn't opted for the five-day hammock ordeal on the Amazon boat.

The minivan stopped next to a Brazilian sports bar/hotel where there was only one room available. Paul said that I could have it and went to a guesthouse down the street. I was stupid enough to assume that I could sit inside the "sports" bar at night and have a beer and chat with some girls. Ha.

The room cost fifteen dollars a night and it was an absolute dump. *Welcome to the third world,* I thought when I opened the door.

The first thing I did when I entered the room was test if the water in the small fountain was running and next I took a dump after holding it in for nearly 24 hours.

Of course (!) the toilet didn't flush and I had to take the plastic garbage bag out of the waste bin and fill the waste bin with water to flush the toilet. Every time I took a shower I filled up the waste bin for flushing water. Those who are poor need to be creative. There were a few water shortages and brown-outs that week.

A reasonable room cost at least thirty-five dollars a night and a good room of western standards would be fifty dollars. No way in hell was I going to pay that kind of money in an old beat-up city like Georgetown.

The bar downstairs, meanwhile, wasn't a sports bar at all but a hooker bar frequented solely by Brazilian miners and prostitutes. The hookers were straight up asking me for money. Of course dem bitches got nothing out of me. The music started playing around four in the afternoon and it was fucking loud. I could feel the bass when lying in bed, and the only way to sleep was to go to bed late or use earplugs. I did both.

As I mentioned, the hookers here had no shame, they straight up asked me for food or drinks without even bothering to at least introduce themselves or have a two-minute conversation first. There were three dark–skinned Colombian hookers, all chubby with huge boobs and ugly faces. They only spoke Spanish and I was figuring out if I should try to bang one of them to get my Colombian flag. I guess I was still pissed about breaking my flagging streak in Colombia. I decided against it to keep my pride. Any normal person would change hotels the next day but I wasn't planning on staying long anyway.

Guyana used to be a Dutch colony in the old days and still had some Dutch street and market names. It became an English colony after the Napoleonic wars in the early 1800s.

It's one of the least visited countries in South America and I now knew why. It was very dangerous there.

I went for a walk to the local market, which was definitely not a part of town where tourists go. People seemed to be surprised to see a white guy in shorts and flips-flops taking pictures and buying a can of Bob Marley energy drink. They tried to make conversation all the time but I had problems understanding the local English, which is similar to Patois, the Rasta English spoken in Jamaica. Guyanans see themselves as more like part of the Caribbean than of South America.

There were bums harassing me a bit but I never felt unsafe, though I'm sure if a white boy like me walked there at night I would be shanked and robbed within minutes.

If you are looking for hot girls, don't go to Guyana. You will have trouble finding anything above a six on the streets, and I'm not a picky guy.

Day game is a waste of time because there's not much to game in Georgetown. The three-storey mall is very small and you can walk through it in less than ten minutes. I saw only one nice looking girl in the four times I went there.

One other time I walked past three Brazilian girls and heard them talking about me. I walked back up to them, opening in English with some question. The hot one dressed in a Brazilian Football shirt and with a banging round ass didn't speak any English, and the short one who was quite cute too kept silent. Just my luck, the only one who spoke English was the ugly fat one. I asked what they were doing in Georgetown and they said they were working at some office.

The ugly one was too ugly to be a hooker but I was not sure about the other two. The hot one kept smiling at me and I heard her say "lindo" (handsom) to her friends.

I asked them out and they agreed to meet me at nine in the evening at the Brazil bar where I was staying. I kept talking with the fat one and even smoked a cigarette with her outside to make sure she wouldn't cock-block me afterwards.

They never showed up. The hot one had given me her phone number but when I looked at my phone I couldn't find it and I probably didn't save it correctly. Too bad, I could have given it another shot even though they didn't show that night. It's not like there was much else to do.

On Friday night I went to Palm Lounge, a club downtown. It was fifteen dollars to get in but at least the place was packed.

There were quite a few hot girls around, but they had bitch shields the size of the Berlin wall. I approached eight girls without any conversation lasting longer than two minutes before I had to bail out. It didn't help that there were a few loud, drunk and annoying American tourists around; they were making horrendous attempts at picking up girls.

At one point I had my eye on four girls standing next to the bar. I walked up to a tall black girl but then noticed that she had horse teeth. Another one in the group was a light-skinned Guyanese girl, and she wanted to dance with me.

By dancing, I mean "daggering", which is basically dry-humping to music. She bent over and I banged her from behind for a few minutes. Till that moment I had only seen dancing like this on music videos or YouTube. Another girl in the group just grabbed me and grinded on me. A short and skinny black girl danced like crazy and at one point she stood on her hands, wrapped her legs around my waist and bounced her ass on my crotch for a few minutes like a wheelbarrow. WTF!!

Lots of people were now watching the show and I felt like a big pimp bumping and grinding with all four girls. I kissed the light-skinned girl a lot and she looked to be into me. Only problem was that there was a guy in their group, trying to do what I was. He looked really pissed off at me and tried to talk the girls out of hanging with me.

Every time I was with the light-skinned girl, the other girls grabbed me and danced with me. I couldn't isolate her and moments later the group left. I did an attempt to get a date with her the next night but that didn't work out.

After they left I approached some other girls but my mojo was gone. I missed my only chance at a Guyanese flag.

The next day I went to another club, but arrived already drunk as fuck because I tried the local rum, named High Wine. It's 69% alcohol and after one strong mixed coke and four bottles of Guinness I couldn't walk straight anymore.

I arrived at the other big club in Georgetown with a Rasta guy I met in the Brazilian "sports" bar below my hotel room. He bought me a few beers there and I returned the favor.

At the door of the club he waited for me to pay his entrance and I told him to pay it himself. He said he didn't have any money but an hour before he'd been flashing his cash around, which was at least twenty-five dollars. He paid to get in and we had a beer there. The club was very posh and full of Indian guys. Like many other Caribbean countries Guyana has a large Indian population, most of whom are well-off and run a business. The guys were smashing their money buying girls expensive drinks and looking with my player eyes I could see none of them was going to get laid that night (or any other club night). I was way too drunk to continue the night and jumped in a taxi. The Rasta guy had suddenly disappeared twenty minutes before. I don't know what kind of scam he was trying to pull on me, but he was obviously a poor guy because I saw him walking around trying to sell sugarcane sticks a few days later.

When I entered my room I sat down on the bed for a few minutes, quickly got up and puked into the sink. The Chinese food that I had been eating all week came out. I kind of blacked out and fell asleep.

When I woke up in the morning with a legendary hangover I had to clean up a huge mess because the sink drainpipe just ended in the shower.. I decided then and there never to drink that rum again.

On Sunday night I went out again, this time with Paul. I drank a beer with him most nights. We visited the water wall, an old three-kilometer-long Dutch dike where people sat in the evening drinking, talking and listening to music.

We walked around a bit and although there were some cute girls around I didn't dare to talk to them with large groups of guys keeping an eye on the white guy. Even though I was there with a Guyanese guy I didn't want to risk getting beat up over a girl.

The Colombian hookers lived across my room and always had their door open. I talked to them a bit in Spanish every once in a while.

At one point there were four of them drinking Johnny Walker Black label, and they were already drunk. As they emptied the bottle they told me that if I got another bottle I could fuck the four of them without paying the ho fee. Well, indirectly it would still be paying a ho, and yes, I did even think about it at one point and decide to check how much a bottle cost at the liquor store. It was eighty-five US dollars, so I said "fuck that". And boy, was I glad I didn't get involved with those pros.

When I returned to the hotel after checking the liquor store and an Internet café, one of the girls was in a fist fight with some guy (pimp?).

All four of the girls were ganging up on the guy and one even lifted up a wooden chair and tried to hit him with it. They were screaming on the top of their lungs and acting batshit crazy. I sat outside watching the whole thing and waited for them to calm down before I went back upstairs. Upstairs they were smiling and calling me over. *Eh, no thanks, I had my share of bat crazy shit in Cambodia already.*

Georgetown in Guyana is not for the inexperienced traveller. Do not go there if you've only ever been to resort-type vacations or only a beaten path backpacker trail.

I had to be there to get a visa for neighboring Suriname and stayed a week in total, but to anyone who does go there, I would strongly advise you to stay in a decent hotel and bring at least fifty dollars a day and only take yellow radio taxis.

In one week I saw two car accidents, three fist fights, one giant bar brawl with chairs flying around and even a few gunshots fired, as well as the whores going bananas. On the other hand, while the city is poor and dirty except for beggars people won't bother you and are generally very friendly.

Lots of guys will shake your hand and make small talk with you. I didn't go into the jungle but had a sixteen-hour drive through it and it's similar to the Brazilian Amazon jungle. Tours are very expensive.

On Wednesday morning I left at 4:00 AM after saying a drinking goodbye to my buddy Paul.

Suriname: Paramaribo

It was time to leave Guyana and move on to a special destination: Suriname, a former Dutch colony that stayed one until well in the 1970s. Getting there was not that easy, though I had already picked up a visa at the Suriname embassy in Georgetown. It is probably the only country in South America where 99% of people need to get a visa first. Although a few days after I arrived, the rules were slightly changed on Independence Day.

I had arranged transportation from Georgetown to Paramaribo by minibus. I was picked up at four in the morning by the giant jolly guy who sold me the ticket. Since I lived right above the "sports" bar there were still drunk and obnoxious people around, and I was glad to leave. The ride to the border was quite comfortable but once we were there, trouble started.

We took a ferry across the river that functioned as a border and had to wait quite a while at Surinamese customs. There was only one customs officer, but a few hundred people in line. I was one of the last to be "helped".

The custom officer didn't trust the picture in my passport, where I look a bit younger and had short, businessman hair, unlike the shoulder-length mane I sported now. He asked me for another ID to check, but the only thing I had on me was my Philippine immigration card. Showing him that really set him off.

The bastard started asking all kinds of questions like I was some suspicious terrorist or something. He asked me how long I had worked in the Philippines and what I did there. I explained that I hadn't been working, that an immigration card is needed to stay there longer than two months and that foreigners aren't even allowed to work in the Philippines unless they have a job a Filipino can't do, but the border guard didn't believe me. "How can you prove this is you?" he said, pointing at my picture. I told him to look at the picture carefully and see all my twenty-eight pages of visa stamps. I was speaking Dutch since that's Suriname's official language. What more proof did the guy want? The moron even asked me if I was Filipino: me, a tall blond white guy who speaks Dutch. What an idiot!

He let me go after searching through my bag, when the bus driver started complaining because I was holding up his ride this way.
The people in the bus had waited an extra half-hour just because of me.

Since I was the last to get on the minibus I had the worst seat, and for four hours I sat with my knees nearly touching my chin. There I was thinking I was used to uncomfortable rides. Can't win, I guess, but that's what you get when you do some real travelling instead of a sanitized traipse to gather photos you can use Photoshop on later.

When we finally arrived, I found a good guesthouse close to the center of town and had a decent room for twenty-two dollars a night. The bathrooms were shared but spic-and-span, clean and with hot water. This was a great improvement over my room in the whore-bar/hotel. It had been a while since I had a hot shower.

The people in the guesthouse were all Dutch, since Suriname is a quite popular destination for Dutch people of Surinamese heritage and older Dutch people. It was nice to get a bit reacquainted with my native language, which I hadn't exactly used much in the past two to three years.

The center of Paramaribo is an official World Heritage site because most houses and churches are made of wood, not unlike Georgetown in Guyana. But I was quite broken from the bus ride, which had lasted ten hours instead of eight, and sightseeing was not on my mind.

I didn't go out on that Wednesday night but was ready for battle the next. I couldn't find anyone to go out with on that Thursday night, but by now I didn't care as much as I used to.

Nowadays I even prefer to roll solo, and I'm not desperately looking for a guy to hang out with in a bar. It's better to man up and go alone than to have a (passive) cock-block standing next to you fucking it all up for you.

Something really weird happened that night. I'd been told Club Touche was the place to be on a Thursday night. I arrived a bit too early and sat down at the bar, ordered a beer and opened the girl sitting next to me; she was in a group of three. It didn't go so well and they walked off and suddenly it hit me.
I can't game for shit when it's not in English.

Suriname is a former Dutch colony and Dutch is the official language there. It should be easy to express myself in my own language but I froze up, and quite frankly I panicked a bit. The last two-and-a-half years I had only spoken and gamed girls in English. I could count on one hand the times I spoke to Dutch girls.

Before I left Holland I couldn't game for shit and had trouble getting a decent girlfriend. I had taught myself lots of things but I learned how to game in English, not in Dutch. This changed everything.

Normally I would walk up to a girl and say something like: "Hey, how are you? Are you enjoying yourself?" and continue to talk from there. I didn't know what to say in Dutch. I wasn't used to Dutch anymore, talking with people at the guesthouse hadn't brought me back to being day-to-day fluent in it. Trying a one-on-one translation from English to Dutch would make it sound insanely stupid, especially since I was clearly Dutch. I had to think this over a bit.

406

I gave it another try in Dutch but wasn't in the right headspace anymore. Talking Dutch was just like all those years ago in Holland, it brought my inability to game right back.

I approached two black girls in English and got somewhere but conversation died after a few minutes. There were loads of Dutch people around and the local people automatically assume you're Dutch if you're white-skinned and speak Dutch to you. This meant the gringo factor was reduced to zero. It even worked against you in a club, because there are always lots of Dutch students there for a three- or six-month internship. Most of the guys were dorky and this rubbed off on the rest of us. My mood been ruined and the drinks went down quick and I left the club a bit disillusioned.

The day after was Suriname Independence Day, and I went to see the military parade. The streets were filled with small stalls and I ate all kinds of quite tasty local foods.

All the people were gathered around a big field and soldiers were parading around a bit. It started raining and it all took very long. There were a few regiments from neighboring Brazil and French Guyana along with the local ones. They were dressed really sharply and had ultra-modern machine guns. The French regiment was part of the infamous Foreign Legion, and was especially dressed to the nines. The Surinamese regiments, on the other hand, were poorly equipped, with old karabiner guns or machine guns from the Stone Age. Same with their tanks and some jeeps. I felt a bit sorry for them.

It started raining hard and most people looked for shelter. I got really bored by the slow progress of the whole thing and went back to the guesthouse. It was time for some rest and to get ready for the night again.

I went out to a club named Zsa Zsa Zsu, but got there too early. There weren't many people inside when I arrived, and I sat at the bar and got drunk. The bouncer told me that it was a Surinamese music night, and I was interested, but soon decided he wasn't so much telling me as warning me.
In most countries I like the local music but this time I couldn't stand it. I made a few approaches, but without success.

The next day being Saturday, I of course went out. I went back to the same place as the day before. I had some manning-up to do. I decided to speak English only and did quite a few approaches that night while pounding a lot of beers. A glass of local Parbo beer costs seven-and-a-half Surinamese dollars, which is like two-and-a-half US dollars.

A Dutch guy walked up to me and we talked a bit. There were so many beta white guys around, the type who would probably wine and dine a girl, that I was getting the feeling that girls weren't looking for quick romance.

Me and the guy went to another room in the club where the music was more quiet and the atmosphere more relaxed.

That part of the club was a big surprise, because I hadn't even seen it the night before. I felt a bit more confident and stepped up to some girls standing by. One of the girls seemed to like me from the get-go and I danced with her a bit. The Dutch guy just stood there drinking his beer and looking at us.

The girl, Vickie, was wearing a sexy red dress, had long hair and a light-skinned complexion. She wasn't exactly a girl anymore, but a woman. She didn't like to speak English with me after she found out I also spoke Dutch. The guy I'd been talking to had disappeared.

After some making-out on the dance floor and a drink, we headed back to my room. She had her own car and that saved me some money on the cab fare, because at night taxi drivers really know how to fuck a white guy over, even though they're all very polite and like to talk a lot. Suriname people are very friendly and super-relaxed.

We arrived at my guesthouse and the night guard saw us but didn't make any problems. He was a very nice guy I'd talked to a few times before going out. It wasn't even forbidden to bring girls back to your room as long as you paid double the next day. If it had been against the rules I still would have sneaked her in and taken the risk of getting kicked out the next day.

We went up to my room and she went to the bathroom to freshen up, so did I after. We kissed and talked a bit while I was taking her clothes off. I couldn't fail anymore! My honor

was saved!! That Suriname flag was mine!!!!
Mwahahahahahaaaa!!!!!!!!!

Just to make sure I asked her how long she'd lived in Suriname, and then she gave me the following answer:
"I'm living for eleven years in Suriname now but I'm from Brazil."
In my head I was cursing a lot. Why did I even ask?

I said something like "Oh, nice". Apparently she'd lived in Suriname for a while, learned the Dutch language and had a few kids there.

I was like *Damn, another Brazilian notch!! I need that Suriname flag; I can't go to a former colony and not (re)capture the flag there.*

Unlike the last Brazilian girl I'd had, this girl was totally not adventurous between the sheets. Afterwards she sneaked out the same way she came in. I never saw her again. I was disappointed and should have seen it coming. When I looked at her picture afterwards I could clearly see she was Brazilian, but the Suriname population is so diverse that it's hard to tell in a club.

Over a third of the population is of South-East Indian heritage, another third are Creoles and the rest are a mix of Maroons (escaped black slaves, also officially named "bush negroes"), Javanese from Indonesia and even Chinese.

Day gaming was pretty much pointless since I didn't really see many great looking girls around and it was very hot outside during the day, with high humidity. All that smoking and drinking made me slow during the day too.

But there were some consolations. One of the greatest things about Suriname was that they sold imported Dutch food. I didn't realize that until I saw Dutch cookies at a supermarket. I bought everything Dutch I could find and came back to the guesthouse with two grocery bags full of Dutch candy and cookies. It is very hard to find the Dutch candy named "drop" outside of Holland. I knew I was going to destroy my bowels and libido (drop is bad for that), but ate it anyway. The only warm meals I ate in those four days were grilled-cheese sandwiches.

Although I liked it a lot in Suriname, the Dutch food

made me long to go back to Holland even more. Food's like that: you taste something from your childhood or from home and you just want to go back there. I had to say goodbye to Suriname after only four days in the capital. Time was running out and I had to move on to the "European" part of South America: French Guyana.

French Guyana

The three-day trip to French Guyana will give a good view on a true off-the-beaten-track travel experience. Though most of the life-on-the-road horror is edited out of the book to save pages, here I'll give you a detailed insight on the shit you can get yourself into while travelling, just so you can't say I didn't warn you. Budget travel will toughen any man up. You'll need lots of patience, creativity, willpower and persistence.

I left the guesthouse in Paramaribo early in the morning and walked to the bus station. It wasn't too far, but enough that you got there with a soaking wet sweaty t-shirt. My backpack weighed around twenty-three kilos and was filled with lots of cookies and candy, a hammock I bought at a local market the day before and a liter bottle of water.

I bought a ticket and the woman behind the counter informed me the bus would arrive somewhere around 1:00 PM. I had to keep an eye on all the buses going in out the dusty square to make sure I found the right one.

I smoked a cigarette and sat down to wait. People at the guesthouse had offered me the tourist taxi to the border, which cost seventy US dollars, but I laughed at them and said I would take the local bus there. A local bus cost only two-and-a-half dollars, so I'd already saved a shitload of money.

A big black woman was breast-feeding her baby right in front of me. I didn't know where to look because I didn't want to be rude, being the only white guy there looking at some giant hooters. She had the biggest nipples I had ever seen in my life. They must have been almost an inch long and I was shocked and intrigued at the same time. The woman just smiled a few times when I took a few peeks.

The local bus arrived and I found a space next to the

410

window in a single row of seats. The bus had about eighteen seats and drove with all the windows and even the door open.

We drove straight to another and bigger bus station where we had to wait for a while. Some other passengers joined us and the bus was now packed with people. My backpack was in the back of the bus and was big enough that it basically used up a seat.

A skinny woman – well, I'm not entirely sure it was a woman, but I think so – wanted me to take the bag on my lap so she'd have more arm space. I refused because I was already packed in between other passengers; the walkway in the middle of the bus had fold-out seats that were now all filled. She started grumping, but I just said no to her.

This bus was overcrowded already and people were eating and drinking, kids were playing on the seats, moms were either yelling at them or breastfeeding them. The skinny woman was on the phone with someone and was cursing. She spoke a mix of Dutch and Neger-Engels, which literally translates to Negro-English, a language used mostly by poor locals.

People started arguing with her because she used so many curse words in front of little children. People in Suriname are very polite.

At one point she was yelling both on the phone and with people in the bus. This went on for half an hour before she finally shut her big mouth.

I was sitting tight against the side of the bus and the guy next to me stank of old sweat, and he had to lean on me since the guy next to him had lots of bags with him. That guy smelled even worse. The guy next to me was loudly telling funny stories and jokes and everyone laughed.

When the bus stopped at a road restaurant, I was incredibly happy to get off the bus and smoke a cigarette. Everyone bought food at the road restaurant and brought it on board, and soon the whole bus smelled of greasy food and old sweat, the kind you get when people sweat a lot, go to bed without a shower and sweat again the next day. The stench was terrible.

The road was only paved for the first hour and the rest

was dusty dirt road, so I couldn't stick my head out of the window anymore to avoid the terrible smell because of the clouds of dust. I had to close the window and suffer. But despite the horrendous conditions, I still like buses like this: taking them means I don't have to feel like some spoiled tourist who doesn't experience anything in the country he's visiting and it gives an insight in the lives of people who don't have it as good as us back in the west.

We arrived at the border, which was similar to the border of the other Guyana: a river separates the two countries.

There's a ferry, but it only goes across once a day, so I choose to take one of the small fishing boats. Young teenage guys ran up to me and pulled my arm to the boats. It was a fight for customers here. I said I needed an exit stamp in my passport and asked where the immigration office was. They said it was far away but as a European I didn't need it. Stupidly enough I was in such a dazed mood that I actually believed them and got on one of the small boats with my backpack.

There was a French girl on board and halfway on the river she told me I definitely needed a stamp if I was going past the border town and into the country. Great. At least it was a nice river, since I had to go across it three times.

Once across the river I asked the boat guy to take me back to the customs office close to the shore in Suriname. He took me back to the starting point and I had to take a taxi to the customs office. The office was already closed, so the driver took me took to some military dude who exit-stamped my passport. Back into the taxi again and later back into the boat again and by now I had trouble my carrying my backpack around. I was exhausted and the worst was yet to come.

The boat guy was really friendly and luckily he was from Suriname, so I could speak Dutch with him. He dropped me at the shore where the French Guyanan police post was and they stamped me into the country. Back into the boat again, and he dropped me off at the small place where the boats docked. I gave him about fifteen US dollars, which is relatively cheap for all the boating he did for me.

As soon as I was in French Guyana, lots of shady Rasta guys came at me, all wanting to take me somewhere. There were no official taxi and it was already dark by now. There I was, with my full backpack with my money, laptop, camera and cell phone.

I didn't feel safe at all being surrounded by all these shady guys but the last thing you should do is let them know that. They asked me ridiculous prices, like sixty or seventy dollars, to bring me anywhere in town, even if it was close.

French Guyana is a very expensive country and the hotels listed in the Lonely Planet book were horribly costly. I had to find something else. The Lonely Planet, aka the travellers' bible, named a guesthouse but didn't give an address. It just said it was somewhere on the way to some small village named St Jean. I cursed the book for its insufficient information.

The friendly boat guy translated for me and one of the guys said he would bring me there for ten Euros. (French Guyana is officially part of France so the local currency is the Euro, which feels weird because it's thousands of miles away from Europe.) I had to take the risk and went in the car with a guy who didn't speak anything but French.

Except for some funny lines my French is non-existent these days, although I was quite good at it in my early twenties. This guy had a good car, so I trusted him more than the guys who drove clunkers. We stopped at two different ATMs along the way and I was lucky they even worked. He drove in the direction of the village but we couldn't find a guesthouse at all. I think maybe he drove past it.

At one point we saw some small houses and it looked like it might be the place. We stopped and looked around a bit, looking for a reception or something.

Suddenly a woman walked out and asked what we were doing there. I pointed at the guy and he explained a bit in French. I couldn't understand what he was saying and suddenly the woman started speaking English. I was so relieved at that moment. I told her that we were looking for a guesthouse but she never heard of it. I asked if I could sleep in the bushes with my hammock. She gave me a strange look, thought for a few seconds and said "You can sleep here if you want". She must have seen the desperation on my face. I paid the "taxi" guy ten Euros and he left.

Bea was a French woman working as a nurse, and had two daughters from an earlier marriage with a Brazilian guy. They were divorced now. The oldest daughter was about fourteen and was a bit scared of me but the youngest one was about seven years old and found me very interesting. I had hit the jackpot and was really lucky to meet this woman.

Bea cooked some dinner for me and gave me a Heineken beer. She had traveled and hitchhiked herself and was excited to hear about my trip. Of course I left out all the stories about girls.

She had prepared a room (with air conditioning) for me and I took a shower and fell asleep around ten o'clock. It had been a very stressful day and I was really exhausted.

The next morning she had to get up very early for work and we ate some breakfast. Afterwards she gave me some extra water and dropped me off at the hitchhikers point in St Laurent de Marconi, the small harbor city I had arrived in the night before. I thanked her extensively for her friendliness.

After spending an hour in the already hot sun trying to get a lift, I gave up and walked back to the harbor which took me about forty-five minutes. I was back where I started.

The hawkers/Rastas came to me and asked what I where I was going. I said that I needed a bus to Cayenne, the capital of French Guyana.

Because most middle-class people have a car and everyone else tries to hitchhike, there's no public transport in this country. There are some private drivers, though, and I was led to a guy who could take me there. It cost thirty-five Euros for a four-hour ride. I had paid two Euros for the same distance in Suriname, but here I had no choice and got on the luxury minivan along with a few others. They paid the same as me, so I didn't feel I was getting ripped off. The prices are just high in this country.

The driver was a very friendly guy who could speak five or six languages. After one hour we had to pass a roadblock and my bag was searched for Surinamese knock-off clothes and my passport was checked by the French cops with their funny hats. The driver dropped us off at some village and we changed buses there.

The new driver wasn't friendly at all and when we arrived in Cayenne he refused to drop me off in the center. I had to walk a kilometer with my backpack again. The sun was relentless and even though it was around noon I was already ready for a nap.

The cheapest guesthouse was supposed to be next to Palm Square, but it was closed down. A guy pointed me towards the second cheapest option in town and I walked over there. Another half-hour walk. At the hotel, they said I had to wait till two o'clock to check in.

The hotel wasn't really nice and only a two-star place, but they still asked forty-five Euros (nearly sixty US dollars) a night and it was strictly forbidden to bring a guest. I could forget about getting a flag here. I left my bag next to the desk and told them I would come back later to check in and would visit an Internet café first.

I walked around the city center, took some pictures, went to an Internet café for an hour, took a shameful dump while a cute Chinese girl was sitting on the other side of the door and afterwards went to the local tourist office.

Luckily there was a young guy there who spoke some English. I asked him about cheap places to stay the night but he didn't know anything.

I decided to leave Cayenne and go to Kourou, one hour away by bus. He was helpful but I still had to pressure him a lot to call several campsites around Kourou for me, because hotels would cost at least a hundred dollars there. He found one that would take me and explained how to get there.

I walked back to the "cheap" hotel to pick up my bag. The staff there gave me a weird look when I just walked in and took my bag and left. I still had to walk quite a distance in the hot sun.

On the way there I bought some chips, cigarettes and a few half-liter cans of beer. I must have left quite a weird impression downing a few beers at four in the afternoon. I arrived at the bus station, where it was hard to get a minivan to Kourou. There were some cute black girls around and I tried to talk to them a bit, but their English was very limited.

People were fighting to get into the vans, but the one to Kourou wasn't showing up. It took ages to arrive and there were some heated arguments between drivers and passengers. There was a Surinamese girl with a baby on the bus and I talked to her a bit as we drove back to Kourou, the place I had passed on my way to Cayenne.

For some reason we changed drivers halfway and my deal with the first one to take me off route to the guesthouse didn't go down well with the other driver. He wanted me to pay five Euros extra, on top of the ten Euros I'd already had to pay. The normal price to center Kourou was five Euros and it wasn't even that far, although the dirt road to the guesthouse was really bad. Lots of arguing later I gave the guy his extra five Euros and knocked on the door of the campsite.

A friendly native Amazon Indian guy opened the gate and showed me a place to hang my hammock. The only other guests were a French family with a cute daughter. They were very friendly; we talked a bit and when I told them I was going to visit the famous Devil's Island they offered me a ride in their rental car to the harbor the next morning because they were planning the same. They gave me some food, too, but I didn't want to take advantage of their friendliness too much.

There seemed to be quite a few French tourists visiting French Guyana. It's super easy for them: they can speak their own language and even pay with Euros while still being thousands of miles away from home. They don't even need passports.

Around ten o'clock I hung up my hammock and fell asleep quickly. I was glad that I could use the hammock, because it hadn't really been cheap and it weighed quite a lot and took lots of space in my bag.

The next morning, breakfast consisted of cookies and candy, just like dinner the night before. We all got into the car and went to the harbor. I was able to book a day trip on the same catamaran as the French family and together with a few others we sailed out.

I'd always wanted to go on a catamaran, it's my favorite type of boat. We were with about fifteen people including the big-bellied captain with a Captain Iglo beard and his wife/girlfriend. She must have been at the end of her forties but still had a good body with big tits loosely bouncing in her shirt. She had long brown curly hair and was sun-tanned all over. Her face wasn't that attractive but she just had that sort of overall raw attractiveness. Weirdly enough I looked at her more than at the young French chick. You don't see a sexy older woman every day. Maybe I was just horny after weeks of not scoring a chick and having only one Same Night Lay. Travelling around on a budget and picking up girls is damn hard, especially in countries where attractive girls are a rarity.

Sailing to the Isles de Salut was amazing: the sun was hot, the waters were blue and even the smell of the ocean was good. The catamaran is a magnificent boat and I loved it. The only problem was that of course I got sunburned early in the day. We arrived at the first island and the boat docked.

The Isles de Salut are famous islands because this used to be the island where French prisoners were send in the old days. They are known as Devil's Island, made famous by the book *Papillion* and the classic movie with one of my favorite actors, Steve McQueen. If getting send to a tropical island doesn't sound so bad then know this: over ninety percent of the prisoners there died within six months. The conditions were terrible.

At first I walked around the island a bit with the French family and another Dutch guy but they took a guided tour and I started walking around alone. I saved eight Euros on the tour – it was in French anyway. It was a good decision because I saw so much more on my own, lots of monkeys, wild pigs and some rare lizards too.

A few hours later we were back on the boat and we sailed to another island close by. The boat stopped and we had to swim about a hundred meters to the shore. I barely made it and was ashamed of my terrible physical state. I coughed my lungs out once I had some steady ground under my feet. The young French girl had a very sexy body. Before she'd been wearing some unrevealing clothes but now that I saw her in her swimming gear she looked so amazing… But what could I do sleeping outside in a hammock with her parents around?

The second island was less interesting and I walked around it twice with the Dutch guy. He was nice, but our views of Holland clashed a bit. He was a lot younger than me and full of idealistic thoughts. He told me that he couldn't find a place to stay and had to pay a hundred Euros a night for a hotel room in Kourou. I'd rather sleep on the streets than pay that sort of money in a dead-end town like Kourou.

At the end of the day we went back. By now I really was quite sunburned. Normally I don't mind that so much, but now I had a 23kg backpack scratching the skin off my shoulders.

I stayed one more night in the hammock and left early in the morning. I said goodbye to the Frenchies. The friendly owner of the guesthouse asked me for less money than we'd agreed on and arranged to have me picked up by a friend, who took me in a car to the Guiana Space Center. It cost me ten Euros, but there was almost no other way of getting there since it was in the middle of nowhere.

The Space Center is the base for a partnership between several European countries for the launch of commercial satellites and rockets.

When I got there the security people gave me lots of trouble because I arrived there with a full backpack and they wouldn't let me leave it anywhere. They said I either had to get it off the grounds or take it with me into the museum and surrounding areas. Like I was going to visit a museum with a giant backpack. After I protested for a while they searched my whole bag and decided I could leave it at the reception while I went to the museum and surrounding sites.

After visiting everything I had to find a way back to Suriname.

I walked off the Space Center grounds and waited for a lift next to the road. It started raining, but I was lucky: one car stopped after a few minutes and took me in.

The driver was a French guy who worked there. As I asked, he took me to the roundabout four kilometers away.

Getting out, I saw a poor black guy waiting for a ride too. I asked him where he was going and he told me St. Laurent, the same place I was going to. I walked past him and waited about fifty meters further up the road so that people would take him first. I had made a sign with a piece of cardboard and the marker Bea had given me.

After only two minutes a car came by and stopped right in front of me. It was a nice big Audi, one of my favorite cars, and the driver told me that he would take me. I threw my bag in the back seat, sat down in the front seat and said to him that the other guy was going to St. Laurent too and he was first. The black dude came over and asked but the driver just said there was no more room and drove off. I felt really bad for that guy, but I also didn't want to take a risk of not getting a ride. I still had some ten hours of travelling, boating, bussing and passport stamping ahead of me before reaching the guesthouse in Paramaribo again. The black guy was in his own country and his own language and had only three hours hitchhiking to do.

The driver was a really nice guy even if he was a bit racist maybe leaving that black guy at the side of the road. He was a retired French policeman in his late fifties who had worked in France and some of its colonies. He told me very interesting stories about Devil's Island and its inmates.

The conditions were horrendous in those years, and the prison was closed in the late 1940s. About eighty thousand prisoners had died there and the ones who finished their sentences were just moved to the mainland, were they often caught by local bandits who enslaved them or sold them.

Some prisoners were so desperate that they mutilated themselves so that they didn't have to work anymore. Some blinded themselves or bought slime/spit from prisoners infected with tuberculosis. It's hard to imagine that people would choose to get infected with a deadly disease.

Another weird story he told me was about how many poor pregnant women from Suriname would cross the river border as soon as their water broke so that they gave birth in French Guyana, letting the baby claim a French Passport and a monthly welfare paycheck based on European standards.

After three hours driving and one roadblock we arrived in St Laurent and he dropped me off at the docking place for the motorized canoes. I took one back to Suriname. I was dropped off at the immigration office next to the water and I was stamped back into the country.

A taxi driver tried to rip me off, saying it was very far to the boat dock where the buses to Paramaribo were. The mofo asked me seventeen US dollars for a four-minute ride. The customs officer even helped him by saying this was true. I told him he was crazy and just walked there in less than ten minutes, even with my backpack.

From there I took a small minivan back to Paramaribo. I paid about sixteen US dollars for this and shared the minivan with a girl and a grandma with a cute little baby. A quick three-hour ride for the same money as what the taxi driver asked me before. I arrived back at my first guesthouse early in the evening.

That was a lot of details, but I just want to make sure you get a sense of how most of my transport went, all over the third world. I had to be constantly careful not to get ripped off or treated like some dumb tourist.

Worldwide, I'd say that the ratio of generally friendly and helpful people to those who try to take as much of your money as possible is about fifty-fifty. This means that you have to make a judgment call with every person you meet. It's easy to treat the good ones as if they weren't, but you have to take that risk.

I made a promise to myself that I would take hitchhikers with me once I was back in Holland.

Suriname: Paramaribo part two

Once I was back at my old guesthouse I showered and started talking to some new guests.

It was Thursday night and I was told that Havana Lounge was the wildest place to go out.

Me, a Dutch guy and an English girl from the guesthouse went there but I couldn't do any damage there – unless you count damage to my liver and my lungs. I was pounding the drinks and smoked like a chimney. The Dutch guy was into the English girl but I could spot him being friend-zoned a mile away.

The club was filled with Dutch girls looking for a Surinamese banana. Dutch girls don't do it for me anymore, so who am I to judge? After all, I'm totally into Asian and Latin girls now.

The English girl went off with some Surinamese guy and the Dutch guy talked to a Dutch woman all night. I tried to hook up with a girl of Indian and Italian heritage, but I couldn't even get a kiss out of her. I went home to get some much-needed sleep.

That Friday I wanted to catch on some sleep before I went out, but after I collapsed I didn't wake up till about one at night. I didn't feel the need to shower, shave, dress up and still go out that night.

Saturday was my last night out in Paramaribo and I had already given up on capturing a flag there. That left me with the all-or-nothing option, and I approached at least ten girls in just two hours – without much success.

But there was a group of four girls hanging around with two guys. I had my eye on the skinny tall dark girl with an amazing round ass. I was pounding beer after beer and didn't see it happening in my mind since I'd already failed at approaching so many girls that night. But suddenly she walked up to me and asked me to dance.

I danced a bit with her and her three girlfriends. That felt a lot better and it was something I had gotten used to: being the center of attention. My player mood was still off, though, and my words came out slow and were still lame. I even mispronounced words a few times.

Back at the bar I talked to the guys and girlfriends a bit. They decided to leave and I exchanged phone numbers with the girl named Rachel. I expected to never hear from her again.

When I woke up the next morning I had an extreme hangover and a vicious cold. I stayed in bed all day and felt a bit feverish and all-over rotten. My nose was clogged and I had trouble breathing. I texted Rachel for a meet-up anyway. I was going to leave in two days but I thought *What the hell*, **a quitter never wins and a winner never quits.**

We met around seven at night in a quiet waterfront bar.

We talked a bit and it looked like she was definitely interested. She even paid for some drinks herself. There was no time for several dates over the next couple of days and I wondered what her plans with me were. I felt truly sick that night.

Rachel wanted to visit a girlfriend who was working at another bar and turned out to be a hottie too with nice boobs. I had fun in that bar with the regulars there. After a while Rachel and I went back to my guesthouse. All the people who were still sitting on the guesthouse porch saw me sneaking the girl in through the side gate, but not the staff.

We took a hot shower together, but this just made me cough only more since now everything in my nose and throat was liquified. I kept as much as possible in but was fighting an uphill battle with my snot reserves.

Rachel had a cute face and her body was simply amazing. I couldn't stop touching her big round butt. It was so firm it was nearly muscular. We kissed a lot and walked back to the bedroom. Her skin was all shiny from the shower gel and although I was quite suntanned I looked pale as a vampire next to her pitch-black skin. I had never made love to such a dark girl.

The two black girls in Brazil were a lot lighter than her. Ever since I'd reached the north of South America I'd made it my mission to find a cute black girl to have sex with and now the moment was there.

She gave me a blowjob and then rode me like a cowboy. She was only twenty-three years old and her body felt so good that night. I was sick as a dog and had a fever but I forgot all about it. We made love for a long time. She kept saying that she couldn't believe I was almost thirty-five.

We were up for a second round when her girlfriend called and asked her where she was. We put our clothes back on and went to meet her friend in another bar. She was accompanied by a guy she'd met in the first bar. He was a loudmouth drunk claiming to be some kind of big gangster. He was all big talk and kept ordering drinks that night. The fever and the drinks were hitting me hard and I said I wanted to go back and sleep. I took a taxi and Rachel came an hour later after she made sure her girlfriend went home safely.

We banged again before we passed out and I was glued to her body for the rest of the night.

The next morning she went home and I smuggled her outside again. Of course some guests saw me and they congratulated me on my score. There were a few Dutch guys of Surinamese heritage around and they kept praising me. She did have a really banging body.

That day I was still sick but I went to a lot of logistical trouble to send a package home. The taxi driver drove all round town to get me to some outside office of a company that sends packages to Holland. I took the bus back to the center and found out that the taxi driver had taken the long way round to make a few extra dollars. "What a bastard," I thought, but it also reminded me of all the times I cheated people about of their money when I was a cab driver myself.

Once I'd sent the package my backpack was about seven kilos lighter and it was a pleasure carrying it around again.

I bought some more Dutch food and longed to go home more than ever. The day I went home was less than three weeks away, but that was still a while.

That evening Rachel came by my place and we had some terrific sex again and I took some naked pictures of her.

We got up in the middle of the night and said goodbye to each other. I still have contact with her from time to time.

A taxi picked me up at four in the morning. This cabbie was in a good mood, talked a lot and brought me to the airport. The sounds of Inner Circle with its famous song *Sweat* rang in my head, but this time I didn't think of Evita in Lima but only of the beautiful black girls I was going to meet in Trinidad & Tobago and Jamaica.

Chapter Seven – The Caribbean

Trinidad and Tobago – Port of Spain

A short flight later I arrived in Port of Spain, the capital of this small island state.

After the usual struggle, which in this case included a local bus and lots of walking in the hot sun, I found my guesthouse. The place was quite a dump and a room without bathroom still cost twenty US dollars. The woman working there was one of the ugliest and least attractive women I had ever seen in my life.

It was obvious that the busy week before had taken its toll on my body. I was still sick and didn't do much more than getting some food and resting a lot.

The weather was terrible so my plan to go to the beach for a day failed. Since I only had three nights there I needed to get my butt in gear and go out at night.

I found a place called Stumble-In, which had a couple of very hot girls inside, but I was too tired to the in the right mood to do anything.

There were no taxis around and a couple of rich kids dropped me off at the guesthouse. It was very nice of them to do so, and they gave me advice on where to go for a good party, but I was too short on time to go there.

I decided then and there it had been a stupid decision to go to Trinidad and Tobago for only three nights.

If I ever go back there it will be for at least a week and with much more money.

The third day I walked around the city as much as

possible to at least get a glimpse of life in T and T. I tried the local specialty called Shark and Bake, a big chunk of fried shark meat on a bun. I really liked it and had the feeling all that protein gave me some extra power.

I went out that night with an Italian guy to Stumble-In again. The night was OK, but it wasn't cheap and pretty much useless since I had no place to take a girl if I succeeded in getting one. The woman who owned the guesthouse had made that perfectly clear to me.

Italian Dude and I walked back together to the guesthouse and two hours of sleep later a taxi picked me up in front of the guesthouse and drove me to the airport.

In my half-sleep in the taxi I nearly had a vision about seeing my friends and family again in Holland. My life would be so different once I returned home, and I had no real plans for the future except for writing and publishing this book.

Jamaica – Kingston

Sleepy as I still was I got on the wrong bus and ended up in Trench Town, the famous neighborhood where Bob Marley grew up. I had not been paying much attention and took the wrong bus after the first change from the airport.

People were staring at me and my backpack in that local bus. You could see in their eyes that they wondered what the hell I was doing there. Trench Town is one of the most dangerous neighborhoods in the world. There are at least two murders in Kingston EVERY day. Luckily I could speak English here and I soon found the right bus without getting robbed or shanked just two weeks before heading home.

The hostel was pretty cool and I met some nice people there. One of them was Mark, an English black guy of Jamaican heritage. I convinced him to go out to Club Quad.

Mark surprised me by walking up to hotties very quickly and started talking to them without hesitation. He didn't get anywhere with them but in his defense, they looked like straight up gold diggers or high-class hookers but it was admirable.

Club Quad, a four-storey club with an expensive top floor was very disappointing and a complete cock-fest, with very few girls.

We walked over from Club Quad to Paddy Royal, a twenty-minute walk. According to Mark it was a mix between a regular club and a strip club. I would say it was more of a strip joint with lots of freelance girls inside.

The entrance fee was low and the beer was cheap. It was a sleazy place inside, with a stage with girls stripping and shaking their asses and lots of dudes around it and some girls too. I think some of the girls were lesbians and they were daggering the shit out of each other.

There were some guys playing pool in the back and lots of girls around who if you gave them some eye contact would grind up to you for half-a-minute and then straight-up ask you some hefty fee, like five hundred Jamaican dollars.

I gave one of them a hundred because that seemed to be the regular price, and she had kind of cornered me and started grinding on me when I came out of the toilet.

Some big Rasta dudes were looking over and I figured I'd better pay her something to avoid trouble. I only did that once because I'm not interested in paying for pussy.

This is also the place I met an English friend of Mark's, named Peter.

Peter was a short, white, poor looking fifty-something guy with greasy hair, a heavy English accent and a Jamaican wife back in the UK. He was always bragging about getting girls, but I never saw him with one (without emptying his pockets). Mark and Peter had known each other a long time and Peter supposedly had a lot of knowledge of Jamaica and especially Trench Town.

According to him he was the only white guy allowed in Trench Town. I wasn't impressed – I'd gone in there and got out alive. He was always high and drunk and I disliked him from the start. He didn't like me either and was jealous I was going out with Mark. I was talking to Mark and Peter was giving him a drunken rant. Mark just kept talking to me without even acknowledging Peter's existence. After a while Peter just walked away. That was the second time I was impressed by Mark.

Most travellers I meet are complete beta males but Mark

had this alpha thing going on. I thought I could learn a thing or two from him and kept an eye on him.

Mark and I went out on Saturday night and ended up in a club named Fiction. The place was half-empty on a Saturday night and barely had any girls inside. Some foreigner with no game was trying to talk up some of the black hotties inside.

It was embarrassing to watch; the guy sat next to the girl and tried to pull some words out of her. She was clearly giving him all the signals that she didn't give a rat's ass about him.

He kept offering her a drink and she said yes, maybe to get him out of her face.

I enjoyed watching this train wreck about to happen. He gave her the drink, sat next to her again, she barely left a spot open on the edge of the couch. As soon she had the drink in her hand, she turned her shoulder on him and his attempts to talk to her. He walked off like a beaten dog with his tail between his legs.

Like I said, there weren't many people inside and most were couples. The crappy music didn't help either. I wanted to see how much of a bitch that girl really was and walked up to her after she ordered a drink at the bar.

Apparently her English wasn't that good and she said something whose true meaning I doubted she knew. She said "I'm stuck up!" I just laughed in her face and kept talking to her; I got her to smile a few times and got a quick dance out of her. The foreign dude was standing in the corner watching the whole thing.

The girls walked off and when I saw her again later I asked her: "Hey, how's the being stuck up going?" She laughed and we talked a bit more. She was a gold digger, though, and I didn't pursue her much further.

Mark had already approached three girls in a corner close to the bar and I approached one of them. She said she lived in New York and I mentioned I was going there next week. We talked a bit; she gave me her number and we agreed to meet again in New York. Her friends left soon after and she joined them. The club was nearly empty now.

We walked back to the hostel and on the way there

stopped at another bar. There were some girls outside and we got talking to them. There were some dudes with the girls but they were drunk and a bit annoying. The girl I was talking to looked OK in the dark, but the more I saw her, especially after we were in a lighter place, the more appalled I became by her.

She was down to fuck and said she had her own place, but I didn't want to get my Jamaican flag by fucking an ugly skank like her and got the hell out of there.

Mark was into the other girl.

In the next days I soon found out he wasn't the guy I thought he was. He was a great opener but a bad finisher, neither alpha nor beta.

Over the next few days he chased the girl we met on the street but got nowhere, saying he didn't want to pay for a hotel.

Mark was pennywise, pound foolish, as they say in England. He was cheap on going out, food and drinks, but he later told me that he was sponsoring the whole of Peter's stay in Jamaica. Everything: his flights to and from Jamaica, the nights in the hostel and even some spending money. When I asked him why he said that Peter knew important people Mark could do business with. Making contacts and doing business was the main reason Mark was in Jamaica.

He sounded like someone with a good sense of business and was obviously well–educated, and I admired him for that, but I just couldn't understand why he was hanging out with Peter. My opinion on Peter was that he was a complete leech who got drunk, stoned and a free vacation at Mark's expense.

At one point Peter was supposed to show up for (business) meetings Mark scheduled and didn't show up till after another night in a strip club. He even missed his flight back to England and kept asking for more money. I couldn't understand how an intelligent, business-minded person like Mark got tricked by a numbnuts like Peter. Perhaps he didn't want to see his own mistakes.

I was planning on moving on to Montego Bay on Sunday but I got up too late after a long night.

The days after that I was so damn lazy that I could barely get out of bed in the mornings. My cold was still terrible and didn't seem to want to get better. Kingston is not a really exciting city to be in. There's not much of a center and you can pretty much forget about day-gaming girls. There just aren't that many attractive girls in the streets or shops.

One afternoon I went to the Bob Marley House Museum but didn't take the tour, which cost twenty US dollars. I was at the end of my trip and also almost at the end of my money. I regretted it later because I'm quite the reggae fan.

I didn't do much during the day except get stoned a few times. I hadn't smoked in a long time and got really high really quickly. It was so bad that I knocked myself out and fell asleep early all the time. It surprised me because I used to be a heavy smoker back home in Holland where quality is good – some say the best in the world.

There was an American guy of Lebanese heritage in the dorm room named Anthony I hung out with from time to time.

We went to a strip club called Pablos a lot and I got a few lap dances from stunningly hot Jamaican girls, a few times for free and a few other times for a few dollars. The dancers were amazing, very flexible and able to shake their big firm asses in every way possible.

I badly wanted to go home, though, and even staying on as a wonderful an island as Jamaica, an island most people want to visit, is less fun when you feel like that. The whole trip had just gone on for too long. I should have gone home a little sooner. Over the last few months, I'd been thinking about seeing my family and friends again a lot, and it had sort of taken my mind off travelling and having fun.

On one of my last days I went to Port Royal with a young Dutch guy. Port Royal used to be the pirate capital of the world, where famous pirates like Blackbeard and Henry Morgan came to spend their money on women and booze.

Port Royal was destroyed twice in giant earthquakes and tsunamis, so there was little left to see. Most of the city is at the bottom of the sea now. We took a bus there and visited Fort Charles.

We also wanted to go to a small island to get a suntan, so we asked the local fishermen to take us there.

The first one asked for way too much money and we went to ask some others. We saw a small group of Rastas and I asked them how much it would cost to take us there and back. Those guys were high as a kite and barely answered.

After two minutes one of them got up and took a jerrycan of gasoline to his small wooden motorboat. We assumed that was a yes.

The Rasta guy had to climb on to two other boats to get to his. He tried to fill the tank of the engine but the jerrycan was too heavy to hold with one hand so he kept spilling the gasoline everywhere while he was smoking a blunt. I was afraid he would set himself on fire but it went well after all.

We climbed of the dock and into the boat and he brought us to the small island. The view over Kingston Town from there was astounding. Two hours and a sunburn later, we went back to the hostel.

The last night in Jamaica the whole hostel group went to a street party. There were large groups of guys and not many girls around. All those guys were really stoned and were listening to the loud dancehall music.

Mark was chasing a rather chubby girl from the hostel; she had some giant boobs but the rest was nothing to be proud of.

Anthony, an American/Lebanese guy, was not that tall but built like a rock and quite muscular too. He was a great guy, a little shy with the girls but at least he had a plan of travelling around the island. He's the only one I keep in touch with on Facebook.

All in all, the street party sucked and I felt it was a bit dangerous to talk to Jamaican girls at the party because there were so many groups of poor, nothing-to-lose guys around. Although most were friendly and smiling a few looked angry at our group of tourists.

It took me a while but I convinced Anthony to go back to Pablos, where we had some drinks and amazing boner-raising lap dances again. I went straight from the strip club to the airport and didn't get any sleep.

It was time for my last travel destination and I had saved the best for last: **New York**

When I look back at my week of Jamaica, I feel bad about going to Trinidad and Tobago. I should have used those days in Jamaica. My time there was just too short to party in the weekend and go for the beach in the next days. I never visited the Blue Lagoon and Errol Flynn's island nor did I go to Montego Bay or Negril like I planned too. I would love to go back and stay at least six weeks to explore the island properly. It's a great place with friendly people, a laid-back vibe and impressive natural scenery.

Chapter Eight – The United States

USA – New York

I was sick and tired of travelling. For the last months I had been longing to return home, to get some luxury and routine back in my life.

It all changed when I looked out of my airplane window and looked over New York. A lifelong dream to visit this city had come true. It was fucking NEW YORK!! A city I had admired since I was a little boy and did a class project on it. I couldn't believe how happy I was to be there and I almost became a bit emotional.

New York, the Big Apple, the city were so many of my favorite movies and television shows were filmed. I loved series like *Seinfeld*, *Friends*, *How I Met Your Mother* and *Law and Order SVU*. I couldn't think of a better place than New York to end my trip.

The American customs were not as strict or hardcore as I'd expected and after a few questions they let me into the land of milk and honey.

An hour later I stepped off the metro. The metros weren't that different from what I'd been in in dozens of other countries, but it all changed when I walked up to the street.

The smell of hot dogs reached my nose and it was like I had stepped into an American movie. There were yellow cabs everywhere; a big school bus drove by. The hotdog guy was reading his newspaper and I asked him to make me a supersized hot dog. I looked around while I was walking towards the hostel. The city blocks with their typical fire stairs were on both sides of me and in my mind I could see a cop chasing down some bad guy, like I had seen so many times in the Hollywood movies.

Fuck nature walks, this was one of the best walks I ever took.

All that was missing were homeless guys warming their hands on a fire in a barrel and the typical crazy lady with a shopping cart full of tin cans.

After walking about eight blocks I arrived at my hostel at 120th and 1st. After some flirting with the Brazilian girl working at the reception I went up to my dorm. It was a big, brand-new luxurious apartment and the bedroom had only four beds. I was the only one in the room so it felt like I had made a great deal on this place for only twenty-five dollar a night. The last time I had seen such luxury was probably the hotel in Jakarta where I stayed with Donna or the love hotels I visited in Rio.

After the first excitement I thought about the fact that I hadn't slept for nearly thirty hours and decided it was best to relax a bit that day. I walked over to the East River Plaza mall and went to Target, one of those giant superstores where you can buy pretty much anything.

In America everything is Bigger and Better, so I couldn't even find some small bags of chips or small bottles of soda. Everything was giant, including the women shopping there.

In the electronics department I saw the same Sony camera I'd bought in Brazil, at half the price. Damn, everything was so cheap here. I bought some food and relaxed the rest of the day.

The following day I walked around all day and took many pictures. I walked across the famous Brooklyn Bridge and back before I headed to the center. Unfortunately the bridge was under construction and it was hard to make a good picture of it.

Half of New York's names were former Dutch names from back when it was New Amsterdam: Brooklyn (Breukelen), Harlem (Haarlem) Broadway (brede weg) and Wall Street are the most famous, but also Flushing, the Bronx, Coney Island, Long Island, Staten island, the Bowery, Bushwick, Greenwich, Flatbush, Hempstead and Yonkers.

Even the words "dollar" and "yankee" are derived from Dutch.

Even more: the first Dutch colonists brought with them a holiday for children named Sinterklaas, who nowadays is Santa Claus in America and the rest of the world. It's still celebrated in its original form in Holland till this day.

I walked towards Wall Street and bought a SIM card along the way in an AT&T store. The girl who sold it to me was a cute girl from the Dominican Republic. She tested out if my number worked with her cell phone and I asked if I could call her later. She said no and also didn't reply to the text I send her. Well, it was worth a shot.

Later that day I walked through Wall Street and took the free ferry to Staten Island to see the Statue of Liberty, which was a lot smaller than I imagined.

That night I went out with Clarisa, a Colombian girl I had met on Couchsurfing. I met up with her and a friend named Rafael, also a Colombian.

We headed to a bar and had some drinks there.

Clarisa, Rafael, a Mexican guy and I went to a club afterwards, drank some beers and had fun. Rafael and I were looking to talk to girls. The club wasn't exactly packed with them but I opened a few girls and Rafael was kind of shocked with the ease with which I walked up to girls. He was more of a shy guy.

We were having fun laughing at two guys who had bottle service and had to stay put at their table to guard their bottle. They were getting drunk but without any girls.

Later some girl walked up to them and I said to Rafael, "Hey, watch, this girl is going to get some free drinks and then dump the guys again." And this is exactly what happened.

Rafael was looking at some girls and I told him he should approach them. He got a bit scared, I guess, and I said, "Let me do it for you" and walked up to the (drunk) girl he liked. I talked to her a bit about my Colombian friend and got her phone number to give to him. The girl left with her friends a few minutes later.

When I joined with the group and gave Rafael the girl's

phone number he was flabbergasted.

When the club closed and we went for after-drinking food where I talked and joked with some more girls. I was on fire that night.

Although New York is an expensive place to go out, I had barely spent more than twenty dollars that night. We said goodbye and agreed to meet again that weekend.

On Saturday afternoon I met up with a girl from Belarus who lived illegally in New York, and we walked through Central park.

It was freezing cold that day and of course I barely had anything warm to wear, so we had to warm up at McDonalds a few times. Later we explored Broadway a bit. It was fantastic; all those billboards and lights were amazing.

We ended up in a Mexican bar where a Belarussian girlfriend of hers worked, and we ended up with free drinks because her friend brought them over without charging.

Although the Belarusian girl was only a six on the hotness scale, I liked her accent, and she was hiding some nice boobs under her sweater. I kissed her in the Mexican bar and we made out all evening.

The problem was that she shared an apartment with some Russians and I lived in the hostel apartment where I couldn't bring anyone. There was simply no place where I could take her and I decided to bail on her and maybe meet her later that week when I might have better options.

She was hesitant when I brought up the possibility of getting together again. She knew I was going to push for the next time. I really wish I'd had a place of my own that night. For sure I'd have got my flag. Good logistics is half your inner game and bang possibility.

I hopped on a metro and an hour later I was back in the hostel apartment. Rafael and Clarisa had been texting me a few times asking me to go out with them again to a birthday party at a club.

Around one at night I walked out of the hostel again and went looking for it. Long story short, it took me over one-and-a-half hours and lots of cursing to take several metros and find that club. When I walked into the club it was already three o'clock. I ordered a beer and tried to text Rafael to locate where he was in the club.

A blonde girl bumped into me and I gave her a smile. I said something lame and she rubbed her tits on me before walking away. I was like, *Damn I screwed that one up*, but she happened to be part of the large group of Colombian girls at the birthday party. Rafael and a few others I already knew were happy to see me.

The girls were acting crazy and there was a bottle of Aguardientes going around. When I said I'd had it before in Cali, Colombia, the group was impressed, and it was a good way to break in my travelling-around-the-world background.

Half a dance later I was making out with the blonde girl and continued to do that for my time there.

Afterwards we all left in taxis and cars for Rafael's house in Jersey and continued to party there. Rafael, who had lived in New York for seven years, had a house full of big flat-screens and game consoles, a giant lounge couch and some reclining chairs. This guy had it made, in my opinion.

We drank and danced away the whole night. The blonde Colombian girl and I kissed a lot and I was also flirting with a skinny Bolivian girl who was pretty hot. A lot happened that night but no banging.

The house had only one bedroom so I had to sleep on the giant lounge couch with three girls. The blond Colombian girl was sleeping on my right and I was fingering one of the other girls, who kept moaning "fuck me, fuck me", but she didn't want to go to the bathroom and actually do it.

The next day everyone was hung-over and I took the bus with the four girls back to Manhattan Island where we said goodbye to each other. I Facebooked pretty much everyone there. I will definitely go back to New York when I have the chance – and it doesn't hurt to make some Colombian contacts either, since that country is high on my list for another visit.

Just a few hours later I met an American girl off the travel website. She was pretty hot, around thirty but still looking very good. She was white, but she came from a mixed bloodline and had some African American features. Her lips were massive and very sexy. She was appearantly complimented on her mixed heritage a thousand times before because she didn't seem to shut up about it until I gave her a compliment about her beautiful features.

We met at Times square and went for a beer in several bars. I spat all my game but she wasn't biting much. When we walked back to her place, I asked her if I could take a pee at her apartment and she agreed. It's one of the best ways to get into a girl's place. (Credit Roosh.)

She had a nice studio apartment in a better part of Manhattan. I tried to kiss her there but she gave me the head turn. She said she wanted to go to bed but I kept hanging around. Eventually I made it into her bed, and all I wanted was to kiss those luscious lips and have sex with her to make it to number 60 on my 80 girls challenge. I pushed pretty far with her. She agreed to a naked massage but when my hand went down to her clean shaven pussy she was dry as a bone and didn't get turned on and wanted to stop.

She said her mind wasn't there because she had lost her job and had to move out in a few days.

I went home at eight in the morning and packed my bags to go to Washington for one night.

USA – Washington

I left a lot of stuff and souvenirs in the locker in my hostel room, dumped my bag in the storage and only took some necessities with me to Washington; it was time to shake hands with Obama.

I arrived at New York's giant bus station around noon and I knew it was already too late, but I had slept at the girl's house so I couldn't complain about it too much. Bus tickets are cheap if you buy them online but expensive if you have to buy a ticket at the counter on the day of departure. A four-hour ride cost thirty-six dollars.

The bus left and I used my laptop and the onboard Wi-Fi to kill some time.

In Washington I still had to walk quite far to the hostel.

It was getting dark and it was pointless to try and do some sightseeing, so I ate some pizza nearby. It was the largest slice of pizza I had ever seen in my life and I only paid

436

five dollars for it. No wonder lots of Americans are obese. The food is cheap and comes in giant portions. It was a struggle to eat all of it but I managed to do it – a full stomach will keep you sober at night.

I met up with a guy named Gmac, who like me has his own website about picking up girls. We went to a club named Marvin's that was quite full for a Monday night. We drank some beers at the bar. We talked about picking up girls and the dating scene in DC, which according to some people is the most horrible in America.

I was still tired from the wild weekend before and not in the mood to chase skirts again, but we gave it a go at another bar where I found out I'd lost my ID card. I had my small driver's license card in my back pocket for almost a year now and I couldn't believe I lost it three nights before heading home. The Dutch government really fucks you over when you apply for a new one. Charging about $110. At that time I thought it would be around sixty and even that pissed me off.

Gmac and I went back to Marvin's, that by now was filled with about 90% black people. I saw three girls in the corner and pointed them out to Gmac, who said it would be hard because they looked occupied with talking. I called bullshit and walked right in there and introduced myself. Those girls were all Ethiopian, and in my mind I was already waving my first African flag. The girl I talked to seemed hesitant and gave me a bitch test, the shoulder turn and whatnot. I had nothing to lose and just kept talking.

Gmac joined us and talked to one of the other girls. It looked like he had a rough time with them. I focused on the sexy girl I was talking to, who now started smiling a bit and told me she lived in New York.

We exchanged phone numbers. When I looked around I couldn't see Gmac anywhere, and the girls went home a few minutes later.

The room we were standing in got cleared and I moved to the other room, looking for Gmac. But he had just disappeared on me. He later told me he had to work early the next morning, but I still found it weird that he didn't even said goodbye. Maybe he was afraid of cock-blocking me.

I walked back from U Street to my hostel and went to sleep at four in the morning. My roomie asked me a million questions about girls that night. The only advice you really need is to be persistent to score with girls. Never give up!

Three hours later I woke up, took a shower and checked out. I had bought an online bus ticket for half-price and had to leave around 13:00. That gave me about four hours to see all the major sites in Washington. I started walking fast and went all the way to the White House, and from there to all the other monuments.

Half of them were under construction, which was disappointing. I had seen the major sights but could only take pictures of the White House from a great distance, and there were way too many trees in the park to get a good clear shot.

The Lincoln Memorial reflecting pools were under construction and completely empty. The National Mall was also being worked on, so I really have the feeling I should return here someday.

I hurried back to the bus station and got the bus back to New York.

My last days in the Big Apple I focused more on sightseeing than on girls. I still had so much to see and I was walking my feet into bloody stumps those last days. I visited the café from the *Seinfeld* series and had a coffee there. *Seinfeld* is my second favorite comedy, my favorite one is still *Married with Children*, the humor is unmatched and something like that won't return with all those feminist groups nowadays.

I went to Columbia University and the riverside park close to it. Some scenes from one of my favorite cult movies, *The Warriors*, were shot there. I also visited a few other locations from that movie but couldn't find the time to visit Coney Island too.

I bought gifts at FAO Schwarz, one of the biggest toy stores in the world. They were for my nephew, whom I had not seen for nearly three years and barely knew because I left home when he was one year old. Of course the Empire State building was on my list and the views were astonishing.

I was nearly walking on my gums but still went out on my last night. I just kept walking on 2nd avenue until I found an open bar and could drink some beers.

The Ethiopian, the Belarusian and the Jamaican girl had all flaked on me in those days. It was too bad because those flags are all quite rare, but quite frankly I couldn't give a damn any more. The only thing that mattered to me was going home now and to see my family and friends again.

It was time for my final destination:

Home!

Epilogue: And then you get home

Well, that was that.

There's not too much to tell about afterwards. I got back to the comforts of home in the First World, and it was great – to an extent. Of course it was great seeing my family and friends again. But in some ways it was weirdly boring, too.

You get used to moving to a different city every few days, and meeting new people all the time.

I'm getting my life back together. It took a little longer than I expected, but that's how the world goes. As you can imagine (having read it!), this book took up a lot of my time.

To the outside observer, it might look as though my three years abroad didn't do much for me. My hair's longer, but aside from that it's not as though spending all my money on wandering the earth did much for me in terms of so-called "real life". Some might say I'm as much of a bum back home as I was on the road, with less excuse. Some might say I'm right back where I started. Some would argue I'm worse off.

Every last one of them is wrong.

I became myself on my trip. I am not who I was. I stand tall. I don't look at the ground, and I have no fear. There's nothing Holland or the world can throw at me I haven't faced up to and bested.

And obviously, my problematic relation with girls has somewhat changed since then.

What did I learn? A great deal. A lot about the world, and a lot about myself.

And also, of course, a lot about girls. Which is the wisdom I will now pass on to you.

Tips and tricks:

Seducing girls

At home and abroad

Style and fashion

You can convey your identity through your style. You want to give off the right vibe: that you are a fun, adventurous and interesting guy.

- Don't be an embarrassment to be seen with. Remember that girls in a club spent a lot of time to look good before they went out, so if you want to approach them wearing your khaki zip-off pants which doubles as raining trousers and a Che Guevara t–shirt, don't be surprised if they don't give give you the light of day.

- Pack a pair of black club shoes, preferably ones that are easy to clean and don't take up too much space in your bag or suitcase. Do not underestimate the importance of having a good pair of shoes. Women always look at your shoes and judge you by them. Wear some clean shiny dark shoes.

- Wear a hip button-down shirt and jeans and at least one interesting bracelet or necklace. Don't wear a t-shirt underneath your shirt and don't tuck it into your jeans. Be careful about wearing an expensive watch. I didn't have a watch my whole trip.

- Work out and look fit. The more you look like an Olympic sprinter the more girls will be attracted to you. I know this sounds weird coming from a guy who smokes, drinks and loves fast food, but I'm the type of guy who gains a maximum of 8 pounds no matter how much unhealthy crap

I eat and still look in reasonable shape. If you are fat, do something about it. Girls saying they are not attracted to a body like Brad Pitt in *Fight Club* are lying as much as guys saying they are not attracted to big tits and round asses. I'm hitting the gym hard now and I'm in great shape btw.

- Backpackers have a bad name for being "dirty", so be and look clean and fresh. That means shaving and grooming. No disgusting "on the road" beards or smelly dreadlocks. It might work sometimes but in general girls are very turned off by this.

- You can't make eye contact or have a flirty conversation with sun glasses on so throw them away. Eyes are half the attraction in your face, don't hide them.

- It's important to always look your best. Especially when staying in hostels. There are new girls in hostels or guesthouses everyday. So if you walk out of the dorm in your striped pajamas while some hot Norwegian girls walk in, you are definitely making the wrong impression.

- Having some chewing gum doesn't hurt your chances either. Especially if you're a smoker.

- If you smoke, remember that it's an advantage for picking up girls because it's easier to make contact with another smoker. I wouldn't start smoking just to pick up girls though. It's still a bad habit.

But above all: having good game trumps having good looks. If you still don't believe this, then look at pictures of Style and Mystery, who are not handsome men by any means and took the rock star look way over the top, but got laid a lot anyway. They looked more like a couple of glam rockers from the mid-seventies, but it didn't matter.

On the other hand, don't believe all those PUA marketers claiming that can turn even an obese, World of Warcraft playing nerd who looks like he got shot in the face with a sawed off shotgun into a Playboy model-slaying womanizer.

442

Game will only get you so far. You need a hell of a lot more than good game to score that kind of girl. In general, having reasonable looks and great style and game can land you girls that are two points higher than you on the 1 to 10 attractiveness scale.

If you are a 5 yourself, then a 7 will be the maximum you can reach. 6 = 8, etc, etc.

Alpha behavior

This is not something you can learn overnight but you can fake it overnight. Fake it till you make it and one day you will notice that you're not even faking it anymore. You will have grown into this personality through all the new things you have experienced and the personal growth you have gone through.

Don't try to turn your alpha-ness on when you're going to a club or bar and turn it off for the rest of the day. It will not work and girls will see through it. And why would you? Don't you want to be a confident man when you're around your friends, colleagues, strangers or family? This goes so much further than only scoring girls. It will improve every facet of your life. So start being alpha as soon as you put away this book and remember to fake it till you make it. The moment of becoming a natural alpha will come very quick if you practice it 16 waking hours a day.

Being alpha and having great inner game are undeniably connected to each other. There are no alphas whose inner game sucks. They are real and confident men. This is one of the things that attract girls the most, more than good looks and money. It's also an integral part of having good pick-up skills.

Let's start with being alpha. The simple fact that you have a dick does **not** make you a man if you don't behave like one. 90% of guys nowadays display beta behavior, which is due to social conditioning. No one taught us to be men. Our parents were beaten senseless by the feminist revolution in the 70s and have nothing to teach us. Almost everything you see on television or read in magazines is aimed at making you a beta nice guy. Most girls live in a fairytale world of soap opera and old reruns of *Sex in the City*. The problem is that men are getting brainwashed to act in the same way as girls. But here's the truth: that lovable loser in the movies who always gets the girl in the end would be alone in real life. Alone!! Adam Sandler and Ben Stiller are good examples of beta males in almost all of their movies. Watch their movies and see why, even if they are funny.

After childhood there are real winners and losers in life.

Which side are you on?

Characteristics of an Alpha male

- Always take up a lot of space. Beta-males always shrink up as if they were apologizing for their own personal waste of space. Put your feet at shoulder width and stand up straight. Keep your chin up. Look people in the eyes when speaking.

- Talk loudly, but not obnoxiously loud.

- Resist the fear that you will piss people off. Be willing to take the lead and end the conversation when you want to.
  Be willing to be distracted when someone is talking to you.

- Confidence: This is simply freedom from self-doubt, and having strong beliefs in your own actions, words and abilities.

- Don't EVER act apologetic. It's OK to clarify something but don't feel the need to explain your actions all the time.

- Be calmer than everyone around you. Stress (talking about it or showing it) is an indicator of beta-male status. Be unaffected by what others are affected by. Heat, cold, stress, being tired, getting lost etc etc

- Time with you is valuable and rare. Don't let other people waste your time when you could be doing things that benefit your own well being.

- Don't make nervous movements or touch your face when speaking. (Touching your face is an indication of lying even if you're are not)

- Be talkative: say whatever is on your mind and don't worry about the consequences. Just be a talkative person.

- Be honest and direct 95% of the time. This will earn you all kinds of respect points.

- A good player **also** knows how to tell a little lie every now and then. Don't tell bullshit stories people can easily see through but it doesn't hurt to lie a bit when dating multiple girls in a short time span. Remember that you are a free man and not too serious with dating.

- Don't take crap from anyone and stand up for yourself. This doesn't mean you have to argue or fight with random guys or always have to have the last word.

- Don't go into endless arguments. You are giving too much value to the other person by trying to prove you're right. You'll win the battle but lose the war.

- Touch people when you talk to them. This is quite normal in many countries outside our feministic western world.

- Don't walk too fast. This is another behavior that is used to break your own frame. Slow down and relax.

- An Alpha is calm, confident and in control around any girl.

- Don't always respond when someone calls your name. When you do respond, turn your head to them slowly.

- Be dominant and in control. If you don't like the conversation...walk away. Start talking to someone else in the middle of the conversation if you feel like it. You are the alpha and you are in charge. Regardless of income, rank etc...you are the leader.

- Don't EVER put yourself down. Alpha males do not do this unless it is an OBVIOUS joke! It's okay to make a joke to convey the opposite of what you are saying in the joke. For example when you say you are a virgin.

- If you treat people like they are much cooler than you are, you are a beta-male.

- If you `put up' with disrespectful behavior, you are a beta-male.

- Taking risks and willing to make a mistake trying to achieve something is Alpha.

- Never stop someone from performing acts of generosity towards you, or be too thankful when they do.

Being Alpha is not being a selfish asshole so the question is:

What is **NOT** Alpha?

- Doing all the things listed above but with really bad body language.

- If everyone sees you are really trying to be Alpha then you're not doing it right.

- Being rude towards people who are friendly to you. Lots of miscommunication is due to language differences.

- Bullying people is not Alpha.

- Starting fights is not Alpha.

- Proving how much you can drink and falling down or slurring your words as result is not Alpha.

- Throwing money around while others take advantage of you is not Alpha.

- Having a big dick makes you fortunate. It doesn't make you an instant Alpha. Knowing how to attract and bang women does.

- Having lots of tattoos or looking like a criminal does not make you alpha. Most guys use tattoos to hide the insecurity. It's ok to have them but don't use them as a crutch to look tough.

- Being arrogant is not Alpha

- Cursing a lot to emphasize your words is not Alpha

"I live for myself and I answer to nobody"

Steve McQueen

Inner game

Are you a shy introvert or an outgoing extrovert? If you are a natural introvert like me then you probably hate the idea of walking up to strangers, even if they are guys. You don't like to ask directions because it makes you feel dumb. You don't like calling strangers on the phone. You have a bad time getting into the "party" mode at places where you don't know anyone. You feel self-conscious in large crowds. You don't like to get public attention and you cringe at the mere thought of walking up to two girls in a club, tapping them on the shoulder and starting to talk to them. And oh my god, you don't even speak the local language. I used to be that guy.

Inner game is the most important part of gaming. This is how you feel inside and you react to others, in particularly girls. If your inner game is weak, then you will have trouble approaching girls and staying strong during conversation and escalating.

The first thing you must accomplish to have strong inner game is to be totally unreactive. Whatever shit is happening during your travels, no matter how the girl reacts to you: it doesn't hurt you. It's like having a force field around you. Nothing can penetrate your protective force field. Every time a girl gives you a funny look, every time a girl puts you down or turns her back on you, even if she laughs in your face, you must stay unreactive, like the insults bounce right off you. This is very, very hard to learn and it will not take a few days or a few weeks. It will take relentless struggling and persistent going out to bars on your own. Yes you read it correct, on your   own!!

There are two unconventional ways of getting rid of the thoughts that are holding you back from the goodies.

1 Turning to the Dark Side

Be very arrogant and think (don't say it) like *this* every time a girl rejects you: "Who the fuck are you to judge me? What do you have to offer besides a pretty face and a surprisingly average fuck most of the time?" Most of the girls that rejected you have never left their own country or even own a passport. I'm Neil Skywalker, who already fucked more girls of different nationalities than most guys in the whole world. And this girl tries to disrespect me? Fuck you, Bitch.

You'll want to be careful about turning to the Dark Side. Using this mindset too often will eventually turn you into a woman-hater. Don't do that. It's whiny.

2 The right way

When a girl gives you a funny or dumb reaction and walks away, just give them a playful smirk and shrug your shoulders. After a while I noticed that when I stayed a bit longer in the conversation girls would open up to me more. I started playing dumb.

The girls will shit-test you hard to see what kind of a man you are. They might give you a bitchy comment or straight up say that they have a boyfriend. I used to just say, "Oh, OK, bye then", but later on I just stood my ground and kept talking. The more I talked the more they opened up and found out that I'm not like the rest of the guys around. Girls will test you for anything: how much money you are willing to spend on them? Are you a needy guy? Do you stand up to her? What do you have to offer her in terms of fun and excitement? Of course you don't have to take this playing dumb to an extreme. If it's very clear that the girl can't stand you then you have to eject out of this situation, because it will make you look bad to other girls in your proximity.

I rarely leave within 30 seconds, and just fire some questions at her.

Focus on the strong points in your character and people will barely notice the flaws. Don't talk about your weak points or things you fear. Build up suspense by keeping your mouth shut from time to time. Having strong inner game and confidence is also about not fearing and even not caring about failure with women or any other things in life you are experiencing.

Think of all the things you see a "nice guy" do in the movies and do

448

the exact opposite, and you will see that you have improved tenfold with all the girls you will ever meet in your life. Romantic movies are the biggest pile of brainwashing crap you can find, so stop watching them as of now. This is the way feministic cat ladies want to see a man.

All the advice and techniques are mostly interchangeable between different situations. It is not restricted to one part of the seduction game. Some things work better in a certain situation than others. Some tips or tricks are more appropriate for clubs and some are better used on a date. I'm not going sum up whole scientific theories on what works or not. Just follow my lead and you will get laid using this. Anyone who claims this stuff doesn't work for him can email me for advice.

Approach Anxiety

An Alpha has great inner game and has no fear of rejection. But even if you still have most Alpha treats under control, in my experience approach anxiety can still scare the shit out of you. It is one of the worst things that can happen to you. You completely freeze up and can't think straight anymore. Thoughts rage through your head and suddenly you can't find words anymore. All of your toughness and self-esteem seem to disappear faster than a chocolate bar in a depressed fat girl. You start to make every possible excuse not to approach. The longer you delay an approach, the harder it will be.

Trust me, I've been there, over and over again.

I've learned that none of my worst fears would come true when meeting a new girl. I've met hundreds of women, maybe even a thousand girls over the last few years – and none (NONE!) have reacted or caused anything to happen that I couldn't handle in the moment.

What if she says something that makes me feel bad about myself?

• This is impossible since you are protected by your force field. No insult can penetrate that and lower your self-esteem. If this is really bothering you, turn to the dark side for a while.

What if she has a boyfriend who wants to beat me up?

• This never happened to me and it's very unlikely. If so, the guy will not start punching you straight away. Finish up talking, say goodbye and walk away with your head up high.

What if I don't have anything to talk about?

• Learn how to tease and how to small talk. Read books or something about the local culture you can ask her about.

What if she thinks I'm a total loser and ignores me?

• Tap her on the shoulder again and keep talking, play dumb, engage her friends. If after half a minute the vibe is still against you, shrug your shoulders and leave.

What if she makes fun of me in front of everyone?

• This almost never happens and is just meaningless fear. Make fun of her when it does happen and most of the times she takes a liking to you for standing up to her. If you can't turn the situation around leave, but not before you make fun of her.

What if she pretends not to hear me?

• Speak loud and this will not happen.

What if she doesn't speak English?

• Most girls feel more insecure about this than you and might brush you off to avoid their own embarrassment. If you know some of the local language, be a man and try anyway. You have nothing to loose and everything to gain.

Rejection is better than regret. Do you remember all the times you came back from a club and regretted that you didn't approach that one girl that even smiled at you a bit? I do!

All those times you're back in your bed and swear at yourself for being a pussy and for being scared of a short girl in a club. You say to yourself: what the hell is wrong with me? Why do I not just walk up to a girl and start talking? I'm a great guy with lots of things going for myself. This is why it is way better to be rejected (which really doesn't happen that much) than to live with your own anger and shame.

Keep in mind that not every girl is interested in meeting someone. Some have boyfriends, some are cold, some are shy, some have problems and are not interested in <u>any</u> guy, not even a handsome rich stud. Some are afraid of being with a foreigner because of all the cultural differences. Some are afraid of being seen as a club slut. Sometimes girls just wanna have fun. Just like the Cyndi Lauper song. Yes, you might even run into some lesbian girls.

And all the time you thought that every girl rejects YOU and you take this personally while she is just rejecting the thought of being with someone at that moment. Every time you go out, you have some approach anxiety to conquer, and how long this will take depends on how your overall vibe is. If you didn't talk to anyone the whole day then it is harder to get your social motor running.

So, you had a shit night out?

You couldn't get any approaches to stick. The girls looked at you funny after you delivered your opener. You were blown off time after time. You're thinking *"What the fuck? I'm a fucking player. I read Skywalkers book! Why is nothing happening tonight?*

Don't worry; this will happen from time to time. If you think you can get laid EVERY time you go out just by reading a book then you are dead wrong. You have to put in hours of struggling outside your comfort zone. This is not easy and you will have setbacks and even approach anxiety will show its ugly face every once in a while.

Do not let this destroy your willpower. Get back into the trenches and keep approaching. Those who keep coming back in the face of failure will ultimately succeed. Draw power from your former successes and keep making mental notes of your accomplishments.

I was so persistent in going out even when I totally didn't feel like it that it felt I was doing a job instead of having a fun night out. People laughed at me when they heard me say: "OK, time to go to work". But I was the one who laughed when I happily put my hands on yet another big round booty and had a passionate make-out with a girl ten years younger than me.

Approach anxiety is greatly reduced with lots of practice and the knowledge that you have a solid strategy. Realize that in most cases you will <u>never ever</u> see the people again when you are travelling.

Go out on the last night of your stay and be prepared to make a fool of yourself sometimes. As soon as you walk out the club you might feel down if everything fails, but this feeling will disappear when you realize that you just walked up to ten or twelve girls and started talking to them.

At least you did something to improve yourself instead of sitting at a hostel drinking with some dudes who are too scared to do what you did and drink their excuses away. Don't leave the club or bar before you've done 10 approaches. Trust me, you will return home a changed man.

Do or do not, there is no try

Master Yoda

Approaching in clubs

I will write about going out alone. It is the hardest form of picking up and it's where the men are separated from the boys. You need strong inner game to pull this off. One of the biggest advantages of going out alone is that you always have someone to go out with. Just look in the mirror and there he is! Your best friend and sometimes your worst enemy.

Going out with hostel crowds or with one or two guys can be fun and I won't really advise against it, but you have to realize that your group sometimes wants to go to several places and wants to leave just when you are talking to a hottie. The group can have people who will cock-block you or stupid people who will embarrass you.

If you go with a group then make sure you know how to find your way home in case you need to ditch them. (Taking a picture of the street name or landmark where you are staying is a good thing to do, especially in places where it's hard to find your way back)
Have money in your pocket for the way back.

Going with just one or two guys can also be fun but you run the same risk as with a group. The guy(s) you are going out with can actively or passively cock-block you.
You will not know how they respond to girls if you don't know them really well, which in the case of a travelling life is almost always the case. Guys can act stupid by bragging, shouting, excessive

452

drinking, telling stupid jokes, breaking into your conversation, acting creepy, needy, aggressive or being overly shy around girls – and that's just the passive cock blocking!

Guys can actively cock-block you by talking you down behind your back or in front of you, trying to pull you out of a conversation, refusing to move around in the club, forcing drinks on you that you don't want, physically obstructing your view and options to touch or openly trying to hit on the girls you opened.

Maybe he speaks the same language as the girl and makes a fool of you. Maybe the guy who was a funny guy back in the hostel turns into a violent guy once he'd too much to drink and starts picking fights. Maybe you have the option to go to a girl's house and your "friend" is acting up and ruining your chances. It's amazing how some guys can travel around but suddenly can't find the way home without your help. I have witnessed all of these behaviors first-hand. You should only go out with guys you trust and know won't cock-block you. Tell the one you are going out with that there is a chance that he has to go home by himself. The ideal guy to go out with is a wingman with some knowledge of picking up girls.

A wingman knows what to do and is willing to keep the other girlfriends company/busy while you talk to your main target. I can't remember anyone who fit that description on my trip.
Another downside is that your inner game is less strong when going out with others. It's so easy to say "Fuck it, I'll just have some beer with my buddies" after being blown off by girls a few times.

Those were the downsides of going out with others. Now let's have a look at the downsides of going to a club alone.

- You will need <u>super strong</u> inner game to be willing to stand around in a club alone and approach girls left and right in an unknown city in an unknown country where you don't speak the language. The less exotic value you have the harder it will be.

- You will have no one to talk to inside or any social proof.

- It's less safe and you have to pay full fare for a taxi back and forth.

- It's hard to get into the right state to be open and talkative and the first approach will build up pressure. You have to be quick on the first approach to counter this feeling. It's good to do some warm up approaches to less attractive girls so you get out of that blocking headspace.

- It's hard to keep two or more girls occupied at once without a wing, and you might just end up with a phone number if she is not willing to part with her friends. Flirting and teasing with one girl and just talking with the other is a difficult thing to do but there's also no guarantee that your buddy will do this for you, so you might as well do it yourself. There's a big chance the girl will flake on you when you call or text her, which makes all your hard work useless.

A final tip is to make just minimal contact with local guys. It's OK to exchange a few words and a few laughs in and outside the club so that you can approach them later that night and make some small talk again but avoid becoming buddies with them. They will cock-block you later. If you are in third world countries where there aren't many foreigners around then young guys might idolize you and never leave you alone. Yes, this happens. They also might try to get free drinks from you since you are the "rich" foreigner. This happens a lot in the Philippines where its culture to share a big bottle with a whole group. Well. guess whose job it is to buy the bottle all the time?

The other end of the spectrum is that people may want to buy you drinks. Not a big problem, but you have to return the favor and this takes away some valuable time. The good thing is that you build up social value when you have people around you who seem to like you.

Goddammit, Skywalker! You make it sound super-hard! Why would I go through all this trouble?

This is why:

You will feel like a fucking superhero if you pull it off. People see you come in alone and approach girls. They will see you talk and have fun with a cute girl and leave with her. You just did something that even most popular local guys can't do. Picking up a hot girl or catching a new flag will give you a powerful and almost godlike feeling that can last for days. You have proved to yourself that you are able to pick up a girl in a strange country and sometimes even in a strange language without any ones help. This will give you all kinds of respect points with both men and women. Remember that all girls love a man who successful with other women.

Ok, so you finally amped yourself up to do the first approach. If you are still scared then walk towards her and touch her arm or tap on her shoulder. There's no way back and you'll have to talk. Even just a "Hey, how are you?" is acceptable. Girls get approached all the time and are comfortable with the situation.

If you smile at them they will often help you out and ask you something. Stand up straight and don't lean into her, that makes you look needy and too eager to talk to her. You don't want to know how many guys already shouted in her ear with beer on their breath. If you worry that she won't hear you over the loud music, just SPEAK FUCKING LOUD! She will definitely hear you and so do her friends who are dying to know what you are saying to their friend.

It's OK to lean in every once and a while or when things get flirty. If you can't hear what she is saying just nod your head a bit and try to get a bit closer. If you keep straight the girl will often come close to you and talk in your ear.
Standing up straight, shoulders back and at a 45-degree angle from your target girl gives you a confident posture. It's best to talk over your shoulder a bit. If you stand right in front of her in the first minutes she might feel limited in her personal space and even scared if you are a big guy. It's a biological build in fear to have no escape route from a possible attacker.

The best possible place to stand is wherever it looks like the girl is talking to you rather than the other way around. This will give you social value and pre-selection with other girls watching you. Position yourself so she has to walk away from you to get out of the conversation. She will lose social points, not you. Lean against the bar, a pillar or a wall so it looks like she is coming on to you. Spin her around, give her a wink and quickly steal her seat at the bar.

Don't circle around the venue looking like you're some kind of sexual predator or socially awkward guy. Girls will notice this and you lose value. You can either take a spot at the bar and stay put for a while and try to approach girls in your direct area or you can move around from one spot to another, but not too fast. Take at least 15 to 20 minutes at every spot. If you're with a friend it's ok to move around a bit. A lot also depends on the size of the venue and the number of bars and dance floors.

The opening line

Let me tell you the secret to getting laid. It's the king of opening lines. One opening line to rule them all. It will work wonders for you. I won't keep you waiting any longer. Are you ready? Here it is:

"Hey, how are you?" or "Hey, how you doing?"

Contrary to popular belief you don't have to come up with a perfect opening line or be a routine stacking freak. Just saying "Hey, how are you?" is enough. The girl will give you some answer and it's your job to give a (funny) reaction to it.

Remember that girls think emotionally, not logically. Say something along the lines of "Are you sure? You look a bit down/sad". You can say this even if she's already smiling. Girls don't want to be perceived as sad or bored, so they will start to qualify themselves to you. Take it from here.
"You look like you're the one having the most fun in here." (credit Roosh) Ask her why she is so happy, take it from there.

Girls who don't have much experience in either the English language or talking to foreigners might react in an insecure way and ask you simple questions like "where are you from?" or "what's your job?" and "how long are you staying here?" Now, these questions are sometimes but not always used for different purposes. Let me explain:

"Where are you from?" = Are you from a rich country? How much money do you have? Can I get free drinks from him? In what currency is this fool going to send me money if I play him right?

"What's your job?" = How smart are you? How much money do you have? Can I get free drinks from him?

The last one is more interesting. She asks how long you are staying. She is probably considering whether she will have a date with you and if she is willing to invest time in you. She might not be comfortable with a one-night stand and is thinking about a date with you first to get to know you better.

If she asks "Where are you staying?" she might be thinking of having sex with you and wants to know if you have a private place to do it.

Look closely for her reactions when you answer these questions.

Don't feel dumb if you stay in a hostel. Say this: "I stay in a hostel but sometimes I have a private room in a hotel if I want some privacy". She now knows that she has the possibility of having privacy with you. It also means that you are willing to pay for the hotel. This is important since most girls are tight with money, even if they   have   it.

I can't stress this enough: Just relax and go with the flow. There is no hurry, and if one girl rejects you or the conversation dies off, it's not the end of the world. Look for another girl to talk with and approach her, and the next one, and the next one. Getting numbers or same-night-lays is still a numbers game. How many numbers or approaches you need depends on how good your game is and the overall impression you make on the girl(s). Girls are not going to appear from thin air. You have to work for it – but the reward is worth the trouble.

A few Don'ts for club approaches

• Don't ever excuse yourself when opening a girl. It's a sign of weakness to be begging for her attention by saying Excuse me.....

• Don't get drunk. It's OK to drink and even OK to drink quite a lot but be sure to stay in the fun zone. The zone where you're funny and witty. Not the zone where you're loose on your feet and slur your words. Stick to beer.

• Don't open big groups of girls if you're alone. This is against most pick-up advice in other books, but those are mostly wishful thinking. Opening and keeping the attention of a large group in a high-energy environment is very difficult and often fails. Stick to two or three girls maximum. Always open a girl who is alone.

• Don't hold your glass up to your chest; leave it hanging to your side. Relax!

• Don't neglect her friends, they will cock-block severely if you ignore them.

• Don't continuously smile at your target. This looks very fake.

• Don't act nervous. Relax! Own the situation.

• Don't be afraid to touch her.

• The moment you suspect the hot girl wants to hook you up with her fugly girlfriend, that's the moment you politely say goodbye and leave. Don't think the hot girl will suddenly be attracted to you if you stay and be a nice guy to her fat friend. It's not going to happen! And you should send a signal to the hot one that standing you up for an ugly friend is not OK with a high-value guy like you.

Flirting signs

You should look for, and be aware of, indicators of interest, also called IOIs in pick-up language. These are things that women do when they become attracted to a man. There are dozens of small signs but these are the most obvious ones. From strong to weak:

Very strong indicators of interest
• She approaches you.

• She stays close to you and puts her hand on your chest while she talks with you. When this happens, kiss her! (A strong indicator that she is aroused)

• She touches herself in a flirtatious way when speaking with you.

• Strong eye contact while smiling at you.

• She'll be eager to introduce you to her friends.

• Her friends go somewhere – bathroom, bar, dance floor or outside and she stays talking to you.

• She calls you a player or a heartbreaker.

• She asks if you have a girlfriend, or she mentions your girlfriend to see what you say.

- She gives you a flirtatious nickname.

- She asks you to dance with her.

- She laughs at all of your jokes. Even the unfunny ones.

- She tries to get your attention when you talk to other girls.

Strong indicators of interest
- She reinitiates conversation when you stop talking.

- She compliments you a lot or compliments you on things of minor importance.

- She tries to keep the conversation going so that you don't leave.

- She teases you about something.

- She touches you.

- She gets physically closer to you. You may even get the feeling she is hovering around you.

- She's the first to ask your name or other personal questions about you.

- She plays with / tosses her hair or adjusts her clothes to look sexier.

Signs that the girl clearly <u>doesn't</u> like you.

- She will do the opposite of all things listed above.

- She will turn her back on you or faces someone else when you try to talk to her.

- She pretends she doesn't hear or understand you for an extended period of time.

- She will say she has a boyfriend straightaway.

- She never asks you anything or sighs and rolls her eyes when you ask her something.

- She looks bored and looks around if she can find other people to talk to.

- She never smiles at any of your jokes because she doesn't want to give off the wrong signal.

- She looks or reacts offended when you touch her.

- She avoids eye contact and keeps a distance between you.

The girl might be shit-testing you to see how strong and confident you are. It's best to keep ploughing for at least a minute before ejecting out of the approach

Teasing

These are "cocky/funny" lines that have to be delivered in exaggerated manner. None should come off as offensive; if they do, correct with "you're cute when you take things seriously".
Remember, the only purpose of these lines is to set the tone of the interaction. Timing and relevance will play a big role since you're really trying to squeeze them in without her noticing too much.

Great lines to tease a girl with.

- You and I are not gonna get along.

- Don't say anything, you're cute. You'll mess it all up.

- You're cool. You can help me pick up chicks.

- You're so cute when you don't know what you're talking about/what to say.

- I love it when you talk mean to me.

- Are you always this shy?

- You kiss your mother with those lips? (When she says bad words or curses)

460

- Your girlfriends would totally laugh at you now.

- You're so lucky I'm not your boyfriend.

- Which one of you girls would win in a fight?

- You guys remind me of the PowerPuff Girls.

- Careful girl, I'm a heartbreak waiting to happen.

- We need to find you a man!!

- You remind me of a bad hair day.

One of the most fun ways to create a flirtatious conversation is to set the frame that she is trying to get into your pants. If you do it in this playful way, she will know you that you are teasing her and will have fun and play along.

Some examples.
- You're hitting on the wrong guy; I'm totally not boyfriend material. That guy looks better for you. (Point to some dorky guy nearby)

- Stop undressing me with your eyes. I'm not a piece of meat damnit!

- You're such a player.

- Hey, I'm not that easy.

- Stop flirting with me.

- My mother warned me about girls like you.

When you learn to listen and you get a feel for what back and forth teasing is, you will realize that women give you all the material you can possibly need to tease them. Once you establish yourself as a flirt the woman treats you that way.

Physical teasing

• FACEPALM when she says or does something stupid, shake your head in disbelief. (Very powerful)

• Give her a high five. Sometimes you can pull your hand away so she misses.

• Say "OK, note to self: do NOT date this girl". (Write on your hand)

• Hold your index finger in front of her face and tell her to wait a second. Keep your finger in the air and talk to someone else until she realizes you are making fun of her and turn back. (Very funny technique)

• You can poke (gently) under her rib cage when she's not looking.

Pre-selection

This literally means what it says. You are being pre-selected by women. Have you ever noticed that when you walk around with a hot girl, you get so much more attention from other girls? But when you're alone and meet the same girls the next day they barely notice you.

If a girl sees you with another (hot) girl, she knows that you are not some anti-social, creepy or threatening guy and that you are capable of attracting and keeping other girls. The girl who is with you already selected you as a fun guy to hang out with.

Being used as a doormat by other girls is NOT pre–selection, so while it's still kinda okay to be in the friend zone you still have to joke around and possibly flirt with them. If the girls you are with are not visibly happy to be around you than no pre-selection has been made.

Pre-selection in real life:
• Have good looking girls around you in social situations like the street, a bar or club or anywhere.
• Greeting and kissing girls anywhere.
• When having an attractive girl with you, make sure you position yourself in a way that it looks like she is attracted to you.

Pre-selection in conversations
• See the article about DHVs
• Mentioning girls in your life in a nonchalant and not so obvious way. Be subtle with this, since a girl's bullshit radar is more fine-

tuned than you think.

When you try to pick up a girl and you sense that she likes to flirt with you but you feel you can't get her to put out, make her your friend. Completely reverse the situation on her and say "let's just be friends". Use her as a pawn when you go out and create pre-selection with other girls this way. The side effect and big advantage of this strategy is that you build good social skills and even might get the girl in the end anyway.

Jealousy

Girls live life on an emotional level and jealousy is one of the strongest emotions out there. Use this to your advantage. Pre-selection combined with jealousy makes seducing her a lot easier since she already sees that withholding sex from you doesn't work. She knows you have options and can get it from other girls than her. It also produces a time limit on her own actions, because she knows other girls will take the prize if she doesn't move fast enough.

Motivation

I guess I'm motivated by the hunt more than the actual pussy. I feel like a winner when I'm totally sweet-talking a girl and can game her into bed. The way she looks at you when you approach her, you see her thinking "Here comes another dude trying to pick me up", the surprise on her face when you actually have an interesting story to tell and you aren't the same as every other guy inside in the club.

I enjoy seeing other guys fail where I succeed. I feel fucking powerful when I see guys throwing money around, buying drinks or acting the tough guy but being shy with girls and I'm dancing with a hot girl and walk out of the club with her. Sometimes I parade her a few times through the club and past a group of guys who have seen me walk up to her and take her away or at least get a phone number, which for most of the average joes is already mind-boggling.

I think you should look at picking up girls more as a sport with winners and losers and not as the only way to get an orgasm besides fapping to late-night porn. Having a goal usually gives a strong motivation to get off your butt and take action. I had my goal to bang 80 girls around the world and score as many flags as possible.

Go out and start gaming.

No excuses.

Just do it

Date game and Conversational techniques

If you did well in a club, but not so well that you got laid the same night, then you should at least have scored a phone number.

Dating is the part of picking up I like the most and is the easiest part. You are alone with the girl. There are no loud distractions or cock-blocks around and you have all the time in the world to game her.

In a club it's much more about quick impressions and looks. Sometimes the girl in the club clearly likes you but her friends pull her away from you or you get majorly cock-blocked by someone else. That's why you shouldn't worry or feel bad if a girl rejects you in a club. She doesn't know anything about you. You can be the coolest person in the world but she didn't even take the time to get to know you. She only saw a snapshot of you.

On a date you can display a whole array of coolness and stories to eventually seduce her. Once I started doing (online) dates in South America I had a major increase in girls I either kissed, banged and/or flagged.

I started doing dates after already two years of travelling and pretty much conquered South America this way. I dare say that I at least kissed 80% of the girls whom I met online and I went out with. IThey came to meet a cool traveller and didn't expect anything else to happen. I just suckered them in.

I won't go into the whole texting thing because the rules are simple; you're not in that destination for a long time, so if you get a number from a club girl text her the next afternoon and forget about the two-day texting rule. Do remember the half-hour rule if she texts you but don't always do this because it's too annoying to have to wait for a text back.

Also, texting is different on different continents. I was bombarded with texts in South East Asia but flaked up a lot in South America. You get flaked on if the girl makes up excuses not to date you or doesn't text you back. If a girl doesn't show up on a date then it's a flake too. This is the worst one because it's a big time waster and fucks up your mojo. Don't worry too much, though, because you can't do much about it. Maybe the girl liked you in the club when she had a few drinks but changed her mind about you the next day. Maybe you kissed her in the club and now she's afraid to meet you on a date because she doesn't want to have sex. That depends on how strong you came on to her. Maybe her friends talked her out of the date. Maybe she gave you a phone number to get rid of you. Maybe she has a boyfriend. Maybe the moon needs to be aligned with the stars.

There can be many reasons for a girl to flake on you. The most important thing is to not care about it too much and move on. I have been flaked on quite a few times in South America. It's part of the game you're playing. If she flakes on you, don't confront her about it next time you see her. Are you the guy who sat around and got upset? Or are you the guy who called over another girl and then forgot all about it?

The following advice is for dating a girl, I mean after you got her phone number or online date. This won't work well in a club because clubs are too loud and too distracting. Clubs are for dancing and more direct game described in the other pick up advice.

You can have the looks of Brad Pitt or the dance moves of Justin Timberlake, but if you can't keep a conversation going with a girl, she will get bored very soon and bail or flake on you. Plain and simple.

So, OK. You got a date with a girl and you're going for a drink. Yes, a drink, not dinner. The first date(s) should always be a drink, not an expensive dinner. Trying to impress the girl with money is wrong and bad for your wallet anyway. Having to pay for expensive dinners and/or gifts/clothes or whatever before the bang is considered non game/pick-up and works only on gold diggers. Something I strongly advise against and will never do. A drink or two is relatively cheap and you can pick up the check without breaking the bank. Schedule your date in the afternoon or after dinner time, around 9:00 or 9:30pm

What do you talk about?

Most new conversations die quickly or contain moments of awkward silence. At some point you just stare at each other and come up with random dumb questions to keep things going. A conversation should be playful, flirty and fun. Your date has to remember how great it was talking to you, so she will agree to a second date or more spicy things. Girls look further ahead than you and want to meet an interesting person to show off to their friends. Depending on good looks or wealth alone is not enough to keep a girl interested in you – Although it sure helps if you have both of them.

If you know where you're going and can predict the time it will take to get there, then be there just on time for the date or five minutes late. Show her that her time isn't that important to you and that you're a busy guy. Never ever say you're sorry for being late or make up excuses. Be aware that girls in South America are notoriously late, so be ready to still have to wait even though you're late yourself. If she asks how long you were waiting for her, always say two minutes. Show up ten minutes late on your second date to show that she is not that important to you. Shrug your shoulders if she is upset and cut her off by telling some random bullshit. "OMG, today I just saw this …. Blablabla"

If in South America always kiss her on the cheek at arrival. No exceptions. Just walk towards her, smile and kiss her check while putting one hand on her shoulder.

One mistake almost all guys make is that they're sitting across the table from the girl. Never do this! Even if you don't know her so well, you're supposed to have a fun animated talk. You're not doing a business deal or applying for a job (or her love).
Sit next to her. The best way to do this is to keep talking while sitting down, so she won't notice it too much or just say that you don't like sitting far away from someone because it's impersonal. This works surprisingly well. She doesn't know you yet so she will accept this. Don't almost sit on her lap or move the chair right next to her, but stay within touching distance.

You should be able to touch her from a comfortable sitting position without having to stretch your arm or lean in heavily. This is important because you have to engage her in the conversation. You must be able to give her a poke, push her away when she playfully insults you and just touch her a lot so she notices that you mean business and you're not scared of touching her. You're a sexual guy, show it! Don't be afraid that you'll scare her by doing this or feel like some sort of perv. If you are giving her signals like this, you are doing it wrong. You can touch her arms, shoulders or poke in her side. Do not touch her hair or face and mess up her make-up, stay away from her legs and other exotic parts. Unless you know what you're doing.

Here's a list of things to talk about. I scraped it together from some gaming websites and came up with a few myself and have field-tested it extensively. Memorize them or make a note on your phone so you can take a peek every once in a while. There's no specific order, use them in whatever order you want. Use it as filler to close a conversation gap. Make her talk about her feelings but be careful not to show too much of your own. Don't be afraid to make fun of her and don't agree with everything she says. It's important to warm the conversation up before you start with these questions. You have to do about 90% of the talking in the first five or six minutes to warm the conversation up because she will hesitant to open up directly.

Many tips, tricks and techniques are interchangeable between club game and date game but I suggest you use the following questions only in a dating situation.

Twenty questions that will get her imagination going and quickly build rapport and comfort.

1. If you could lead someone else's life for a week, who would it be?

2. If you could have any job in the world with no chance of failure, what would you want to be? And don't say "Princess".

3. What would you do if you were the opposite sex for one day?

4. If you would be ruler of the world from now on, what would you change?

5. If you could have three wishes, what will they be?

6. If you win five million dollars in a lottery tomorrow, what would you do with the money?

7. If from tomorrow on, you had no fear of anything, what would you do?

468

8. Which day in your life would you want to do over again and would you change anything?

9. If someone invented a pill so you don't need to sleep anymore, what would you do at night?

10. If you could be the best at any skill, what would it be? (for example: singing, dancing, acting, sports, writing)

11. If you could travel in time, would you go backwards or forwards in time? And to what date would you go?

12. If you had no chance of failure, you can be anybody or anything in the world, how would you want your life to look?

13. What do you have going for you besides your good looks? Look around here, there are a lot of pretty girls, what sets you apart?

14. Would you call yourself a good girl or a bad girl? Why?

15. If you could choose a superpower, which one would it be?

16. Who do you think lies more? Man or women? And who is better at it? (Actually, women train men to lie, because every time they ask us if they look fat in a new dress or whatever, we HAVE to lie!)

17. If you could commit any crime, and get away with it, what would it be?

18. If there's one country you could go for a few months, which one would it be? Why ?

19. Would you like to be famous? In what way?

20. What has been your worst date ever? Why?

Use these questions and have fun with the answers. You will never seduce a girl with facts and logic so keep the conversation light and fun. Fun is the keyword: don't be too serious and don't go through the list as if you were interviewing her. It's an excellent way to find out anything about her personality and it shows you're not only interested in getting in her pants. Of course you and I are and this will help you get there. Don't be too shy or embarrassed to ask the deeper questions, but don't start off with them. I usually start with question nr 6. It's a fun way to fantasize about things or you can call her out as a shopaholic. Be prepared that she will ask you the same, so think of good answers to give for the whole list or the ones you choose to use.

Golden tip
No matter what you're talking about, always look for opportunities to talk about sex and love (but not relationships) Her willingness to talk about these subjects is a good indicator on how open she is for sex and how fast she is willing to escalate.

Use these questions a lot and you will see results quickly. My style is to have fun and make fun of the girl a lot. Be tough in certain subjects, be soft on others. I sometimes laugh if I hear myself talk unbelievable bullshit. Train yourself, practice makes perfect. You can ask these questions to anyone, so practice. You have nothing to do during the day? Ask the questions to some ugly girl in a hostel. Practice a fun vibe. When you make fun of a certain thing with your date you can use it as a recurring joke. One of her wishes (#5) is ridiculous? Make fun of it when you see her the next time.

These questions work best with educated women. I found out that girls who are not that educated or well-traveled have trouble answering most questions, so stick to the simple ones with them.

Be ready to get a surprised reaction when you start asking a question like those listed above. If she asks or shit-tests you by saying "Eh? what?" or just gives you a dumb look then throw it back at her and say something like: "Or I can just ask you a boring question like 'What's your favorite color' " and wait for her reaction.

Remember that girls do not expect dreamy subjects but secretly love them. I have received impatient looks from girls just waiting for me to ask another dreamy question (whilst knowing they are being gamed). Getting called out may happen, but I wouldn't think too much about it. I used to worry about the same thing until I realized that it never really happens and when it does happen, there's still no reason to worry about it. Just give a ridiculous reaction to it. Say something like "All right, you got me. I'm secretly doing research for Playboy magazine after photographing naked girls got too boring for me."

You don't care because players don't care and live in a world of abundance. There are cute girls everywhere. As a guy you get more interesting year by year. Girls get older year by year. If you are a

470

couch potato who never chases girls or does nothing interesting with his life, you will get old soon too. So, do something about it.

A few no-go areas
It's still possible to talk about these subjects but I would keep it to a minimum if you're inexperienced in picking up girls. Especially with foreign chicks who are not used to the western style of humor.

Weird sex: talking about sex is good, but don't try to impress her with knowledge about anything that's considered perverted by most people. Talking about a threesome should be the borderline. Do not ask about how many partners she's had or tell them about yours. If you are a cool guy, than she already knows you have (many) girls in your life.

Status or wealth: a cool guy doesn't openly flash cash or talks about how much his house/car/watch/clothes costs. It should be obvious to the girl already that you have money. If you're kind of broke, don't make a secret of it.

Violence: do not try to impress her by telling her about kicking some guy's ass or how people are scared of you. Don't make a scary impression on her either or act the opposite: a wimp. Again, it should be obvious that you're a man, not some wimpy guy.

Blood and gore: horror movies, things in the news that are shocking like rape or child abuse. Do not try to show the girl how much of a caring guy you are or how much you are offended by certain things.

Bad past relationships: come on, nobody wants to hear you whine about how you broke up or got your heart broken. Don't complain about past relationships either. No one likes a complainer and she will think you will do the same with her.

Politics: do not act like a green environmental guy or have strong opinions on immigration or human aid. Girls are softer on those subjects and don't think as logically or realistically as most guys (unless they're softies). A lot of foreign girls are not really up-to-date or, quite frankly, have a clue about what's going on outside their own   country.

Religion: always a touchy subject, avoid it or mention that you are not religious.

Racism and racial jokes should be obviously avoided or treated with caution.

Cursing: a cool guy doesn't need to curse to underline his words. It's a sign of weakness. Once or twice is OK but don't make it a habit.

And the most important one is: **don't** talk about things that are gross or sickening like dirty toilets, diseases, weird conditions or disgusting things about food like the time you ate a rotten egg or stepped on a cockroach with your bare feet and saw his guts coming out. This will put an image in her head picturing you in this situation. She has to be sure you won't tell a gross story when meeting her friends or family, so she won't be embarrassed by you. Remember that girls girls think emotional, not logical.

One mistake a lot of guys make is that they don't recognize the signals girls are giving them. You have eyes and ears, so use them. You have to watch her reaction and act upon it. If she's not comfortable talking about certain subjects then drop it and move on to something else. The right mindset is that you have to assume that the girl likes you and talk to her like she's an old friend you haven't seen in a while.

Be relaxed, you're not in real hurry and you won't die if she doesn't like you from the start. The most important thing you have to remember is that you're a fun guy with a fun life. The girl will put her guard up unless you are a fun guy to hang out with and you know how to build rapport with her. This goes for night-life gaming also.

472

DHV – Demonstration of Higher Value

Talking about the cool people, events or exciting stuff you know is a huge DHV for a lot of girls, since the hottest girls are very value-oriented, so the more value you or your life has, the more value you have to them.

Instead of telling several short DHV stories it is also possible to tell a major DHV story in which you display a lot of high-valued characteristics. It is important that it sound genuine and not over-the-top. Use a story that is party true so you don't mix up the details. I used something that is partly made up by old school PUA Style (the gypsy part) and something from my own experience. It may sound like utter bullshit to you because men have a logical and solution-focused brain but girls think on an emotional level. Don't try this with a cold-hearted, short-haired career businesswoman.

Example story:

Ask her: *"Do you believe in magic or spirituality?"*
She will either say yes or no but will probably ask why.

"Well, it's a long story but two years ago when I was travelling in Russia for a couple of months, I met a Russian girl in the train to …. It was love at first sight and we had a few amazing and very romantic days together. Unfortunately I had to leave the country since my visa had run out and I had no way of extending it.

She was a beautiful girl and I kept in touch when I continued travelling in Japan and South Korea. We emailed all the time and I was proud to have a Russian girlfriend who was a bikini model when she was a bit younger. My friends back home warned me about a possible scam but I had been at her place and knew she had a good job as an accountant.

We met again in China; she came to a small border town just across the Russian/Chinese border and I sat two days in the train to see her. We had a great weekend together but had to say goodbye again. We kept in touch again and she visited me in Thailand half-a-year later. She had saved up all her money to see me again.

We spend three weeks together, traveled across Thailand and had a heartbreaking goodbye after. I was almost ready to give my trip up and thought about living in Russia.

Six months later we met again in the Philippines and spent two weeks on a tropical island together. We had a great time but the love between us had dimmed down a bit. My strong feelings for her were not completely gone but it was just different. She was very disappointed and cried for months. We broke up but she still tried to convince me to see again in South America. I asked her not to come because I didn't want her to spend all her savings on me again."

So far this is all true. (I guess I'm a pretty cool guy after all.) What I didn't tell is all the banging of other girls I did. In real life I would add some more details to make the story more believable but you get the drift. From now on I start telling the fairytale:

"So here's the crazy thing. When I was travelling in Argentina I started dreaming about her at night. I had already had a Brazilian girlfriend but I kept seeing Julia in my mind. It was almost like a vision. The dreams felt real and I felt like I could almost touch her. I even felt her presence next to me when I woke up.

I developed strong feelings for her again. I didn't know what to do and decided to call her on Skype.

After some talking she admitted something to me. Well, I know it sounds really crazy but this is what she told me: she couldn't get me out of her mind and was determined to get me back. She took a bus to a very small village a few hours away from her city. She visited an old gypsy woman and the gypsy witch put a love attraction spell on me. This happened around the same time as I got the dreams. I must say I freaked out a bit when she told me this and asked her to stop it and break the spell. I don't want anyone to influence my mind, it was almost scary. It stopped a few days later and the dreams haven't returned since."

"What do you think? Can this be real or what happened?"

Almost all girls will take this seriously and talk about some spiritual thing that happened to her. This story builds some very high value. Girls will read between the lines and see what a great guy you are.
Let's see what she heard in this story:

I traveled alone in Russia for months, which means I'm adventurous. I picked up a beautiful Russian girl who was a bikini model before. We had romantic days together and she now knows I had sex with

474

her very shortly after meeting her. She can now figure out the romance and sex must have been really good because the Russian girl fell in love with me. She was so crazy about me that she spent all her money to see me again in unknown exotic destinations twice.

We emailed all the time, which means I keep in touch with girls I meet. She works as an accountant, aka she is intelligent. I was almost willing to give it all up for love. She cried for months after losing me. She desperately tried to see me again in South America and was willing to spend her money again. She went to a gypsy to put a spell on me.

These are all big-time DHVs and real value builders.

There are a few minor DHVs in the fictional part of the story. By now the girl you're telling the story to is thinking *My God, what kind of guy is this? He must be very special.* I know all you non-believers are thinking: "What a load of crap!" But this stuff really works if you know how to bring it.

The story she heard contains things all women love: an almost Hollywood-like love story, drama, mystery and lots and lots of pre-selection. It's almost like a soap opera. That's why stories like this work well in countries where soap operas play a major role in a girl's life, like in South America or South East Asia. The level of fairytale drama they endure in only half an hour of telenova soap is unbelievable. You can add more DHVs by adding extra details in between the story. In this case I could describe the things we did on the holiday, parts of my travelling, the old gypsy woman.

Even if the girl laughs at you and doesn't believe the gypsy part, she has still heard all these value-building things about you. Keep a straight face and shrug your shoulders. Just say: "I'm not sure what happened but I'm telling you the truth." Shrug your shoulders and try to change the subject. Never ever admit it wasn't true.

You can make your own DHV story. It can be anything as long as you add values like love, excitement, drama and pre-selection to it and don't make it sound too obvious you're telling a story where you highlight all the positive things. You need to convey that you are a sexual person. You should feel confident when talking about sex. Make sure you add an element that displays that you have limited time, so she is pressed for time if she wants to get with you.

Sit down and think of something in your life that you can spin into a DHV story. You can use the gypsy part of the story if you want and combine it with your own story. Write it down and practice your storytelling. It has to be something which is partly true and of which you can remember all the details. You can wake me up in the middle of the night and I can tell this story. That's because 90% of it is true.

If you are an excellent liar then make up a good DHV story that isn't true. If you're only in the city for a few days then you can tell the girl pretty much anything. Not something I do though.

Learn how to tell a good story with the right facial expressions, body movements and tone of voice. Speak slowly and you will not lose her attention. Use vivid language and words that are easy to understand. It's hard for people to create a mental image of your story if they don't understand what you're saying. Talk with passion and it doesn't matter anymore what the subject is. A passionate man is an attractive man. Even Adolf Hitler, possibly the most evil man on earth, had tons of female admirers.

Golden tip

Last but not least, a tip that will drive girls crazy and keep them re-approaching you in any setting. This should be done if you already know the girl for a bit (anything longer than 10 minutes of talking) and should be said in a flirty manner.

Me: "You know, there are 3 things I really like about you."

Girl: "Hmm, what are they, tell me!" (Already curious)

Me: "Well, the first thing I like about you is the way you smile/look/smell..." (Whatever)

Girl: "Oh, well thanks. What more?"

Me: "The second thing about you is the way you move/walk/talk/dance..." (Whatever)

Girl: "ah ok, what's the third thing?" (Or something similar)

Me: "well, it's just how you.... Nah, I can't say it. Maybe you get angry. Forget it..." (Put a big grin/smile on your face)

The girl will go mad all right. She might ask you to tell her 10 times. She's dying to know. She might walk away but she'll come back later and ask again. I've had girls call or text me in the middle of the night.

You can keep this up a long time and sometimes pull her into a date this way. If you have to say something eventually, make something a bit insulting or funny. Say something like: I just love how your nose

476

wiggles when you laugh.

This works in clubs but especially in places you visit more than once, like a bar or restaurant. It works well on bar maids and waitresses, receptionists, girls working in a store. It's easy to pull off and girls abroad don't know old-school tricks like this.

When a waitress walks past you in the bar or restaurants a few times, say this with a flirty smile:

Me: "Hey you again? You like being close to me/hanging out around me, do you?"
Girl: "Haha"
Me: (make some small talk and then say) "I think you will return soon, I can see it in your eyes."
Girl: "hahaha, blablabla…"
Me: (later) "See, you are back again. I knew you couldn't stay away."

If she likes the bit of flirting, when you're done eating/ drinking/ buying something say this:

Me: "You know what, you're a nice girl. I think I'm gonna call you later."
Girl: "You think so? But you don't have my number."
Me: "You're right." (take out your phone and hand it over to her, don't ask) "Put your number in there."

If she doesn't want to give you her number, say this:
Me: "Hmm, what? I can't hear you. Speak slower. So your number is 555…?"

A lot of times she will give you the number anyway but chances are higher on a flake.
The last two tips are also very doable in a club setting with a normal girl.

Another one for a waitress is:

Me: "You know what? You're a bad girlfriend. I can't remember the last time we kissed. You know what? It's over between us."

Or (this one works in a club too)
Me: "You know what? You are a bad girlfriend! I'm breaking up with you. Tomorrow I'm coming by your place to have break-up sex and

to get my CDs."
How to talk in third world countries

I can't stress it enough that you need to take your time to talk to a foreign girl. Unless she has very good English, you have to speak slowly and clearly. Use easy words and don't try to impress her with all kinds of logical facts and your grand intelligence.

They don't care for what they don't understand and it doesn't make a good impression when you make them feel stupid. Girls in Cambodia or any other South East Asian country cling strongly to their own culture. They watch Thai or Cambodian soap operas which are all drama all the time and are on every hour of the day. They don't watch American comedy shows, so they don't understand that kind of humor.

They can watch an episode of *Friends*, *Seinfeld* or whatever show you find funny and not smile once. They'll just take the remote control and put on *Tom and Jerry* cartoons and laugh their asses off. I noticed this all over Asia. She will not understand your fast English and witty comments with slang or English sayings.

Most of the time they aren't stupid at all but just don't understand you because of their limited English and cultural differences. This is even more important when you have a heavy regional accent. Ever heard a Scotsman talk at full speed? Yeah, that's why.

Your country's humor might not work and sarcasm, cynicism and irony might not be funny to them. The less educated she is, the simpler words you have to use, especially in third world countries. Emails and texts should be handled the same way. Always write your texts in full and stay away from abbreviations like *btw* (by the way) or *c u ltr* (see you later). Even things like *I'm* (I am), *we're* (we are) and *xxx* at the end of a text or email should be avoided. Her reply will be the question: *What means xxx?* If you do get this question, text this back: *I will show you the next time we meet.* Writing your emails and texts in full is vitally important because some girls will use Internet translation to find out what you are saying.

I use my version of the KISS technique. **K**eep **I**t **S**low and **S**imple.

Escalating for the bang

Now, I assume that most of my readers aren't virgins anymore and have some techniques of their own for this part. I'm just going to explain a few useable techniques that I've found to work in my case.

Escalating consists of these three parts: touching the girl, kissing and, in the end, going for the bang.

This is something guys fear because they can be rejected by the girl for touching or wanting to kiss. That's why you have to start with the touching first, to literally feel her out. It's the man's job to initiate the kiss and unless she is very turned on by you and makes the first move she will wait for you. If you are a nice beta dude, then this will be hard and can give escalation anxiety.

Touching
I aim to touch the girl as soon as possible. It breaks the touching barrier early in the conversation and gets her used to the fact that you are a touchy guy. Start with harmless touches to win her trust, like a shoulder touch or her arm. It's hugely important to **not** look at where you're touching and make it look as nonchalant as possible. She has to feel this isn't anything unusual for you.

It's best to look away when you touch a girl the first few times, for example if she says something funny or a bit insulting to you.

Touch her shoulder while looking at her friends and ask: "Is she always like this?" If there is no-one around, you can still make the same touch and look away while shaking your head in disbelief. Do not repeat the same thing twice in the same conversation. I'm quite rough with girls and will touch them quickly, sometimes giving them a hip bump or a shoulder push, saying "Sorry, I didn't see you there". Do this ONLY when you were already talking to her and she's flirted with you a bit. I make fun of girls a lot and they will touch, gently push or pull, just like I do with them.

The only way to get a natural feel for this is to do it a lot. Pull her hat or cap over her eyes while you're verbally teasing each other. Smile when you touch or look serious in a funny way. Do NOT look like you're really trying. That's just creepy. Make it seem natural to you. Practice on unattractive girls or girls you're just friends with if you want to see some of the reactions you get.

Do the spin-move described in the travel part. Girls love it. Just grab her hand and do it. Make sure you've already at least exchanged a few words together. Saying "Give me your hand" in a manly way also usually works. If she refuses or is afraid, grab the hand of her (fat) friend and spin her around, saying, "See, it's not so difficult".

Although it is possible to do this with a strange girl on the dance floor I advise against it. Girls get scared easily when you just grab them out of nowhere. At least exchange a few words or have extended eye contact first.

Touching techniques
• Feel her muscles if she says she works out or something like that.

• Grab her hand and look at her rings and make some comment about it (short diamond ring routine). you can do the same with a necklace.

• High-five or fist-bump her.

• Take her hand and read her palm. Hold her hand and slowly and gently touch her lines while proclaiming some bullshit like *Your fun line shows you are in for a good night*, etc etc. All girls love this and some even get giddy from the semi-erotic touching.

• Hook your arm in hers while you walk.

• Play fighting, ticking, poking her in her side.

• Hitting her with a pillow (inside the house).

• Gently pulling her hair.

• Slapping her ass (with a newspaper, towel, your hand, anything) is only for experienced players

• Say "What's that? Look there" and poke her boob with your finger when she looks away. This is the experienced level, so be careful.

• Walk behind her, crouch down a bit when she doesn't see it, grab her calves hard with one hand and make loud dog biting/barking sounds. She will jump up and scream in panic and will laugh hard afterwards. Only do this if you've known the girl for at least a short while.

• Last but not least: dancing!

Kissing

Sometimes I see guys wildly kissing a girl, slobbering all over her face and holding her tight. Such amateurs. That's no way to turn on a girl. Girls want to be kissed like they see in the movies. Slow and soft.

How to (first) kiss good:

Gently grab her by the back of her head with your right hand (fingers spread and woven into her hair), pull her towards you, and make the C-shaped stroke from her hair, behind the ear towards her chin with your left hand. Look her in the eyes and kiss slowly her on the lips. No pecking kisses and no tongue for at least the first 10 seconds.

Kiss slowly and gently bite and suck on her lips. This is the fastest way to make her panties wet. Always keep one hand free to touch her body while kissing her. Use your left hand to explore her body a bit. Stroking the side of her body and touching and squeezing her buns.
She might resist a few times or pull your hand away but if you're doing it right she will give in.

After a good ten seconds start using your tongue and kiss her neck and lick her earlobes a bit. Work your love making magic from here.

Girls will give you the head turn sometimes. This can be embarrassing but you have to persist and just try again a minute (or two) later. Unless she specifically says that she doesn't want to kiss and just wants to be friends, nothing is lost. If she persists in just being a friend, you have to be careful with using her for pre-selection. She might actually cockblock you if she sees you going for someone else later. If she head-turns on you but stays close, then she's still interested in you but you are moving a bit too fast. Try again later.

Going for the bang

I have described countless bangs in the travel part of this book and won't go into it too much. The best results come from first or second dates. I rarely went over the second date mark. As you can read for yourself, same night lays are quite possible, but it takes a certain kind of girl. Alcohol is almost certain to be involved in either small or very large amounts, so be sure you can stand your ground when you start drinking with a girl. Do not go head on with a Russian girl drinking Vodka, you will lose. I usually stick to beer but that's also because it's the cheapest drink. Booze loosens up a girl and takes away her anti-slut defenses.

Some pick-up artists say that they will only leave with the hottest girl in the club and get a same night lay out of it. Don't believe that crap. Not every girl is up for a same night lay; in my opinion, it's only girls who have done it before who will, and most of the time it will only happen if you're sending out strong alpha sexual vibes and the girl is clearly attracted to you. Don't think you'll talk a shy church girl into bed or that the girl you've fancied for a long time will suddenly end up with you because of your newfound pick-up skills.

There are two ways to escalate to the bang. One is to kiss her and make her horny; she'll know that you are going to want to have sex with her when you get to your room. You can almost always be certain that the bang is going to happen if she agrees to come back to your room after midnight. This usually works with girls who have done it before. I don't like the words "slut" or "whore" and almost never use them. These girls just have a strong sexual appetite, and there's nothing wrong with that. Where would you be if they didn't? I wouldn't marry them though.

The second option is to not kiss her beforehand. This requires some subtlety from you: you have to give all the signals that you do want to kiss her but that you're OK with postponing it for a short while. Some girls are not fond of public displays of affection, and in some cultures it is so looked down on that the girl will not even think about it. Accepting this will make a good impression.

In this situation it's wise to invite the girl to your room and give her the impression you're going to kiss her there. Some girls love this scenario because that's all they want, just kissing. If your escalation game is tight you can have sex with her anyway, but sometimes you need one more date.
Take her inside your room and make her feel at ease. Don't be in a hurry if she isn't but keep her busy and don't give her time to change her mind. Play some music. Talk a little bit and make sure you have some mixed drinks in your room. Don't be ashamed if you have a cheap-ass room. Don't even mention it and never apologize for it. Most girls don't really care about that if they're already into you. In poor countries they are not used to fancy rooms anyway.
Whether you have sex with her is up to her. Just make sure you bang her like there's no tomorrow if you want to see her again.

Whatever you do inside your room, have fun doing it.

Cheap travelling:
The Backpacking Casanova way

Accommodation

Accommodation is the number one cost of travelling. The more special or remote the city or village you're staying is, the more you pay. The language barrier is also a problem when you want to find a cheap place. Conning touts or taxi drivers will always take you to the place from which they receive the highest commission. The Lonely Planet is a reasonable guidebook, but as soon as those recommended guesthouses are in there, they starting charging a lot more. Booking a hostel online is not a bad idea either; most have pictures, prices and route descriptions on there. In the cheaper countries it's very possible to get a hotel room for 3 to 25 dollars. In more expensive countries, this will be 25 dollars and up.

How to save money on accommodation

- When staying in place of minor importance (transport hub, or place where there will be no girl chasing), swallow your pride and stay in the cheapest place possible. Nothing wrong with cold showers and squatter toilets. Man up!

- Couchsurfing: a free place to stay and most people will show you around and treat you as their guest. Never turn away from free food and drinks.

- Stay in cheap dorms and guesthouses, which are also a place to pick up chicks. Banging in a dorm room is not uncommon; just hang some sheets around your bed.

- Find a girl who will accommodate you. Spend money on her as long as it cheaper than getting your own place. Of course the girl herself is a bonus too.

- Bargain for a room. It's very possible with most guesthouses and hotels. No guts, no glory.

- Book a place for only one night and start walking and asking around for better and cheaper places.

- Share a double room with somebody, possibly a girl so you can have some nightly action too. Ask her if she wants to share a room for the costs, work your magic and end up using the other bed to lay your bag on.

Food and drinks

Food and drinks are the second most expensive part of travelling. Drinking especially can ruin your budget. In a lot of countries, going out means spending more on drinks than on food and accommodation put together. In some places food will also be costly simply because there are just no cheap restaurants around or you're sick of eating the same cheap food over and over. (For example: rice and noodles. They get boring pretty fast.)

How to save money on food and drinks

Food:

- Eat lots of street food. Your stomach will get used to it eventually, and going to more expensive places is no guarantee of not spending a day or two on the toilet. Stop washing your hands every 10 minutes and build up some tolerance.

- Eat the breakfast included at your hostel. It will be a shit breakfast, but hey, it's free. Personally I can't stand those toast-with-jam breakfasts and will eat out, but if you're really counting pennies this is one time not to imitate me.

- Cook for yourself if you are in more expensive countries. Again, this isn't what I do, but if you can it'll save you money. I almost never cook and will go to a fast food place or street market instead to get my belly filled. I'm lazy and don't know how.

- Never refuse when people you meet offer you food. It's rude and bad for your wallet.

- When dating girls in poor countries, you will be the one paying for everything (though exceptions apply). Bite the bullet on this one. You can't expect them to pay for their food and drinks when they make three dollars a day. It shows no respect if you ask them to split the bill and you will make a fool of yourself. Don't go overboard with this either; when a girl eats rice seven days a week and wants to go to a five-star restaurant with you, dump that gold digger. She has to like you, not your wallet.

- Find places with cheap food. Chinese restaurants are a good option. Buffets and places where you get free food are another.

- Take a girl out to McDonalds; just say you haven't had a Big Mac in months and you're craving it. If the girl really likes you, she won't mind.

- Go eat at a cheap local place and tell the girl you love her country and their tasty food; don't mention you've been eating rice in every possible form for the last year. Look excited when reading the menu.

Drinks:
- As said before: drinking can kill your budget faster than a speeding bullet. The best solution by far is to stop drinking alcohol. This is also the most boring and unsociable solution.

- Drink water instead of Coca Cola during the day; it's much cheaper, healthier and better for your teeth. Stay away from juices too; they're full of sugar and always pricy. And why drink coffee at a Starbucks when McDonalds sells it for a quarter of the price. A bottle of water and three candy bars or a bag of chips will get you through the day if you have a decent breakfast and know you can get a big meal in the evening.

- Find out when the happy hours are or get drinks for free.

- Drink in if you're the heavy drinking type. If you want to pick up girls, go out and drink moderately. No girl likes a slurring apeman.

- Do not go to expensive clubs with hefty entrance fees and 10-dollar drinks. It's no guarantee of anything. Clubs like that are frequently used by prostitutes or bitchy gold diggers who are not looking for broke backpackers.

- Don't drink out of boredom in trains, planes and busses. Find somebody to talk to and you might get some free drinks.

- And last but certainly not the least: Charm girls into buying you drinks.

Transportation:

Transportation is the last major reason why your wallet is always empty. The rule is that the slower you travel, the cheaper it gets. Unfortunately, we cannot teleport from one place to another so we have to take a bus, train or airplane to get there. You can live as cheap as you want, but if a ticket to some destination costs 50 dollars, you just have to bear with it.

How to save money on transportation.

- Hitchhiking is the cheapest way to get from A to B; I don't have much experience in it so far, so you'll want to find out someone else's advice on this.

- Local transport is always the cheapest paying option and most of the time the most fun as well. Ask locals where to find the bus station and how much they pay for a ticket if it's not posted. Avoid travel agents. The downside is that it may take a lot of time and sometimes have a lot of hassles.

- Bargain hard anywhere and anytime. Taxi and motorbike drivers are especially notorious for ripping you off. Walk off at the first sign of overpricing and most of the time the prices suddenly drop 50% or more.

- Walk around; you can easily do 4 or 5 kilometers an hour, and it's a great chance to meet people on the streets – and who knows how one thing can lead to another. You will not meet girls sitting in a taxicab.

- A bus is almost always cheaper than a train and a train is almost always cheaper than an airplane. Travel slow and save money. Read the stories and see how I met some girls on buses and trains.

- Plan ahead. Book airplanes online and as far ahead as possible. Use budget airlines and look for the hidden costs. Strange advice from a guy who almost always travels by the day or week, but I spent way too much money on this.

Does this all mean you can never stay in a fancy room, eat a descent and tasty meal, smash 50 dollars on drinks? Of course not; you're travelling to enjoy yourself and have a good time. And a good time is the reason you went away in the first place.

Just keep in mind that the more you spend the shorter your trip will be and the sooner you will be back at a boring job.

What to bring on your trip

Backpack:
- **A good durable backpack.** I bought a solid military backpack (Berghaus Vulcan 2) from a guy working in a military airbase nearby my hometown. It was brand new but I only paid 100 euros for it instead of the retail price of 270 Euro. I wonder why...

- **2 small padlocks for your backpack.** You can also use them for locking a hostel locker

- **A couple of karabiners,** multipurpose.

- **A hidden pocket,** to wear under your clothes. Not a money belt, those things are for chumps and are good only for a pair of sweaty balls. An experienced pickpocket can still take it from you.

- **First aid kit,** some bandages, tape and other stuff. Just buy a cheap set. You'll hardly use it. Buy some valium in a cheap country without prescription. And take whatever (vitamins) pills you need.

- **Cable with lock,** so you can lock your backpack to a (bunk) bed, steel pipe or something. There's hardly any control on who walks in and out of hostels and your room there. It would be easy to just grab a bag and walk out of there.

- **Some plastic bags** for your flip flops, clothes, laundry, shoes and stuff. Bring some solid ones

- **Sheet bag**, for times you're sleeping in disgusting places, dirty beds or when the guesthouse or hostel doesn't supply sheets, which happens a lot in poorer countries.

Clothing:
- **Jeans,** for going out or colder countries. Buy a normal pair, not one all cut up with holes. It might be normal back home but that does not mean it will be where you're going. Not to mention that the cut-up ones will wear out even faster.

- **Shorts.** Buy some cool fashionable shorts with some big side pockets, big enough to put a bottle of a book in.

- **A beanie**, for colder days or for looking cool.

- **Swim shorts**. Not shorter than knee-length, no speedos or other gay-looking stuff. Not that there's anything wrong with gays, but we're aiming for girls. Avoid the Borat look.

- **Several pairs of underwear.** You can buy cheap knock-offs in a lot of countries if you need to replace them. Buy tight, cool boxers, not Sponge Bob or other funny-looking undies. Nothing kills the mood faster than a girl bursting into hysterical laughter when you take your trousers down.

- **5 or 6 T-shirts.** Don't buy the same shirts everyone is wearing. I'm sick of those shirts and so are girls. Make sure you're not out of style but don't look like you're slavishly following fashion either. Personally I bought shirts with tough-looking Clint Eastwood, Charles Bronson cowboy prints and a few surfer brand shirts. Got nothing but compliments on it.

- **A pair of sneakers.** Nikes, Adidas, Puma; not with too many flashy colors, you're not in high school anymore. Great for hiking the city or outdoors.

- **2 pairs of flip flops,** one pair for outside and one pair for in the shower. You do *not* want to touch the shower floor in a hostel in a third-world country.

- **A pair of black dancing shoes,** to get into the clubs and not look like a backpacker bum.

- **A jacket,** for colder or rainy days. Don't bring rain clothing; you look dumb and that's why they invented umbrellas.

- **A good shirt** for going out to clubs. Buy a nice one, but nothing too flashy. No funny or crazy prints.

- **2 fluffy towels.** Don't buy those blue easy dry towels, they starting stinking after a while and aren't comfortable at all.

Toiletries:
- **A toiletries bag,** one you can hang on a hook or door. Many showers have no hooks or anything.

- **Toothbrush, shampoo, soap + soapbox.**

- **A razor, not a shaving machine. Man up!**

- **A comb, scissors**

- **Creams** and whatever stuff you need to keep you looking young, World travelling is tough.

- **A shitload of condoms.** Don't be an **idiot**! In fact you should have condoms in every pair of jeans, shorts and bag you have. Some girls have been around the block, no matter what they tell you. Never leave your room without a few rubbers.

Technology:
- **A laptop**. I can't travel without one, being a blogger and internet junkie. I have mixed feelings about it. After I bought the laptop, I did a lot less sightseeing and socializing. But it's damn handy to have one.

- **A laptop lock cable,** just lock it to your bed or something solid, so you can leave the room shortly or protect it from being stolen when you're passed out (or occupied) in bed.

- **A phone,** for texting and calling all the chicks you're going to meet. I have a phone with a qwerty keyboard. The keyboard is priceless. In countries like Indonesia and especially the Philippines you'll get 50 to 100 texts a day if you're a player.

- **A camera with video function**, for all the beautiful pictures you're going to take worldwide and naughty videos with girls. I have a Sony Cybershot. Don't be shy to send me your action shots.

- **A good pair of headphones.** You will spend countless hours on trains and buses, you need some quality headphones.

- **A world electricity converter plug.** Make sure it has every possible plug option.

Other Stuff
- **A cigarette lighter.** Anyone will do as long it looks normal. Don't use a Zippo, those things are for sailors and poseurs.

- **A passport.** Leaving aside the EU, you can't leave the country, or get into a new one, without one. Preferably a big one with extra pages. My business passport has 64 pages and most of them are full.

- **Money,** preferably in dollars or Euros. Don't bring travel cheques. Those things are worthless in a lot of countries. I never used them.

- **ATM card.** Check with your bank and make sure you can use it overseas; check the costs of use abroad.

- **Some bracelet and necklaces.** There's lots of cheap cool-looking local stuff you can buy anywhere you go.

- **A deck of cards,** for drinking games. Only play drinking games when there are girls around. Otherwise you're getting drunk for no reason.

- **A spork,** a spoon, fork and sometimes knife all in one.

- **A lot of passport photos,** you'll need them at border crossings and embassies a lot.

- **A bit of duct tape,** multipurpose

- **Tissues,** for toilet emergencies. Yes, you will have them too. It's best is to always carry a small pack anywhere you go.

- **Sun block and anti-mosquito stuff**

- **Earplugs,** for dorm rooms

Stuff I paid a lot for, never used and chucked out.
A flight bag, Travel hammock, walking shoes for mountains, walking sandals, drinking flask (the ones you see in the movies), travel alarm, mosquito net, T3 oil, camera holder, an eating bowl, clothing line (you can use floss for that), multitool, travel pillow, survival book, emergency blanket, Maglite flashlite, knife (actually got stolen), calculator, pepper and salt shaker, washing powder, can opener, electric razor, books and paperwork.

So there you have it, that's all you need. But the most important one is free: a big smile on your face!
You can also bring your own pots and pans, a sleeping bag and a tent and hike outside the city and find a place to camp while you cook your own food. I'm sure that there are lots of hot Latina chicks wearing a nice dress and high heels who want to join you in your tent and make hot love all night long.

In case you couldn't tell. That was a joke.

Conquering the language barrier

One of the major problems a travelling player or regular traveller has abroad is conquering the language barrier. Although the best way would be learning the language of the country you'll be in before you go, this is nearly impossible for most people. In my case, first of all I didn't have the time to learn a language for every country I visited, and second I didn't want to either.

So, here's my trick list to still have some fun with girls who only speak a few words of English or even girls who speak good English but who you want to surprise with some funny words. A lot of times some of these words will become nicknames or recurring jokes. You can use these words in any language, so translate them if necessary. It's best to ask a local for translation to make sure you get the right words. Sometimes the dictionaries don't get it right, or there are regional variations you're not aware of. You don't want to be the guy who uses "Baise" in France, thinking it means "kiss" when it actually means "fuck".

The trick is to actually pronounce the words very well so that you're not misunderstood. I asked some hot girls working in hotels or stores to translate the words for me into their language and that was already fun. Once they hear the words you want to translate you've already got pre-selection going, because these are the words a player would use. I had my friend Gustavo from Chile translate this list to Spanish and it works fine.
The word for "shorty", which in Spanish is: "Enana" (which literally means "dwarf girl") is golden. I'm a tall guy, 1.88 meters, so most girls are way shorter than me. I never used it without getting a big laugh out of it and girls punching me in the arm. From there you can transition to other words, saying she's aggressive or bossy or whatnot; use your imagination. My other friend Nico taught me the sentence "Te quiero dar un beso", which means "I want to kiss you".

I'll use my Indonesian list as an example because that's where I came up with this technique. In Asia, where the local guys are polite, this is dynamite. Go there and playfully insult your targets. Remember to say everything with a smile! I've added the Spanish translations too.

Remember that this is only a basic EXAMPLE list. The more you know of the actual language, the more you will enjoy your trip and the easier it will be to get laid in that country because it doesn't limit your chances to only English-speaking girls

Basic language knowledge for the traveling player

Words	Indonesian	Spanish
How are you?	Apa kabar ?	Cómo estas?
What is your name?	Namamu siapa?	Cómo te llama?
My name is _____	Nama saya _____	Me llamo _____
Thank you	terima kasih	gracias
No.	tidak	no
How much? (Price)	ini berapa?	cuánto cuesta?
Monkey	moyet	Mono / macaco
Liar	bohong	mentirosa (f)
Big	besar	grande
Small	kecil	pequeño
Girl	wanita	chica
Beautiful girl	wanita cantik	chica bonita
Bad girl	wanita jahat	chica mala
Naughty	nakal	chica mala
Love	cinta	amor
Good	bagus	bueno
Sweet (girl)	(wanita) manis	dulce
Crazy (girl)	(wanita) gila	(chica) loca
Lazy (girl)	(wanita) malas	(chica) floja
Shy (girl)	(wanita) malu	(chica) timida
Joke	bechanda	broma
Tiger look	kucing garong	-
i	aku	yo
You	kamu	tú
Drink	minum	trago
Shorty (short girl)	pendek	enana
Playboy	gila wanita	galán
Slut	gila lalaki	puta
Kiss	cium	beso
Dancing	manari	bailar
Big boss	boss besar	la jefa
I love you	aku cinta padamu	te amo (serious)
I like you	aku suka kamu	te quiero
Crazy Dutch	belanda gila	Holandés loco
Hug	berpelukan	abrazo
Kill	bunu	matar
Lips	bibier	labios
Ass	pantat	culo
Ugly	jelek	fea
Tickle	geli	cosquillas
Jealous	cemburu	celoso

Travel route and dates – Around the world in 80 girls

Location	Date	Location	Date
Netherlands	01-05-09	Kaohsiung, Taiwan	17-10-09
Berlin, Germany	02-05-09	Taipei, Taiwan	22-10-09
Warsaw, Poland	05-05-09	Ho Chi Minh, Vietnam	24-10-09
Vilnius, Lithuania	09-05-09	Nha Trang, Vietnam	27-10-09
Riga, Latvia	12-05-09	Da Lat, Vietnam	10-11-09
Tallinn, Estonia	16-05-09	Buon Thuot, Vietnam	12-11-09
Helsinki, Finland	20-05-09	Kon Tum, Vietnam	13-11-09
St-Petersburg, Russia	21-05-09	Ngoc Hoi, Vietnam	14-11-09
Moscow, Russia	26-05-09	Hoi An, Vietnam	15-11-09
Kazan, Russia	05-06-09	Hue, Vietnam	17-11-09
Yekaterinburg, Russia	13-06-09	Vinh, Vietnam	18-11-09
Astana, Kazakhstan	15-06-09	Hanoi, Vietnam	19-11-09
Almaty, Kazakhstan	22-06-09	Bangkok, Thailand	04-12-09
Novosibirsk, Russia	02-07-09	Pattaya, Thailand	07-12-09
Irkutsk, Russia	03-07-09	Bangkok, Thailand	11-12-09
Listvyanka, Russia	03-07-09	Surat Thani, Thailand	12-12-09
Ulan-Ude, Russia	04-07-09	Ko Samui, Thailand	12-12-09
Naushki, Russia	05-07-09	Phuket, Thailand	20-12-09
Ulaanbaatar, Mongolia	06-07-09	Bangkok, Thailand	26-12-09
Ulan-Ude, Russia	13-07-09	Arany Prathet, Thailand	02-01-10
Chita, Russia	15-07-09	Siem Reap, Cambodia	02-01-10
Khabarovsk, Russia	22-07-09	Sihanoukville, Cambodia	06-01-10
Vladivostok, Russia	26-07-09	Phnom Penh, Cambodia	14-01-10
Niigata, Japan	30-07-09	Don Deth, Laos	02-02-10
Tokyo, Japan	31-07-09	Pakse, Laos	06-02-10
Kyoto, Japan	11-08-09	Vientiane, Laos	07-02-10
Nara, Japan	12-08-09	Vang Vieng, Laos	12-02-10
Kobe, Japan	13-08-09	Nong Khai, Thailand	21-02-10
Kyoto, Japan	13-08-09	Bangkok, Thailand	22-02-10
Hiroshima, Japan	14-08-09	Phnom Penh, Cambodia	28-02-10
Fukuoka, Japan	15-08-09	Sihanoukville, Cambodia	10-03-10
Nagasaki, Japan	16-08-09	Phnom Penh, Cambodia	18-03-10
Busan, South-Korea	17-08-09	Battambang, Cambodia	24-03-10
Seoul, South-Korea	22-08-09	Bangkok, Thailand	28-03-10
Beijing, China	03-09-09	yangon, Myanmar	02-04-10
Harbin, China	10-09-09	Bagan, Myanmar	05-04-10
Suifenhe, China	11-09-09	yangon, Myanmar	08-04-10
Harbin, China	14-09-09	Bangkok, Thailand	12-04-10
Dalian, China	17-09-09	Koh Lanta, Thailand	16-04-10
Beijing, China	21-09-09	Ko Phi Phi, Thailand	18-04-10
Xian, China	23-09-09	Krabi, Thailand	23-04-10
Shanghai, China	27-09-09	Langkawi, Malaysia	24-04-10
Hong Kong, China	02-10-09	Kota Bahru, Malaysia	02-05-10
Macau, China	07-10-09	Pulau Perhentian, Malaysia	03-05-10
Taipei, Taiwan	09-10-09	Jertih, Malaysia	14-05-10
Tianchiang, Taiwan	14-10-09	Kuala Lumpur, Malaysia	15-05-10
Ken Ting, Taiwan	16-10-09	Manila, Philippines	19-05-10

Location	Date	Location	Date
Banaue, Philippines	01-06-10	Paihia, New Zealand	05-03-11
Manila, Philippines	04-06-10	Auckland, New Zealand	10-03-11
Cebu, Philippines	04-06-10	Turangi, New Zealand	16-03-11
Boracay, Philippines	07-06-10	Auckland, New Zealand	19-03-11
Cebu, Philippines	20-06-10	Buenos Aires, Argentina	24-03-11
P Princessa, Philippines	27-06-10	P de Iguazu, Argentina	05-04-11
El Nido, Philippines	05-07-10	Foz de Iguacu, Brazil	09-04-11
P Princessa, Philippines	11-07-10	Ciudad de Este, Paraguay	09-04-11
Cebu, Philippines	13-07-10	P de Iguazu, Argentina	10-04-11
Tagbilaran, Philippines	20-07-10	Rosario, Argentina	12-04-11
Cebu, Philippines	22-07-10	Cordoba, Argentina	15-04-11
Manila, Philippines	25-07-10	Mendoza, Argentina	11-05-11
Cebu, Philippines	16-08-10	Santiago, Chile	22-05-11
Manila, Philippines	01-09-10	Valparaiso, Chile	01-06-11
Angeles, Philippines	05-09-10	Santiago, Chile	03-06-11
Kota Kinabalu, Malaysia	07-09-10	Valparaiso, Chile	08-06-11
Sandakan, Malaysia	12-09-10	Santiago, Chili	12-06-11
Sepilok, Malay Borneo	14-09-10	La Serena, Chili	13-06-11
Kota Kinabalu, Borneo	15-09-10	Calama, Chili	16-06-11
BSB city, Brunei	17-09-10	San Pedro, Chili	17-06-11
Miri, Malaysian Borneo	19-09-10	Arica, Chili	20-06-11
Batu Niah, Borneo	20-09-10	La Paz, Bolivia	21-06-11
Kuching, Malay Borneo	21-09-10	Copacabana, Bolivia	11-07-11
Singapore, Singapore	24-09-10	Cusco, Peru	16-07-11
Melaka, Malaysia	02-10-10	Machu Picchu, Peru	21-07-11
Dumai, Indonesia	05-10-10	Cusco, Peru	23-07-11
Medan, Indonesia	06-10-10	Nazca, Peru	27-07-11
Bukit Lawang, Indonesia	08-10-10	Lima, Peru	28-07-11
Medan, Indonesia	12-10-10	Máncora, Peru	03-08-11
Samosir, Indonesia	15-10-10	Guayaquil, Ecuador	08-08-11
Bukit Tinggi, Indonesia	21-10-10	Quito, Ecuador	08-08-11
Jakarta, Indonesia	23-10-10	Tulcán, Ecuador	16-08-11
Yogyakarta, Indonesia	27-10-10	Cali, Colombia	17-08-11
Kuta, Indonesia	02-11-10	Pasto, Colombia	23-08-11
Travangan, Indonesia	16-11-10	Quito, Ecuador	24-08-11
Kuta, Indonesia	20-11-10	Trujillo, Peru	27-08-11
Jakarta, Indonesia	26-11-10	Lima, Peru	28-08-11
Singapore, Singapore	04-12-10	Nazca, Peru	29-08-11
Cebu, Philippines	05-12-10	Puno, Peru	30-08-11
Davao, Philippines	17-12-10	La Paz, Bolivia	01-09-11
Cebu, Philippines	24-01-11	Uyuni, Bolivia	05-09-11
Manila, Philippines	28-01-11	San Pedro, Chile	07-09-11
Singapore, Singapore	02-02-11	Sucre, Bolivia	08-09-11
Darwin, Australia	04-02-11	Santa Cruz, Bolivia	09-09-11
Sydney, Australia	05-02-11	Asunción, Paraguay	14-09-11
Blue Mountains, Austr.	10-02-11	Montevideo, Uruguay	24-09-11
Melbourne, Australia	11-02-11	Porto Alegre, Brazil	28-09-11
Sydney, Australia	17-02-11	Florianópolis, Brazil	28-09-11
Auckland, New Zealand	01-03-11	São Paulo, Brazil	03-10-11

Location	Date	Location	Date
Rio de Janeiro, Brazil	13-10-11	Cayenne, French Guyana	29-11-11
Salvador, Brazil	24-10-11	Kourou, French Guyana	30-11-11
Morro De Sao Paulo	27-10-11	Paramaribo, Suriname	01-12-11
Salvador, Brazil	30-10-11	Trinidad and Tobago	06-12-11
Belém, Brazil	02-11-11	Bridgetown, Barbados	09-12-11
Manaus, Brazil	07-11-11	Kingston, Jamaica	09-12-11
Boa Vista, Brazil	15-11-11	New York, USA	15-12-11
Georgetown, Guyana	16-11-11	Washington, USA	19-12-11
Paramaribo, Suriname	23-11-11	New York, USA	20-12-11
S-Laurent, French Guyana	28-11-11	**Netherlands**	23-12-11

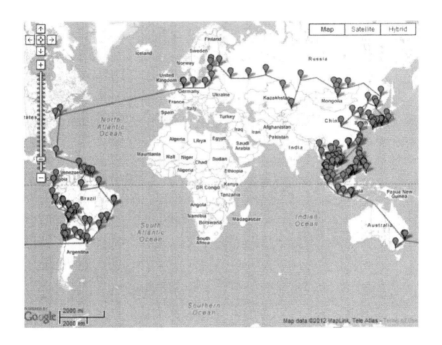

496

My round the world trip in numbers

In a time of **2** years and **8** months I have visited **42** countries, some for a (very) short time and some for a long time.
I went through customs **67** times including 2 very tricky ones in Kazakhstan and Russia.
I took **9** boats, **33** (overnight) trains, **37** airplanes and **94** (overnight) busses. Besides that I took **hundreds** mini vans, local busses, taxis, tuk tuks, motorbike taxis and rickshaws. I have slept in **countless** guesthouses, hostels, houses and even on the street once or twice.

I have slept in **188** different beds and that's without counting many changes of beds in hostels and sleeping on overnight busses and trains. Quite an accomplishment for a guy that hated sleeping in other beds than his own back home.

Google maps calculated that I have traveled 120021 kilometers but that's calculated in straight lines so the real distance must be at least 150000 km. That's nearly 4 times the circumference of the world.

I'm fluent in Dutch and English and can manage myself in the German language. Besides that I have communicated in **24** other languages most of the times with hands, feet and a notebook. I learned to speak some Russian and Spanish along the way and also learned quite a lot of Philippine, Indonesian and Portuguese words.
I had sex with **59** girls of **25** different nationalities and kissed dozens others.
I paid with **36** different currencies and filled **39** pages with stamps in my passport.

It was the best time of my life and I would do it all again in a heart beat.

Special thanks to:
My family for standing by me in my crazy trip and the writing of this book.

Jonathan, for showing me how cool the life of a backpacker can be and making the decision to leave everything behind easier.

Julia and Jenna, for giving me their true love and dedication.

D-Lux, for having a good time with in three different countries, letting me stay in his house for five weeks for free and helping my out with designs for business cards and website headers.

Darren, for six great weeks of traveling and fun in Indonesia, one of the best parts of my trip.

Gustavo and Nico from Chile, for being good friends.

That beautiful girl working at Vladivostok Airport for keeping me out of Russian prison.

J. M. for the editing wizardry.

Ranilo Cabo aka Line14 , for designing an awesome cover at 99designs.

My willpower, for putting up with the idiotic amount of hours I spend on creating this book.

And of course you the reader for reading this long book all the way to the end. I would of course highly appreciate a review.

Neil Skywalker

Neil.skywalker@live.com
www.aroundtheworldin80girls.com